POLITICAL LEADERSHIP IN A GLOBAL AGE

Political Leadership in a Global Age
The Experiences of France and Norway

Edited by

HARALD BALDERSHEIM
JEAN-PASCAL DALOZ

LONDON AND NEW YORK

First published 2003 by Ashgate Publishing

Reissued 2019 by Routledge
2 Park Square, Milton Park, Abingdon, Oxon, OX14 4RN
52 Vanderbilt Avenue, New York, NY 10017

Routledge is an imprint of the Taylor & Francis Group, an informa business

Copyright © 2003, Harald Baldersheim and Jean-Pascal Daloz

Harald Baldersheim and Jean-Pascal Daloz have asserted their right under the Copyright, Designs and Patents Act, 1988, to be identified as editors of this work.

All rights reserved. No part of this book may be reprinted or reproduced or utilised in any form or by any electronic, mechanical, or other means, now known or hereafter invented, including photocopying and recording, or in any information storage or retrieval system, without permission in writing from the publishers.

Notice:
Product or corporate names may be trademarks or registered trademarks, and are used only for identification and explanation without intent to infringe.

Publisher's Note
The publisher has gone to great lengths to ensure the quality of this reprint but points out that some imperfections in the original copies may be apparent.

Disclaimer
The publisher has made every effort to trace copyright holders and welcomes correspondence from those they have been unable to contact.

A Library of Congress record exists under LC control number:

ISBN 13: 978-1-138-70823-5 (hbk)
ISBN 13: 978-1-315-19869-9 (ebk)

Contents

List of Tables and Figures   *vii*
Preface   *x*

INTRODUCTION

1 Comparing France and Norway: Why? How? Towards a Contextual Analysis
 Harald Baldersheim and Jean-Pascal Daloz   1

2 Reflections on the Comparative Study of Political Leadership
 Jean-Pascal Daloz   17

A CHANGING INTERNATIONAL ENVIRONMENT

3 The Globalization Debate in France: The Attitudes of Political Leaders
 Sébastien Ségas   35

4 The Norwegian Globalization Debate
 Øyvind Østerud   55

NATIONAL CLEAVAGES AND POLITICAL PARTIES

5 French Political Parties and Cleavages: Why is there no Christian Democratic Party?
 Emmanuelle Vignaux   67

6 Political Parties in Norway – National Institutions, Locally Anchored
 Knut Heidar   93

7 The One and Indivisible Republic? The Constitutional Debate on Corsican Autonomy
 Raino Malnes   109

ROOTS AND REGIONS

8 French Regional Leadership and Economic Strategies in a Globalizing World
   Michel-Alexis Montané — 125

9 Norwegian Regions as Development Agents – County Councils on the Defensive
   Harald Baldersheim — 137

10 Interest Group Leadership and Territory: The Case of Bordeaux Wine Producers
   Andy Smith — 155

LOCAL DEMOCRACY AND MANAGEMENT

11 Proximity and Social Cohesion in French Local Democracy: Answers to the Increase in Abstention and Political Disaffection?
   Laurence Bherer — 169

12 Local Political Participation in Norway: Does Globalization Make a Difference?
   Lawrence E. Rose — 193

13 "Management" and Urban Political Leaders in France
   Stéphane Cadiou — 219

14 Is Local Democracy Under Pressure from New Public Management? Evidence from Norway
   Morten Øgård — 231

CONCLUSIONS

15 France – Return of the Girondins? Norway – Rise of the Jacobins?
   Harald Baldersheim and Jean-Pascal Daloz — 245

EPILOGUE

   Towards a Local-Global Leadership? A Research Agenda
   Claude Sorbets — 255

Index — 267

List of Tables and Figures

Chapter 1

| Table 1.1 | Summary of Contextual Features | 14 |

Chapter 3

| Figure 3.1 | A typology of globalization frame proposals in French political discourse | 43 |

Chapter 5

| Appendix | Electoral results of French parties in parliamentary elections, by percentage of votes in the first ballot | 84 |
| Appendix | Presidential elections – Percentage of votes obtained by candidates | 86 |

Chapter 6

Table 6.1	Parties' share of the vote at parliamentarian elections (percentage), selected years 1945-2001	96
Table 6.2	Parties' share of Storting representatives (percentage), selected years 1945-2001	97
Table 6.3	Governments and party composition 1969-2002	98

Chapter 9

Figure 9.1	"European integration has led to increasing competition among regions." Responses from regional policy committee members	143
Figure 9.2	Policy choices of regional politicians. Percentage in favour of indicated policy type	144
Figure 9.3	"More responsibilities for development functions should be transferred from regions to municipalities." Responses of regional and urban politicians	145

Figure 9.4	"More responsibilities for development functions should be transferred from state bodies to regions." Responses of urban and regional politicians	146
Figure 9.5	Participation in networks international and overall. Regional politicians	147
Table 9.1	Policy learning: How many politicians are able to nominate pioneering regions/cities. Percentage of total who can identify pioneer	148
Figure 9.6	Policy learning index: Ability of regional councillors to nominate pioneering region/city	149

Chapter 10

Table 10.1	The presidents of the FGVB	157
Table 10.2	The presidents of the CIVB	158
Table 10.3	The CIVB's promotion budget	162

Chapter 11

Table 11.1	Electoral turnout in municipal elections 1947-2001	172
Table 11.2	Electoral turnout in municipal elections 1983-2001, according to the number of inhabitants	173

Chapter 12

Figure 12.1	Voter Turnout in Local Elections in Norway, 1901-1999	194
Figure 12.2	Citizens reporting different forms of local political participation in Norway, 1993 and 1996 (percent)	196
Figure 12.3a	The interrelationships between globalization, identity and political behavior – a simple model	197
Figure 12.3b	The interrelationships between globalization, identity and political behavior – a more complex model	198
Figure 12.4	Percentage expressing "strong" identification with selected geographic areas (1993) and "strong" solidarity with other people living in these areas (1996)	200

Figure 12.5	Percentage of the population in 16 countries expressing greatest identification with "the town or locality where they live"	202
Figure 12.6	Percentage reporting having undertaken selected forms of local political activity	204
Figure 12.7	A typology of citizens based on their cognitive orientations to local and international areas	205
Figure 12.8	Percentage reporting having participated in a volunteer project for the benefit of their neighborhood, local community or municipality according to differences in cognitive affiliation	206
Table 12.1	Rates of selected forms for local political participation among persons with different cognitive affiliation profiles. Percent and eta	208

Chapter 14

Table 14.1	Administrative innovation: mean score of the indexes by country	233
Table 14.2	Correlation matrix for the indexes' openness, measures directed towards citizen participation, used freedom of choice and market/competition orientation	237

Preface

This book is the fruit of contacts and meetings between scholars from the political science departments at the universities of Bordeaux and Oslo. Relations between the two *milieux* are of long standing. Since the early 1980s, joint seminars, mutual study visits and student exchanges have taken place, often at the initiative of individual scholars who found kindred spirits in the other department. We should like to mention our late colleague, professor Francesco Kjellberg, as an especially devoted and successful organizer of these Franco-Norwegian meetings. The volume edited by Francesco Kjellberg and Vincent Hoffmann-Martinot, *Décentraliser en France et en Norvège*, was the outcome of a joint seminar organized in Bordeaux in 1993. The success of that venture inspired a second seminar, this time in Oslo in 2000, with a follow-up in Bordeaux in 2001. The topic was chosen so as to involve a broader segment of colleagues, with expertise on international relations, political parties and constitutional issues, in addition to that of regional and local governance that formed the backbone of the former volume. The political response to globalization, in terms of leadership and institutional changes, was a topic of high scholarly and political salience in both countries. A mutual exploration of Franco-Norwegian responses to globalization at all levels of governance was seen as an interesting heuristic device to enhance the overall understanding of the topic. The present volume is the outcome of these efforts. We are deeply grateful to the French-Norwegian *Aurora* programme for financial support for the seminars that resulted in this book. Translations and final editing of the manuscript were completed with expert assistance from Lesley Daloz, Jostein Askim and Ole Kristian Brastad. Their diligence and good spirits helped us through the delicate hurdles of a tri-lingual game.

Bordeaux and Oslo, September 2002

The editors

Chapter 1

Comparing France and Norway: Why? How? Towards a Contextual Analysis

Harald Baldersheim and Jean-Pascal Daloz

The purpose of this book is threefold: First, to present updated, parallel accounts of institutional change and political leadership in two European polities – France and Norway – that are rarely thought of as a likely pair; in this sense, the book may be read as an introduction to politics and institutions in the two countries. The second purpose is to try to ascertain the extent to which institutional change is driven by the common challenge of globalization and the extent to which globalization drives a convergence of political forms. The third purpose is to analyze the role of leadership in framing responses to globalization at various levels of government – national, regional and local. The choice of the unlikely pair of France and Norway is justified as a contextual strategy of analysis, i.e. an exploration of ways in which contexts condition leadership and responses to globalization. For this purpose the choice of *contrasting contexts* is an important heuristic device.

Our angle on globalization is that it creates *opportunities for political leadership*. Leadership is a rare phenomenon in our highly developed and institutionalized societies. Leadership belongs to an extra-institutional and personalized logic that democratic mass-society has sought to escape. Leadership is the mobilization of personal loyalties for group-specific ends. Admittedly, the leader-follower nexus may involve several links of interpersonal relations, so that all followers do not necessarily stand in direct and immediate, daily contact with the leader – there may be several intermediaries. However, relations of personal loyalty and allegiance are core features of leadership. The governance of modern society mainly relies on instruments of the marketplace and large-scale bureaucracy, impersonal mechanisms of coercion and compliance. The central institutions of democratic mass politics – the political parties – have also acquired the features of bureaucratic machines while their strategists increasingly seek to emulate the behaviour of the firm, including the help of ad men and spin doctors in the pursuit of the popular vote. Leadership is primarily called for in cases of institutional breakdown or in the construction of agendas across institutional boundaries. As globalization exerts pressure on established institutional patterns it also drives a throwback to more basic modes of governance – those of leadership, loyalty and group politics. These modes are likely to be more culturally specific than institutions are since they are more personal in character and will therefore reflect local or national contextual features. These notions of leadership are more fully presented in chapter 2.

Globalization is both real and constructed. It is real in the sense that transactions involving the exchange of information, culture, finances and goods across continents and national borders occur at increasingly greater volumes and speeds; these transactions do have some real consequences for nations, communities and individuals. Money is moved across borders, so are factories, goods and information. Globalization is constructed in the sense that it is very much open to debate and interpretation as to what the consequences of those transactions are, and how important they are. Many observers emphasize the universal benefits of globalization, others mainly see threats to workplaces or cherished lifestyles; even the nation-state is sometimes set to vanish. These competing claims open up possibilities for the construction of new political agendas and movements or for shoring up faltering political careers and organizations.

For our purposes, Nye and Keohane's definition of globalization is a useful point of departure: "Globalization is the process of increasing globalism", which "is a state of the world involving networks of interdependence at multicontinental distances" (Nye and Keohane 2000:7/2). In consequence, as economies become increasingly integrated across national borders, nation-states may lose some of their room to maneuver in terms of policy-making and self-determination. Globalization exerts pressure on existing institutions and modes of governance. Still, Nye and Donahue do not agree that globalization necessarily signals the decline of the nation-state. They maintain, however, that the responses of the nation-states to globalization will vary, e.g. with their type of economy, the institutional set-up and political culture and traditions. Change and adaptation is to be expected. Such responses can be expected to be highly context-bound. What is under pressure in modern welfare states of the type that France and Norway represent, is "The compromise of embedded liberalism that created a social safety net in return for openness (of the economy)" (Nye and Keohane 2000:36). The most realistic political response to the new world order in terms of governance, the authors claim, is that of "networked minimalism". Governance through the pooling of resources through issue networks rather than through hierarchy and command will be the norm. Minimalism will characterize governance since the scope for choice in domestic politics will be severely reduced.

The nexus between globalization and leadership lies primarily in the pressure that globalization exerts on the institutions of the nation-state, setting in motion processes of shielding, reconstruction, adaptation or counter-moves, including supra-national alliances and strategies such as the EU or the WTO. In a neo-liberal and technology-driven world order borders are porous – and traditional shielding strategies are difficult to implement or may have lost their legitimacy. The perceived impact of globalization is frequently that of increasing exposure to competition – competition emanating from foreign firms, regions or nations. As leaders seek to respond to the challenges of competition processes of change are set in motion. Globalization – real or constructed – is, therefore, a general force of change. We do not take a stand on the issues of the newness or intensity of globalization. We do note, however, that globalization is an increasingly discussed topic in many countries, including France and Norway, and that globalization is more and more often invoked as a reason for reform. Paradoxically, the post-modernity that emerges out of the responses to globalization includes a stunning embrace of pre-modern political forms, viz. that of leadership. The terminology of post-modern governance celebrates networks, partnerships, identity politics, regionalism etc as the ways of the future. The common denominator of these modes of governance is a reliance on old-fashioned leadership dressed up in the garbs of the media and the computer age.

How may globalization more specifically open up new opportunities for leadership? Following Kehoane and Nye, globalization is likely to reinforce the political competition for the middle ground since the scope of politics is becoming more restricted. As economic and social change accelerates, established cleavage structures are likely to erode. Second, citizen interest in and participation in politics are likely to wane since politics matters less. Third, the volatility of politics and parties is likely to increase since the established cleavages and the concomitant political loyalties are weakened. This again may provide fertile ground for a cesarist type of political leadership.

However, globalization is not only a force of standardization, driving a convergence of political, cultural and economic forms. Coca-cola and Hollywood may have penetrated most corners of the world, but national and regional peculiarities are not disappearing. The view taken here is not exactly the opposite of the convergence thesis; our contention is rather that responses to globalization are highly context-bound. National, regional and local contexts condition the way leaders respond or the leadership that emerges in response to the challenges of globalization and internationalization. Institutional crises that may occur in the wake of globalization bring out culturally specific patterns of leadership in so far as there is a response at all. So with regard to political leadership, at least, globalization is expected to affirm diversity and cultural specificity rather than increasing uniformity. Such an expectation is what justifies our choice of cases for comparison.

France and Norway have been chosen as cases well suited for a test of the contextuality thesis. As is argued below, the two countries represent starkly contrasting contexts at all levels of government that are included in our analysis, i.e. national, regional and local institutions. Globalization is expected to bring out the "Frenchness" and "Norwegianness" of leadership rather than obliterating it. The debate on globalization and how it is framed in France and Norway respectively is further analyzed in chapters 3 and 4.

France and Norway – European contrasts

At first glance, France and Norway may seem an unlikely pair for comparison. France is among the largest states of Western Europe, Norway is among the smallest. Indeed, the population of the latter barely surpasses that of Greater Paris.

France is a Great Power and a driving force in European integration. Norway's international position is marked by carefully managed dependencies and deep euro-scepticism to the extent of having twice rejected EU membership in national referenda. In the realm of culture and ideas, France has been an exporter of political inventions and cultural models, Norway has been on the receiving end; the Norwegian constitution of 1814 carries the combined imprints of the French Enlightenment and the French Revolution; later administrative developments borrowed heavily from Napoleonic precepts. French cuisine is an international byword for excellent cooking whereas Norwegian fare may appeal to minorities with a taste for arctic flavours. The time and money a French family spends in the culinary field is perhaps matched by the average Norwegian family's passion for home (re) decorations. The Mediterranean, Latin and Catholic culture of France speaks of a Roman heritage that stands in contrast to the North Sea and Protestant ambience to which Norway belongs. The Concorde and the TGV bear witness to successful French high-tech industries, perhaps matched by the Norwegian oil industry in Northern waters. In the field of public finances Norway is in the enviable position, however, of running huge surpluses on its state budgets whereas France has had to make serious economies to comply with the Maastricht criteria.

Frenchmen and Scandinavians may represent *the other* to each other. What is that they see as striking or defining features when they look at each other? The Dane Uffe Østergård, in his outlook on European history, pinpoints the *French Revolution* as the key event that shaped French development, even as a defining force for those opposing it (Østergård 1992: 192ff). The issues and clashes of the Revolution reverberate through subsequent periods of French history to this day: rationalism, republicanism, universalism, centralism. To the Swedish historian Johansson, the defining issue is *regionalism*, or rather the regional diversity of France (Johansson 1992: 172 ff). French history, especially from Louis XIV onwards, is depicted as a struggle of the central government to control and come to grips with the provinces, with their cultural and linguistic plurality. In this perspective, the Revolution represents continuity rather than a break, continuity characterized by even more insistence on centralization and the use of more brutal means. Also this battle is not finally won: one president resigned over the issue of power to the regions (de Gaulle after the referendum of 1969) and a minister of the interior has recently resigned in protest over concessions to Corsica.

Scholarly works dealing with Norway from a French point of view are not numerous. However, a recent edition, *Passions Boréales. Regards français sur la Norvège*, seeks to present Norwegian history, society and tradition to a general French public. Much space is devoted to the Viking past; and the Viking connections to French history (Rollo) is pointed out. The Norwegian enrapture with Nature and the passion for hiking is lovingly portrayed. Particularities pinpointed are the parallel senses of patriotism and local roots (urban Norwegians often make a point of detailing not only the rural community – *bygda* – from which the family hails but also the farmstead of their origin). Egalitarianism and moralism may be mores shared in large measure with other Scandinavian countries but may reach leveling proportions in Norway (Eydoux 2000: 117). However, it is also suggested that "…ce siècle n'a guère produit en Europe que trois personage que l'on pourait qualifier de "gaulliens": le Maréchal Mannerheim, le Général de Gaulle, le roi Haakon VII" (François Kersaudy 2000: 222).

Marginality is a recurrent theme in analyses of Norway's position in the world. Norway's distant location on the outskirts of the European continent has a counterpart in the country's suspicion of deep international commitments, of which its attitude to European integration is a logical expression. Marginality has not meant that Norway has remained untouched by European upheavals, however. These historical interventions have often had traumatic overtones: in 1814 when the post-Napoleonic settlement resulted in a transfer of Norway from Denmark to Sweden, in 1940 with the German occupation, and in 1949 when Norway broke with its traditional policy of neutrality and joined NATO in the wake of the communist coup in Czechoslovakia. Whereas Norwegian NATO membership originally served to reduce Norway's marginality, the post-1989 events have, of course, also had repercussions for Norway, especially in terms of changing its relations with Russia and have added to Norway's marginality as the Northern areas have diminished in strategic importance. A feature of Norwegian politics often noted, a preference for a consensual decision-making style (Eckstein 1966, Katzenstein 1985), may be closely related to the marginality phenomenon as well as the egalitarian tradition.

There are, however, also commonalities between the two countries. They are both stable European democracies. They are both highly developed welfare states. They are both founding NATO members (France admittedly with more reservations than Norway, as a sort of counterpoint to Norway's euro-scepticism). They are both undergoing a transition from an industrial society to a service and information economy.

They also face many of the same challenges that are common to the open European democracies and capitalist economies today. As democracies they are experiencing the emergence of new political cleavages related to issues of immigration, European integration and global competition. As the Cold War waned and new security issues have come to the fore, foreign policy and international commitments have had to be rethought. The pressure of global competition has led to re-considerations of the role of the state as an economic regulator. A switch to more regulation through the discipline of the market rather than the command of the state has caused debate and resistance in both countries. Worries about the sustainability of the welfare state in its present form and concomitant reform initiatives have given new twists to the traditional left-right cleavage that has been so dominant in both cases.

A contextual approach

Against the combined background of contrasting socio-political contexts and common challenges it is pertinent to ask more precise questions about how the two nations and their leaders at various levels respond to these challenges and especially how variations in context shape those responses. It is our contention that by analyzing the unlikely pair of France and Norway in parallel, a deeper understanding may be gained of options of and preconditions for political leadership in our societies. The approach adopted here may be termed *contextual* and *reflexive* rather than comparative in the strict sense of the term. French and Norwegian specialists in various fields have been paired and asked to write parallel essays on selected topics. The essays are informed by deep contextual knowledge of the respective countries. The contextual understanding is enhanced by a reflexive strategy, i.e. the juxtaposition of two contrasting contexts, France and Norway.

The leadership challenges that we seek to explore are defined along four contextual dimensions: the respective countries' position in the world, their features of state- and nation-building, and their internal structures in terms of central-local relations and local life. How do leaders and elites in the two countries see challenges and options in these four spheres of political life?

World position

As suggested above, the position of France in European and world affairs is imbued with the heritage of a Great Power tradition, a nation "qui n'est réellement elle-même qu'au premier rang" in de Gaulle's terms. The ambition to maintain this tradition has been pursued in the form of vigorous European leadership and the development of a Franco-German axis while keeping a distance to the Atlantic alliance without completely alienating the American and British partners. The position of one foot inside and one foot outside NATO is a curious parallel to Norway's relationship to the EU. The colonial past is also a defining feature of France's position in the world. France tries, first of all to maintain a special relationship with its former colonial territories, above all in franco-phone Africa. A sense of a "mission civilisatrice" is often said to motivate French cultural efforts abroad. The colonial legacy also haunts French present-day politics as a large-number of foreign-born and second- and third-generation immigrants from overseas territories have settled on French soil since the late 1950s. Many of them still only half assimilated, their fate represents a durable cleavage in French politics, nurturing a right-wing reaction to their presence.

Norway's status as a fully independent state in the modern age dates only from 1905 when she broke out of the Union with Sweden. Norwegian independence was only possible with the consent of the great European powers of the time, especially that of Great Britain. The relationship with Great Britain has since been of paramount importance to Norway for economic and geo-strategic reasons. For example, de Gaulle's 'no' to British membership of the Common Market in 1962 also meant the suspension of Norway's ambition to join. In international affairs in general, Norway has traditionally been an adapter rather than a player, watching her steps and hedging her bets, a typical small state syndrome, perhaps (Katzenstein 1985). It took the trauma of 1940 and 1949 to break with this tradition and join NATO. Whether Norway's recently acquired reputation for international peace-brokering represents another break with the spectator role or rather a confirmation of it is a matter for debate. It may also reflect the idealistic and missionary strands that have been a long-standing feature of Norwegian foreign policy.

Arguably, the Norwegian economy may be presented as more globalized than that of France. Almost 50 percent of the production of Norwegian firms is sold in foreign markets as against around 25 percent in the case of France (Frankel 2000:50). This, of course, reflects both the difference in size of the respective home markets (the export shares of Italy and the UK are much the same as that of France) and also the importance of Norwegian oil exports. At the same time, Norway's share of total world production is naturally much smaller than the French share. Nevertheless, "globalization" has become a concern in public debate in both countries, a worry to some, a new promise to others.

Globalization and its concomitant challenges to the "embedded liberalism" of the welfare states drive a common agenda across Europe: integration of European markets as a response to higher efficiency requirements, institutional overhaul to achieve higher cost discipline in public services and a quest for legitimacy to counter the political strain engendered by reforms. Market integration means giving up national sovereignty to European institutions. Cost discipline is sought through the recommendations of the New Public Management school, whereas the quest for legitimacy drives reform in central-local relations, granting more autonomy to local and regional institutions in an effort to bring decision-making closer to the citizens.

What are the contents and connotations of the debate in the two countries, the Great Power and the Small State? Conceivably, the debate might run along very different lines in France and Norway respectively; globalization might perhaps be seen as offering new opportunities to the Great Power and mainly threats to the Small State. However, as demonstrated by the two articles on the globalization debates (Ségas and Østerud), the patterns are much more complex in both countries. In fact, debates on globalization issues seem to be structured more by the existing patterns of political cleavages rather than by the respective countries' position in the world.

State- and nation-building

The start of French state-building is to some extent a matter of definition. If an ambition to gain control over territories beyond the traditional lands of a clan and the establishment of institutions of governance of a certain permanence are important features, then the late Middle Ages may mark a watershed, viz. the reign of Philip le Bel (1285-1314). Nevertheless, France remained culturally and economically highly heterogeneous well into the 19th century, divided into regions with languages and patois not mutually comprehensible and with little contact with each other. French state- and nation-building have been seen, as mentioned above, as a long struggle to manage and master this heterogeneity. "Who can govern a country with 350 different cheeses?", de Gaulle once exclaimed. A certain idea of republicanism, with strong Jacobin strands, became an integrating force just as much as the French language. The resulting centralism became a byword not only for administrative rationalism but also for Parisian dominance culturally and politically. "France: Paris and the desert", is a famous summary of long standing (Gravier 1947). Republicanism has therefore served to keep the centre-periphery cleavage in the background in French politics to the extent that it is possible to talk about a republican hegemony. An awakening regionalism has not met with a great deal of understanding in Paris despite the establishment of regional governance structures since the late 1960s and some measure of functional devolution since 1981. It is highly significant that the proposal to grant some elements of home rule to Corsica almost split the Jospin government in 2001. The republican idea is unitary and universal, not federal or plural. The Corsican case is therefore a lens through which the French cleavage structure is interestingly reflected, as shown by Raino Malnes' chapter. That the new prime minister, Jean-Pierre Raffarin, has made transfer of power to the regions one of his core issues may become a test of the political system's capacity to adapt under the pressure of a new global agenda. However, the republican idea also became defined by anti-clerical struggles of the latter part of the 19th century, with secularism becoming an important component of the idea. Furthermore, from the time of Louis XIV and Colbert the state has been a modernizing force in the economic sphere, not only as provider of infrastructure but as owner of substantial means of production. Deregulation is therefore an especially difficult issue in France.

With regard to Norway, embryonic state-building may probably be identified at an even earlier date than in the French case. The legal codifications of Magnus Lagabøter may perhaps mark the emergence of state institutions of some permanence. However, the introduction of the Christian religion backed by the sword of aspiring kings from around 1000 meant that State and Church became closely linked, the establishment of the new religion becoming a legitimation for the new overlordship of the kings. In this respect, the Christianizing mission of the Church became an integral part of the state-building process. Some of the traditional institutions of local and state governance survived the Danish period. Under the Union with Sweden state-building, kick-started with the constitutional assembly of 1814, took on an increasingly nationalistic and anti-Swedish tenor. A complete set of national institutions were brought into being by the 1814 Constitution, including a National Assembly and a separate Norwegian Army and Navy, functioning more and more independently of Swedish kings. Two of the fundamental cleavages of the 19th century can be understood as reactions to the successive overlordships of Denmark and Sweden, viz. that of peasants vs Crown Servants and that of *Høyre* vs *Venstre*. Crown Servants (*embetsmenn*) were often of Danish stock, speaking a foreign language and seen by the peasants as serving an alien, far-away regime bent on extracting a maximum of taxes and administrators of hated labour services. These Crown Servants became the ruling elite of the new state. Thus the gulf between rulers and ruled remained. It was gradually transformed into a centre-periphery cleavage that was to remain a characteristic feature of Norwegian politics. The *Høyre-Venstre* split arose in the 1880s as a direct response to attitudes to Swedish rule and the issue of the continuation of the Union. *Høyre* was more favourable to Sweden whereas *Venstre* became the party of the radical secessionists. The modern-day version of the cleavage is one between integrationists and sovereignists, i.e. those favouring

Norwegian EU membership, a loyal role in NATO and extolling the virtues of WTO vs those who prefer to maintain a distance to the former institutions while pursuing Norwegian interests through the UN and bilateral treaties. In Norway as elsewhere, industrialization gave birth to an urban working class that added a new dimension to the left-right cleavage. Since the 1930s the Social Democratic Party (*Arbeiderpartiet*) has been the preferred party of the working class but its rise to power was also in large part due to its ability to forge an alliance with important rural groups, especially the smallholders. This alliance has proved extremely durable and has provided the main continuity of Norwegian politics until now, resulting in deep social democratic imprints on Norwegian institutions that also the Conservatives have learned to bow to.

Following Lijphart's classification the political systems of France and Norway can be described as *majoritarian-unitary* and *consenual-unitary* systems respectively (Lijphart 1999:248). However, neither system fits neatly into these categories. First of all, this classification overlooks the distinction between republic and monarchy that so strongly colours the national identities of Frenchmen and Norwegians. Second, the presidential power of the French system does not rest on a parliamentary majority but on an independent presidential mandate. Third, the split character of the French executive that has become so apparent during recent periods of *cohabitation*, has introduced elements of consensus-style governance into the French political system. Therefore, a contextual understanding must supplement the constitutional contrasts between the two countries with data on political culture and attitudes.

Based on analysis conducted as part of the volumes on *Beliefs in Government*, Norwegians appear as stronger believers than the French. They are more often party members and also more often members of voluntary associations. Around 12 percent of Norwegians and 4 percent of the French say they are party members (Widfeldt 1995:140). Still, party membership is declining in both countries, and so is party identification among voters – the latter is a general West European trend, however (Schmitt and Holmberg 1995: 121). French parties seem somewhat more aloof from their supporters than Norwegian ones do. In terms of social and ideological representativeness parties on the right as well as on the left tend to be more distant from their supporters than in the Norwegian case (Widfeldt 1995:171). This should not be taken to mean that Norwegian parties at all times faithfully reflect the views or the social status of their supporters, however. Norwegians, furthermore, have greater confidence in their institutions than the French do. Confidence is particularly high with regard to the police and the legal system and much higher than in the French case. Interestingly, there is one case where French confidence is higher and that is in major companies (Listhaug and Wiberg 1995: 304). Not surprisingly, against this background, the proportion of politically apathetic citizens is larger in France than in Norway (32 against 11 percent) (Topf 1995: 84), which may reflect what one observer has characterized as "the remoteness of the regime from the people" (Wilson 1994:171). The other side of the coin is the French tradition of street politics, such as wild strikes, spontaneous demonstrations and disturbances to try to make authorities listen, which stand in sharp contrast to the cozy Norwegian corportatist arrangements at all levels of society, from the workplace to the ministries.

As regards cherished values there are also discrepancies between Norwegians and Frenchmen. Meritocratic attitudes seem to have spread faster in France than in Norway. In France, for example, there is increasing support for the notion that a faster worker should also be better paid, so that in 1990 80 percent thought so whereas just half of the Norwegians agreed (Thomassen 1995: 404). These days, in both countries, people's tolerance towards new minority groups is being increasingly tested. Judging from the prevalent attitudes it does not seem likely that the integration of such groups will take place without frictions. Few citizens would wish to welcome as their neighbours people of a different race or of a minority religious background. In this respect the French and the Norwegians seem fairly similar (Thomasen 1995: 398). And so their respective polities may face similar problems with the new issues of internationalism and multiculturalism that the organizers of the project on *Belief in Government* by way of conclusion think will figure prominently on the future political agendas (Kaase and Newton 1995: 172).

Since the French elite is a driving force in European integration, while at the same time French voters seem more alienated than Norwegians, French politics may be more exposed to a possible electoral backlash from an alienated electorate. For the same reason – European integration – France is under greater pressure to overhaul its institutions and to introduce economies in its public household. This, however, may intensify the left-right division, which is more pronounced in France than in Norway to begin with. Therefore, such reforms may be more needed in France than in Norway but will be more difficult to implement. There is a potential in both countries for a permanent cleavage centred on issues of multiculturalism and sovereignty. Levels of tolerance clearly have their limits. Whether this will transform existing parties that become either more or less tolerant, or will give rise to new parties, is an open question at the moment.

What is the agenda associated with globalization likely to do to the French and Norwegian parties and electorates? Will a shift to governance through "networked minimalism", as predicted by Nye and Keohane, gradually make traditional political parties obsolete? Political parties are essential components of representative democracy and a parliamentary chain of command. Networked governance conjures up images of much more diffuse lines of influence and decision-making in which political parties at best have to compete for a role. One may wonder, though, how new networked governance really is to many European countries. Networks may seem a good term to describe traditional corporatist arrangements, which have co-existed hand in glove with political parties for a long time. However, if a dissolution of cleavage structures are under way, the foundations for political parties may weaken, leaving the stage to networks of various kinds.

The evolving cleavage systems and party structures of the two countries are further discussed in the chapters by Heidar and Vignaux.

Roots and regions

As suggested by Rokkan's model of nation-building, the integration of disparate regions into a larger national entity was at the core of the nation-building projects in Europe. Integration took place in stages, from territorial domination, via cultural standardization, democratic inclusion and redistribution. Does the pressure of globalization amount to nation-building in reverse with a return to regional prides and peculiarities and rejection of national standards? And economic self-sufficiency *via* world markets with no need for the redistributive state?

France is very much a country composed of "lands" with long historic roots and with distinct cultural traditions, such as Bretagne, Gascogne, Languedoc or Bourgogne. Many lands were controlled by semi-independent lords within an overarching feudal order. Until 1789 a distinction was maintained between *pays d'état* and *pays d'élection*, the former enjoying wider privileges than the latter. Attempts at introducing a uniform administrative order did not really break the traditional privileges and exemptions until after the Revolution although the *intendants* of Richelieu and Louis XIV did their best to control local parliaments and other institutions of local governance. The standardized system of *préfet* governance introduced as a part of the Napoleonic administrative system was, ironically, a decisive victory for the ideas of the Revolution. Today, France has a two-tier system of regional governance: 22 *régions* and 100 *départements*, both of which are headed by directly elected assemblies. The reforms of decentralization and democratization of the early 1980s, after Mitterrand's first election as president, strengthened the regional levels substantially. Powers were transferred from the prefects to the elected bodies and new functions taken over by the regions. Interestingly, the present regional subdivisions correspond in large measure to the historic *pays* of France. The reforms were accompanied by an awaking of cultural regionalism in which many regions try to assert their cultural identities more vigorously. France now allows teaching of five different official languages in its public schools (Basque, Occitan, German, Breton, in addition to French), which may amount to a second Revolution (or a Counter-Revolution?). Development policies have acquired more than before features of partnerships between state and regions. Through the instrument of the *contrat de plan* negotiations take place between the levels of government as to the choice and funding of development and infrastructure project throughout the country.

With respect to Norway, too, regions could be said to have a longer history than the state. Of course, the state-building project of the middle ages was one of suppression of regional chiefs and regional legal institutions. However, the kings for a long period had to seek elections by the various ancient regional parliaments (*ting*). Since the Norwegian aristocracy was almost wiped out by the Great Plague of the 14th century there was no elite to organize any resistance to the centralizing initiatives of the Danish King from 1660 onwards. From the 1660s, the King's Crown Servants ruled largely unopposed in Norway except for a few local peasant revolts that were quickly subdued (still, Norwegian peasants enjoyed greater freedoms than their counterparts did in Denmark). During the Danish period the regional subdivision largely corresponded to that of the bishoprics. Modern regional governance dates from 1837 when new Local Government Acts also introduced a regional tier of government with indirectly elected assemblies. The role of the assemblies (composed of mayors from the rural municipalities of the region) was largely that of advising the prefects in the performance of their duties. The regions became important agents in the modernization of agriculture and education and also with responsibilities for infrastructure. In 1976, reforms of regional governance were introduced with many of the features of those of France of the 1980s mentioned above: directly elected regional assemblies, right to levy regional taxes, an administration separate from that of the prefect, an enhanced role in planning, etc. The Norwegian regions (*fylke*) were to perform functions that in France were split between the departments and the regions: i.e. planning as well as extensive service provision. However, during the 1990s Norwegian regions came under severe criticism for excessive bureaucracy and incompetence in service provision, especially in the field of hospital management. A question mark hangs over their future. Many regions are imbued with the famous "counter-cultures" (centring on differences with regard to language, religion, consumption of alcohol) that have defined the centre-periphery cleavage of Norwegian politics. Still, these counter-cultures have not given rise to a regional identity revival in the way it has happened in France.

Since the early 1980s many observers have claimed to be spotting the emergence of a "Europe of the regions" (Sharpe 1993). This trend is driven in part by financial pressures on the state, in part by vigorous identity politics, and in part by European integration. Regions have not only been given more tasks in service provisions, they are given wider powers in economic planning and development and they collaborate extensively with regions in other countries. "Para-diplomacy" is a term that has been coined to capture this trend in cross-border co-operation.

To what extent can developments in France and Norway be said to correspond to such a trend? Paradoxically, France being at the eye of the European whirlwind may feel the centrifugal pull of regionalism strongest. Consequently, we should see strong initiatives by French regions towards developing their own policy responses to meet the pressures of international competition. We should also expect to see willingness to change regional institutions and to enter into partnerships with private and state institutions and also keenness on cross-border co-operation. The same responses are likely to occur in Norway since regions often learn from each other. However, the Norwegian responses are expected to be weaker and more hesitant. The Norwegian periphery, the periphery of the periphery, is expected to seek the shelter of the state rather than enter into vigorous cross-border co-operation or establish cross-institutional partnerships. The Norwegian regional trust in the state is likely to be reinforced by the well-filled state coffers that signal a capacity to maintain the redistributive welfare state. The institutionalization of the centre-periphery cleavage at the national level will work in the same direction.

Developments in France and Norway in this respect are discussed in three chapters (Baldersheim, Montané and Smith).

Local government and participation

At the local level in France are found the famous 36.000 communes, each of them headed by a strong mayor who is usually the leading figure of the local party branch to which he or she belongs. French mayors make a point of developing good connections to higher levels of government. The *cumul des mandats* has a long tradition; it is now being curtailed somewhat, however, but its legacy is that the larger cities always compete in trying to entice a leading national figure to take on the role of mayor. National connections are all-important. Chaban-Delmas, for example, was mayor of Bordeaux from 1948 until 1994. After him, Alain Juppé has taken over. Faced with such an array of powerful mayors national governments will always think twice before launching any initiatives of large-scale municipal amalgamations. In an official inquiry into appropriate local government structures in 1976 the following was stated as guideline: "Every single commune of France is irreplaceable... It is in the communes that democracy is closest to the people and their problems... As long as there are people living in a village, it is a community with the right to decide its own future..." (Quoted from Norton 1994:143). Despite the cherished position of the commune participation in local elections is not very high by European standards. Around 40 percent of the electorate turned out for the last local election.

Norwegian governments have had fewer inhibitions with regard to amalgamations. In the 1960s the number of municipalities was reduced from 730 to 454 and it now stands at 434. Nevertheless, average size is just 9.000 inhabitants and over half have less than 5.000. Many think this is still too small and would like to see further amalgamations. Advocates of amalgamations are especially vociferous in the Conservative and Labour parties. Debates on the size of local authorities have been put on hold for the moment but may surface again in the wake of a possible restructuring of regions. Norwegian communes have a wider range of functions than their French counterparts; responsibilities include primary health care and primary education. Norwegian communes try to maintain a stricter line of demarcation between the political and the administrative sphere than is normal practice in France. There is no mayoral responsibility or involvement in daily affairs of the commune. The mayor may often be no more than the speaker of the local council and the ceremonial figurehead of the commune. Recently, there are concerns over the democratic legitimacy of local councils since turnout has dropped from a high of 83 percent to only 59 percent in the last election in 1999.

Concern over the democratic quality of local government is widespread in Europe. Experiments aimed at enhancing the level of local democracy are proliferating. More reliance on new information and communication technologies is one of the solutions being offered. In many cases, these concern are clearly reflections of the quest for a renewal of political legitimacy that the pressures of globalization engenders in the nation-states. The necessity of overhauling or redesigning institutions has the side effect of wear and tear on the politicians shouldering responsibility. Policies of proximity and transparency have been launched in many countries as a response to the problem of the distant polity. With more feelings of alienation and a more distant elite it is to be expected that the politics of proximity should be pursued with greatest vigour in France. At the same time, France has more of a protest culture than Norway. Therefore, the political culture may make the actual implementation of such policies more unlikely in France.

These are questions discussed by the two chapters on local participation (Bherer and Rose).

The democratic quality of communes is also affected by the quality of their management. Management has become hot topics in later years, such as transparency issues or demands for the enhancement of citizen orientation in service delivery. A reform movement under the label of *New Public Management* has made inroads into traditional ways of running communes. Ségas and Øgård discuss the extent to which NPM can be found in French and Norwegian communes respectively and present evaluations of the impacts such notions have had. At the outset, it seems reasonable to expect NPM to be more widespread in Norway than in France given the more pronounced administrative character of Norwegian communes (cfr. for example the strong position of the chief administrative officers in Norway). Also, Norwegian communes have wider service responsibilities, which may make NPM seem more relevant.

Table 1.1 Summary of Contextual Features

FRANCE		NORWAY
Great Power/cultural centre; Mission civilisatrice	*World Position*	Small state/ Marginality; Peace mission
Gradual containment of regional diversity through revolutionary republicanism; Europe and immigration drive a shifting party pattern	*State- and Nation-Building*	Gradual absorption of counter-cultures into national institutions through consensual style of governance; relatively stable party pattern despite European and immigration issues
Lingering identification with regions; challenges to centralism and universalism from regions	*Roots and Regions*	Weak regional identification; will democratic regions survive?
Extremely small-scale local govt.; distant political style, low turnout; Mayoral colonization of national govt.	*Local Government and Participation*	Moderate-to-small-scale local govt.; falling turnout; national colonization of local govt.

References

Eckstein, Harry (1966). *Division and Cohesion in Democracy: A Study of Norway.* Princeton: N.J.:Princeton University Press.

Eydoux, Éric (2000a). "De la Norvège et des Norvégiens, culture et traditions", in Éric Eydoux (ed.). *Passions boréales. Regards français sur la Norvège.* Caen: Presses universitaires de Caen.

Eydoux, Éric (ed.) (2000b). *Passions boréales. Regards français sur la Norvège.* Caen: Presses universitaires de Caen.

Frankel, Jeffrey (2000). "Trends in Globalization", in Joseph S. Jr. Nye and John D. Donahue, *Governance in a Globalizing World.* Cambridge, Mass: Brookings Institution Press.

Gravier, Jean-François (1947). *Paris et le désert français: décentralisation, équipement, population.* Paris: Le Portulan.

Johansson, Nils (1992). *Historiens återkomst.* Lund: Studentlitteratur.

Joseph S. Jr. Nye and John D. Donahue (2000). *Governance in a Globalizing World.* Cambridge, Mass: Brookings Institution Press.

Kaase, Max and Kenneth Newton (1995). *Beliefs in government,* Vol 5 Beliefs in Government. Oxford: Oxford University Press.

Katzenstein, Peter J. (1985). *Small States in World Markets: Industrial policy in Europe.* Ithaca, N.Y.:Cornell University Press.

Keohane, Robert O. and Joseph O. Nye Jr. (2000). "Introduction", in Joseph S. Jr. Nye and John D. Donahue. *Governance in a Globalizing World.* Cambridge, Mass.: Brookings Institution Press.

Kersaudy, François (2000). "Haakon VII et Charles de Gaulle ou la solitude des grands hommes", in Eydoux, Éric (ed.) *Passions boréales. Regards français sur la Norvège.* Caen: Presses universitaires de Caen.

Klingemann, Hans-Dieter and Dieter Fuchs (1995). *Citizens and the state.* Vol 1 Beliefs in Government. Oxford: Oxford University Press.

Lijphart, Arendt (1999). *Patterns of Democracy. Government Forms and Performance in Thirty-Six Countries,* New Haven, Conn.: Yale University Press.

Listhaug, Ola and Matti Wiberg (1995). "Confidence in Political and Private Institutions", in Klingemann, Hans-Dieter and Dieter Fuchs. *Citizens and the state.* Vol 1 Beliefs in Government. Oxford: Oxford University Press.

Norton, Alan (1994). *International Handbook of Local and Regional Government. A Comparative Analysis of Advanced Democracies.* Aldershot: Edward Elgar.

Schmitt, Hermann and Søren Holmberg (1995). "Political Parties in Decline?" in Hans-Dieter Klingemann and Dieter Fuchs. *Citizens and the state.* Vol 1 Beliefs in Government. Oxford: Oxford University Press.

Sharpe, L.J. (1993). *The Rise of Meso Government in Europe.* London: Sage.

Thomassen, Jaques (1995). "Support for Democratic Values", in Klingemann, Hans-Dieter and Dieter Fuchs *Citizens and the state.* Vol 1 Beliefs in Government. Oxford: Oxford University Press.

Topf, Richard (1995). "Beyond Electoral Participation", in Klingemann, Hans-Dieter and Dieter Fuchs, *Citizens and the state.* Vol 1 Beliefs in Government. Oxford: Oxford University Press.

van Deth Jan W. and Elinor Scarbrough (1995). *The Impact of Values,* Vol 4 Beliefs in Government. Oxford: Oxford University Press.

Widfeldt, Anders (1995). "Party Membership and Party Representativeness", in Klingemann, Hans-Dieter and Dieter Fuchs. (1995) *Citizens and the state.* Vol 1 Beliefs in Government. Oxford: Oxford University Press.

Wilson, Frank L. (1994). *European Politics Today. The Democratic Experience.* Englewood Cliffs, N. J.: Prentice Hall (2nd ed.).

Østergård, Uffe (1992). *Europas ansigter: Nationale stater og politiske kulturer i en ny, gammel verden.* København: Rosinante/Munksgaard.

Chapter 2

Reflections on the Comparative Study of Political Leadership

Jean-Pascal Daloz

In spite of the publication of impressive *summae* intending to provide theoretical syntheses,[1] one must admit that the scientific study of leadership remains rather unsatisfactory.[2] Basic disagreements still exist with regard to definition, not only between but also within scientific disciplines.[3]

For instance, in political science, if many authors seem tempted to resort to this concept, it is generally on the basis of discordant premises. What poses a problem is that, too often, one tends to make leadership a convenient synonym of power relations dealing with relationships between the governors and the governed, rulers and the ruled, political elites and the masses, the elected and the electors, the representatives and those represented: these are indeed "thinkable" pairs but correspond to analytically different logics.

Our discipline often suffers from notions which are too inclusive or interchangeable. However, scientifically speaking, it is in our interest to refine these concepts. Then, and only then will they become potentially operative and useful in the interpretation of certain kinds of interaction. The relatively narrow approach to leadership we are advocating is largely based upon an inductive method. It is from numerous field observations that we have reached the conclusion that a current (but not necessarily universal) type of political relation was worth being clearly distinguished and that the leadership concept was the one best able to cover this object of analysis.

However, taking into consideration that the notion of leadership had already formed the subject of a considerable literature, we could not ignore this and could hardly propose a complete reconstruction out of nothing. In our view, there are often highly pertinent intuitions in certain standard texts on leadership. But unfortunately, the reflections are not always taken to the end of their logic, or there is a mix-up between constituent dimensions.

First and foremost, we would like to insist on the scientific advantages of sticking to a precise and restrictive conception of political leadership, akin to the ideal-type approach. Next, some reflections on the non-universal nature of leadership are presented. Finally, the issue of leadership dynamics in a period of globalization is discussed, with special emphasis on how cultural logics may prevent standardization of the forms of leadership.

Theories of leadership revisited

The literature on leadership is like a gigantic labyrinth with multiple hidden recesses containing more or less coherent elements worthy of interest. Undoubtedly, we also find many dead-ends. And yet, in our opinion, a main thread spread out among certain scattered propositions here and there can clearly allow one to make sense out of this and show that leadership is not quite reducible to other types of political links.

Five constitutive points seem fundamental to us: We would like to stress, first, the relational nature of leadership; second, its inter-personal character; third, its particularist character; fourth its logic of exchange; fifth, its informal or even extra-institutional side.

The relational nature of leadership

For a long time, there has been and still is (to a large extent) an amalgam in the political science literature between perspectives in terms of elites and those in terms of leadership.[4] But it is important to understand that these phenomena do not at all amount to the same thing.

First of all, when considering the object of the study, works on elites are generally centred on the very person holding political power. This is true, whether a positional or reputational approach is adopted and whether one is interested in the composition, recruitment, attributes, reproduction of elites, networks, logics of accumulation, etc. By contrast, as some political scientists emphasize so much, the study of leadership tends to move away from this starting point focused on *positions* at the top of a hierarchy and concentrate instead on the *relation* between those who lead and those who follow or are led.[5]

Even if studies of elites are rid of the elitist connotation they originally had (Pareto or Mosca in particular), we have to acknowledge that this intellectual tradition still poses a problem with many authors who hesitate to use the term.[6]

From a methodological point of view, the main point of interest regarding approaches in terms of leadership is precisely that the leadership relation is not reduced to leaders' personalities. Except for those holding on to old debates inherited from the 19th century between "Great Men" theories of history and "leaders-do-not-matter" determinist schools,[7] it is essential to grasp that everything does not proceed from the leader even when we consider charismatic figures. Research must therefore be centred upon the relation between the leader and those following him/her (and what his/her legitimacy is based on) much more than upon the individual characteristics of the leaders and the composition of their reference groups (even if these two dimensions obviously need to be taken into consideration). In other words, the heart of the analysis should be the interaction itself taking into consideration that followers and supporters are also real actors.

The inter-personal character of leadership

Leadership is not rulership. It is important to understand that it is by no means a universal and remote relation between the governors and the governed. To consider that a relationship between the government and member-citizens of a nation would pertain to leadership is not of much interest, unless one wants to have two synonyms.

On the contrary, political anthropology tends to show us the importance of proximity in the leaders-followers relationship.[8] The leadership relationship seems to us adequately described when referring to relations "immersed" in an atmosphere of affective communication, which is also as direct as possible. A ruler delivering a "catch-all speech" by addressing all his fellow-citizens through the media does not seem to us to express a leadership logic. Admittedly, modern ways of communication may give the illusion of a relatively direct relationship but this is not really leadership because in most cases, the receivers themselves will never be able to address the transmitter. So, there is neither a real exchange, nor a real gathering in the concrete sense of the term. By this we mean that a simple objective relationship between the top and the bottom would not suffice. A high level of interaction and a strong subjective consciousness is needed. Or else we are talking about something other than leadership.

It would be wrong to think that this dimension is applicable to small groups alone. In extremely personalized political systems (as in sub-Saharan Africa for example) there are many cases where leaders want to control everything including the demands of the most lowly assistant. It is essential to appear attentive to everybody's expectations and to provide the "protection", on which a reputation depends.

In our view, it would be very difficult to see leadership relations as being impersonal, and this is not stressed enough in the literature. This neglect may create analytical confusion when there is an accumulation of situations: for example, a politician may be considered as a leader in the face of his fellow-party-members; as a ruler, a statesman in his ministerial position; and even perhaps with another status when collaborating with his counselors or administrative team. From this point of view, politicians often have to manage relatively contradictory situations, especially if they willingly accumulate their mandates (as is often the case in France).[9]

The particularist character of leadership

As this has frequently been emphasized since Janda's[10] classic article, leadership is a specific form of power relationship which is practised with respect to a reference group. Burns pertinently specifies that "leadership is dissensual".[11] In other words, the leader's goal is not to achieve a sentiment of indiscriminate universal affection. It is in his interest to choose sides and even to make enemies. If we often notice a rhetoric in favour of unity, this is usually directed at the insiders of the group in question and not the whole of society according to a logic defending the general interest.

This particularist relation with a group supporting you is obviously linked to what has previously been said on the inter-personal character of leadership. However, these two points do not exactly coincide. To use standard political science terms, we would say that leadership hardly concerns "public and indivisible goods" which a national group may collectively enjoy. What counts in leadership is rather a concern with targeted distribution. This does not at all mean that the leadership relation can be reduced to a pure logic of patronage, because, as Burns points out, leadership is not only transactional, but also holds an ideological dimension.[12]

In terms of political representation, leadership is not about endeavouring to seduce an omni-directional electorate, but rather about becoming the champion for the interests of a particular group. Sometimes, the leader appears as the simple emanation of a political community. In this case, (s)he would enjoy legitimacy all the more as (s)he truly incarnates the group through personal characteristics and strong support of the group's values and objectives. Sometimes, it is rather the leader who makes the group: a very banal hypothesis where factional struggles are concerned. In the second case, the leader's margin for maneuver is certainly more important, but (s)he is, however, never in a position of total autonomy. This brings us to the next point.

Leadership as (political) exchange

It is well known that in the elitist tradition most of the great classical authors (to a lesser extent Mosca) set down (as an axiom) the idea that an elite rules to the detriment of a dominated and amorphous population. Quite obviously, too, in the Marxist tradition, the upper class is supposed to exploit the others. But this vision, in terms of a near-absolute subordination of the majority, is sometimes debatable in certain contexts.

In our opinion, the most interesting approaches on political leadership stem from another kind of intellectual tradition. We are particularly thinking of the Weberian approaches to authority, or even Mannheim's perspectives on asymmetrical reciprocity. These perspectives take us into the domain of political exchange.[13]

In other words, the advantage of the leadership concept is to allow us to depart from approaches dealing with manipulation and pure domination. With Burns for example, we find a clearly anti-machiavellian dimension (the difference with the elitist Italian school is felt very well here). In the same way, Welsh emphasizes strongly that "leadership involves authority and authority implies legitimacy".[14]

The difficulty here is that the problem of legitimacy is of a rather philosophical nature and leads to endless normative debates, which certainly go beyond the social scientists' field of inquiry. As far as leadership is concerned, this could bring about debates to know for example if Hitler could be qualified as a leader or not. The answer is "no", if we take on a moralist position according to Burns. "Yes", if we admit that with regard to his reference group, the dictator could also use persuasion and not only coercion.[15] Contrary to what Blondel states, the question of the leader's legitimacy should not be evaded in favour of a focus on the "recognition" of the leader by his followers.[16] What simply matters is to pass from the ethical discussion of legitimacy to the scientific investigation of power legitimation, that is to say the acquisition of legitimacy.[17]

What we are arguing is that leadership is not only a typical top-down relationship[18] but also vice-versa, hence both ways. Possibly, this can even lead to real blackmail by supporters on whom a leader depends.[19]

The infra-institutional character of leadership

Contrary to many authors, we think that, analytically speaking, there is much to be gained by clearly differentiating leadership from power relations linked to an institutional position. Following Friedrich, we would say that leadership which gets institutionalized becomes "rulership"[20] and corresponds to rather different logics. In a similar perspective (although he would rather speak in terms of the passage from leadership to "headship"), Gibb stresses that when the relationship between a leader and his supporters takes on a more institutionalized form, there is an entirely different perspective. According to him, leadership is precarious, always liable to be transformed into formal headship, and in that case, the term "leadership" is no longer appropriate.[21] Consequently, the leadership relation as we seek to define it (that is: a two-way, top-down and bottom-up relationship, closely linked to a reference group, according to a particularist logic of political exchange) tends to be substantially more informal than a rulership role within an organized structure.

Following Weber (also as revised by Merton and Blau), we suggest that the institutionalization of roles tends towards the elimination of the personalized character of relations: authority resides more in the *positions* of power than in the individual holding them for a shorter or longer period. Consequently, there is less room for targeted exchanges, for transactions (as Burns interprets them), even if both could hardly disappear completely. In this case, people find themselves in a more formal universe at the opposite extreme of a leadership relationship, which implies flexibility and the ability to sort out the problems beyond a formally defined sphere of competence, within the context of a kind of "moral particularist economy".[22]

In his enlarged version of Stogdill's *summa*, Bass lays much stress on the cleavage between these two (narrow and wide) conceptions of leadership. We hardly see the point of the wide conception, except to have a synonym for ruler or governor. On the other hand, the narrow (informal and extra-institutional) conception allows one to refer to a very different type of situation: where there is not a very clear differentiation of the leader, who in any case never enjoys a permanent position.

The question of the universality of leadership

Defined in this way, leadership refers to an ideal-type precise enough to get rid of the ambiguities or even contradictions, which frequently remain in literature. One can confront it with precise empirical cases within the framework of a comparative approach. With this approach, political leadership is expected to be unevenly distributed in today's world and (contrary to what many authors seem to imply[23]) not really universal.

The main problem in several of the major works which have contributed to establishing the leadership concept in political science during the 1970s, is over-ambitiousness or normative drift. In fact, sometimes, the presentation of the leadership approach proclaims a sort of new paradigm. For example, Page announces (at the end of his chapter on "Political leadership: challenge to political science") an extraordinary programme:

> Attention needs to be focused upon political leadership in relation to major fields such as political theory, national politics, comparative politics, and international relations; to major paradigms for political analysis such as power, decision making, cybernetics, structural-functionalism, value allocation, the new political economy, and Marxism-Leninism; to single polity studies such as those of China, the Soviet Union, India, the members of the United Nations, and other political communities; to types of political systems such as monarchies, military dictatorships, and single-, two-, and multiparty systems, to institutional components of political systems such as parties, bureaucracies, the military, legislatures, courts, economic institutions, and patterns of citizen participation; and to political processes such as policy making, budget making, diplomacy, elections, revolutions, peace, and war.[24]

In short, an "emerging field" is launched by the author, who is, at the same time, greatly offended by a "surprising lack of disciplinary focus [...] upon the concept of political leadership".[25]

In other cases, the purpose of work on leadership is directly subject to an ethical necessity linked to a type of regime regarded as ideal. For example, as early as the 1950s, Seligman emphasized the necessity of political leadership studies for creating or maintaining a democratic society.[26] Another example: in his very large book of 531 pages (with many innovative reflections), Burns stresses the superiority of leadership with regard to "brute power". Or again, he sees it as a modern form of political relationship preferable to authority, which corresponds (in his opinion) to tradition.[27]

Because they conveniently went no further than extremely loose definitions, many authors seem to see leadership as an omnipresent phenomenon for which it would suffice to differentiate "styles". Or yet again, they see it as a sort of model towards which political systems should all tend. A bit like Pareto who considered that "history is a graveyard for aristocracies" (that is, elitism could not be evaded and that it is a good thing after all), many authors defend a universalizing and/or normative vision of leadership.

Our approach is fundamentally different. We envisage leadership as a particular form of political power, observable at certain times and certain places. If it is important to underline its advantages and its disadvantages as a concept, we are endeavouring to consider it in an axiologically neutral way. From our point of view, it does not by any means amount to a universal tool of analysis which may be applied alongside any other tool. Analytical models should not be dogmatically hardened by setting a deductive approach in terms of leadership against other analytical traditions such as those of class or elites, for example. On the contrary, what we are proposing consists in adopting an inductive perspective according to which the object of study is more or less in leadership situations (such as defined above). There are cultural areas favourable to its rapid expansion and maintenance (especially in some non-Western countries), and others a lot less favourable.

Before providing some illustrations of our perspective, we shall recapitulate the five aspects of leadership developed in the first section of this paper by confronting them with several issues. The relational character and exchange dimension of leadership will be considered with regard to what we call the "gap issue". The inter-personal character of leadership will be dealt with in relation to the development of mass society. Finally, the particularist and extra-institutional character of leadership will be considered as a contrast to the institutionalization of political roles.

The gap issue

We have previously emphasized that the political elite approaches were generally centred upon the very person of the political ruler, whilst the study on leadership tends to consider rather the relationship that the people at the top maintain with their own supporters. We have also mentioned that in the elitist tradition, most of the great classic authors advocated the idea that the elites rule to the detriment of politically negligible masses. In contrast, the perspectives in terms of leaders and followers tend to stress political exchange and authority.

Rather than presumptively convincing oneself of the advantages of one model over the other, it is important to take into consideration the situation being studied. When elites are obviously cut off from the rest of the population, the elite approaches are appropriate.[28] By contrast, when one is dealing with logics of a vertical nature between leaders, brokers and supporters, it is likely that leadership perspectives will be suitable. Unlike the classic elitist thesis on the gap, approaches in terms of leadership have the advantage of putting emphasis on the *limited autonomy* of the people at the top. This being particularly frequent in certain contexts.

In other words, it is important to understand that *elite* status like leadership can be located empirically and that elite studies are no less worthy of interest than leadership studies. Not only does one need to admit that "not all political elites are leaders" and that "many leaders are not elites"[29] but one also needs to adapt one's corpus of theoretical references and methods (i.e. emphasis placed rather on the dominant position or on the relation) to the case in point. Comparatively speaking, the respective approaches will prove more or less relevant according to the areas studied.

Leadership and the issue of representation in a context of mass society

Modalities of the progressive passage (in certain areas of the world) towards mass societies are well known. The decrease or even the disappearance of community structures, the atomization of populations which amalgamated more and more within an undifferentiated "entity", the triumph of the nuclear family as well as the consolidation and widening of perceptions have been widely studied since the very beginning of social sciences.

In the political sphere, the consequences of modernization have also been the subject of numerous analyses. Without elaborating on the subject, let us mention: political professionalization and specialization, the advent of democracy and citizenship, horizontal cleavages which take precedence of traditional, vertical layers, and logics of political marketing.

In our view, such evolutions can only lead to a decline in leadership as we have defined it above. This happens for example as politics is exercised increasingly through the mass media. In modern democracies, the political elite is (in principle) accountable before the whole society in view of the decisions they make. This is obviously linked to a conception of the public interest and public policies. In other words, those exercising political power – whether they are rulers, elected representatives or designated officials – are obliged to render accounts to all fellow-citizens. Politics is polarized around (regular but spaced out) crucial electoral moments.

From the point of view of political representation, politicians are more and more inclined to try and transcend socio-political cleavages, to attempt to win as many votes as possible for themselves, even if it entails varying messages according to audiences, crystallizing the aspirations of different classes of the population. In this type of system, according to a (sometimes contestable) Downsian approach, it is considered that "leaders are completely controlled by mass preferences, in a manner similar to the control exercised by the consumer in the economic theory of the firm" or that "leaders are vote maximizers".[30] We think that the leader notion here is very debatable and confusing because there is no longer any direct relationship with followers but rather a logic of political entrepreneurship facing a multitude of anonymous voters who must be convinced.

Leadership (as defined above in a narrow sense) tends to only residually persist in this type of context, even if subtle differences from one country to another are inevitably noticed. In a country such as the United States, the persistent fragmentation of communities and multi-cultural claims can, on the other hand, allow for a relative maintenance of leadership, from the bottom to the top. The now well-studied links between political practices and catholic (with its stress on personalized ties, its spirit of patronage...) or protestant (more individualist, moralizing, abstract, ideological) cultural codes also deserve to be taken into account from a comparative point of view.[31]

Having said this, with the road to mass societies not being a universal phenomenon, the decline in leadership could not be so either. There are other contexts, especially in non-Western countries where political success mainly continues to go through the ability to satisfy such and such a supportive fraction or faction. This is done in a particularist manner and from day to day. In this case, the relation is less between politicians and voters and more between leaders and their followers, which make up the fundamental structure of the political system whilst institutions are at best only a façade.

Leadership and the issue of institutionalization

We certainly agree with perspectives emphasizing that: "leadership is not something that inheres in the person of the leader"[32] and what matters is the relationship with followers. However, we must acknowledge that the person of the leader is not something indifferent, especially if we consider the relationship under the angle of trust and loyalty. We know that (since the works of Almond and Verba) considerable contrasts of a cultural nature exist between societies in this respect.[33]

The question we want to ask here concerns the maintenance of a leadership logic when dealing with personalities who would be largely interchangeable and would tend to take a back seat behind the roles they are more or less provisionally holding. In Western democracies, rulers (more or less sincerely) tend to affirm the institutions' superiority and only present themselves as temporary occupiers of posts of authority that they will sooner or later be led to abandon. According to this logic, the institutions also represent the supreme legitimacy of power. This formalization and institutionalisation tend rather towards the weakening of a leadership with a transactional and particularist nature (even if the latter could not completely disappear).

To take up Burn's words, "bureaucratic behaviour [...] is antithetical to leadership [..]".[34] Within the context of a real state, in the Weberian sense of the term, the people in power lose any ownership rights over the public weal whose management they are only in charge of. Simultaneously, political exchange is structured according to more abstract and more general criteria, because of political enterprises able to transcend the stage of identity allegiances or clientele exchanges. Frequently, an increase in legitimacy results precisely from a widespread acceptance of supra-personal norms. In this respect, Norway, even more than France, proves to be a remarkable case.

On the other hand, there are situations where prestige and influence remain closely linked to the capacity of permanently supplying tokens of goodwill to supporters who constitute the basis of legitimacy. One can possibly seek to accumulate leader positions, but to transform oneself into an impersonal ruler does not make much sense.

Leadership and globalization: from evolutionist interpretations to cultural perspectives

The points we have just discussed have rarely been examined under the angle of leadership but rather through developmental perspectives, stating that all countries converge towards the same (institutionalized, codified and democratic) model. Drawing his inspiration from Parsons' "pattern variables", Hoselitz could envisage for instance that all societies go through development or modernization as particularism, ascription and diffuseness are replaced by universalism, achievement and specificity.[35] By studying the evolutions of many "developing countries", it is however necessary to note that the "euro-centrism" or teleological presuppositions of American political science are far from being confirmed over the last decades. What would strike the observer more, are the logics of cultural resistance facing a Westernization of systems, which were only superficially imposed and accepted. Keeping in mind that with globalization discourses presuppositions of an ineluctable convergence come back to the fore, we would like to discuss the evolutionist conceptions regarding leadership. We will then contrast these with a cultural interpretation based on ground observations.

A model of evolutionist interpretation of leadership

Such as we have defined it above, we maintain that leadership corresponds to a kind of intermediary stage between primordial solidarities and a real institutionalization of the political system (characterized by an emancipation of the state from society). Drawing inspiration from development studies, intended for both developing countries as well as for the United State's internal political evolutions for example, we propose the following schema.

At a stage evolutionists would describe as "traditionalist", the solidarities could be only but primordial, within a "circle of trust" where blood-ties, ethnical or even religious ties are fundamental. This corresponds to the pre-colonial stage in African societies, or to the initial nationalist regrouping of new settlers arriving in the United States for example. It leads to an imperative need for loyalty.

The enlargement of reference and competition spaces (colonization, advent of nationalist elites and finally independences in the African case; development of political machines in the North American case) obliges one to enter upon a logic of alliances and factions. The pressures of modern political competition demand that political leaders surround themselves with an ever larger number of dependants, beyond their own community reference. Political leaders need to widen their support base continually. They seek to establish principles of mutual aid, of patron-client reciprocity, based on the model of kin and family relations. These, however, are less solid, more evanescent and depend almost entirely on the extent to which the networks are properly nourished. This second stage would make up the golden age of leadership logics such as we have defined them. In fact, it all rests on particularist relations of exchange between leaders competing and the (sub-) communities they claim to represent.

At a later stage, because of the advent of more horizontal logics, of the passage to mass society, there is a gradual establishment of habits which are more codified, more institutionalized and less particularist, less personalized. We are then coming out of a logic of redistribution of "separable goods" between rival factions to enter upon a logic of public policies redistributing the "public goods" according to ideological cleavages linked to programmes of competing (and more or less conservative or progressive) political enterprises. The voters' support is not obtained through primordial or clientele interdependences but it has to be earned by proving to be more convincing than one's adversaries.

In the line of "New Political Culture" analysts, we could even think of a fourth stage in certain highly developed countries, according to which leadership no longer comes from parties or unions, is no longer based on class politics but on very specific issues under the auspices of very specialized leaders.[36]

Generally, according to evolutionist perspectives,[37] the empirically noticeable differences are simply interpreted in terms of a delay with regard to a dominant model considered as superior and inevitable.

With the globalization phenomenon, there is an plethora of universalising interpretations. The question of convergence of political systems according to a predominant model is again raised. The problem is that we very quickly fall back on normative discussions. Some welcome the promise of a planet unified by a universal democratic culture. Others deplore a regrettable uniformity asserting itself to the detriment of a rich diversity of identities (and possibly concealing secret agendas). Be that as it may, whether we rejoice in or despair of it, we would again enter a global logic, in such a way that any change made somewhere would have repercussions (more or less and sooner or later) elsewhere.

The empirical evidence of enduring differences

Nevertheless, when political systems seem to resist certain dynamics from generation to generation, it is justifiable to examine the universal validity of the dynamics in question.

Field research and analyses that we carried out lead us to conclude that, as regards leadership, certain regions of the world refuse to go beyond what we have defined above as stage no. 2. That is to say a stage with leaders at the head of factions, where power legitimacy essentially continues to depend on particularist distribution.

Sub-Saharan Africa is an example of an area where a particularistic relationship between leaders at the top, myriads of middlemen and followers matter much more politically than do universalistic, institutionalized regulations. They *durably* tend to strengthen vertical cleavages and solidarities, meanwhile preventing the emergence of class antagonisms and favouring factional struggles. Finally they are decisively *informal*, constantly re-negotiable and therefore largely inimical to the development of genuinely institutionalized patterns of relationships. The originality of our interpretation is to emphasize that what could be interpreted by developmentalists as a rather archaic stage (which must be surpassed) constitutes, on the contrary, a form of political modernity, but at the opposite extreme of the Western model of development. In other words, in this part of the world, political relations go no further than leadership logics (in the stricter sense as we have defined earlier) not really wishing to reach rulership.

Maintaining a form of extra-institutional accountability presents advantages and disadvantages.[38] Non-institutionalization leads to a relative fragility. In a situation of (economic/political) crisis, the leader will often be considered as the one personally responsible. But extra-institutional accountability can also prove to be a resource because the leader is looked to for everything. Why would leaders not continue to make the most of these types of extra-institutional relations (knowing well that for their demands for protection, assistance and development, their supporters will continue to rely on them, and that their reputation depends upon their capacity to meet these expectations)?[39]

Major events like the fall of the Berlin wall, the Soviet Union and Eastern European communist regimes have led us to believe that we are coming out of "longue durée" logics. Western-style democracy and market economy would become inevitable after the collapse of communism. Globalization would be precisely the moment precipitating and accelerating this global change, whilst relations intensify extremely.

Many actors know perfectly well how to make speeches to this end, as a political resource within a domestic perspective and with respect to the developed world. At the national level, recourse to new fashionable slogans (democratization, market economy) are commonly used to de-legitimate ex-top leaders. At the international level, the triumph of liberal ideas and imported Western models are no longer defined in terms of subordination but of opportunity to obtain financial support.

However, if some actors seem inclined to apply what they call the "the right formula", it is necessary to acknowledge that practice does not follow intentions. Behind the speeches set to please the indispensable donors, the observation reveals that, quite often, the same particularist logics continue to be predominant. The legitimacy of formal principles emanating from a modern state framework is seen as inferior to the commandments ensuing from the priority of factional interdependences, which make sense locally and are always easily "instrumentalized". Consequently, in a comparative perspective, globalization does not seem to be driving a convergence of forms of leadership.

On the Norwegian and French cases

By contrast, according to the narrow perspective we have proposed above, leadership would appear as a rather rare form of power in France like in Norway. Just by taking into consideration the deep-rooted presence of a strong state in both countries, or cultures emphasizing the institutionalization of power, it is obvious that particularist and informal exchange relations can only but be exceptional.

In the Norwegian case, the respect of the inhabitants for the State, which has somehow been the major instrument of the country's triumph over poverty and still proves very generous in this period of economic prosperity, may have led to habits of reliance. In such a context, any over-personalization of public relations would tend to be suspect. Admittedly, the ideal of a certain proximity between politicians in charge and citizens is very strong but it makes sense within a political culture where the bureaucratic machinery matters more than the individuals who administer it. Following our approach, in Norway we are dealing more with stances of rulership and headship than with leadership. Possibly Christian Michelsen, the Prime Minister who took Norway out of the Union with Sweden in 1905, would be the exception? In more recent times, Anders Lange, founder of a populist movement and his successor Carl I. Hagen have developed relationships with their supporters which somewhat correspond to our ideal-type. However, it is not at all certain that these relationships have survived the institutionalization of the Progress Party (Harmel & Svånsund 1993). Like in Sweden, Norwegian politicians tend to reject the term "elite". They adopt a rather modest profile and above all consider themselves as representatives of the people. They might accept to be designated as leaders, but only in the sense of personalities who think that they have a strong mandate on a moral basis.

As for France, even though the (political) culture is different in many respects (for instance when considering the display of external signs of power[40]), leadership as we understand it seems just as exceptional. Since political parties have become institutionalized, heads have been much more predominant than leaders. Specialists of business administration show that Anglo-Saxon style leadership cannot easily be established within French firms, because hierarchical power distance generally triumphs over employee's individual skills.[41] This would be very true for the political sphere as well. In a unitary and very state-controlled country like France, leadership logics can be observed only at the local level[42] and within some political parties where a certain informal proximity can sometimes be discerned. J.-M. Le Pen, as the founder of the "National Front", certainly appears to be a leader in the eyes of his supporters. When F. Mitterrand re-constituted the Socialist Party, he could be considered as a leader. But that was not the case anymore after his election as President of the Republic. Actually, after 1981, he was to take cover under the institutions of the Fifth Republic, which he had for a long time criticized. Even Ch. De Gaulle, who had elaborated a doctrine on the chief's necessary aloofness as early as the 1930's, and who claimed to embody the whole country above political cleavages, was hardly a leader according to our definition. In this case, it is important not to confuse charisma with leadership. The General, who placed so much emphasis on the reinforcement of institutions when he came back to power in 1958, belongs to a long French tradition where rulership clearly prevails over leadership.

However, we are quite ready to accept the idea expressed by many authors that political power relations are not reducible to mere rulership in France.[43] As far as Norway is concerned, one may equally think about the fact that political authority is never entirely taken for granted. Even the major actors certainly have to argue most of the time and prove to be convincing. Notwithstanding what has been said above, this certainly makes the investigation regarding leadership in the two countries relevant. However, this can only be done analyzing the singular history and the specific trajectories of the countries studied. It is not a question of defending an immobile vision. On the contrary, one needs to show how these deep structures have been able to evolve and adapt with regard to a changing world environment.

References

Almond, Gabriel A. and Sidney Verba (1965). *The Civic Culture: political attitudes and democracy in five nations*, Boston: Little Brown.
Badie, Bertrand (1983). *Culture et politique*, Paris: Economica.
Bailey, Frederick George (1969). *Stratagems and Spoils: a social anthropology of politics*, Oxford: B. Blackwell.
Bass, Bernard M., ed. (1981). *Stodgill's Handbook on Leadership*, New York: Free Press.
Beetham, David (1991). *The Legitimation of Power*, Basingstoke: Macmillan.
Blondel, Jean (1980). *World Leaders: Heads of Government in the Postwar Period*, London and Beverly Hills: Sage.
Blondel, Jean (1987). *Leadership: towards a general analysis*, London and Beverly Hills: Sage.
Burns, James MacGregor (1978). *Leadership*, Harpercollins.
Chabal, Patrick and Jean-Pascal Daloz (1999). *Africa Works: Disorder as Political Instrument*, Oxford: James Currey Bloomington, Indiana: University Press.
Claeys, Paul-H. and Andre-P Frognier, eds. (1995). *L'échange politique*, Éditions de l'Université de Bruxelles.
Clark, Terry Nichols (1989). "Why [sic] causes political Cultures? Sources and dynamic processes" in Harald Baldersheim, Richard Balme, Terry Nichols Clark, Vincent Hoffmann-Martinot, Håkan Magnusson, eds. *New Leaders, Parties and Groups: Comparative Tendancies in Local Leadership*, Bordeaux-Talence: Cahiers du CERVL.
Clark, Terry Nichols and Vincent Hoffmann-Martinot, eds. (1998). *The New Political Culture*, Boulder: Westview.
Daloz, Jean-Pascal (2002a). *Elites et représentations politiques: la culture de l'échange inégal au Nigeria*, Bordeaux: Presses Universitaires de Bordeaux.
Daloz, Jean-Pascal (2002b). "Ostentation in Comparative Perspective: culture and elite legitimation", *Comparative Social Research*, vol. 21.
Elgie, Robert, ed. (1995). *Political Leadership in Liberal Democracies*, Basingstoke: Macmillan.
Fiorina, Morris P. and Kenneth A. Shepsle (1989). "Formal Theories of Leadership: agents, agenda setters, and entrepreneurs", in Bryan D. Jones, ed. (1989). *Leadership and Politics: new perspectives in political science*, The University of Kansas.
Friedrich, Carl J. (1970). "The Theory of Political Leadership and the Issue of Totalitarianism" in R. Barry Farrel, ed., *Political Leadership in Eastern Europe and the Soviet Union*, Chicago: Aldine.
Frolich, Norman, J.A. Oppenheimer and O.R. Young (1971). *Political Leadership and Collective Goods*, Princeton: Princeton U.P.
Gibb, Cecil A. (1969). "Leadership", in G. Lindzey and E Aronson eds., *The Handbook of Social Psychology*, vol. 4, 2nd edition, Reading (Mass.): Addison-Wesley.
Harmel, Robert and Lars Svånsand (1993). "Party Leadership and Party Institutionalisation": Three Phases of Development", in *West European Politics*, 16/2.

Hofstede, Geert (1997). *Cultures and Organizations: software of the mind*, New York: McGraw-Hill, second edition.
Hoselitz, Bert F. (1971). "Economic Growth and Development. Non economic factors in economic development", in Finkle, Jason L. and Richard W. Gable, *Political Development and Social Change*, 2nd ed. [article first published in 1957].
Huntington, Samuel (1968). *Political Order in Changing Societies*, New Haven: Yale U.P.
Inglehart, Ronald (1988). "The Renaissance of Political Culture", *American Political Science Review*, vol. 82/4.
Janda, Kenneth F. (1972). "Towards the Explication of the Concept of Leadership in Terms of the Concept of Power " in Paige. [First published in 1960].
Jones, Bryan D., ed. (1989). *Leadership and Politics: new perspectives in political science*, The University of Kansas.
Kellermann, Barbara, ed. (1986). *Political Leadership: a source book*, Pittsburgh: University of Pittsburgh Press.
Kitschelt, Herbert (2000). "Linkages Between Citizens and Politicians in Democratic Polities", *Comparative Political Studies*, vol. 33/6-7 (August-September).
Lagroye, Jacques (1985). "La légitimation", in M. Grawitz and J. Leca, eds., *Traité de science politique*, volume 1, Paris: PUF.
Nay, Olivier (2000). "Representation Roles and Institutionalism: the Case of the French Regions", in Rao, Nirmala, ed., *Representation and Community in Western Democracies*, Basingstoke: Macmillan.
Paige, Glenn D. (1977). *The Scientific Study of Political Leadership*, New York, the Free Press.
Paige, Glenn D., ed. (1972). *Political Leadership: Readings for an emerging field*, New York: the Free Press, London: Collier-Macmillan.
Parry, Geraint (1970). *Political Elites*, New York: Praeger.
Sartori, Giovanni (1987). *The Theory of Democracy Revisited*, Chatham: Chatham House Publishers.
Seligman, Lester G. (1950). "The Study of Political Leadership", *Amercian Political Science Review*, vol. 44/4.
Smith, Andy and Claude Sorbets, eds. *Le leadership et les territoires: les cadres d'analyse en débat*, Paris: La Découverte (forthcoming).
Tucker, Robert C. (1981). *Politics as Leadership*, Columbia: University of Missouri Press.
Welsh, William A. (1979). *Leaders and Elites*, New York: Holt, Rinehart and Wintson.
Ysmal, Colette (1985). "Elites et Leaders", in M. Grawitz and J. Leca, eds., *Traité de science politique*, volume 3, Paris: PUF.

Notes

[1] E.g. Burns' chapter 16 (1978) is entitled "Towards a general Theory", whilst one of Blondel's books (1987) is headed "Leadership: Towards a General Analysis".

[2] Slightly attacking Burns' (1978) or Blondel's (1987) famous *summae*, Jones (1989) again emphasises this in the introduction to a quite sophisticated collection of articles, but whose lack of cohesion still betrays some of the profound disagreements on the concept.

[3] The handbooks available on leadership provide abundant illustrations on this. See for example Bass (1981) and Kellermann (1986).

[4] For example Blondel (1987), who immediately slips to a study of "chief executives", after discoursing a little on the notion, within a rather traditional comparative perspective.

[5] On this point, cf. Welsh (1979) and Ysmal (1985), for example.

[6] It would seem that (since the 1960s), the general trend in the literature builds up a conception of leadership that also includes actors not at the apex of political systems. Welsh (1979, p. 17) emphasizes, however, that "the shift has been as much one of semantics as of genuine change in the focus or methods of research".

[7] Whose main representatives are of course Thomas Carlyle and Herbert Spencer (respectively) who astonishingly keep appearing in the manuals although they have been widely considered as out-dated. See Elgie (1995) for example.

[8] See especially Bailey (1969).

[9] Nay (2000).

[10] Janda (1972, p. 58) (Originally published in 1960).

[11] Burns (1978, p. 453).

[12] Burns (1978). See also Frolich, Oppenheimer and Young (1971); Bass (1981, chapter 24).

[13] Claeys & Frognier (1995).

[14] Welsh (1979, p. 18).

[15] Tucker (1981).

[16] Blondel (1980, pp. 13-14).

[17] Lagroye (1985), Beetham (1991).

[18] Contrary to what Blondel (1980, p. 3) says.

[19] Daloz (2002a).

[20] Friedrich (1970).

[21] Gibb (1969).

[22] Burns (1978) verges in this direction (see p. 295 ff) even if the whole of his book is not always very consistent in this respect.

[23] Blondel (1980) begins his book by saying: "Leadership is as old as mankind. It is universal. It exists everywhere [...] ".

[24] Paige (1977, p. 8).

[25] Ibid p. 9 and 11.

[26] Seligman (1950) as quoted by Paige (1977, p. 44).

[27] Burns (1978, p. 24). And yet, following Max Weber, one may think that there are modern forms of authority.

[28] Let us add that they are preferred to approaches pertaining to social classes when the logic of domination is not mainly of an economic nature. On this point, see Parry (1970).

[29] Statement made by all those endeavouring to differentiate elites and leaders. This quotation is taken from Welsh (1979, p. 17). In the same way, Blondel (1987, p. 13) says: "Some leaders do not hold top positions; some holders of top positions are not leaders".

[30] Jones "Leader/Follower Interactions in Mass Democracy" in Jones (1989, p. 42). These approaches are discussed in this collective book.

[31] See Badie (1983) or also Clark (1989) for example.

[32] Fiorina & Shepsle in Jones (1989, p. 36).

[33] Almond & Verba (1965). See also Inglehart (1988).

[34] Burns (1978, p. 296).

[35] Hoselitz (1971), first publication in 1957.

[36] Cf. Clark & Hoffmann-Martinot (1998).

[37] See also Huntington (1968), Sartori (1987), and an alternative perspective in Kitschelt (2000).
[38] This issue will be elaborated on in our paper "Légitimation infra-institutionnelle et cultures politiques: plaidoyer pour une refonte de la théorie du leadership" above-mentioned.
[39] The consequences at the country's macro-level are often catastrophic but at the micro-level of leaders and their respective networks, they maintain a certain rationality in the context studied. This is what we call the "political instrumentalization of disorder". Cf. Chabal & Daloz (1999).
[40] Daloz (2002b).
[41] See for instance Hofstede (1997).
[42] See Paoletti's chapter in this book on the question of proximity (to be contrasted with Cadiou's one in terms of expertise).
[43] Cf. Smith & Sorbets (forthcoming) in this respect.

Chapter 3

The Globalization Debate in France: The Attitudes of Political Leaders

Sébastien Ségas

In this chapter, I am going to focus on the social use of the term "globalization" by a special type of social actor (political leaders) in a specific country (France). The word needs special attention. Since the early 1990s, the word "globalization" has regularly appeared in the discourse of French leaders to the extent that it has even become a subject of debate, or what I would term the object of a struggle of meaning (cf. for example José Bové's movement against an "unruled" globalization). More fundamentally, I think that the use of the word "globalization" helps political leaders make sense of (local and national) situations and define their commitment within these contexts in front of different audiences. In other words, this term is used to form *framing proposals* that seek to define reality in particular ways. What I will try to do here, is to show how these new structures are integrated into the traditional leaders' discourse as a *genre* and how they may fit into various linguistic contexts.

My work is based upon two different types of material: on the one hand, studying the quotations of political leaders on globalization in the well-known French newspaper, "*Le Monde*" over the course of the year 2000 and, on the other hand, analyzing the discourse of rural political leaders whom I interviewed in 2000 for a project on local development. This material may seem heterogeneous, and in fact it is, but in an interesting way, it shows how two different types of leaders (national party or government leaders vs. local leaders) can use the same word in two different contexts (a "national" audience: the "*Le Monde*" readers vs. a face-to-face conversation with a social scientist). This heterogeneity can finally be considered as a heuristic device.

Globalization and frames: globalized frames and frames on globalization

This part of the analysis is aimed at identifying the different uses of the word "globalization" by national and local French leaders. The first thing that struck me was that none of these leaders seems to question the "reality" of globalization. Both national and local leaders agree upon the existence of a trend that can be described as a growing international exchange of goods, cultures and persons. Even José Bové does not deny the reality of globalization. Of course, as I will demonstrate further, they do not necessarily agree on the way this trend should be interpreted, explained and judged but they do all consider that "globalization" is something that can be grasped and that the word "globalization" refers to the same "piece of reality". Although French leaders disagree on the *meaning* of the word "globalization", they agree on the existence of the *reference* this word is supposed to point out in reality.

The word globalization is considered to be a good answer to the question "what is going on *now* in our world?". By our leaders, it is considered as a good description of a changing reality and none of them is saying the reality is not changing or that growing international exchange is not new, which are two possible ways of contesting the relevance of this concept. On the contrary, the word globalization serves, for these leaders, as a basis of reality framing proposals or as an object of moral evaluation (is globalization a good or a bad thing?) or as discussion about its logical nature (is globalization a necessity or something we can change?).

A frame, in the classic conception developed by E. Goffman (inspired by G. Bateson), can be defined as an answer to the question: "What is going on there?". Frames, however, are more than simple cognitive tools. Not only do frames enable actors to understand situations, they also enable them to act in the situations that frames define. In other words, frames define the actor's *commitment* to the situation i.e. the way he can act, what he can do or must do, when he is supposed to act and not supposed to, the opportunities in the situation for action and creation, etc... More than a *cognitive* concept, frame in E. Goffman's perspective is a *pragmatic* one. Moreover, by describing what the situation is and what we can do in it, the frame enables us to compose the "face" that we will try to protect in this interaction, i.e. what we are (or what we want the others to think we are) in context. To define a commitment consists in defining the possibilities of action and discourse, and also the possible (in situation) presentations of self.

My theory is that the use of the word "globalization" helps political leaders to make sense of situations and define their commitment to situations in front of different audiences. We can distinguish different forms of framing in our empirical material by using the two analytical components of frames: cognition and commitment. The cognitive criterion refers to the interaction between the meaning of globalization and the context to which it gives meaning. The commitment criterion distinguishes between different answers to the question "what can or must leaders do in this frame?".

We have just said that we have found that actors agree that globalization is a valid description of reality. In actual discourses, however, the meaning of globalization can vary: it may be considered as a good or bad thing (moral meaning), as a necessity or the fruit of human will (historical meaning), as a cause or an effect (logical meaning), etc.

In my typology[1] of French leaders' use of globalization, I will first distinguish between frames referring to globalization as a given fact and frames for which globalization is a subject of action. I will try to show how these frames define what leaders can and must do and what "face" they can or must put on for their audiences.

Globalization as a given fact

In this category, I will of course include all the discourses that present globalization as a historical law but also all the discourses that present it as a context of or for action, in the sense that you can act *within* it but not *upon* it.

Globalization as an historical or natural law

In this type of discourse, the trend growing exchange of commercial and cultural goods can be specified by their necessity, in the sense this word takes when it is opposed to contingency. This trend expresses a direction of History and can be resumed to a causal law. Here, globalization is not only the name of a movement but the name of an "untouchable" determinism that causes "effects". The notion of "natural frame" can help us to go further.

For E. Goffman, a natural frame, by contrast to a social frame, enables the identification of situations not oriented by human will, that are purely "physical". In this case, globalization is presented as a movement that human will cannot control or change, a frame in which we live but that we have not chosen and cannot modify. So globalization can be presented by leaders as a *quasi-natural* frame that they can use to explain situations to their audience.

We can find explicit expressions of this conception in articles from *"Le Monde"* written by newsmen, economic experts or officials. We must note now that politicians (except for someone like A. Madelin[2]) do not generally expose this kind of frame (I shall return to this issue later). We can take the example of A. Fontaine's response to those who think that globalization is the product of human will: according to him, the word globalization "is today used at random (many designating this as a policy, and to be more exact, an undertaking of capitalist domination) whilst it is about a fact established by the abolition of distances and the technological revolution".[3]

In this newspaper, those in favour of a perception of globalization as a quasi-natural frame are often convinced of its benefits:

> So, globalization can mean that the rich share the largest portion of the economic cake between themselves, but the cake has become so big that even the poor have a bigger portion. Of course, economic reasons are not the only ones nurturing opposition to globalization. But there again, we have encouraging signs, as growing exchange with the world economy has provoked many surprising social and political changes. For example, the country practicing an offensive globalization has spent more in secondary and academic education [...] Expenses have also increased for health, access to social housing and other social programmes [...] Strangely enough, these are the countries where political freedom and individual rights are respected more and more.[4] (Paul A. Laucidina, general director of the Global Business Policy Council-A.T. Kearney)

"Actually, the liberalization of exchanges is beneficial for the society as a whole, even if certain groups briefly suffer from increasing foreign competition".[5] (F. Larsen, Director of the European International Monetary Fund.)

But we must not overlook the fact that the same kind of frame can be used with a very different meaning as when a local leader in a French village says: "I can do nothing about the local repercussions of globalization and world wide exchange for our local industry". Globalization is here a quasi-natural frame, which enables a leader to explain a situation (and his attitude: non-action), which is said to be out of reach for human (and thus political) will. Globalization is here also a cause, which has effects, but these effects are no longer considered as good ones. Here, globalization is considered to be more an expression of *fatality* than history itself.

In the two versions of this kind of discourse (the triumph of democracy through liberalism vs. the adverse historical forces), there is no place for (political) action. The world is framed and dominated by international economic forces or trends, which are not worth opposing (an opposition which is not even desirable in the case of pro-globalization). The political leader who uses this kind of frame is powerless (a sort of "low" profile) but non-responsible or guilty.

Globalization as a context for action

Globalization is here also a given fact in the sense that we live in a "globalized" world and it would be too idealistic to want to change this. But this globalized world is seen as being open, where action is possible. Globalization is no longer a law excluding men, it is a context in which men live, act and explore opportunities. Let's see how a newsman describes the report on globalization produced by the European Union's Committee of the Regions (composed of local councillors from member countries): "The text also supports job creation schemes without denying the necessities of globalization which, "being registered within a dynamic of opening and complex fixation of the world, conceals a formidable growth potential". For all that, it is also out of the question to succumb to its charms: those elected locally are in the right position to know that, if globalization is recognized as a "zero sum game", it produces winners and losers both among companies as well as among regions".[6] In this zero sum game, local councillors have to make strategic choices and the committee advises them that: "in the committee's opinion there are two possible approaches as regards reinforcing competitiveness... It is not in favor of the first solution, which consists in helping companies [...]. The regional committee, instead, prefers a long-term approach, based on cooperation from the public and private sectors, research and production, and also based on the association of a real quality of life and modern infrastructures".[7]

In this frame, political leaders are presented as actors in a globalization context and not as victims or agents of it. They are rational actors that adapt themselves to a context, develop strategies, and choose the objectives and means to achieve it. This rational attitude does not exclude creativity: you can invent new means or new objectives, but this creativity does not express itself in a normative or value-based way as when globalization is seen as an object of action and human judgment.

Globalization as an object

As for this second type of discourse, I shall analyze respectively presentations of globalization as a) an object of social struggle and modification and as b) an object of control. What these two approaches have in common is that they do not consider globalization as a quasi "natural frame", non-modifiable by human action but as an object of social action: humans can decide to stop this process or choose the degree and/or the extension of its development.

It is important to note that the reality of globalization as a process is not denied: this reality is a necessary basis for its control, modification or annihilation. You cannot fight against something which does not exist; you cannot control globalization if the reference indicated by the word is non-existent for you.

Globalization as an object of social struggle

In these discourses, globalization, in its current form, is judged as a bad evolution of society that political action must fight against by trying to modify its nature. José Bové has become famous for expanding on such topics with his desire to switch from a "liberal globalization" to a "democratic globalization". But traditional political leaders express similar theories, both on the left wing and on the right wing. On the left wing, R. Hue, the leader of the French communist party (PCF) expresses his determination to fight against a liberal globalization and denounces the EU as a "a springboard for liberal globalization". A. Lipietz, a leader of the Greens, can declare: "all these Briton flags, these ATTAC streamers, saying that the world is not a piece of merchandise, it's just the 1960s coming back. People are again beginning to think that they can change something. They are not resigned in the face of the market anymore as in the 1980s. Demonstrating against the black tide, denouncing bad quality food, fighting against the effects of globalization and denouncing lorries in the alpine massifs, it's all the same."[8]

The Jacobins of the leftist anti-European party (the MDC) fight against globalization because "globalization is the new word for imperialism and capitalism".[9] S. Naïr, one of the leaders of this party, employs highly martial expressions referring to the idea of a true social struggle: "We are all involved in the struggle against haphazard globalization".[10] The MDC discourse departs from that of the Green leaders because the response of the former to globalization is not linked to a (postulated) global awareness and democratization at world level (as in the case of J. Bové), but is instead a call for the reinforcement of the traditional Nation-State: "By breaking up the nation, we are denying ourselves of one of the last counterbalances to the triumph of haphazard globalization".[11] [S. Naïr] This kind of discourse comes close to that of the right-wing "souverainiste" leaders such as P. Seguin and C. Pasqua.

Political responses to globalization can also be in the form of advocacy of a new form of international governance. According to the French prime minister L. Jospin: "To organize globalization, so that mastery over it is more democratic, new forms of collaboration must be invented within stronger and more legitimate multilateral institutions [...] Political globalization therefore remains to be constructed. This type of globalization bears a name: regulation [...] We cannot allow so-called natural economic laws to guide the evolution of our societies. This would mean renouncing our political responsibilities. We must on the contrary seek to govern the forces which are at work in the globalization of the economy".[12] In his view, "the world is not just a market, our societies need rules and the economy must be at the service of man and not the reverse [...] Faced with the often excessive appetite of market interests, the right of the human person, the quality of our environment and our resources, have to be defended. This is one of the essential assignments of a modern State".[13]

In these kinds of frames, leaders present themselves as people who use their creativity normatively in order to point society in a new direction. They do not accept globalization as a context, they denounce it as a norm: globalization is a trend which serves an ideology (the liberal one) and they propose new or different norms and ideologies to guide actions. Consequently, they start to oppose those supporting the existence of a "natural law of globalization".

Globalization as an object of control

Globalization is, in these discourses, an overall positive trend, but the direction of which has to be controlled. This is clearly the position of the president of the French Republic, J. Chirac: "It [globalization] is ineluctable, inevitable. Today, globalization is by definition the great force of progress, in so far as it allows for the increase and acceleration of exchanges, which, in our day, create wealth. But it involves serious dangers [...] If we are not careful, it will considerably accentuate the phenomena of exclusion. The second danger is the development of international crime [...] And the third danger is that globalization, through the race for profits it engenders, seriously risks implicating our global ecosystem [...] it can only be controlled by an international agreement. Making profits is absolutely legitimate, but not at all costs".[14]

This desire to control can take the form of the protection of a particular domain, for example, the defence by the French government of an "exception culturelle" before the World Trade Organization. We find another spectacular example of the will to control the specific drawbacks of this ineluctable movement in the MNR (extreme right) election platform which advocates a "sanitary inspection at the borders to limit the epidemiological risks linked to globalization".[15]

In this frame, the leader is no longer a person proposing a new vision of Globalization or a change in the nature of the process. He is seen as a man who can control the trend: the main idea is that he can fine-tune the degree of society's "globalization" or keep some domain outside the reach of globalization. To a certain extent, globalization is subject to human (and therefore leaders') will. In this kind of frame, the leader is seen as the person defining the desirable degree of globalization, i.e. like persons who act *upon* globalization.

The traditional face of the French leaders

In the preceding sections, we have isolated specific forms of commitment or "faces" that politician leaders want to project. Next, to understand how the different frames we have identified can challenge the traditional relation between the leader and his audience, I will try to identify what is the *typical form* of leaders' commitment in French political discourse.

We suggest that leaders project certain faces in their discourses and they have to respect some "conditions of felicity" if they want to be taken seriously [Goffman, 1974]. But do these faces and conditions differ from one context to another, or can we define a number of common "features" in the faces that French politicians project in their discourses?

The analysis of C. Le Bart may help us answer this question. In his opinion, there are at least two ways of analyzing political discourse: we can consider it as a whole and examine it in terms of *genres* (just as there are literary genres – poetry, drama, novel, etc., there would be discourse genres and political discourse would be one of them) or focus on discourses in their singularity and also look at their *styles* (as in the case of books, all the discourses would have their own style). But, if every discourse has its style, determined by the usage context and the biography of the speaker, each discourse has to respect the rules of the genre if the speaker wants its audience (who have expectations) to identify what is termed as a (good) political discourse, a discourse that partakes of this specific genre. C. Le Bart has tried to identify the rules[16] (that he calls "abstractions") that define political discourse as a genre in France. From these rules we can deduce the common figures of French political faces projected in discourse: each political discourse can project a specific face (even for the same politician), but each specific face must be in agreement with the rules of the genre.

Of course, a genre can evolve: innovators can create new rules and try to re-define a genre with more or less success (as we will see, A. Madelin's discourse can be interpreted in this way). Consequently, the typical face that we are going to identify is no more than a historically constructed form that may be dismantled at a later stage. In fact, I think some uses of the word globalization pose a threat to the traditional typical face of the French leader or a traditional political condition of Felicity.

According to C. Le Bart, political discourse *as a genre* is based upon and serves as a vehicle for four fundamental "abstractions" [P. Bourdieu, 1982, calls them *"illusio"*]:

- Social reality is transparent: the social world is simple, easy to understand. The politician must appear as a person who can understand and explain this reality.
- Political authority is legitimate: political discourse can legitimate a politician as a particular person but also (and often at the same time) as a role and social position.
- Politicians can rule social reality: political discourse "tells about" the power of politicians, it shows them as men who can change the world, who

do things (we can think about the work of self-appraisal made through discourse: "I was the one who did such and such...", "It is thanks to me (to my support) that this could (or could not) happen...", etc.).
- Discourse can construct identities: by using categories (like citizen, French people, the nation of Norway, the German enemy...), political discourse imposes an identity on the receptors in the communication contract (an identity that people can disagree with: "I am not French, I am Basque" for example). By showing a community, by identifying its enemies, politicians confirm their representative role, i.e. to be an "I" who speaks in name of a "we" (a community) reinforced by a "them" (the enemies of the community).

From these *illusio* we can deduce the image of politicians that political discourse as a genre conveys: a politician is someone who knows reality better than the common run of people, who rules the world and has the right to do it, who represents us.[17] So, we have an idea of the political face that politicians try to maintain in their discourses and interactions with people.

Before going further, I would like to warn the reader not to be misled by the word *illusio*. It does not imply that politicians are cynical actors who claim to do things that they cannot do (or that they have not done) in order to maintain the public in an illusion that serves their interests. In fact, this cynical attitude is one possibility but it does not exclude the other possibility: a politician can believe in these four *illusio*. For C. Le Bart (1998), the belief in these *illusio* could explain a politician's arrival into politics, cynicism beginning later (with experience and political failures). This last theory can seem a little bit far-fetched but it stresses the point that cynical actors and men with a "militant" attitude meet the same "constraints": both must reproduce these *illusio* in their discourse if they want to be re-elected (Will you vote for someone who tells you: "I will not change anything because social reality is too complex"?). However, sincere actors follow the rules without thinking about them. As G. Deleuze (1969) said (but in another context), only surface has importance, what is hidden behind faces (sincerity, cynicism, or secret intentions in general) does not have any importance in our analysis: only the political face projected through communication is important.

Figure 3.1 A typology of globalization frame proposals in French political discourse

Nature of globalization	Status of globalization	Possibility of action	The leader's form of Commitment
Globalization as a given fact	Law/fatality	Non-action	Leader without power and without responsibility
	Context	Actions in context/ opportunities	Strategic decider
Globalization as an object of action	Movement to control	Action of context	Controller
	Movement to modify	Social fight against context	Leader as creator of a new world (new identity, new norms)

The limits of globalization: frame limits and the face of the leader

Our typology of the frames built around the concept of globalization would be clear if we were to distinguish between two levels of discourse: discourses about globalization and discourse "with" globalization. I think that we cannot understand the French use of the term "Globalization" if we do not isolate the strong debate on globalization and the specific use of the term to explain concrete situations (and the attitude of the leader-speaker in front of these situations). These two levels of discourse correspond to two different types of repercussions in terms of the speaker's commitment: at the situational level, new types of "faces" of the leader are proposed whereas at the reflexive level, some frames reinforce the traditional image of the leaders as we have identified it.

The situational level

At this level of discourse, the role of the word globalization is that of a resource enabling one to give a meaning to a concrete event, action or project (or references if we use a linguistic vocabulary). To play that role, globalization may appear as a given fact in our world and not an object of struggle of meaning. To propose interpretations based on globalization as a given fact, our speaker can at least use two registers: the fatality register and the opportunity register.

The "fatality" register

In this frame, globalization appears as a bad evolution of our society that one does not have the ability to fight. As a register, it can be used to give meaning to a concrete situation and define the speaker's degree of commitment. For instance, a mayor of a small town undergoing a textile crisis can launch an anti-attribution process by using a globalization register: "It is not my fault, we cannot compete with the price of the Southern-Asian economies in these days of globalization...". The reference to "globalization" is here a way to protect a feature of the leader's political face: he is not politically responsible because it is an international economic event which destroys employment. But, if his responsibility in so far as a community (a "we") representative is partly preserved (on condition that his audience accepts this explanation), another component of his "political face" is not respected. A politician who uses this kind of register to give meaning to a concrete situation admits that there is at least a part of reality that he cannot rule, he loses (his) face as a ruler to preserve his responsibility (his face as a community representative). And, actually, it could sometimes seem better to admit a lack of power than a lack of action.

These frame proposals leave a new kind of political face to the citizens' judgment that we can call, in reference to the "traditional" one: a *truncated face*. The leader is a person who understands reality but who cannot act upon it, and consequently, cannot be judged responsible before the community he represents. But this kind of frame is evidently limited: leaders cannot present this "face" too frequently if they do not want to seem to admit their uselessness (for instance a leader can admit his powerlessness in the economic sphere but not in others).

The opportunity register

In this register, globalization is not given as a fatality but as a context where actors live and can develop strategies. Globalization is here a challenge for concrete communities and institutions, which have cards to play in this new world (or game).

This register is particularly used to give an evaluation of a decision or strategy ("this decision is not good for France in a globalized context") or to expose political programs. We can take the example of mayors from two big French cities when campaigning: in Bordeaux A. Juppé defended "an offensive strategy of towns within a context of permanent competition born out of globalization."[18], whereas in Toulouse, P. Douste-Blazy defined his platform in this way: "by drawing on the remarkable achievements of this exiting municipality [...] it is possible to prepare Toulouse for the great challenges of globalization and technological revolution, so that this town becomes the big French economic capital of the 21st century."[19] In the same vein, a rural leader of the Médoc[20] presented us with his analysis of the (and his) local situation thus: the return of the petrol industry is a dream because of international competition; we have to adopt a new developmental strategy adapted to a globalized context based upon our prestigious and world-renowned agricultural products (wine and the *agneau de Pauillac*).

We may note that the same type of register is used to give a comparable meaning to three different references (a project for Bordeaux, one for Toulouse and another for Médoc!). At the relational level i.e. the "face" level proposed by this kind of discourse, the political leader appears as the person defining strategies for his city (or country or whatever) in a new world. This register draws the portrait of a leader who, if s/he cannot change what is given (the globalized context), will adapt her/his city to the situation and will obtain the better part in that context. The leader is no longer a ruler (a person who can change or modify the rules of the game or use his creativity at the normative level), s/he is seen as a player in a game that s/he cannot define. But our leader "saves" (his) face as an extraordinary person as s/he shows her-/himself to be the better player, the person who knows the game (the leader knows reality) and is able to create the best strategies to win. In other words, this kind of discourses substitutes (at least for a moment) a new kind of projected face (the leader as a game-player) for the traditional one (the leader as a ruler of reality).

To sum up, putting globalization in context can be a way for a leader to attribute a fact he is reproached with (fatality register) to a blind and uncontrollable mechanism or a way to redefine his face as a game player and strategic actor.

The reflexive level

By discourse "about" globalization, I mean discourses in which globalization forms the subject. It is the kind of discourse that has drawn the attention of analysts and journalists because it has become of great importance in France at least since the birth of J. Bovey's movement (ATTAC). But, because of their ignorance concerning the other level of discourse "with" the word globalization, analysts and journalists overlook the specific nature of this kind of discourse.

These discourses are discourses *about* frames and not only framing *proposals* for specific situations. What is at stake in the former type of discourse is the validity of globalization as a general frame in order to understand our world, to act and place ourselves within it. Globalization is here an object of debate between two extreme positions with some intermediary ones.

The first position includes those for whom globalization is a "quasi natural frame", a historical evolution that you cannot fight without risking isolation, losing competitiveness and finally being thrown out of the run of history. This position is on the whole defended by economists, experts and journalists more than by politicians. A. Madelin and his partisans, however, are often close to this line of thought.

The second position denounces the former one as an ideology which prompts "laissez-faire" attitudes: they think political action can modify globalization, they want to change the "run of history". Those found in this position are most of the party leaders from the Communists, the Greens and the "souverainistes" from the right wing. For J. Bové, "globalization is not a meteorological phenomenon, it is a deliberate de-regulation".[21] According to many "souverainistes", globalization is the "mask of American hegemony".

Between these two extremes, we find those who want to keep globalization in check to avoid its undesirable effects. Here we can include most of the leaders of the Socialist party and of traditional right wing parties.

The nature of the debate is clear: is globalization a necessity or something you can act upon? H. Joas (1999) would probably describe this debate as a "democratization of globalization", the actors becoming aware that the existing globalization, constructed by or through human action can become an object of action, i.e. an object of social struggle between those supporting a historical law of globalization and those who want to make a subject of social reflection and voluntary choice out of globalization. This reflection and this choice would determine the extent to which France should open up to globalization (for instance in which area) and/or if we should cease or modify this process (with perhaps a global action). It is obvious that this debate has a moral background: speakers have to determine if globalization is a good thing in some contexts and a bad thing in others.

This level of discourse can be specified by its *reflexivity*. Leaders are talking about a general view of the world, trying to determine the status of globalization: is it a natural frame or a social one, i.e. one that can be modified by action? We come across this partly creative restructuring of a "view" of the world in contexts where this kind of general reflection is appreciated: in prestigious newspapers like *Le Monde*, in books written by politicians but also on traditional occasions where politicians are supposed to propose and expose their "vision" of society: programs for national elections, greetings to the nation, etc.

One of the stakes of this discussion (which is a frame discussing the validity of a frame) on the status of globalization as a frame is relational in the sense that it affects the face that the speaker (the leader) projects before his audience. In fact, we have just seen that political discourse, as a genre, nurtures the ideas that politicians rule the world and that national (and infra-national) communities exist (and must continue to do so). But globalization, when it is understood as a natural frame, is linked to the idea that trade (and in particular economic trade) rules the world (in particular its economy) and that the notion of frontier is inefficient. In other words, the growing importance and autonomy of the economy would involve a withdrawal of politicians from the economic sphere to the benefit of the international market and would challenge the frontiers which are a fundamental element for registering the political community within space. This frame goes against the *illusio* of the political ruling of the world and gives us the impression that politicians are subjected to the social world. So, the debate on globalization can be reformulated in a relational perspective: have political leaders lost (their) face or are they still rulers or our world?

Those supporting globalization as a law of history are against the idea of a political rulership as understood in France, which can explain why few politicians adopt this perspective, except A. Madelin who proposes a new definition (for a French audience in any case) for a politician's role and face: a politician who would respect the autonomy and the superiority of the economic sphere. This view can be seen as a way of coming to grips with the actual situation: the faces built in context to respond to situations (the leader as a strategist or as a man without changing power) become elements of a reflexive discourse where the role of politicians is redefined: its area of action is restricted to a "laissez-faire" perspective.

Globalization seen as an object of control or social struggle transforms the traditional commitment of French politicians to reality: leaders can rule and even change the world. Moreover, this kind of reflexive discourse can reinforce the image of the politician as a man able to understand reality and as a creator of new values and identities (cf. José Bové and his "world citizen" concept for instance).

Frame limits

In a Goffmanian perspective we have to question the limits of the frames we have defined, the point where a frame proposal is no longer relevant, the point where a frame has to yield its place to another frame. Although a serious study of these limits would surely involve an empirical study on the audiences' reception of political discourses, I think our analysis can help us make some hypotheses on them. These limits are linked to the usage context: in contexts, some elements are or can become relevant and make the use of a specific frame difficult. In the following discussion, I will try to show how some of these elements: the framed problems, the economic conjuncture and the position of the speaker linked to the expectations of his audience related to his position, can define and/or modify the limits of a frame[22] (which actors may eventually try to break).

The position of the speaker

Every speaker is not likely to generate the same type of expectation. For instance, the mayor of a small town in a rural area will probably not resort to the same discourse on globalization as a prime minister. The first one will tend towards using the fatalistic register because he and his audience will not understand how a rural mayor could claim to struggle with an international trend. In contrast, a politician who pursues a national career may appear more legitimate as having a strong position upon this problem because people generally consider that general options can be taken at this level: a prime minister of a western country can say that he will combat the bad effects of globalization without being made fun of. Even at the national level, people could have doubts about the ability of leaders of a middle-sized nation like France to control or rule an international and powerful international trend. But national decision-makers may have recourse in their discourse to the help of international political organizations like the E.U. Thus, J. Chirac can declare that "there is no alternative to European construction if we want [...] to maintain and defend our own values in the face of globalization, which conveys progress but also risks, which Europeans will only be able to master together".[23] Likewise for A. Lipietz, "We need a European constitution to give the floor to the citizens of Europe. And the social forces opposing liberal globalization must take care of European construction in the same way progressive forces have set the establishment of a Welfare State against the all-powerful Market in the past".[24]

A leader also has a biography (a man who has been anti-globalization would have more difficulty in shifting to a pro-globalization discourse) and political baggage which partly limits his field of discourse. Thus, the word "globalization" has become what we could call a term-marker of political baggage for the anti-globalization parties (The green Party, the MDC, the right-winged "souverainistes" of the RPF).

By using certain terms and registers a politician can show his adherence to a party by reproducing its doctrine (or more subtly, he can show his heterodoxy, his singularity, his modernity by using words that he is not expected to use as a member of a particular party). In fact, language, which is obviously a system of expression, can act at the same time as a system of recognition (Ghiglione, 1989). By listening to the particular language of politicians, we can generally say whether it is a communist or a conservative talking. We may identify what F. Bon called *ideo-systèmes* (Le Bon, 1991) marked by specific terms. Hence, in our case in France, the term-markers are different between the pros and the cons when politicians talk of globalization: in fact, if pro would talk of "globalization", the cons would use two terms to distinguish the process from the ideology that sustains it.[25] For instance, P. Seguin distinguishes "globalization as an objective reality" from "globalization as an ideology of standardization" which would serve as a "pretext for doing away with politics".[26]

These markers are "entries" in two different linguistic registers: one which is opposed to, or has reserves concerning globalization, one which presents globalization as a positive opportunity or fatality. By using the right terms a politician can show that he is a good anti-globalization militant for instance. But these linguistic rules can enable one to show his heterodoxy by breaking them: a leader could show his singularity by defending his heterodox opinion but will have to face the reaction of his party companions. Thus, in 2000, a text of D. Cohn-Bendit, which was said to be too allusive and not "aggressive" enough with regard to globalization, became a controversial subject.

The economic situation

A bad economic situation (for example, a mayor faced with the collapse of a firm) can launch a process of non-responsibility referring to a fatality register: "It is the global market that fixes the rules today and we can do nothing about it". The reference to globalization is here a way to protect the leader's political face: he is not politically responsible because the international economic trend is inimical to employment. The bad effects of globalization can also serve as a basis for a discourse of mobilization based upon the idea of a struggle against or a control of that process.

In a good situation, these uses of the term "globalization" are likely to diminish. The fatalistic register seems to be a negative one, it is not a process of self-attribution but of hetero-attributions ("it is the mayor's fault..."). It does not refer to action but justifies a lack of action ("there is nothing I can do against globalization"). It does not confirm a political *"illusio"* but protects the electoral interests of a politician. In the same way, the idea of controlling the international economic forces can become less relevant if the national growth rate is high, and then the discourse against globalization can focus on the ethic or cultural aspect of the process (the hegemony of the American culture, the cult of profit). On the contrary, in a good economic conjuncture, leaders are more likely to present globalization as an opportunity for strategist deciders.

The problem

The word "globalization" does not only indicate economic movements. It can also be used to describe the growth of cultural trade: this aspect can be judged positive even in a discourse that denounces the economic consequences of globalization. Thus, there is a discourse on the opportunities offered by Internet when it comes to increasing our knowledge of other cultures and communication with people all around the world. But in France, globalization is described by the principal political leaders as a menace to French identity confronted with a movement of cultural homogenization or Americanization.

According to J. Chirac, France leads a true struggle "in the name of all creations, all identities, all cultures. If globalization is rich in promises, it threatens the national and cultural identities [...]". Today, to France, "being the motor of cultural diversity in the world is for her a modern way of remaining true to her own universalism since 1789".[27] To J. Lang, one of the leaders of the Socialist party, "A counter-power needs to be established against globalization that so strongly influences people's minds. If we want our people to keep their originality, it is essential for the governments to fight to preserve their national existence."[28]

The same political actor can take up different positions depending upon the nature of the problem. In France, those who are pro-globalization in the economic field are not always partisans of a global culture. We have just seen that J. Chirac, in his desire to control economic globalization, wants to stop the cultural globalization process in a logic of social struggle. For this struggle, French leaders do not have recourse to the EU or any other international organization: it is the French society and state, guided by its political leaders who are leading the struggle. As we can see, the limits of the frame can vary according to the problem (or reference) that is indicated.

Even in the economic domain, the use of the term "globalization" is likely to change if the speaker talks about the textile industry (threatened by strong international competition) or high-tech firms (which export their products and for which globalization seems to be an opportunity).

Conclusions

Most French analysts describe globalization as a process that weakens political power. In their view, the growing economic, cultural and human worldwide transactions create a world that politicians do not control anymore. I hope that this chapter has shown that the situation is more complex than it may seem when we look at the word "globalization" as a component of French leaders' discourses.

Some leaders like A. Madelin construct and project a new and *modest* political face through their globalized frames. However, the term is also used by politicians to preserve features of their faces, following their failures (fatality register), to build new programmes and even to become a subject of debate. As long as globalization becomes, at least in discourse, an object of political action, the leader re-projects his traditional face in front of his audience: a person capable of understanding and ruling reality, who can create norms and identities, and who is legitimized to do so.

Moreover, some leaders can, according to the usage context or the subject or area in question, change their register and frame, and project a plurality of discursive faces in space and time and not necessarily a single and universal (i.e. in all contexts) "modest face" in a world which has become largely apolitical. But it is important to note that the audience can (when they pay heed to the message) re-interpret and refuse the faces and the frames proposed to them: they can think the frame inappropriate to the indicated *reference*, that it has no *meaning* or has a bad one, or, at the *intentional*[29] level, that the proposed face is only an easy mask for the leader. Actually, projected faces are not always assured of a good mirror.

References

Austin J. L. (1970). *Quand dire, c'est faire*. Paris: Seuil.
Berger, P. (1966). *Invitation to sociology*. London: Pelican Books.
Blanchet, A., Ghiglione, R., Massonat, J., Trognon, A. (1987). *Les techniques d'enquête en sciences sociales*. Paris: Bordas.
Bourdieu, P. (1982). *Ce que parler veut dire*. Paris: Fayard.
Deleuze, G. (1969). *Logique du sens*. Paris: Editions de Minuit.
De Luze, H. (1997). *L'Ethnométhodologie*. Paris: Economica.
Edelman, M. (1991). *Pièces et règles du jeu politique*. Paris: Seuil.
Ghiglione, R. (1989). *Je vous ai compris*. Paris: A. Colin.
Goffman, E. (1974). *Façons de parler*. Paris: Editions de Minuit.
Goffman E. (1974). *Les rites d'interaction*. Paris: Editions de Minuit.
Joas, H. (1999). *La créativité de l'agir*. Paris: Cerf.
Le Bart, C. (1998). *Le discours politique*. Paris: Que sais-je?.
Le Bon, F. (1991). *Les discours de la politique*. Paris: Economica.
Schapp, W. (1992). *Empêtrés dans des histoires*. Paris: Editions du Cerf.

Notes

[1] This typology is analytic in the sense that real discourses are often mixed forms. For instance, the same leader can successively adopt different types of frames or combine several frames in the same discourse.

[2] The leader of "Démocratie Libérale", a right wing party, partisan of the "laissez-faire".

[3] "est employé aujourd'hui à tort et à travers, beaucoup désignant par-là une politique, et, pour mieux dire, une entreprise de domination capitaliste, alors qu'il s'agit d'un fait, engendré par l'abolition des distances et la révolution technologique", *Le Monde*, 27 April 2000.

[4] "Ainsi la mondialisation peut signifier que les riches se partagent la plus grosse part du gâteau économique, mais le gâteau est devenu tellement grand que les pauvres ont également une part plus grande. Bien sûr, les considérations économiques ne sont pas les seules qui alimentent l'opposition à la mondialisation. Mais, là encore, il y a des signes encourageants, car des échanges croissants avec l'économie mondiale ont provoqué des changements sociaux et politiques nombreux et surprenants. Par exemple, les pays pratiquant une mondialisation offensive ont dépensé plus dans l'éducation secondaire et universitaire [...] Les dépenses ont également augmenté dans la santé, l'accès au logement social et autres programmes sociaux [...] Ce sont les pays où, curieusement, les libertés politiques et les droits de l'individu sont de plus en plus respectés", *Le Monde*, 10 October 2000.

[5] "En fait la libéralisation des échanges est bénéfique pour la société dans son ensemble, même si certains groupes souffrent à court terme, de l'intensification de la concurrence étrangère", Le monde, 19 September 2000.

[6] "Le texte va également dans le sens d'une promotion de l'emploi, sans nier les impératifs et les bienfiats de la mondialisation qui, 's'inscrivant dans une dynamique d'ouverture et de complexifixation du monde, recèle un formidable potentiel de croissance". Pas question, pour autant, de succomber à ses charmes: les élus locaux sont bien placés pour savoir que, si la mondialisation est reconnue comme "un jeu à somme nulle", elle fait des gagnants et des perdants tant chez les entreprises que parmi les régions.

[7] "l'avis du comité analyse les deux approches possibles en matière de renforcement de la compétitivité et fait clairement son choix. La première solution, qui consiste à aider les entreprises [...] n'a pas ses faveurs. C'est pourquoi le comité des régions préfère une démarche de long terme, fondée sur la coopération du public et du privé, de la recherche et de la production, et sur l'association d'une vraie qualité de vie et d'infrastructures modernes", *Le Monde*, 18 January 2000.

[8] "tous ces drapeaux bretons, ces banderoles d'ATTAC, disant que le monde n'est pas une marchandise, c'est l'atmosphère des années 60 qui revient. Les gens recommencent à croire qu'ils peuvent changer quelque chose. Ils ne sont plus résignés face au marché comme dans les années 80. manifester contre la marée noire, dénoncer la mal-bouffe, lutter contre les effets de la mondialisation, dénoncer les camions dans les massifs alpins tout cela, c'est pareil", *Le Monde*, 8 February 2000.

[9] "la mondialisation c'est le nouveau mot pour parler d'impérialisme et de capitalisme", *Le Monde*, 2 September 2000.

[10] "Nous sommes partie prenante du combat contre la mondialisation sauvage", *Le Monde*, 31 August 2000.

[11] "En cassant la nation, on se prive d'un des derniers contre-poids au triomphe de la globalization sauvage", *Le Monde*, 23 August 2000.

[12] "Pour ordonner la mondialisation, pour que la maîtrise en soit plus démocratique, il faut inventer des formes nouvelles de concertation au sein d'institutions multilatérales plus

fortes et plus légitimes [...] La mondialisation politique reste donc à construire. Cette mondialisation porte un nom: la régulation [...] Nous ne pouvons pas laisser des lois économiques prétendument naturelles guider l'évolution de nos sociétés. Ce serait abdiquer nos responsabilités politiques. Nous devons au contraire chercher à gouverner les forces qui sont à l'œuvre dans la mondialisation de l'économie", *Le Monde*, 27 June 2000.

[13] "le monde n'est pas qu'un marché, nos sociétés ont besoin de règles, l'économie doit être au service de l'homme et non l'inverse. [...] Face à l'appetit souvent excessif des intérêts marchands, le droit de la personne humaine, la qualité de notre environnement et de nos ressources, doivent être défendus. C'est là une des missions essentielles d'un Etat moderne", *Le Monde*, 4 January 2000.

[14] "Elle [la mondialisation] est inéluctable, inévitable. La mondialisation est par définition le grand facteur actuel de progrès, dans la mesure où ellle permet d'accentuer, d'accélérer les échanges, qui sont aujourd'hui les plus créateurs de richesses. Mais elle comporte des dangers sérieux [...] Si l'on n'y prend pas garde, elle va accentuer considérablement les phénomènes d'exclusion. Le deuxième danger, c'est le developpement de la criminalité internationale [...] Et le troisième danger, c'est que cette mondialisation, par la course au profit qu'elle génère, rique de mettre en cause gravement notre écosystème mondial. [...] elle ne peut être maîtrisée que par un accord international. Faire des profits, c'est tout à fait légitime, mais cela n'autorise pas tout", *Le Monde*, 15 July 2000.

[15] "contrôle sanitaire aux frontières pour limiter les risques épidémiologiques liés à la mondialisation", *Le Monde*, 3 October 2000.

[16] In our mind, rules are both constraining and enabling (they enable to produce political discourses).

[17] We have to notice that, by projecting this face, the politician proposes a definition of the listeners (you are less intelligent than me, you are a whole that I represent, etc.). Thus, the leader who presents himself as a leader in his discourse defines his listeners as followers (and tries to impose his definition).

[18] "une stratégie offensive des villes dans le contexte de concurrence permanente née de la mondialisation", *Le Monde*, 11 April 2000.

[19] "en s'appuyant sur le bilan remarquable de la municipalité sortante [...] il est possible de préparer Toulouse aux grands défis de la mondialisation et de la révolution technologique, afin que la ville deviennne la grande capitale économique française du XXIème siècle", *Le Monde*, 2 February 2000.

[20] The Médoc is a rural area near Bordeaux, famous for its wines.

[21] "la mondialisation n'est pas un phénomène météorologique, c'est une dérégulation délibérée", *Le Monde*, 22 June 2000.

[22] Other factors can have an influence upon discourse: for instance, the audience (a leader will surely not say the same thing about globalization in front of unemployed persons or in front of company managers) or the medium used (public speech, TV, radio). This sensibility of discourse to context must make us conscious that there is not a good discourse (i.e. acceptable everywhere).

[23] "il n'y a pas d'alternative à la construction européenne si nous voulons [...] conserver et défendre les valeurs qui sont les nôtres face à une mondialisation, porteuse de progrès mais aussi de risques, que les Europ_ens ne pourront maîtriser qu'ensemble", *Le Monde*, 20 June 2000.

[24] "Il nous faut une Constitution européenne pour rendre la parole aux citoyens et citoyennes d'Europe. Et que les forces sociales qui s'opposent à la globalization libérale s'emparent de la construction européenne comme jadis les forces progressistes opposèrent

l'édification d'un Etat Providence à la toute puissance du Marché", *Le Monde*, 13 December 2000.

[25] Like any important term, the word 'globalization' forms the subject of a distinct struggle of definition: each side tries to monopolise the legitimate use of this term and to impose its definition.

[26] "alibi à l'effacement du politique", *Le Monde*, May 2000.

[27] "au nom de toutes les créations, de toutes les identités, de toutes les cultures. La mondialisation, si elle est riche en promesses, menace les identités culturelles nationales [...] Aujourd'hui, pour la France, être le moteur de la diversité culturelle dans le monde est sa façon, moderne, d'être fidèle à l'universalisme qui est le sien depuis 1789", *Le Monde*, 17 July 2000.

[28] "Il faut établir un contre-pouvoir contre la mondialisation qui rabote les esprits. Si on veut que nos peuples gardent leur originalité, il est essentiel que nos gouvernements se battent pour préserver leur existence nationale", *Le Monde*, 4 August 2000.

[29] Intention (and feeling) is the third level of the construction of signification. Cf. D. Dennett's strategy of the interpreter.

Chapter 4

The Norwegian Globalization Debate

Øyvind Østerud

During the 1990s globalization emerged as the Grand Narrative of our time. The full-fledged story said that economies, cultures, and social formations were disconnected from their territorial frameworks, and that the world was now woven together in a network of new kinds of contact, collective agents, dependency relationships, and self-constructions (Castells I-III 1996-98, Held et al, 1999).

This epochal diagnosis has rather dramatic implications. National and parliamentarian democracy becomes impotent and irrelevant within the new power relations of globalized networks. Representative democracy is tied up with a political system that is narrower than the supranational structures that permeate social life – economically, politically, culturally, and even linguistically. Thus the nation-state and its political institutions recede as remnants from bygone times. Democracy, traditionally conceived, becomes an illusion that is veiling the new, borderless modernity.

Still, the globalization debate has not arrived in such a neat packet. There is a plethora of globalization debates both within and across political boundaries. Globalization – economically and culturally – is an uneven process of development, with winners and losers. The debate of globalization, accordingly, is a reflection of this uneven process as well as a formative element upon it. Furthermore, there are, paradoxically, national specifics to the debate; it comes in versions emerging from the national scenes and discursive traditions in various countries. The debate of globalization, then, is not really a global debate, even if some features of the general theme have diffused globally.

The topic here is the specifics of the globalization debate in Norway as it has emerged over the last few years. Some basic characteristics of the debate will be explained against a double backdrop: the peculiarities of Norway's foreign policy debate prior to the themes of globalization; and the peculiarities of Norway's structural conditions – economically and politically – in relation to the transforming forces. First, however, some more general features of the debate on globalization will briefly be spelled out.

The coordinates of the globalization debate

"Globalization" is one word for a multifarious phenomenon – from financial transactions to the Internet, and from the power of the transnational firms to the network of personal encounters in multicultural societies. Even if we restrict the focus of the debate to economic affairs, which actually triggered the new diagnosis in most countries, there are vastly different ways of perceiving the situation both in the professional literature and in the general discussion.

Roughly, we might organize the terrain of the debate in two major camps. The so-called hyperglobalizers argue, firstly, that globalization implies a qualitatively new stage of development, secondly, that the development is driven by economic and technological factors, thirdly, that neoliberal modes of governance tend to emerge everywhere, and fourthly, that change is basically exogenous (Held et al, 1999, Tranøy and Østerud 2001).

The premises for the qualitatively new stage were primarily set at the end of the Cold War. Francis Fukyama gained fame for his thesis of "the end of history", implying that liberal democracy and liberal market economies would now dominate politically and economically. Overall harmony would replace the bipolar contestation of principles and societal systems (Fukyama 1992). Ricard O`Brien followed suit, postulating also "the end of geography" as the result of an instant financial market across borders and defying distance, with an increasing irrelevance of delineated political units (O' Brien 1992).

Economic-technological determinism, ironically, is shared by neoliberals who are in favour of globalization and neomarxists who are opposed to it. The basic common argument is the economic imperatives that follow from connected markets and transnational networks for trade, production and finance. Capital is then instantly able to relocate, forcing its favoured policies upon labour and upon national politicians alike.

The premise of political and institutional convergence on a neoliberal model follows from national competition for investments. The general policy implications strengthen convergence – tax cuts, careful financial policies, cutbacks in welfare expenditures, a more flexible labour market with weakened trade unions, a restrictive monetary policy aiming at price stability. Mobile capital, moreover, is supposed to reinforce itself in the spread of deregulation from one country to the next.

Finally, the premise of exogenous change implies that intensified foreign competition everywhere renders the state obsolete as a framework for economic organization, and thus progressively deprives it of popular legitimation. The nation-state – as a remnant from the industrial epoch – is supposed to dissolve in the borderless information society (Ohmae 1990).

There are variations between the hyperglobalizers, but these are the major perspectives and premises. They have been met with empirical critique from various angles, contesting their basic premises and claims. We shall indicate the sceptical arguments in four different directions, following the lines of reasoning above.

Firstly, it has been argued that the contemporary inter- and transnational market system is not unique in world history. It has, on the contrary, a predecessor in the liberal epoch during the last quarter of the 19th century to the outbreak of the First World War. In percentage of GNP for the economically advanced countries, international trade and foreign investments were equally high in 1913 as in the late

1990s, with a contraction during substantial parts of the 20th century. Financial transactions now certainly move faster, and inter-firm transactions have an unparalleled scope, but for some major indicators the thesis of globalization as a qualitatively new stage is refuted. Similarly, the national home base is still vital to the competitiveness of most multinational firms (Hirst & Thompson 1996, Dickens 1998).

Secondly, the idea of a unilinear causal chain from technology and economy has been contested. It is pointed out that deliberate policy-making was central to the reemergence of a global financial market, and that legal rules of competition were designed to favour specific interests – national or private or both (Helleiner 1994). The centrality of the political dimension also implies that state and market is no zero-sum game. They may be complementary institutional forms, but state policies may even be important as driving forces in the process of globalization. The public sector is now substantially bigger than it was during the liberal epoch pre-1914, with a wider range of methods to protect the citizens from international market fluctuations; there seems to be a positive correlation between an open economy and a large public sector, with improved ways to compensate uncompetitive groups; and robust public institutions – legal institutions, infrastructure, high education, extensive research and development – make for a more efficient competitive edge in a more globalized economy (Evans 1997). The modes of state governance may have changed, rather than states generally obliterated (Weiss 1998).

Thirdly, it has been argued that capitalism now comes in different models – a continental European type, an East or South-East Asian type, a North American type, a Russian type, with various institutionally specific minor versions (Hall & Soskice 2001, Whitley 1999). Alfred Chandler distinguished between the competitive managerial capitalism of the US, the personal capitalism of Britain, and the cooperative managerial capitalism of Germany, with managerial-personal and competitive-cooperative as the two dimensions (Chandler 1990). Within this context, Francis Sejersted has characterized the Norwegian type as "democratic capitalism", tempered by small-scale enterprises and stung norms of popular legitimation (Sejersted 1993). The major points in the globalization debate is that some of the dynamic features of capitalism is embedded in its non-standardized character, and that divergence may be reproduced in the comparative advantage of specific forms as attractive to different agents of investment. Multinational firms may invest in comparative institutional advantages as they are shaping their strategies of localization. Educational standard, political-economic stability, and legal framework are among the likely advantages. There are thus strong modifications and exceptions to the supposed globalizing trend of neoliberal convergence.

Fourthly, some of the recent developments in the OECD area and elsewhere may be due to parallel endogenous processes rather than to exogenous pressure. Governments may be motivated to reduce public expenditure because of a structurally induced fall of productivity (a shrinking industrial base), a self-propelled increase in welfare demand, and an ageing population in the old industrialized world. Policy learning from the mistakes of the 1980s – when the credit markets were liberalized – may also account for some of the convergence in strict monetary policies with more autonomous central banks from the 1990s. Therefore, the thesis of exogenous compulsion may be overstated, even if globalization may have increased some policy constraints.

Within the terrain of the general globalization debate, there has been a simplification of the normative contestation. Those arguing for a return to Keynesian credit controls have been marginalized, due to the fact that reregulation nationally is politically far harder to attain than was deregulation. "Keynesianism in one country" is not widely perceived as a realistic option. The current neoliberal hegemony has, however, been challenged by movements in favour of international – or supranational – governance. *Attac* is now the most well organized movement arguing for control of financial transactions by taxing them, presumably to the benefit of distribution and social and environmental concerns. Originating in France, from the editors of *Le Monde Diplomatique*, in 1997-98, *Attac* spread to the Latin world, to Europe and to North America and Asia, focusing on the meetings and gatherings of the institutions of the international economy. It is a broad coalition of fractions, from socialists, agriculturalists and trade unionists to mild versions of international social democrats and social liberals, but it does, nevertheless, embody a new normative schism in the globalization debate, challenging the neoliberal hegemony of the post-Cold War years.

These are the major coordinates of the general debate. Now we will explore the specific character of the Norwegian variety.

The latency period

The immediate aftermath of the Cold War, and particularly the years from the contest and referendum on EU membership in the early 1990s and until the awareness of heat from "globalization" in 1997-98, may be called the latency period in the Norwegian globalization debate. These years – with the foreign policy issues that were paramount – should be seen in historical context (Heidar 2001, Riste 2001).

Norwegian foreign policy in the post-World War II era has consistently been a balance act between internationalism and national self-assertion. In the early nineteen-nineties the balance act was symbolically expressed by the Oslo Peace Agreement between Israel and PLO on the one hand and the insistence on limited commercial whaling on the other. The dual image of Norway at the time was simultaneously the idealistic and harmless small power in engagement for the improvement of the world – and the self-righteous little country in defence of its national interests against worldwide moral indignation.

This balance of a dual image goes at least back to the early 20th century, after the dissolution of the union with Sweden. Norway was a sea-faring country with limited resources, bound to accommodate the interests of fishermen, whalers, and polar explorers. It was also a small country in search of legality and cooperative order in international affairs, as protection against the risks of power politics. There was an uneasy balance between these two strands during the mid-War period, without a stable elite compromise. Arctic nationalism occasionally got the upper hand, as in the infamous Greenland occupation leading to defeat at the International Court of Justice. Otherwise Norwegian diplomacy leaned heavily on the flawed prospects of the League of Nations, advocating the rule of law behind a tacit security guarantee from Great Britain. In one lucky strike the nationalist and the internationalist strands coincided, when Norway extended its territorial borders with the Svalbard Treaty after World War I, as the harmlessness of a small country made Norwegian control appealing as a compromise between contending Great Powers in the Arctic.

The peculiar domestic elite compromises were settled in the post-World War II period, first in security policy and later in economic affairs.

In security policy the Norwegian consensus solution after 1945 was Nordic defence cooperation with an informal US guarantee, but this solution failed because of Swedish resistance. NATO was formed as the Cold War intensified after the Czechoslovakian coup in 1948. Norway joined with reluctance and skepticism both from a fraction of the political center-right, who feared an infringement on national sovereignty, and also – with outright resistance – from the left wing of the Labour party in charge, who saw NATO membership as a risky cementation of the Cold War. The outcome was an elite compromise on NATO that elevated security policy above partisan politics, with the exception of consistent opposition from the radical left.

The compromise on NATO was designed to satisfy the needs for Western integration from a broad coalition of elites in business, politics, administration, organizational life, and military circles, without endangering this policy through political opposition from the traditional center and the moderate left. The solution was NATO membership with reservations designed to strike a balance between international integration and national shielding. The other side of this balance was a compromise between an American-led deterrence posture against the Soviet bloc on the one hand, and a reassurance of peaceful and non-provocative intentions towards the Soviet Union on the other. The shielding from the West and reassurance towards the East was worked out by reservations like a policy of no military bases on Norwegian soil, no depots for nuclear weapons in times of peace, and no NATO exercises in eastern parts of Norway in the far north, towards the Soviet border. The compromise on security policy worked quite well during the whole Cold War period, although the radical left gained some strength with the establishment of the anti-NATO Socialist People's Party from 1961. After the Cold War, NATO as such is next to non-controversial in Norway, although new discussions have erupted about out of area operations in the Balkans and elsewhere. There are affinities between a posture favouring territorial defence as a paramount priority and a skeptical stance against erosion of sovereignty from globalization.

The compromise on the issue of the European Union was worked out after a long and rather bitter strife. EEC membership was first put on the political agenda in the early 1960s. The Labour government of the day decided to apply for membership, but the door was closed before a final decision was made, when president de Gaulle excluded Britain, and by implication Denmark and Norway. In

1972, when Britain and Denmark obtained membership, the Norwegian government again chose to join, but the entry was blocked by defeat in a referendum on the issue. The referendum was formally advisory to the National Assembly, being outside Norway's constitutional arrangements, but it was politically regarded as decisive. It was imperative for the Labour party in charge to avoid a devastating split of the party, and a referendum eased some of the direct pressure on party representatives and made disagreement tolerable.

Still the campaign up to the referendum was a fairly bitter contest. Substantial parts of the elites in politics, mass media, administration, and business were in favour of membership, while the opposition was a broad popular coalition from trade unions, peripheries, farming and fisheries, radical movements like student, peace and women organizations, academic institutions, and cultural life. Labour Party leaders were out of step with substantial parts of their rank and file, while the Socialist People's Party and the agrarian Center Party mobilized against membership and against the predominantly pro-European Conservative Party. It is probably fair to say that Norwegian elites generally favoured membership, with a notable exception of Academia and cultural life, while broad popular movements were against, and with regional strongholds in the peripheries.

This pattern was amazingly stable during the new referendum on EU membership in 1994, despite the fact that academic and cultural life now was more divided on the issue, and despite the fact that the agrarian population had numerically declined. The peripheries, the rural areas, and the public sector were consistently against membership, helped by the favourable econmic position of oil-producing Norway outside the EU. So the outcome of the new referendum duplicated the results from twenty-two years earlier, even if Sweden and Finland now had opted for membership.

But the remarkable feature of the European issue in Norwegian politics in the last decade of the century is a new political compromise: the treaty of the European Economic Area. The EEA was conceived by the Labour government in Norway in the early nineteen-nineties as an antechamber for EFTA members queuing for EU membership. After the new Norwegian "No", the EEA became a more permanent solution that regulated EU relations for Norway, Iceland, and Lichtenstein. It secured a rather complete economic integration, while preserving some of the national prerogatives in the regime for natural resources, fisheries, farming, and regional policy. Norwegian business accepted this solution, and so did substantial parts of the political milieu on both sides of the issue. For the dominant party in the minority center government from late 1997 to early 2000, the Christian People's Party, the compromise was even top priority, preferable to full membership on the one hand and a renegotiated trade agreement with the EU on the other. To substantial parts of the political-economic milieu, the compromise was regarded as better than the prospects of a consistent and unpredictable strife about Norway's links to Europe.

In NATO, Norway has been a member with reservations intended to balance shielding with integration in the West and reassurance with deterrence in the East. As for the EU, Norway is an integrated non-member eager to take part without abandoning all those aspects of sovereignty which figured high in the national contest about Europe. These political compromises are characteristics of Norwegian foreign policy and they betray the peculiarities of Norway: the political need to balance internationalism and nationalism – idealist as well as pragmatic participation on the one hand and shielding of sovereignty on the other.

This ideological and political context is far more than a backdrop to the globalization debate from the late 1990s. It has framed the debate of globalization with political lines and mental maps. The privileged position of a robust welfare state rich on natural resources on the one hand, and the persistent frontlines of the EU debates on the other, have dug the tracks into which the incipient globalization issue was trailed.

"Globalization" hits Norway

The word "globalization" ("globalisering" in Norwegian) was rarely used in Norway before 1997-98. A few trendy academics and journalists had picked it up from international sources, but it surfaced only occasionally in the mass media, and it was not a catchword for political controversy or intellectual fashion. The themes which later were brought together in the syndrome of globalization – the implications of European integration, of the fall of the Berlin Wall, of deregulation of capital export, of transnational mergers and acquisitions, of immigration, of the Internet, and of the universal aspirations of human rights – had been parallel issues, with rather disconnected debates. The closest one could get to a common denominator to these themes was the idea of the obsolete nation-state, with post national intellectuals criticizing the very idea of a national community, and with the contest about EU membership as the most focused issue. Here was a very strong Norwegian resonance to the supranational wave of "globalization" as it rolled up to the shores of Norway in the late 1990s. Pro-EU commentators quickly adapted the new theme to the cleavages of the EU debate, and argued for an emerging *pro* and *con* globalization pattern along the lines of the EU referendum, implying that denationalization – and thus the national issue – was the core of both globalization and Europeanization. The Norwegian EU contest echoed into the reception of "globalization". Globalists and Europeanists were painted in similar colours.

The real breakthrough for the public debate on globalization, however, was somewhat different. An immediate shock wave in the media was produced by the publication in Norwegian of a German book – *Die Globalisierungsfalle* (Martin & Schumann 1996/98). It was presented in March 1998, and this was the start of the high profile of "globalization" in Norwegian media and politics. A major newspaper, *Aftenposten*, brought a long series of articles on the topic throughout most of 1998.

The message of *Die Globalisierungsfalle* (The Globalization Trap) was incongruous with the frontlines of the subsequent Norwegian debate. The importance was agenda setting rather than the message itself. The message was concentrated in the subtitle, "the threat against democracy and welfare". The globalization trap was a sombre prospect: mass unemployment would increase dramatically due to work saving technologies; welfare distribution would become increasingly unequal also in the rich world, with extreme vulnerability to global market fluctuations; transnational firms would gain power and influence at the expense of political institutions; rich countries would be hit by a welfare crisis as capital flew to more profitable low cost areas.

The way to avoid the globalization trap, to the German authors, was supranational governance by closer EU integration. In principle, this was a consolation to EU protagonists in Norway, but membership was now beyond the horizon, and the point did not loom large in the Norwegian reception of the message. The message rather confirmed economic scepticism as to the blessings of a post national world, without deterring those inter- and supranationalists who greeted globalization for cultural encounters and communication and rights across and beyond borders. The two basic questions were translated into Norwegian and played out in a peculiar setting: (1) Was globalization real or was it a myth? (2) Was it good or was it bad?

Globalization with a Norwegian twist

To the socialist left, in Norway as elsewhere, globalization was real, and it was basically bad. To the liberalist right it was real and it was good. The intellectual debate – in journals and newspapers – was not wholly consistent with this cleavage. Two aspects complicated the issue. One was the conceived difference between globalization in economic versus cultural terms. The other was the shadow of the EU contest.

There was a tendency towards a split between academic disciplines. Commentators from social anthropology and history of ideas greeted globalization for its cultural border crossings, "glocal" hybridization, universalization of rights, and trendy modernization. Political scientists and economists were more concerned with nation-states as frameworks for representative democracy and the welfare state, and tended to be more sceptical towards the consequences of globalization and the obliteration of borders. Some also argued that the open borders could backlash into neo-tribalism, renationalization, and political fragmentation, as globalization meant a threat to stability, security, and the sense of belonging for broad sections of the unprivileged non-elite (Østerud 1999). Historians and historically oriented social scientists also put globalization into a long-term context, arguing that some of its aspects had had an earlier heyday before the First World War, and that national economies now were far more robust in welfare protection and stability measures than was the case in the liberalist epoch a hundred years ago (Glimstedt & Lange 1998, Østerud 1999). Nobody disputed the novelty of the Internet or the radicalness of speedy financial transactions, but also in Norway some aspects of the thesis of hyperglobalization were soon branded as mythmaking.

In Norway, it was particularly easy to see that economic globalization was no natural force, but that it was brought about by political decision-making a few years back, at the time of deregulation of capital control. It was easy to see because of the paramount peculiarity of Norway: the country's prosperity and rich natural resources, making a wide scope of maneuver for political measures and public governance. This privileged position became the backbone of collective reassurance in the globalization debate: Norway was not, and less so than nearly every other industrialized or postindustrial country, caught in a globalization trap. The eschatological images of *Die Globalisierungsfalle*, though instrumental in triggering off the Norwegian globalization debate soon receded into the background, called to life only when some business consultant urged for a radical, adaptive modernization of Norwegian industry and entrepreneurial spirit. "Globalization" was thus referred to as a call to action rather than as irrevocable fate.

The other side of this coin, also due to Norway's undeniable prosperity, was that Norwegian politicians rarely, if at all, employed globalization for the purpose of blame avoidance, as was the case in many other countries. It was not generally regarded as credible that globalization was putting Norwegian prosperity and welfare in immediate danger.

Still, Norway was transformed by forces of globalization – in the economy, with mergers and acquisitions across borders; in information and communications technology; in demographic terms, with fast immigration; in the legal field, in terms of loss of sovereignty. Some of these areas drew serious debate, while others did not.

The debate on business mergers and acquisitions was unstable, with politicians wavering behind the news. It was unstable because politicians wanted strong Norwegians actors and firms to meet intensified international competition, while they were reluctant to the same concentration for sake of domestic competition. It was, as always, difficult to square the circle. The new business debate was consistently haunted by this dilemma, each time a major merger raid was on the agenda.

The debate on the new technology was primarily a debate about means and conditions for innovation and competitiveness; here the new world as such was taken for granted and above contestation.

The radically transforming force of immigration was also shielded from serious public debate, because the hegemonic norms of political correctness trapped the worried voices into a morally compromising corner.

The sphere of legal sovereignty was another matter. Here the implications of denationalization were increasingly obvious, with a string to the EU debate (Tranøy & Østerud 2001). Norway is now woven into a wide set of legal obligations which goes beyond the interstate system that is regulated by international law. The most notable of these supranational obligations are the EEA agreement and the European human rights regime.

The EEA treaty implies that the parties are obliged to follow EU regulations, laws and directives in areas that are not explicitly exempted from the treaty, like agriculture and offshore resources. The major EU regulations of the terms of economic competition are thus also applicable to Norway. The crux of the treaty, as far as legislative sovereignty is concerned, is the clause saying that EU regulations have priority above national law in case of conflict. The parties may veto certain decisions that are considered as detrimental to their interests, but the political barriers towards activating the potential veto are high.

Legal experts have criticized the EEA treaty for transferring nearly as much sovereignty as would have been the case with full EU membership, but without participation in the legislative institutions. The Conservatives and the social democratic leadership take this as an argument for full membership, while the Center party argues for terminating the treaty in favour of a re-negotiated trade agreement with the EU. In relation to the EU, the farmer interests have been weakened because gradual adaptations to more commercially oriented agriculture have been enacted by Government with reference to the WTO.

Another mode of supranational jurisdiction is the evolving regime of human rights. Norway is one of the signatories of the European Human Rights Convention, and in May 1999 this convention and two other human rights treaties were integrated by adoption into Norwegian law. The adoption was also referred to in a new clause in the Constitution, and the act itself stated that in case of conflict with other parts of Norwegian legislation – past or future – the Human Rights Act should have priority. The radical implication of this regime is that the supreme judiciary in these matters is not the Norwegian Supreme Court but the European Court of Human Rights. Here, the final, authoritative interpretation of what is Norwegian law then resides in a supranational institution.

The Norwegian Parliament enacted this radical transfer of sovereignty without strong reservations, while there was some reluctance and scepticism within the bureaucracy and the legal profession. There was no widespread public debate, and the mass media was generally favourable to supranational harmonization in the field of rights. Here, globalization and Europeanization *cum* legalization and judicialization found Norway wide open and in accordance with its double tradition as a legalistic Small Power and as a champion for human rights.

The new internationalization

In February 2001, there was a new turn to the globalization debate: Attac came to Norway. Like in France and elsewhere, editors and journalists from intellectual journals played an active role in preparing for the establishment of *Attac Norway*, and like in France and elsewhere, both trade unionists and youth activists played a part. But there were Norwegian peculiarities. *Attac* was welcomed to Norway by a curious alliance between the Marxist or left socialist daily *Klassekampen* and the intellectual late modernist weekly *Morgenbladet*. Post national humanitarians joined forces with ecological movements, moderate social democrats, globally concerned conservatives, and the Marxist left. The foreign minister (Labour) expressed strong sympathies for the general idea of global governance and the specific idea of the "Tobin tax" on financial transactions. A former prime minister (Conservative) also expressed clear sympathies for *Attac*, together with other Conservative notables. The Conservative party leadership, however, was highly critical, and branded *Attac* as a threat to the universal advantages of liberalized trade.

Attac certainly is an umbrella organization with a wide variety of motivations and concerns beneath it. In Norway, it seemed to be unusually wide. From the start, some warned against turning the organization into an anti EU membership tool, and it came out as an extremely broad plea for global governance, redistribution, ecological concern, and social stability. It succeeded in giving the variuos worries about globalization an alternative to renationalization. It also succeeded in building a bridge across the EU divide in Norwegian debate, at least in the interim period up to the formal foundation of *Attac Norway* in June 2001. It was principally the pro EU faction who wanted the Norwegian branch to be silent on the EU issue. But the price for the broad appeal was a question mark after the "plus" in "Tobin tax plus", like in other countries, and a further price was what seemed to be an even less specific alliance than elsewhere. Even here, the legacies of the EU contest were heavy, because that cleavage was now something to avoid despite those bipolar connotations, attachments, and attitudes that remained.

Attac as such went beyond the Norwegian EU debate, because the distant aim was some sort of repoliticization and governance at the global level. Factions from the *pro* and *con* EU camps tried to meet here, and they could do so provided the solutions were not too ambitious or specific. Thus the general dilemma of *Attac* was intensified in the Norwegian context.

The peculiarities of the Norwegians – a summing-up

The globalization debate got quite specific features in Norway. It was shaped by the dilemmas and ambiguities that were inherent in Norway's relations to the outside world, and it was molded by the structural characteristics and outstanding affluence of the country. Globalization was not really, at least not widely, perceived as a dramatic process.

Two aspects had direct implications for the ways of the globalization debate. One was the specific character of Norwegian capitalism, with the state as the leading capitalist owner, with the small scale nature of private enterprises (yet under pressure), and with a notable stability in political and economic affairs. These specifics were able to absorb some of the potential shocks of the globalizing trends.

The other aspect was the long shadow of the EU contest, and the consistent balance of autonomy and internationalism that was built into the compromise solutions here. When an alternative to both denationalization and to neo-liberal globalization was imported, in the shape of *Attac*, it was mandatory to build bridges across the old schism. That effort did not solve the tensions of the movement, but it rather intensified them with a peculiar Norwegian flavour. Negotiated silence on the EU issue in Norway meant that the issue was screaming in its absence. Many aspects of the Norwegian globalization debate had EU connotations.

References

Castells, M. (1996-98). *The Information Age: Economy, Society and Culture*, I-III, Oxford: Blackwell.
Chandler, A.D. (1990). *Scale and Scope*, London: Belknap.
Dicken, P. (1998). *Global Shift*, London: Chapman.
Evans, P. (1995). *Embedded Autonomy*, Princeton: Princeton University Press.
Fukyuama, F. (1992). *The End of History and the Last Man*, London: Hamish Hamilton.
Glimstedt, H. and E. Lange, eds. (1998). *Globalisering – drivkrefter og konsekvenser*, Bergen: Fagbokforlaget.
Hall, P.A. and D. Soskice, eds. (2001). *Varieties of Capitalism*, Oxford: Oxford University Press.
Heidar, K. (2001). *Norway. Elites on Trial*, Boulder: Westview.
Held, D. et al. (1999). *Global Transformations*, Oxford: Polity Press.
Helleiner, E. (1994). *States and the Reemergence of Global Finance*, Ithaca: Cornell University Press.
Hirst, P. and G. Thompson, *Globalization in Question*, Oxford: Polity Press.
Martin, H-P. and H. Schumann (1996). *Die Globalisierungsfalle*, Hamburg: Rowohlt.
O' Brien, R. (1992). *Global Financial Integration: The End of Geography*, London: Pinter.
Ohmae, K. (1990). *The Borderless World*, London: Collins.
Riste, O. (2001). *Norway's Foreign Relations – A History*, Oslo: Universitetsforlaget.
Sejersted, F. (1993). *Demokratisk kapitalisme*, Oslo: Universitetsforlaget.
Tranøy, B.S. and Ø. Østerud, eds. (2001). *Mot et globalisert Norge?* Oslo: Gyldendal.
Weiss, L. (1998). *The Myth of the Powerless State*, Cambridge: Polity Press.
Whitley, R. (1999). *Divergent Capitalisms*, Oxford: Oxford University Press.
Østerud, Ø. (1999). *Globaliseringen og nasjonalstaten*, Oslo: Gyldendal.

Chapter 5

French Political Parties and Cleavages: Why is there no Christian Democratic Party?

Emmanuelle Vignaux

Political parties reflect longstanding cleavages in society.[1] Stein Rokkan highlighted four main cleavages in European societies, with their roots in two revolutions. The "national revolution" produced two types of cleavages: one between the State and the Church, based on the Church's claims of supremacy and control in matters of conscience (the State-Church cleavage). Another line of division was the tension between the cultural norms of the centre and those of the subjected populations living in the peripheries (the centre-periphery cleavage). The industrial revolution created a cleavage between the owners of the means of production and the employees (workers-employers cleavage), and a second cleavage between the rural populations and the urban ones (urban-rural cleavage). These cleavages crosscut each other and initiated strategies in defence of the interests of the various groupings associated with the respective cleavages. Political parties, formed during the era of the extension of the suffrage, articulated some of these interests.

This approach is helpful in understanding both the Norwegian[2] and the French party system since it opens up for a comprehension of contrasts between parties that are outwardly similar.

The larger Norwegian parties were founded during the latter half of the 19th century, and the party system has remained relatively unchanged since the early 1970s. The French party system was structured later than the Norwegian one, and has undergone more change, at least with regard to the name of the party organizations and to their number. It stabilized after the beginning of the Fifth Republic, but the present system shows a multiplication of parties. However, entirely new parties appeared later in Norway than in France. This is the case of Christian political forces, which emerged with a different timing. The French Christian party of the 1940s is the offspring of an old force in French politics. While it can be included in the broad European movement of Christian Democracy, the Norwegian Christian party is of a fundamentally different nature. The two parties do not stem from the same cleavage.

We shall first present existing political parties in France. It will be emphasized that no single party really enjoyed a long-term hegemonic position. One should rather talk about block domination. Inside each block, symmetric tendencies are visible, towards division or union. We then turn to the Christian forces in France and in Norway. While one seems to disappear, the Norwegian counterpart is steadily growing. We will then see why the Norwegian Christian People's Party does not belong to Christian Democracy as it is understood in Southern Europe.[3]

The tectonics of French parties

The current French political system is characterized by a tendency towards bipolarization, which is the result of several factors. But this bipolarization is recent and does not necessarily limit the number of political parties, whose candidates are represented in other types of elections: European, parliamentary, regional, and municipal. Bipolarization is stimulated by the ballot type used in the presidential elections, which obliges the candidates of several parties to form alliances for the second ballot of the election, where only two candidates can stand.

After the constitutional reform of 1962, following which the president came to be elected at a majority uninominal poll with two ballots and universal direct suffrage, the party system underwent changes. This new electoral system tends to favour big parties since it obliges the different parties to unite for the second ballot, the largest seeking the support of the others. Thus, middle and small parties tend to gravitate around the largest party of either block, a process which has contributed to the creation of a leading party at the expense of the others. The party system is thereafter characterized by multipartism, but with a dominant party in each block.

During the Third and Fourth Republic,[4] French parties were very loosely structured, with little disciplinary authority over the members of Parliament, who consequently enjoyed a relative freedom and independence. No real party leadership existed. The Fifth Republic, by contrast, is characterized by a much stronger control by the parties over their elected members. This leadership is also visible at the partisan level. The new regime produced by the Fifth Republic is of a presidential type, with a strong personalization of power. As a result, political parties have to present a candidate who can be seen as a potential president. Therefore, the party leader is almost "naturally" the future president. He tends to overshadow the rest of the party leaders.

Even so, French parties have had few strong leaders during the Fifth Republic. Charles de Gaulle and François Mitterrand succeeded in making the union within their own parties, because of their strong leadership and personality. Their succession corresponded to a split within the Left wing and the Right wing. Along with Jean-Marie Le Pen, leader of the National Front, they certainly are the most visible leaders the Fifth Republic has produced, within the limits inherent to each organization.

The French presidential and parliamentary elections in 2002 produced rather unusual phenomena and sent tremors through the party system. Whether this election will have a profound and long-lasting impact on the party system remains an open question. It was, for sure, a highly emotional political period for the French electorate.

In April 2002, the presidential election process developed in ways quite contrary to what was expected. Beginning with an electoral campaign perceived as highly boring, the elections eventually ended with a million people demonstrating in the streets.[5] Consequently, parties felt the need for organizational reform as well as for ideological questionings. This led, as we shall see, to a political union on the Right and to an electoral union on the Left. Several aspects characterized these elections, all of them interrelated.

First, the rates of electoral abstention were remarkably high: 35 percent and 38 percent respectively for the first and second ballot. These are the highest figures for the Fifth Republic.

Second, there was an extreme scattering of the votes, due to the inflated number of candidates. There were 16 candidates in the presidential election of 2002, the highest number ever.

Third, the high score received by the extreme right parties in the first ballot totaled more than 20 percent of the votes.[6] The rise can be explained by several factors: the high abstention rates; the absence of perceived difference between traditional parties of the Right and of the Left, whose ideological identities had been blurred by five years of smooth power-sharing (*cohabitation*); the scattering of the votes, encouraged by the coupling of the increased number of candidates with the traditional ideological vote of the first ballot[7]; the appeal of the rhetoric of J.-M. Le Pen to voters confused and frightened by the growing unpredictability of the future in the wake of globalization, unemployment, felt urban insecurity, immigration. Furthermore, the extreme-Right has acquired an increasing aura of credibility and normalization with the young generation. Voting Le Pen is undeniably becoming less and less a taboo. Last but not least, the personality of the National Front leader is important in explaining the vote: J.-M. Le Pen is very charismatic, and his paternalistic style seems to meet many voters' expectations.

The results of the first ballot indicate a rejection of the major traditional parties. Indeed, if the Socialist Party was eliminated from the first ballot, the Right party also lost a great number of supporters in comparison with the previous elections in 1995. Instead, people chose the smaller parties and the extremes: both Right and Left. The extreme Right increased its score by 90,0000 voters since 1995.

Several new features were also visible in the legislative elections of June 2002: for example, the first application of the act on gender parity for parliamentary elections.[8] Some parties preferred to pay the financial fine rather than present more women candidates.[9] Like the presidential election, the legislative election witnessed an inflation of candidacies, mainly due to the financial incentive represented by the Act of 1988.[10] Yet, the Left was united because of the presidential results.[11] The National Front could not repeat its presidential score, and polled 11.34 percent of the consolidated votes for the first ballot, and only 1.85 percent for the second ballot.

The unusual results of the presidential second ballot indicated that J. Chirac's support came from the voters of the traditional left.[12] Thus, this election was seen by many as a decision on the future of the regime rather than a real partisan choice. Indeed, most of the parties officially called for the support of J. Chirac. However, these events have confirmed some changes in the functioning of the regime: a trend towards more weakening of the presidential function and powers. These had already been dwindling with the failed dissolution of Parliament of 1997, the cohabitation, and many attempts at legal action against the president. This might be the most important impact of the last electoral outcomes, more than any change in the cleavage structure.

Within the two main blocks, the Left and the Right, several parties have flourished. In terms of electoral support, three large parties co-exist with mid-sized and small parties. These parties are the Socialist Party (PS), the Union For the Republic (RPR), and the Union for French Democracy (UDF).[13]

The progressive union of the Left wing

On the Left, Norwegian and French parties are comparable. They originate from the same functional cleavage, and can be divided roughly speaking into the Social Democrats and the Communists. Historically, the Norwegian Social Democratic Party has proven much stronger than the French one. This is true on two levels: electorally and organizationally, although the latter has known many structural modifications over time.[14]

The French Socialist Party emerged in 1969 from the old SFIO (French Section of the International Labour). The SFIO was founded in 1905, but the majority of its militants left the party in 1920 to build the French Communist Party (PCF), which joined the Third International. Subsequently, Communists and Socialists reached an agreement in 1934 with the Radical Party,[15] which led to the creation of the *Front Populaire*, a coalition which won the elections in 1936.

Right after the formation of the PS, François Mitterrand became its leader in 1971, and managed to unite the different factions while reducing the differences between them.[16] Unity of the non-communist Left was realized during an historic meeting at Epinay, June 1971, when the new strategy of the Socialist Party was built: the Left tried to present a unified front against the Right. This would require several developments such as a possible union with the Communists, the rallying of the party to the institutions of the Fifth Republic, and the construction of a governance-oriented program. As soon as 1972, the "Common Program" was established with the Communists.

The PSU (Unified Socialist Party) led by Michel Rocard, joined the PS in 1974. PSU was the name given in 1960 to the PSA (Autonomous Socialist Party), a formation created in 1958 as a secession from the Radical Party[17] and led by Pierre Mendès-France. The PSU had a reformist agenda with a strong emphasis on social rights, and stood also for desalinization.[18]

The Communists and the PSU supported the first candidacy of F. Mitterrand for the presidential election in 1965. Partly due to these efforts, and after nearly twenty-five years of right-wing hegemony, a Socialist was elected as president in 1981. This was considered by some as a little revolution, and the arrival of the Russian tanks in Paris was believed to accompany the one of F. Mitterrand at the head of the State.

F. Mitterrand experienced the first cohabitation, in 1986, when Jacques Chirac, from the RPR, was designated Prime Minister. F. Mitterrand's leadership was at stake, but this did not really weaken the PS leader. The Socialists had already realized much of their program, and could continue in office after the cohabitation interlude.[19]

After some years in power, the Socialist Party underwent a series of ideological changes: it abandoned the principle of the "rupture with capitalism",[20] self-management, the defence of the working-class, and economic planning. These changes were salient at the economic level, when the government decided on the politics of economic "rigor" in 1983-84: the main components of this new direction were the control of inflation, a freeze on prices and wages, the denationalization of major industrial firms and the progressive introduction of flexibility in the labour market. Many left-wing people felt betrayed by these changes, which were justified by some specific priorities, among which European integration was paramount.

The PS has also known changes in its electorate: it tends to recruit less now in the working-class, and more among the middle and professional classes. These trends are also noticeable in the composition of the party: there is still an overrepresentation of teachers, while the intermediary categories and the upper classes are growing and the blue-collar workers are declining.

In the presidential election of 2002, the PS came third after the FN. After this result, Prime Minister L. Jospin immediately resigned. The defeat of the Left has been explained by the lessening ability of the socialist organization to represent and bring in new ideas. The party was also perceived as increasingly removed from the traditional social concerns of the working-class. It also had difficulty highlighting the results of the work done in government. François Hollande now represents the socialist leadership. The party has been shaken: fierce internal critics, the advent of numerous new adherents in a short time,[21] and internal rivalries. Nevertheless, the need for a clear re-organization required by the recent events remains unanswered: the choice of L. Fabius (representing an economically liberal wing of the party) as the new party speaker and the absence of power-sharing between the old party elite and the new politicians[22] clearly illustrates this.

The Socialist party underwent a major split, with the creation by Jean-Pierre Chevènement of the *Mouvement des Citoyens* (MDC) in 1993. One may note that since the very beginning of his engagement on the Left, J.-P. Chevènement distanced himself from the SFIO, by for instance, creating a distinct organization, within the SFIO.[23] The leader of the MDC advocates centralization and national sovereignty, and opposes, for example, a federal European Union. He positioned himself very strongly against the Maastricht Treaty in 1992, criticizing its liberal orientation. Jean-Pierre Chevènement has built most of his political strategy on his reputation for integrity. He resigned three times from government,[24] the last one in 2000, over the Corsica issue. He presents himself as an alternative in French politics, which led to the choice of the campaign slogan "the third man" in the 2002 presidential election. The opinion polls indeed placed him in the third position, right after J. Chirac and L. Jospin. As a candidate in the presidential elections, he was supported by an extremely large spectrum of politicians, from former members of the Communist Party to right-wing persons. Finally, the ability of the MDC to rally such different forces lay in the strong personality of its leader as well as in the traditional orientation of its programme. The latter could be characterized by concepts such as security, unified France, and the repeated idea of "republic". The persistence of the MDC and its potential success illustrated the strength of the European issue in French politics, which has activated a cleavage between advocates of national sovereignty and partisans of supranationality.

The creation of the MDC is the institutionalization of a strong and ancient trend within the PS. Capable of making the union between various Left tendencies, F. Mitterrand gave the party the strength necessary to gain power. His succession provoked tensions inside the PS, some of which led to a split.

The other historic political force on the Left is the Communist Party (PCF). According to Rokkan's typology, a third revolution, the "international" one, drove the split between followers of the Bolshevik revolution and the others, the reformists. This explained the division within the SFIO in the 1920s and the creation of the French Communist party.

The party benefited greatly from its participation in the coalition government in 1936 and grew strongly until after the Second World War. At that time it became the major political force in France, obtaining 25 percent of the votes. It benefited also from the active involvement of its members in the Resistance movement. It briefly joined a coalition government in 1946-1947, but experienced an electoral decline afterwards. PCF weakening contributed to its participation in an alliance with the Socialist Party in 1972. Different phenomena explain the decline of the PCF: the growth of other parties (Gaullist, Socialist and Centre), the loss of the intellectuals, like Louis Aragon, who had supported the party, the diminishing significance of the attachment to the Eastern block especially after its collapse. The PC entered the Left-wing government in 1981, after receiving the lowest vote since 1945 (15.5 percent). In 1993, its long-standing leader Georges Marchais, handed over the office to André Lajoinie, then to Robert Hue, and now to Marie-Georges Buffet. Moreover, the party ideology has undergone radical change: in 1976 it abandoned the reference to the dictatorship of the proletariat and became more critical towards USSR. New electoral strategies have been adopted such as opening the electoral list for European elections to non-party members. However, the party electoral strength is in a continuous decline. The presidential and parliamentary elections of 2002 represent the sharpest decline for the party: it did not gain more than four percent of the votes. Some elements of explanation of this steady weakening lie in the desegregation of the working-class, from which the party still mainly recruits, and in the diminishing reference by R. Hue to the traditional themes of the Communist Party.

Another party on the Left is the Movement of the Leftist Radicals (MRG) created in 1973 from the Radical Party. Its program centered on the "socialist revolution" and the party took a clear stand against Gaullism. In the 1990s, the program of the MRG refers to the values of the Left: laity,[25] tolerance, anti-racism, social justice. Bernard Tapie, a very media-oriented, self-made man, became minister in 1992, during F. Mitterrand's presidency. At the European elections in 1994, the MRG list, led by B. Tapie, obtained 12 percent of the votes. Its electorate is young and quite working-class. In 1996 it became the Left Radical Party (PRG).

The Greens can be included in the Left block as well. The Green Party (*les Verts*) is the most recent formation, which did not emerge as a split from an existing party. The first environmental issues, which attracted a large audience in France, appeared in the 1970s. Two issues in particular provided the focus: one concerned the nuclear project and the other the expansion of a huge military camp in the centre of France, in the Larzac region. Without any party ticket, the ecologist René Dumont presented his candidacy at the presidential elections in 1974, obtaining 1.03 percent of the votes.

The Greens long remained critical of the traditional parties, which caused them to refrain from creating their own party until 1979. They obtained 4.4 percent of the votes at the European elections in 1979. Soon after, the Movement of Political Ecology (MEP) was formed, renamed in 1984 to become the Greens. Inside the party, two main factions can be identified. A radical one led by Antoine Watcher, who, as candidate of the Greens at the European elections in 1989, won 10 percent of the votes. Excluded in 1994, he created the Independent Ecology Movement (MEI). The representative of the second, more leftist faction, Yves Cachet, was the militants' chosen candidate for presidential election of 2002, but was replaced by Noël Madera, also a media-oriented person.

The Greens reached an agreement with the leader of the Ecologic Generation (GE); a party founded by a former member of the PSU, Brice Alone, and obtained 7.8 percent of the votes at the parliamentary elections in 1993. In 1995, Dominique Ovine, candidate for president obtained only 3.3 percentage of the votes. In 2002, N. Madera obtained 5.25 percent of the votes. However, for the legislative election that followed, the party received only a small score, with 3.2 percent of the votes.

Obtaining seven members of parliament at the elections in 1997, the Greens have turned to the PS to reach an agreement, which gave them one minister in the L. Joplin government (they later got two).[26] They again did well in the European elections in 1999: 10 percent.

The Greens advocate an economy that respects the environment and favour sustainable development. They criticize productivist and consumerist society, and want to promote alternative means for the production of energy. They espouse a distinctive organizational form: the party is characterized by a decentralized structure, a joint leadership divided in four, a rotation of mandates, and a great weight is placed on the rank and file of the party.[27]

These five Left parties reached an electoral agreement for the parliamentary election of 1997 and formed a government under the premiership of Lionel Jospin.[28] However, this "plural Left" (*Gauche plurielle*) encountered problems of cohesion. It was dominated by the Socialist Party, and the other parties, especially the Greens and the Communist Party, had to make concessions in order to stay in government. They were often criticized and misunderstood by their own rank and file. The leader of the MDC, Jean-Pierre Chevènement, reaffirmed his distance from the PS by resigning from his position as minister of the Interior. The Left success at the 1997 parliamentary elections reinforced the PS and the position of its leader, Lionel Jospin. However, this collaboration did not seem to be profitable for the smaller parties, as their poor results at the 2002 elections show.

The Right wing towards more divisions

The Right was in power without interruption during the first twenty-five years of the Fifth Republic. Benefiting from a charismatic leader and his heritage, the Right is now facing problems of succession. The parties on the Right are as numerous as those of the left block, and, until recently, had not reached any agreement on a common platform. Moreover, the internal fragmentation was growing within the main parties of the bourgeois block before the 2002 presidential election.

The largest rightist party is the Union for the Republic (RPR), which claims the heritage of the former Gaullist party. After the Second World War, General de Gaulle founded the RPF (Union for the French People), which intended to be a movement rather than a party. The RPF was the second largest party after the Communist party, in terms of voters. Partly because the RPF members of parliament did not follow de Gaulle's injunctions to remain distinct from the other parties, the RPF disappeared in 1955.

De Gaulle was called back to office in 1958 by the President of the Republic, René Coty, to solve the Algerian problem. One of the conditions raised by de Gaulle was the revision of the constitution; however, a new one was eventually written. De Gaulle was elected as the first president of the Fifth Republic by an electoral college via indirect suffrage. The Union for the New Republic (UNR) was created in 1958 to support de Gaulle. The party changed its name to the Union of the Democrats for the Fifth (UD Fifth) in 1967. De Gaulle rejected partisan divisions and harboured distrust towards parliamentarism. Indeed, Gaullism claimed to be different from other parties, and sought to unite the French people. The electorate of the Gaullist party at that time was socially mixed. The Gaullist agenda was the rallying of heterogeneous masses.

In 1968, the party changed its name to the Union for the Defence of the Republic (UDR) but internal dissent led to the emergence of several candidates for the presidential elections in 1974. Again in 1976, the party changed its name, to become the present RPR whose first leader was Jacques Chirac. He claims the heritage of de Gaulle, but the party has, to a great extent, lost its popular support since its electorate is now less representative of French society and more dominated by the better-off classes. The platform of the RPR is the return of order, the defence of the French nation. Another difference with the old Gaullist party is the acceptance by the RPR of economic liberalism whereas de Gaulle was in favour of State intervention. This party, or movement (Gaullism), has no equivalent in Norwegian politics. The present RPR can be compared to the Norwegian Conservative Party in terms of electorate - both are supported by the middle and well-off classes – and in terms of agendas – both advocate a certain economic liberalism. But Gaullism gathered around the personality of de Gaulle, and when he disappeared, the movement had difficulties staying united. Gaullism is often presented as a French exception. Gaullism was the carrier of a "certain idea of France", the core of which was a great and independent France, both politically and economically, a strong, renewed State, and a united society (i.e. without social divisions). The personalization of power is a major component of Gaullism, with the use of instruments such as referenda, public orations, and assimilation between the person and the state.

Like the Left parties, RPR is divided on the European issue, maybe to an even greater extent. Two important figures of the party, Philippe Séguin and Charles Pasqua, took a negative stand on the European issue, while the RPR advocates European integration. Taking his distance from the RPR on this issue, C. Pasqua left the party and created in 1999 the Union for France (RPF) with Philippe de Villiers. The latter, leaving the Republican Party, had previously created his own party, the Movement for France (MPF), in 1994, after the good electoral result he obtained at the European election (12.3 percent).[29] He was clearly against the Maastricht Treaty in 1992 and campaigned for a negative vote. But C. Pasqua and P. de Villiers could not manage to stay united and eventually split. Once willing to be a candidate for president in 2002, P. de Villiers chose not to run, in order, in his words, "not to add division to division and confusion to confusion". He has recently published a book where he reaffirms his hostility towards the idea of European integration.[30]

After the election of Chirac as President of the Republic in 1995 and the Right's loss of the parliamentary elections in 1997,[31] the Right wing seemed more divided than ever.

In 1978, the creation of the UDF (Union for the French Democracy) put the RPR in a less dominant position. UDF corresponds to the gathering of different centrist forces: the Republican Party (PR), which is the remains of the old Radical Party, and the CDS (Centre of Social Democrats),[32] the heir of the Christian-Democratic party. It is indeed more like a confederation than a party.

It obtained 21 percent of the vote during the parliamentary elections of 1978 and maintained its score at around 18 percent afterward. The members of the party belong to the well-off classes, the electorate is composed of the middle-classes, non-salaried classes, and its structure is very similar to that of the RPR (Ysmal 1989). UDF reached an agreement with the RPR in 1981, and in 1995 did not present any candidate, while supporting one of the two RPR candidates, Edouard Balladur. The party is generally accepted as the centre party in French politics, though this could hardly reflect the diversity of its standpoints. It actually claims to be distinct from both Left and Right. Still, the party is more conservative than would indicate its "liberal" origin. Attached to traditional values such as the family, the party also represents the traditional Catholics.

UDF does not escape from divisions either: Christine Boutin, a former member of UDF, has recently created her own party, the Forum of Social Republicans (FRS), which has had difficulties building an identity distinct from the UDF one.[33]

At the other end of the spectrum is the party founded by Alain Madelin, Liberal Democracy (DL), the new name of the PR, representing the most liberal parts of the UDF. The so-called French Liberals have little to do with the Norwegian Liberal Party, the old *Venstre*. "Liberalism", in Norway, is the present translation of the "Left", the first party that appeared to fight for independence and the defence of rural interests. It is now a party of the political centre, supporting the Conservatives' and Social-Democrats' propositions depending on the issues, but more often allied with the former. By contrast, the Liberals in France are the economic ultra-liberal branch of the RPR, standing for minimal state intervention and for individual initiative, and are morally very conservative.

In the autumn of 2001, in an attempt to create a union of the right-wing parties – in reality, to rally support around the candidate of the Right – partisans of J. Chirac created a new organization, the Union in Movement (UEM). However, UEM found it difficult to reach its goal. The results of the first ballot of the presidential elections in April 2002 urged and accelerated the creation of a new party. The forming of UMP (Union for the Presidential Majority) between the presidential and the parliamentary elections was clearly a reaction to the political upset that characterized the 2002 presidential election. Under pressure from Chirac's followers, UMP was launched to unify the Right in order to resist a potential threat coming from the National Front and to win against the Left. If Liberal Democracy and The Movement for France joined the RPR in this new formation, UDF leader F. Bayrou would eventually stand apart, though some of the UDF members were candidates under the UMP banner at the National Assembly elections. The strategy proved efficient since the UMP won an absolute majority of the Assembly seats (47.3 percent of votes).

The new party's goal is now to present a candidate for the next presidential election, under a condition of unity. Nevertheless, the new federation-like party does not erase the traditional divisions of the Right. Liberal, Conservative, and Traditionalist are still the main factions on the Right and each one is determined to keep its identity.

The chaotic existence of the extreme Right

In contrast to the Norwegian case, the extreme Right in France is an old political force, which is still alive and well. The National Front (FN) is a fairly recently established party. The Second World War brought discredit on the extreme Right and destroyed for a time the will to create a party. However, extreme-right currents appeared during the Third and Fourth Republic. These may be viewed as the forerunners of the FN, though the party also originates from another ideological trend, inherited from the French Revolution and characterized by Catholicism, traditionalism, and monarchism. The National Front was created in 1972 by the coming-together of several groups. Among them were those who had fought for a French Algeria, like Jean-Marie Le Pen. During the 1980s, the FN made some electoral advances due to particular political circumstances: Left and Right were both criticized while the FN offered a series of simple proposals such as to solve the problem of unemployment, the fight against immigration and to defend moral values. Institutional reasons also provide an explanation for the electoral breakthrough of the FN: the short-lived introduction of the proportional representation at the municipal and parliamentary elections respectively in 1983 and 1986 allowed it to gain thirty-five members of parliament. Subsequently, at the presidential elections in 1988, it obtained 14.4 percent of votes.

Until the 1990s, the electorate of the FN was dominated mainly by bourgeois voters who traditionally voted for the Right. It attracted more voters from modest backgrounds, with the growth of the working class in its electorate.[34] In 2002, the electorate of J.-M. Le Pen was composed of 30 percent unemployed people, 24 percent blue-collar workers, 20 percent young voters and 17 percent private sector executives.[35] This is evidence of a protest vote.

Old themes of the extreme Right in France are exploited by the FN: the defence of national identity ("national preference" in economic and social matters) and traditionalist moral values. It is coupled with a populist discourse criticizing bureaucracy, denouncing corruption, and alleging the existence of a "plot". Nevertheless, FN is not only populist – which actually is quite recent – but also racist and anti-Semitic, despite its denial of being so.

Observers of the discourse of J.-M. Le Pen have pointed out its ambiguity, which allows many interpretations. But this discourse has been softened after several "scandals" and since it tended to discredit the FN leader's pursuit of credibility (Schain 1987). In 1987 for instance, J.-M. Le Pen said that the "gas chambers were a point of detail in the history of the Second World War", provoking strong reactions in the political class as well as in the population.

The strong internal leadership of J.-M. Le Pen did not leave any room for discussion within the party, and was criticized by some members of the FN. Bruno Mégret (ex-member of the RPR), who represents the ideological and bourgeois branch of the FN, created the Republican National Movement (MNR) in 1998. In the short run, this division had negative consequences for the extreme Right. At the European election of 1999, the MNR obtained 3.3 percent and the FN 5.7 percent of the votes, while in the municipal elections held in 2001, their scores were lower in most of the municipalities. Still, the two were candidates for the presidential election.[36] B. Mégret presents an agenda similar to Le Pen's, but he tends to be more offensive than Le Pen, who is in search of respectability. He affirms his will to "solve the question of those who do not respect French customs and values and who do not come to our country to work but rather to live like parasites, from state subsidies and trafficking".[37]

The other parties in general took a strong stand against any sort of alliances with the FN, but some RPR candidates publicly accepted the transfer of the FN votes for the second ballot of the parliamentary elections in 1997, despite the critics of the RPR.

The 2002 elections were turbulent events for the FN: an unexpected result at the presidential election, followed by a defeat at the legislative elections. FN became the second largest party in terms of votes, ahead of the PS, with nearly 17 percent of the votes. Consequently, J.-M. Le Pen became the candidate against J. Chirac for the second ballot of the presidential election.[38] Since the FN leader is about to leave the leadership, due to his age, there will be a succession problem. Several challengers seem to be on the list, among them his youngest daughter Marine, as well as Bruno Gollnisch. Populist and anti-system parties in Europe are characterized by a high identification of the party with its leader, who is often a charismatic figure. Consequently, typical for this type of party, one of the greatest problems is the survival of the party after the disappearance of the leader.

Christian parties: vanished in France, flourishing in Norway

France is a forerunner when it comes to Christian political formations: the expression "Christian Democracy" was uttered for the first time in France in 1791, during a speech in the Legislative Assembly (Maier 1992). It was in France as well that the first party called "Christian Democrat" appeared, in 1896 (Letamendia 1995). Although the State-Church cleavage was the first cleavage to emerge in French society after the Revolution, there is no Christian Democratic party at the moment. The Catholics have long remained divided over several issues. The form of the regime and the State were especially divisive issues, particularly during the Third Republic, when most of the Christian Democratic parties were already founded elsewhere in Europe.

After the Second World War, the Catholics, who had played an active role in the Resistance movement, united in a party named the Popular Republican Movement (MRP).[39] There were many earlier attempts by Catholics to organize a permanent party, but the projects aborted rapidly.[40] Founded in 1944, the MRP obtained 28 percent of the votes in 1946 (its best score ever), becoming a major political force in France. The MRP participated in most of the Fourth Republic governments, first with the Communist and the Socialists, then with the Socialists and the Radicals. However, its electoral strength did not reflect a similar strength of the party militants. The organization was much weaker. MRP was unevenly rooted, as strongholds of the party corresponded to the most devout areas, especially the Western parts of France. There was an obvious correlation between church attendance and MRP vote. MRP progressively slipped towards the centre-right, as one of the leader of the party, Georges Bidault, stated, "MRP is a party pursuing Left-wing policies with a Right-wing electorate".

The MRP, with great figures such as Robert Schuman, became a fervent defender of the European construction. The party advocated "respect for personal rights and the freedoms of citizens",[41] was a reformist party, and advocated social reforms and family assistance. It was attached to the social teaching of the Catholic Church.

It quickly suffered from the creation of the Gaullist party and declined in the legislative elections of 1951. After having stated in 1958 their affinity to Gaullism, MRP leaders maintained a distance in 1962.[42] As the various strands of the party joined other political forces, the party disappeared and was replaced in 1966 by the Democrat Centre (CD). This latter positioned as a third way, rejecting both the Left wing and the Right wing, advocating freedom and solidarity. At the parliamentary election held in 1967, it obtained 14 percent of the vote. In 1970, it became the CDS (Centre of the Social Democrats), and joined the UDF, after many divisions over the strategy to be adopted. The CDS became, under the leadership of François Bayrou, the Democratic Strength (FD) in 1995. The latter rejects ultra-liberalism, defends Europe and propagates, to a certain extent, the Christian heritage.

MRP was part of European Christian Democracy, a prominent political movement after the Second World War in Southern Europe.[43] The presence of Christian Democracy in Europe is generally analyzed from a State-Church cleavage perspective. Its emergence is linked to a reaction to a lay-liberal confrontation with the Church. In a context where the struggles between Church and State have historically been highly significant, it is striking to note the weakness of a Christian Democratic party in France. Some explanations have been offered to account for this paradox: the difficulties for the Catholics to form a unified front against the lay Republicans during the Third Republic because of their strong divisions. Some were rallying to the Republic, while others remained strongly royalist. Moreover, within the pro-republican group, Catholics were divided between a social branch and a more liberal one. The Christian Democratic movement could not succeed in unifying these tendencies until the Second World War. Up to then, the movement lacked leaders. During the Fifth Republic, the movement was the victim of bipolarisation, and suffered from a loss of identity. The emergence of a strong political force on the right (RPR) corresponded to the decline of the MRP. Finally yet importantly, the Christian Democratic Party could hardly go against the Catholic vote's traditional preference for the Right.

These different factors may explain the difficulty for a Christian formation to grow stronger. But this movement has shown, by surviving, its ability to adapt to political and institutional changes. Elsewhere in Europe, some CD parties could not survive, a few exceptions got stronger, like in Italy or Germany where they became more like conservative parties.

While CD forces of Southern Europe are declining,[44] or vanishing, as the French one has done, the Christian party in Norway has proved to be a durable formation and is now among the leading political forces of the country.

The Norwegian Christian People's Party (*Kristelig Folkeparti*, Kr.F) was formed in 1933 from a split within the oldest party, the *Venstre*. At first very regionally located in the Western parts of Norway (Hordaland region), it quickly competed with the other parties, constituting a real alternative. Becoming a national party in the 1950s, it remains weakly established in two types of areas: the urban ones and the Northern and Eastern ones.

Rivalled by two other centre parties, the Kr.F nevertheless claims to represent the views of the Christian people in Norway, which is far from the actual situation. Notwithstanding its will to be different on this particular issue, it is obliged to compromise with other parties when it comes to forming a government. Coalitions are particularly difficult to form with the Social-Democrats and the Conservatives, because of ideological distances on moral issues. Nevertheless, in a system characterized by proportional representation and by the lack of any majority party since the end of the 1960s, the central position of the Kr.F. is highly strategic in the formation of coalitions. The Kr.F. has thus participated in nine coalitions since the beginning of the 1960s, and two Prime Ministers were from the Kr.F., Lars Korvald in 1972 and Kjell Magne Bondevik in 1997 and 2001.[45]

For students of Christian Democratic movements it may be difficult to understand the presence of Christian Democratic parties in countries characterized by a significant distance from Rome, both geographically and spiritually. In theory, countries with a homogeneous Protestant denomination, where the Church is established, should not have Christian Democratic parties.[46]

This line of reasoning, quite common in the literature, cannot account for the existence of Christian parties in the Nordic countries. In this area, they are neither

Christian Democratic parties, nor do they have the same ideological nature as the Southern European Christian parties. Nordic Christian parties do not have equivalents in the South.

Similar names but different nature

The Norwegian Christian People's Party is overwhelmingly Lutheran, although it tends now to be more open to other confessions. It remains, anyhow, a strongly denominational party, which distinguishes it from the Christian-Democratic parties of Southern Europe. Moreover, the latter have largely abandoned their religious ties, as religion is relegated more and more to the private sphere.

Nevertheless, Christian Democratic parties in Southern Europe and the Kr.F share a common attachment to Christianity and to the Bible. Another common denominator is the weight of the believers and churchgoers in the electorate of the Christian parties, be they from Southern Europe or from the Nordic countries.[47] Many studies have shown the importance of the religious variable to explain the vote to the Christian parties. An indirect consequence of this is the interclass character of all these parties. Members of all socio-professional categories support them, precisely because religion is not linked to a specific class membership. The only exception is the under-representation of employees. Moreover and to a great extent, Christian Democratic parties attract more women than men. The French MRP electorate, for instance, clearly indicated this.

The large Christian parties of Southern Europe[48] have long constituted an alternative between right and left. Positioned at the political centre, they have enjoyed a strategic situation, been able to govern with different kinds of parties.[49] Although the electoral weight of the Kr.F has long remained lower than that of Christian Democratic parties, Kr.F belongs to the same political configuration: it has formed governments with other parties of the centre and with the Conservative Party.

Common points stop here: interclass parties, with a reference to the Holy Scriptures with variable intensity, and a central position in the political system. Still, they differ from two points of view: their religious ties are variable in intensity, and their ideological direction is distinct.

If one looks more closely at the religious tie, differences quickly appear. Despite very high percentages of Church membership and of attendance to religious *rites de passage* in Norway, the Kr.F has not been able to mobilize proportionately.[50] The Norwegian Christian party does not appeal to all the Christians believers of Norway, but mostly to the most active and "peripheral" part of them.

The relation to the State is of a fundamentally different nature in the Scandinavian countries, which have State Churches (except for Sweden since the year 2000). Thus, the creation of a Christian party is not a reaction against the liberal positions of a lay state, struggling for sovereignty against Rome, as in South European countries. It represents more a reaction against the secularization of society represented both by morally progressive parties and by the High Church.[51]

In Norway, the latter has always represented the establishment, be it under Danish domination or after. The positions of the establishment are considered too liberal by the traditionalist members of the Low Church, also called "lay people". "Lay" refers to the Protestant meaning: non-ordinate believers, but who, by virtue of the universal ministry, claim the right to preaching the Gospel and giving the sacraments. The lay people in Norway are the most fervent opponents to the State Church. They are highly traditionalist, and for some of them fundamentalist in orientation.[52] They are opposed to the submission of the Church to the State laws, and some defend the separation of the two institutions. Consequently, a religious cleavage does exist, but it involves two parts of the same Church.

In Southern Europe, the Christian parties have been established to fight *against anticlericalism*, while the Norwegian party has been established to fight *against clericalism*. This anticlericalism is apparent in a distrust of the established structures of the Church, often considered unable to maintain orthodoxy and purity.

The religious tie is much more important in the Norwegian case. Most of the large CD parties in Southern Europe have abandoned the religious discourse and Christian-oriented policies. This can be illustrated by the party's attitude to the state of Israel. Despite some recent modifications the party has a long tradition of support for the Israeli state. This is the result of a particular reading of the Bible, much more than any geopolitical considerations.

Another illustration is the continuous attachment of the party to prohibition of alcohol. This issue, totally absent from other DC parties in Southern Europe, has always constituted a clear position of the Christian party. It derives from a puritan religiosity developed in the 19th century in reaction to the ways of life and attitudes of the bourgeois class. Prohibition was a culture developed by the periphery against the representatives of the centre.

The second difference lies in the distinct ideological agenda of Christian parties.

First, one can find dramatic differences in the ideological content of the agenda. Christian Democratic parties in Southern Europe do not constitute a monolithic block, as the European issue demonstrates so clearly, at least in its origins. Yet, the leaders of the large Christian Democratic parties remain pillars of European integration.[53] Christian Democracy is characterized by an emphasis on civil society (*corps intermédiaires*): family, regions, profession, and supranational unity. The common point here is the principle of *subsidiarity*, which means that man has a sphere of autonomy in each unit, be it lower or higher.[54] Actually, "local authorities' right to independence holds only so far as it is consistent with the needs of the wider community to which they belong", as Fogarty recalls.[55] The leaders of the large Christian Democratic parties promoted the European institutions, considered of great importance to keep the peace in Europe after the First and the Second World Wars. Since that time, the European feeling has remained strong among Christian Democrats. The French MRP contributed to the European construction right after the Second World War: Robert Schuman proposed the formation of the CECA (European Community of Coal and Steel) in 1950, which led to the formation of the European Economic Community.

In contrast, the Norwegian Christian party has officially taken a negative stand on Norwegian membership in the European Union. Raised twice in Norwegian politics (1972 and 1994), the issue provoked tensions within the party, the leaders being relatively more favourable than the militants. From this particular perspective, the Kr.F does not belong to the vast movement of Christian-Democratic euro-believers.

The map of the Norwegian referenda results shows a greater proportion of "no" votes in the rural areas, in particular those of the West and South, which are the strongholds of the party. Christian fundamentalists are very hostile to Norwegian membership of a European Union, which to them symbolizes the "Catholic countries", and "liberal manners". To some fundamentalists, Europe may evoke an apocalyptic imagery, as the 1972 debate showed: the Beast of the Apocalypse stood for Europe.[56] This extreme position is marginal in the party, however, at least among the leaders. All the same, the Norwegian Christian party is reluctant to promote European integration, and in this respect, the party is very distinct from Christian Democracy on the Continent.

The Christian Democratic parties in Europe are all members of the European Popular Party, a liberal movement clearly anchored on the right. This leads us to the second point of difference: a contrast with regard to ideological direction. The Christian Democratic parties of Southern Europe are leaning towards the Right. Large CD parties have become *the* Conservative party, as in Italy and Germany. The Norwegian Christian party has remained in the political centre, even though it has mainly professed centre-*right* positions.

The Norwegian Christian party cannot be considered as belonging to the Christian-Democratic movement. It does not share the common attitudes and symbols of the Christian Democratic movements of Southern Europe. Its existence can only be understood as the institutionalized expression of *a conflict between the centre and the periphery*. In this conflict, Kr.F is the party of the periphery. Such an understanding of the Kr.F accounts for the numerous differences between the Christian Democracy agenda and the Kr.F one. The core issues defended by the Kr.F derive from a particular reading of the Bible; leaders and militants are carriers of a Biblicist vision: a literal reading of the Bible, thanks to which one can find precepts for political conduct and action.

Conclusions

French political parties are facing an era of extreme fragmentation within the two main blocks, while the Norwegian party system has remained relatively unchanged. This is partly due to institutional factors: Since WWII, France has known three different Republics, with very distinct political practices. Political parties had to adapt their structure and organization in order to build viable strategies to gain power. In contrast, the Norwegian political institutions have not undergone major transformations since the introduction of parliamentarianism at the end of the 19th century. The only exception occurred when the European issue was raised in 1972. It had dramatic consequences, especially during and after the referenda debate. The European issue, as indicated, is also important in French politics in explaining the creation of new parties. However, it is difficult to mobilize voters around this issue apart from election campaigns that are dominated by the European issue. Indeed, the European issue has divided the parties along different lines that do not correspond to "Right" and "Left". The division also crosses party lines, creating internal conflicts that could eventually lead to splits. Furthermore, the party leaders are more the products of particular institutional contexts than personal attributes. The presidential election and the personalization of politics are factors that may contribute to the emergence of strong leaders in each party. At the same time, other tendencies lead to fragmentation and multiplication of parties, which in turn tends to a blurring of the political space: a great many party leaders appear but only a few remain for the long haul.

The emergence and development of the French parties can be explained with the four cleavages grid and the crosscutting cleavages. Some of the cleavages did not find any conspicuous political expression during the mobilization era, while others appeared to be highly significant, for instance the State-Church cleavage. A major line of division between French parties is, indeed, the lay-religious one. But because of strong historic divisions among French Catholics and a tendency to identify with the Right – thus creating difficulties with regard to keeping a distinct identity – a specific Christian-Democratic party could hardly survive in the party system. The disappearance of the MRP as the political institutionalization of Christian Democrats in France does not invalidate the applicability of the model. Indeed, the existence of a cleavage in a society does not necessarily mean the permanence of a political party representing the interests related to this conflict. However, in the long run, it is generally relevant to speak about political parties as expressions of a social conflict. It is particularly helpful for understanding the identity of parties such as the Norwegian Christian party. The Christianity reference is not sufficient to characterize the party, nor is it grounded in a State-Church cleavage. Instead, the centre-periphery cleavage has to be invoked to account for the party's staying power.

In France, a functional type of cleavage has been important for party developments: the largest parties are positioned along the workers-employers line of cleavage. This is the most fruitful line in explaining the present configuration of parties. Urban-rural and centre-periphery cleavages appear to be secondary. Few political parties have actually been able to mobilize along both of these cleavage lines, although the existence of some small parties can be explained from this perspective. They become evident in the discourse of the largest parties, seeking to mobilize a larger spectrum of voters. Thus, the Left-Right dimension accounts for the existence of most of the parties, located in a one-dimensional space rather than in a multi-dimensional one.

APPENDIX

Electoral results of French parties in parliamentary elections, by percentage of votes in the first ballot

1958

Party	Percentage of votes
PC	18.9
UFD	0.9
SFIO	15.7
Radical Party	8.2
MRP	10.8
UNR	20.3
Independents	24.2
Ext. Right	1.0

1968

Party	Percentage of votes
PC	20.0
PSU	3.9
FGDS	16.6
UDR	46.4
PDM	12.5
Diverse	0.6

1978

Party	Percentage of votes
Ext. Left	3.3
PC	20.6
PS-MRG	25.0
Left Diverse	1.1
UDF	21.4
RPR	22.7
Right Diverse	3.5
Ext. Right	0.5
Greens	2.2

1988

Party	Percentage of votes
Ext. Left	0.36
PC	11.32
PS	34.76
MRG	1.10
Presidential Majority	1.65
RPR	19.18
UDF	18.49
Right Diverse	2.85
Ext. Right	0.13
FN	9.65
Greens	0.35
Regionalists	0.07

1997

Party	Percentage of votes
PC	9.94
PS	23.53
UDF	14.21
PRS	1.44
RPR	15.70
FN	14.94
Greens	6.81

2002

Party	Percentage of votes
Left Diverse	1.27
PC	3.26
PRG	2.15
PS	35.26
Republican Pole (MDC)	0.06
UDF	3.92
UMP	47.26
Right Diverse	1.29
FN	1.85
Greens	3.19
Regionalists	0.14

Presidential elections – Percentage of votes obtained by candidates

1974

Candidate	First ballot	Second ballot
F. Mitterrand (PS-PC-Radicals)	36.8	49.19
V. Giscard d'Estaing (UDR)	32.6	50.81
J. Chaban-Delmas (UDR)	15.10	
J. Royer (UDR)	3.17	
A. Laguiller (LO)	2.33	
A. Krivine (Ext. Left)	0.36	
R. Dumont (no ticket)	1.32	
J.-M. Le Pen (FN)	0.74	
E. Muller (MDSF)	0.69	
B. Renouvin (no ticket)	0.17	
J.-C. Sébag (Regionalist)	0.16	
G. Héraud (Regionalist)	0.07	

1988

Candidate	First ballot	Second ballot
F. Mitterrand (PS)	34.09	54.02
J. Chirac (RPR)	19.94	45.98
R. Barre (CDS)	16.54	
J.-M. Le Pen (FN)	13.39	
A. Lajoinie (PC)	6.76	
A. Waechter (Greens)	3.78	
P. Juquin (Communist)	2.01	
A. Laguiller (LO)	1.99	
P. Boussel (MPPT)*	0.38	

* Movement for the Workers' Party

1995

Candidate	First ballot	Second ballot
L. Jospin (PS)	23.31	47.36
J. Chirac (RPR)	20.73	52.64
E. Balladur (RPR)	18.54	
J.-M. Le Pen (FN)	15.07	
R. Hue (PC)	8.69	
A. Laguiller (LO)	5.32	
P. de Villiers (MPF)	4.75	
D. Voynet (Greens)	3.32	
J. Cheminade (no ticket)	0.28	

2002

Candidate	First ballot	Second ballot
J. Chirac (RPR)	19.88	82.14
J. M. Le Pen (FN)	16.86	17.85
L. Jospin (PS)	16.18	
F. Bayrou (UDF)	6.84	
A. Laguiller (LO)	5.72	
J. P. Chevènement (MDC)	5.33	
N. Mamère (Greens)	5.25	
O. Besancenot (LCR)	4.25	
J. Saint-Josse (CPNT)	4.23	
A. Madelin (DL)	3.91	
R. Hue (PC)	3.37	
B. Mégret (MNR)	2.34	
C. Taubira (PRG)	2.32	
C. Lepage (Cap 21)*	1.88	
C. Boutin (FRS)**	1.19	
D. Gluckstein (PT)***	0.47	

* Environmental party led by a former minister under RPR A. Juppé's government.
** Forum of the Social Republican, Conservative party.
*** Workers' party.

References

Bell, David S. and Byron Criddle (1987). *The French Socialist Party. The emergence of a party of government*, Oxford: Clarendon.

Bull, Martin (1996). "The Italian Christian Democrats", in Gaffney, John, ed., *Political Parties and the European Union*, London: Routledge.

Fogarty, Michael P (1957). *Christian Democracy in Western Europe, 1820-1953*, London: Routledge.

Garvik, O, ed. (1983). *Kristelig Folkeparti. Mellom tro og makt*, Oslo: Cappelen.

Hanley, David (1986). *Keeping Left? CERES and the French Socialist Party, a contribution to the study of factionalism in political parties*, Manchester: Manchester University Press.

Irving, R. E. M (1979) "Christian Democracy in post-war Europe: Conservatism Writ-Large or Distinctive Political Phenomenon", *West European Politics*, 2/1.

Karvonen, Lauri (1996). "Christian Parties in Scandinavia: Victory over the Windmills?", in Hanley, David, ed., *Christian Democracy in Europe, a Comparative Perspective*, London: Pinter.

Letamendia Pierre (1995). *Le Mouvement Républicain Populaire. Histoire d'un grand parti français*, Paris: Beauchesne.

Letamendia, Pierre (1997). *La Démocratie Chrétienne*, Paris: PUF.

Maier, Hans (1992). *L'Église et la démocratie. Une histoire de l'Europe politique*, Paris: Critérion.

Mayer, Nonna (1987). "De Passy à Barbès: deux visages du vote Le Pen à Paris", *Revue Française de Science Politique*, 37/6.

Mayer, Nonna and Pascal Perrineau, eds. (1996). *Le Front National à découvert*, Paris: Presses de la FNSP.

Michelat, Guy and Michel Simon (1977). *Classe, religion et comportement politique*, Paris: Presses de la Fondation Nationale des Sciences Politiques.

Michelat, Guy and Michel Simon (1985). "Religion, classe sociale, patrimoine et comportement électoral: l'importance de la dimension symbolique", in Gaxie, Daniel, ed., *Explication du vote, Un bilan des études électorales en France*, Paris: Presses de la FNSP.

Paterson, William (1996). "The German Christian Democrats", in Gaffney, John, ed., *Political Parties and the European Union*, London: Routledge.

Rokkan, Stein and Seymour M. Lipset (1967). "Cleavage Structures, Party Systems and Voters Alignments: an Introduction", in Stein Rokkan and Seymour M. Lipset, eds. (1967), *Party Systems and Voters Alignments: Cross-National Perspectives*, New-York: The Free Press.

Schain, Martin (1987). "The National Front and the construction of a political legitimacy", *West European Politics*, 10/2.

Schonfeld, William R. (1985). *Ethnographie du PS et du RPR. Les éléphants et l'aveugle*, Paris: Economica.

Stephens, John D. (1979). "Religion and Politics in three Northwest European Democracies", in Tomasson, Richard E. ed., *Comparative Social Research*, 2.

Tarr, Francis de (1961). *The French Radical Party from Herriot to Mendès France*, London: Oxford University Press.

Vialatte, Jérôme (1994). *Les partis Verts entre ville et nature: un réalignement urbain en Europe Occidentale*, Economica: Paris.
Vignaux, Emmanuelle, *Luthéranisme et politique en Norvège. Le parti Chrétien du Peuple*, to be published.
Villiers, P. de (2002). *You liked animal flour, you will adore euro*, Paris: Albin Michel.
Ysmal, Colette (1989). *Les partis politiques sous la Ve République*, Paris: Montchrétien.

Notes

* We would like to thank the Department of Political Science, Stanford University, for hosting us, and Belinda Yeomans for her patience with the reading of the final manuscript.

[1] See for instance Stein Rokkan and Seymour M. Lipset (1967).

[2] For precisions on the Norwegian party system, see the article of Knut Heidar, in this book.

[3] Vignaux, Emmanuelle, *Luthéranisme et politique en Norvège. Le parti Chrétien du Peuple*, to be published.

[4] Third Republic: 1875-1946. Fourth Republic: 1946-1958.

[5] Together with trade unions, people expressing their opposition to extreme Right totalled more than one million all over France, on May 1.

[6] In some regions, J.-M. Le Pen polled between 23 percent and 25 percent, before J. Chirac.

[7] The first ballot of the presidential election is usually interpreted as an "ideological vote" (*vote préférentiel*), whereas the second one is a "useful vote" (*vote utile*). This means that voters tend to vote, at the first ballot, for the candidate whose ideas they feel closer to, knowing that he/she would not remain in the second ballot.

[8] Law from 2000.

[9] UMP presented 19.7 percent of women candidates, PS 36 percent and FN 48.5 percent. The figures for elected women are far lower. Parties that do not comply with the law have to pay a fine.

[10] According to this law, the parties that present at least 50 candidates receive subsidies from the state for five years. This subsidy is calculated on a two-fold basis: half is given for the number of votes received and half for the number of candidates elected.

[11] Only MDC candidates did not receive the support of the PS.

[12] It is said that J. Chirac got a banana republic score. More seriously, the very high support also means as many people for democracy.

[13] See the electoral results of the parties at the end of the article.

[14] See for comparison the tables in this article and in Knut Heidar's contribution, same book.

[15] The Radical Party was founded in 1901, but traces back to the Third Republic (1875-1946), when the main political issue was the nature of the regime. The Radical Party was a union between the Republicans, the Moderates and the Socialists. Republicans and Moderates stayed in power during most of the end of the 19th century, seeking to accomplish their agenda: separation between Church and State, anticlericalism laws, social and economic reforms. The Radical Party was supported by two main categories: the intellectual bourgeoisie and the small craftsmen, merchants and industrials. After the creation of the SFIO, the Radical Party moved more towards the centre, remaining a party with strong different tendencies, and could not avoid a series of future schisms.

[16] On the different trends existing within the PS in a comparative perspective with the RPR, see Schonfeld, William R. (1985).

[17] Tarr, Francis de (1961).

[18] Especially in the case of Algeria.
[19] A second cohabitation occurred during the Mitterrand presidency, with the nomination of Edouard Balladur in 1993.
[20] Bell, David S. and Byron Criddle (1987).
[21] Between the two presidential ballots, in a two-week period, a great number of people adhered to the democratic political organization. PS claims 13000 new members, RPR 2500, PCF 3500, and the Greens 2000, Le Soir, Bruxelles, 05-06-2002.
[22] F. Hollande announced that the next congress debate would be opened to the partisans of institutional changes, gathered around MP Arnaud Montebourg. The latter is the co-founder, together with other MP's and social sciences scholars, of a growing organization called "Convention for the Sixth Republic" (C6R), advocating constitutional reforms and claiming nearly 2000 members.
[23] The Centre for Socialist Studies, Research and Education (CERES). See Hanley, David (1986).
[24] The first one when he was minister of Industry and Research in the first Socialist government (he was opposed to the policy of economic austerity), the second time when he was minister of Defence at the beginning of the Gulf War. Concerning the third dismissal, see the special chapter by Raino Malnes, same book.
[25] Laity refers in France to the 19th century political and philosophical battles between Republicans and Liberals ("lay") on one hand and Catholics on the other. The word laity is associated with anticlericalism and atheism, i.e. non religious standpoints.
[26] Dominique Voynet was minister of Environment and Planning of the Territory under the Premiership Lionel Jospin until June 2001, which gave the Greens new important responsibilities over the borders of the sole "environment" portfolio.
[27] Vialatte, Jérôme (1994). The latter assumption needs to be qualified though: recently, the leadership of the Greens did not respect the results of the primaries.
[28] There are more parties on the Left. They are relatively minor, though lasting. Suffice it here to mention Labour Struggle (FO), led by Arlette Laguiller, and the Revolutionary Labour Struggle (LCR) led by Olivier Besancenot.
[29] He stands for a veto right in the European institutions, the maintaining of the national and monetary independence of France. On economic and fiscal matters, he is very liberal. He is very willing to restore familial and moral values.
[30] "You liked animal flour, you will adore euro", is the title of the book, published in 2002 (Paris: Albin Michel).
[31] In 1997, President Chirac decided to dissolve parliament in order to increase his legislative support. The loss of the Right led to another period of cohabitation, with Lionel Jospin as Prime Minister.
[32] See further for developments on the CDS.
[33] C. Boutin became well-known as MP's, she was the most fervent opponent to the 1999 Law on PACS (Civilian Pact of Solidarity), an attempt to acknowledge non-marital situations, between partners, homosexuals, or family members. C. Boutin is a member of the Opus Dei and the founder of a pro-life organisation.
[34] Mayer, Nonna (1987). See also Mayer, Nonna and Pascal Perrineau, eds. (1996).
[35] Le Monde Diplomatique, 29-04-2002.
[36] Each candidate has to obtain the signature of 500 elected persons. This measure creates a "natural" filter to some potentially "unserious" candidacies. It penalises small parties which have fewer networks or means to mobilise in order to convince 500 persons.
[37] Le Monde, 06-12-2001.

[38] The absence of a Left-Right cleavage was entirely new, though in 1969, there was also no Left candidate, as Gaullist G. Pompidou faced centrist A. Poher.
[39] Protestants were also present, but to a lesser extent. In fact, French Protestants have generally been more attracted by radicalism.
[40] Divided over the regime, the Catholics formed two political organisations: the Popular Liberal Action (ALP) in 1902, which defended the religious liberties, and the League of the Young Republic (LJR) in 1912, characterised by its attachment to social Catholicism, and to social reforms. Then in 1924 is created the Popular Democratic Party (PDP).
[41] MRP status, article 2.
[42] Opposed to the constitutional reform which led to the election of the president at the direct universal suffrage, MRP deputies were also more euro-enthusiastic than de Gaulle. They eventually join the opposition. One may note that this rightist direction is the one taken by a great part of its electorate, as pointed out in Michelat, Guy and Michel Simon (1985).
[43] See Fogarty, Michael P. (1957) and also Irving, R. E. M. (1979), pp. 53-68.
[44] See the contribution of Daniel-Louis Seiler, *Bilan des partis démocrates-chrétiens et conservateurs à l'aube du XXIe siècle*, Colloque du CEVIPOL, Bruxelles, 10-11 mai 2001.
[45] See the electoral results of the Kr.F at the end of the article.
[46] "The absence of religious struggles in Scandinavia, the national and very established character of the Protestant churches did not allow predicting the emergence of democratic parties with a Christian inspiration", Letamendia, Pierre (1997), p. 64. Stephens even talks about a kind of rule, following which "the homogeneous Protestant countries do not develop explicit religious parties of great importance". See Stephens, John D. (1979).
[47] Michelat, Guy and Michel Simon (1977). See also Karvonen, Lauri (1996).
[48] "Large" refers more to the past, since Christian Democracy in Southern Europe presently knows a sharp decline.
[49] The Right in Germany, the Left in Italy, both Right and Left in France.
[50] See further the Kr.F results at the parliamentary elections.
[51] Inside the Lutheran Church of Norway, one can distinguish a High Church and a Low Church. The High Church is composed of the members of the Church hierarchy while the Low Church is composed of active lay Christians. The two Churches were opposed mainly on theological issues, the High Church being more progressive and liberal than the Low Church.
[52] The term "fundamentalist" is taken here in its sociological meaning: a spiritual trend which has influenced some Protestant Churches, where biblical literalism is particularly highlighted. Biblical texts are seen as expressions of timeless truths. Fundamentalist Protestantism accentuates the direct link between God and the believer, who can, thanks to a personal and direct reading of the Bible, interpret the Holy Scriptures. In this conception, it is understandable that both exegetic works on the Bible and scientific discoveries are considered as direct threats, and therefore criticised and rejected.
[53] Paterson, William (1996) and also Bull, Martin (1996).
[54] As Fogarty puts it, "The Catholic phrasing stresses rather the inclusion of these small units of society in greater wholes, within which however they have a sphere of autonomy on which they have a right to insist", Fogarty, M., *op. cit.*, p. 41.
[55] Fogarty, M., *op. cit.*, p. 98.

[56] "If Norway joins the kingdom of the Antichrist, thousands will fall in the devil's traps and be damned. If you love Jesus, if you love Norway and the Norwegian people, do not vote for the Common Market, but pray for our country and support the opposition movement as much as you can", booklet by Oddens, Guri: "The Roman Empire and the Common Market in the end", quoted in Botnen, Bjarte, in Garvik, O. ed. (1983).

Chapter 6

Political Parties in Norway – National Institutions, Locally Anchored

Knut Heidar

Since the introduction of parliamentarianism in 1884 political parties have been the central actors in Norwegian politics: Parties have organized political activists and supporters through formal membership organizations. They have trained politicians and structured the mass vote as well as the vote in representative assemblies. Politics in Norway is by and large party politics – individual politicians either rise through the parties or with the help of parties. Politicians depend almost entirely on their party for future political careers. They must in general support the policies of the party to which they belong, even though they of course may advocate changes in those policies inside the party if they so wish. National politicians changing party affiliation are extremely rare.

In this chapter I start with a discussion of the political cleavages that have generated and sustained the party system in Norway. This is followed by a presentation of the individual political parties. Thirdly, I look at the central issue of Norway's position in European co-operation followed by a short exposure of the formal and informal international contacts of the major parties. I end by with some reflections on the role of elites in Norwegian politics in general.

The cleavages

Parties reflect different periods of historical development; they are organizational sediments of past struggles. The Norwegian social scientist Stein Rokkan coined the term "political cleavage line" in order to identify the major effects of decisions at critical junctures in the history of "nation-building" (Rokkan 1970). Inspired by the functional approach of Talcot Parsons he identified four critical "lines of cleavage" in the modern political history of Western Europe: First, between subject and dominant culture; second, between Church and government; third, between the primary and secondary economy and; fourth, between workers and employers. Following his general ideas on this, he later – with Henry Valen – presented an empirically based model of the Norwegian conflict system. (Valen and Rokkan 1974). They argued that in the history of "Norwegian mass politics there emerged seven cleavage dimensions that were crucial in the structuring of the party alternatives and in the alignment of the electorate" (Valen and Rokkan 1974:326).

One such cleavage was based on geography, three on culture and three on economy.

First there was the geographical cleavage between the eastern centre in and around the capital, Oslo, and the two peripheries: one in the "counter-cultural" South West, the other in the "class-polarized" North. This centre-periphery cleavage was particularly important during the struggle between the Left (*Venstre*) and Right (*Høyre*) parties when they were founded in the 1880s. An important sentiment in the Left Party movement was the feeling – strongly present in the peripheral constituencies – that their values and interests were not properly represented in and accepted by the state. Even today, all large Norwegian parties have an internal element of this cleavage. What made the Labour party so successful in the 1930s and later so dominant in the electorate was precisely the fact that the party managed to forge an alliance between the rural underprivileged and the urban working class. Part of the strength of the agrarian Centre Party (*Senterpartiet*) is based on this peripheral opposition to the urban centres. Also the strong opposition against EU membership in the Norwegian electorate is fuelled by this cleavage.

Three cultural cleavages have been formed over language, alcohol and religion. First, the linguistic cleavage is rooted in the fact that since the late 19th century protagonists of the rural *Nynorsk* language ("New Norwegian") have antagonized the defenders of the established central standard, the *Riksmål*. The second cleavage arose from recurring struggles over moral issues, foremost among them the question of alcohol. Prohibitionists wanted a ban, but there have been all variant positions in the continuous debates; from no sales at all, over controlled sales and/or increased prices to the position that alcohol should be treated like any other commodity in the market and with a minimum of state interference. The third cultural cleavage has been over religion. Central elements in this cleavage have been who should control the State Church and what should be the impact of Christian values in state affairs. How to teach religion in the public schools for example has been a recurrent theme in the debate, and from the 1960s the issue of abortion has been extremely important. Historically, this was a conflict mainly within the Church itself between the orthodox Lutherans organized in lay movements and the more liberal university trained clergy. Today – although the question about a State Church is still on the agenda – this is more a conflict between the active, practicing Christians and the secularized majority of nominal Church members. These "counter-cultures" joined the centre-periphery cleavage as an integrated part of the conflict between the liberal Left Party and the conservative Right during the formative years of the party system in the 1880s. Also the founding of the Christian People's Party in the 1930s can be seen as based on these cultural cleavages.

Three economic cleavages have their origins in the markets for commodities and for Labour respectively. In the commodity market there has been the old urban-rural conflict between producers and consumers. This materialized in "the battle between market farmers and the various urban interests over the control of prices and subsidies" (Valen and Rokkan 1974). The cleavage was operative at the time when parties were first founded in the 1880s. The liberal Left party was predominantly a rural peasant's movement, challenging the illiberal privileges and state control of the urban elites. The second economic cleavage sprang from the rural class struggle between labourers and smallholders in the countryside on the one side and the peasants/farmers who controlled land and capital on the other. This cleavage contributed to party splits in the Left Party on several points in time. It was also important in giving the Labour party political capital to recruit voters outside of industrial areas. Third, there was the industrial class struggle between owners/employers and their workers. This has no doubt been the dominant cleavage in 20th century Norwegian politics, giving rise to the division between the "socialist" and the "bourgeois" block of parties. This divide placed the Labour party (and subsequently its later off-springs, the Communist party and the Socialist People's Party/Left Socialist party) on one side and the different non-socialist or bourgeois parties on the other. Although still used in political debates today mostly – for polemical reasons – the socialist-bourgeois divide had its origin in the industrial age and is less useful when discussing the party system today. The problem is also that the Labour party cannot meaningfully be described as "socialist" any more. If "socialism" is taken to denote an ideology advocating the socialization of industry, meaning state take-overs, then Labour left the socialist path, in practice, in the early 1930s, in its programs in the 1950s. The party itself, however, waited till 1981 to remove the term completely from its programs, but then it had long described itself as social-democratic.

Most parties are political coalitions in the sense that they encompass more than one of these cleavages. The left-right cleavage alone presents a much too simple picture to do justice to Norwegian party politics. The Labour party for example is generally to the left in matters involving the economic role of the state in society. But Labour has also been on the restrictive side in the issue of liberalizing public policies on the sale of alcohol and pursued an active policy of economic transfers to the districts. Most parties, however, stand out more distinctly on one or two of these cleavages. The left-right cleavage is still the most important one in defining the major battleground of Norwegian politics – both in competing for the voters or in positioning the party for governmental power. In broad terms Labour and the Left Socialist Party have been to the left, the agrarian, the Christian and the liberal parties in the middle, and the Conservative and the Progress Party on the right. The electoral support of these parties and their presence in parliament is shown for selected years in tables 6.1 and 6.2, and their government experience in table 6.3.

Table 6.1 Parties' share of the vote at parliamentarian elections (percentage), selected years 1945-2001

Party	1945	1961	1973	1985	1993	1997	2001
Red Election Alliance [1]			0.4	0.6	1.1	1.7	1.2
Communist Party	11.9	2.9		0.2		0.1	0.1
Left Socialist Party [2]		2.4	11.2	5.5	7.9	6.0	12.5
Labour	41.0	46.8	35.3	40.8	36.9	35.0	24.3
Liberals	13.8	8.8	3.5	3.1	3.6	4.5	3.9
The Liberal Peoples Party [3]			3.4	0.5			
The Centre Party [4]	8.0	9.4	11.0	6.6	16.7	7.9	5.6
Christian People's Party	7.9	9.6	12.3	8.3	7.9	13.7	12.4
Conservative	17.0	20.0	17.4	30.4	17.0	14.3	21.2
Progress Party [5]			5.0	3.7	6.3	15.3	14.6
Others	0.3	0.2	0.5	0.4	2.6	1.5	4.2
Turnout	76.4	79.1	80.2	84.0	75.8	78.3	75.5

Notes

[1] In 1989 the "County lists for Environment and Solidarity".
[2] Socialist People's Party until 1973. In 1973 Socialist Electoral Alliance includes, among others, the Communist Party.
[3] Called "The New People's Party" until 1980. Reunited with the Liberals in 1988.
[4] The Farmers' Party until 1959.
[5] "Anders Lange's Party" until 1977.

Sources: Adapted from Knut Heidar and Einar Berntzen, Vesteuropeisk politikk, Oslo: Universitetsforlaget, 1998, p. 53 and Official statistics of Norway, Historical Statistics 1994, Oslo: Statistics Norway, 1995.

Table 6.2 Parties' share of Storting representatives (percentage), selected years 1945-2001

Party	1945	1961	1973	1985	1993	1997	2001
Communist Party	7.3						
Left Socialist Party		1.3	10.3	3.8	7.9	5.5	13.9
Labour	50.7	49.3	40.0	45.2	40.6	39.4	26.1
Liberals	13.3	9.3	1.3		0.6	3.6	1.2
The Liberal People's Party			0.6				
The Centre Party	6.7	10.7	13.5	7.6	19.4	6.7	6.1
Christian People's Party	5.3	10.0	12.9	10.2	7.9	15.2	13.3
Conservative	16.7	19.3	18.7	31.8	17.0	13.9	23.0
Progress Party			2.6	1.3	6.0	15.2	15.8
Others					0.6	0.6	0.6
Number of representatives in Stortinget	150.0	150.0	155.0	157.0	165.0	165.0	165.0

Source: Adapted from Knut Heidar and Einar Berntzen, Vesteuropeisk politikk, Oslo: Universitetsforlaget, 1998, p. 55.

Table 6.3 Governments and party composition 1969-2002

Year	1969	1971	1972	1975	1976	1977
Month	Sept	March	Oct	Oct	Jan	Sept
Prime Minister	Borten	Bratteli	Korvald	Bratteli	Nordli	Nordli
PM's party	C	Lab	Chr	Lab	Lab	Lab
Left-right position [1]	C-R	L	C	L	L	L
Conservative	6					
Christian People's Party	3		4			
The Centre Party	3		6			
Liberals	3		5			
Labour		15		15	16	16
Number of ministers	15	15	15	15	16	16
Gov't share of MPs in parliament (percentage)	50	49	26	40	40	49

Year	1981	1981	1983	1985	1986	1989
Month	Feb	Oct	June	Oct	May	Oct
Prime Minister	Brundtland	Willoch	Willoch	Willoch	Brundtland	Syse
PM's party	Lab	Cons	Cons	Cons	Lab	Cons
Left-right position [1]	L	R	C-R	C-R	L	C-H
Conservative		17	11	10		9
Christian People's Party			4	4		5
The Centre Party			3	4		5
Liberals						
Labour	17				18	
Number of ministers	17	17	18	18	18	19
Gov't share of MPs in parliament (percentage)	49	34	51	49	45	37

Year	1990	1993	1996	1997	2000	2001
Month	Nov	Oct	Oct	Oct	March	Oct
Prime Minister	Brundland	Brundland	Jagland	Bondevik	Stoltenberg	Bondevik
PM's party	Lab	Lab	Lab	Christ	Lab	Christ
Left-right position [1]	L	L	L	C	L	C-R
Conservative						10
Christian People's Party				9		6
The Centre Party				6		
Liberals				4		3
Labour	19	19	19		19	
Number of ministers	19	19	19	19	19	19
Gov't share of MPs in parliament (percentage)	38	41	41	25	39	38

Note

[1] L = left, C = centre, R = right.

Source: Adapted from Knut Heidar and Einar Berntzen, Vesteuropeisk politikk, Oslo: Universitetsforlaget, 1998, p. 55.

The political parties

Labour

The Labour Party (*Arbeiderpartiet*) that entered government in 1935 was contrary to much "socialist" party rhetoric, a pragmatic social-democratic party. It was also a party with a revolutionary past. From 1919 to 1923 it had been a member of the Komintern, the Moscow based communist international, advocating armed revolution by the working class avant-garde to create a true people's democracy. In 1921 a social-democratic party split off to the right, but this was reunited with Labour in 1927 – after Labour had left the *Komintern*. The break with the Moscow communists in 1923, however, lead to a party split and the founding of the Norwegian Communist Party.

The Labour Party became the hegemonic party in Norwegian politics for more than 30 years after 1935. From 1945 to 1961 it commanded a majority in parliament, and a "parliamentary situation" could only arise – according to an explicit statement from the leader of its parliamentary fraction in the late 1950s – if the Labour party itself so wished (Stavang 1964: 144ff). And even when the coalition of centre-right parties took over from 1965-71, the change in political direction was not great. The war experiences and the moderation of the Labour governments of the 1950s had prepared the ground for increased political convergence of the major political parties. A corporatist mode of decision-making including private industry and interest organizations outside the "Labour family" contributed also to a low-conflict political system, a new "Social-Democratic Order" (Furre 1992: 248-253). This "order" from the early 1950s to late 1970s had several characteristics in politics and society, which made it special compared to the periods both before and after. Labour was the "natural party of government" in the period. During the thirty years from 1950 to 1980 the party was out of office for less than eight years and Labour never ruled in a coalition with other parties. Social progress was founded on a more or less continuous economic growth during this period. The state gave priority to industrial development and a strong belief in progress as such permeated society. Planning was a central instrument in state economic policies and sectors like agriculture, fishing and transport were all strongly state regulated. The social-democratic order was also marked by a belief in a strong state. Primary public goals were full employment, social equality and a high level of welfare. Redistribution of resources was accordingly a major objective, and it was considered the responsibilities of the state to provide free education, free health care and to look after important cultural institutions. In short, markets were to be guided private solutions few and the chances for "opting out" restricted.

Labour has never entered a coalition government in peacetime. But because of its size it has remained the main governmental alternative in Norwegian politics since 1945. In the following 50 years Labour spent 37 in office. During the 1950s and 1960s the Labour Party pursued a reformist course – at least when compared to its more radical *Komintern* past – building a modern, industrial society. The Party also laid the foundations of the new welfare state on the basis of a mixed economy. Private capital, in part foreign investments, was crucial in building the new economy, but the policy was for the state to control commanding positions in major industries like iron and steel production. The party leader for most of this period was Mr. Einar Gerhardsen who was chairman for 20 years and Prime Minister for about 17 between 1945 and 1965. He also became – particularly in retrospect – a "father of the nation"; a rock solid captain having led the Norwegian nation safely through the rough waters of Cold War and into increasing prosperity.

The 1970s were turbulent years for Labour. The European issue split the party and new issues like the environment added to the old left-right and Cold War divisions within the party. There was also a shift of generations that weakened the party. Labour was traditionally a "mass party" with a high membership and a robust – the left-wing opposition would say "Leninist" – party culture. In 1981, Mrs. Gro Harlam Brundtland took over both as party leader and as Prime Minister. She stayed on as a party leader until 1992 and held the position as Prime Minister on and off for 10 years until 1996. During the 1980s, Labour changed both organizationally and politically. Through a "modernization" drive the party aimed at becoming more open and less dependent on closed "processes". The party was also more open to criticism (e.g. the unintended effects of) of its own welfare state project. Public solutions to problems in society were not automatically considered best: child nurseries needed private supplements not only for reasons of low capacity, but also for improving services through competition. In the 1990s the European Union issue returned to divide the party in the run-up to the new referendum in 1994. Within Labour, however, the issue was now handled much less controversially vis-à-vis the party minority fighting against membership. The election of 2001 was a disappointment to Labour, however, with a record low of 27 percent of the votes. The downward slide has continued in subsequent opinion polls with Labour trailing behind the Conservatives and even the Progress Party in the popularity stakes.

The Conservative party

The conservative "Right Wing" party (*Høyre*) was founded as the instrument of the old upper class, as represented by higher state officials and the merchant bourgeoisie. These state officials were thrown out of government in 1884 when parliamentarianism was practiced in full for the first time. The Conservative Party returned to government office repeatedly between 1889 and 1928, but then had to wait until the 1960s before its next appearance (again excepting the wartime coalition 1940-45). Of the 13 years the Conservative Party has been in government after 1961, 11 have been in coalition with the centre parties.

The Conservative has been the party of the well-to-do and in terms of their voters' social profile it still is. Ideologically, it has a dual heritage from the paternalist old state officials' culture stressing the responsibilities of the state and from the urban bourgeoisie a liberal market philosophy advocating individual responsibility and limited state interference. The party was a fierce critic of the post-war "Labour Party State" with state industries, increasing taxes and disdain for private initiative. The conservatives did not appreciate Labour's emphasis on redistribution and equality by taxation and mass (i.e. low quality) education. The Conservative Party formed a one-party minority government from 1981 to 1983, which was at the time of the so-called "right-wing-wave" in Norwegian politics. This brought Høyre from a 17 percent support at the 1973 election to 32 percent in 1981. In the years of "thatcherism" and "reaganomics" the ideological climate was favourable. Also, the party's organization opened up for more input from the districts and the party's profile approached more of a "people's party". After the conservatives left government in 1986 voter support dwindled and in the 1993 election it was back to "sub 20" – at 17 percent. During these years the party experienced a political squeeze between an increased competition from the "modernized" Labour on its left and the populist Progress Party on its right. The issue of EU-membership gave the conservatives few opportunities to present a distinct political profile to the electorate. If the party wanted Norway to join – and it very much did – it had to play second fiddle to the Labour Party. Changing the party leader four times between 1985 and 1994 did not help much either.

The parties of the centre

The Norwegian Liberal Party (*Venstre*) was founded as the party that succeeded in seizing power from the conservative right in the 1884 debacle. Later, the Liberal party alternated with the conservatives in government for more than 40 years. The Liberal politicians were frequently in government until Labour finally broke the "bourgeois" hegemony in 1935.[1] The Liberal Party mobilized the social and cultural forces in opposition to the "Officials' State" – in the peripheries to the south and the west, in the lay church movement, among the teetotalers and among the adherents of the "New Norwegian" language. These groups made up a political coalition under the umbrella of a liberal ideology – the ideologues were, however, mostly to be found in the urban centres around the capital.

There were in-built tensions between the different segments in this coalition opposing the Officials' State and some subsequently formed parties of their own. First, parts of the agrarian segment broke out to form the Farmers' Party in 1920.[2] In the early 1930s the Christian People's Party was created by dissatisfied "lay-church" segments. The overall history of the Liberal Party after 1945 is one of electoral decline, and in 1972 the EU membership issue split the party. This contributed to making its parliamentary existence a matter of life or death in the 1980s and 1990s – in spite of a later party reunion. While the liberals in the first decades after 1945 scored around 10 percent, the party after 1970 had its top score at the *Storting* elections of 1997 with a 4.5 percent vote. The Liberal Party was without representation in parliament for two periods from 1985 to 1993. During these years the liberals could not quite decide whether their party's "social-liberal" ideology was sufficiently liberal to give it a place in the bourgeois group of centre-right parties or sufficiently social to make it a natural ally of the new Labour emerging in the 1980s. Having (re)turned to its liberal heritage in the 1990s, the party again entered parliament and became a coalition party in the government of centre parties formed after the 1997 election.

The Centre Party (*Senterpartiet*) was named "The Farmers' Party" until 1959. Up till then it literally was a party of farmers for farmers and their families. During the 1960s the party's policies broadened to make a party in defence of rural and general "district" interests, electorally expanding into the periphery sectors of fisheries and small-scale industry. Still, as the farming population declined, the party's share of the vote went down from about 14 percent in the inter-war period to 8-10 percent after the war and further to a low point in 1989 with 6.5 percent of the votes. The debates on EU membership in the early 1970s and 1990s stimulated the support for the party. In the view of many people voting against EU membership the Centre Party directed its no-campaign with skill and effective leadership. At the 1993 election the party polled 17 percent of the vote and became the second largest party in parliament. The Centre Party continued to present itself as the party defending the interests of the peripheral districts, but at this election it also put much emphasis on the need to deepen national democracy (which it perceived as threatened by the EU and the bureaucrats in Brussels). The party vigorously claimed that the old left-right divide by now had become obsolete, and distanced itself from one of its coalition partners, the Conservative Party. In 1990 the Centre Party broke with the centre – right coalition – led by a conservative Prime Minister – over the policies of EU rapprochement. Later the party claimed victory both in the 1994 EU-referendum and when the three parties of the centre (the Christians, the Centre Party and the Liberals) formed a coalition government in 1997. This "centre government", they claimed, was a truly independent alternative, independent of the old left-right rivalries.

The Christian People's Party (*Kristelig Folkeparti*) was founded in 1933 and at first ran for election in the West Coast counties only. It became a national party after 1945. Originally, it was the party of the lay Christian movement, later for the broader, although decreasing Christian segments in Norwegian society. The party focused on the struggle against secular trends in a changing, modernizing society and in particular defended the place of religion and the Lutheran State Church within the school system. When the abortion issue entered the agenda in the late 1960s the Christian People's Party turned vigorously against a proposal to permit abortion on demand within the first 12 weeks of pregnancy. Such a law was adopted in 1978 after a long and bitter struggle. Labour had proposed a new abortion law in their 1969 program. Even after the other centre-right parties all had accepted it, the Christian People's Party refused to sit in the new conservative government in 1981: They would not be part of a government which had to administer an unacceptable abortion law. Two years later, however, they decided to join the government coalition in spite of the law, hastened by the Centre Party who had grown impatient with their close ally.

The Christian People's Party polled between 8 and 12 percent of the vote throughout most of the post-war period. At the 1997 election, however, they broke a downward trend by getting close to 14 percent – its best result ever – and the party became the second largest in the *Storting* (shared with the Progress Party). The party also got the Prime Minister in the new government, Mr. Kjell Magne

Bondevik, a long time MP and party leader. The party leadership has tried to make the party more broadly based in terms of support and policies. Mr. Bondevik has made no secret of his wish to transform the party into the more Christian-Democratic type, i.e. more similar to the centre-right parties on the European mainland – possibly more to the centre than to the right, like the "Christian Democratic Appeal" in the Netherlands.

Left and right and some smaller parties

The Left Socialist Party (*Sosialistisk Venstreparti*) was created in 1975 by a "left of Labour"-merger. These parties had just successfully fought Norwegian membership in the European Community at the 1972 referendum. The bulk of members and voters came from the former Socialist People's Party. This party had been created in 1961 to fight against the threat that nuclear arms might be placed on Norwegian territory and also against the "right-wing drift" of the Labour government. Although new forces joined the Left Socialists in 1975 – from the old Communist Party and so-called "independent socialists" – the new party basically turned out to be a continuation of the old Socialist People's Party. Ideologically the party was proclaimed a "third way" party[3] – i.e. neither communist nor social-democratic – and SV gained momentum from the leftward trends manifested particularly by the young (student) generation of the late 1960s. During the 1970s and 1980s the party made environmental protection part of its platform, transforming ideologically from a 1960s "new left" party towards a more "green" party in the 1980s. Organizationally, the party did not, however, in the end adopt the extreme mode of grass roots decision-making and the political action strategy found e.g. in the German Greens. It still considers itself a socialist party advocating an active state in the development of the Norwegian society. Originating from an anti-Cold War platform in the 1960s and 1970s, however, the party has during the 1990s increasingly found itself in search of new policies.

The Progress Party (*Fremskrittspartiet*) entered Norwegian politics in 1973 on a low tax, anti-state platform – inspired by a similar Danish populist revolt at the time. In 1978 the party elected Mr. Carl I. Hagen as their chairman, and he still serves in this position in 2002. During the 1980s Hagen proved himself to be a very skilful media performer. At elections the party profited from a broad-based voter resentment against politics and politicians, and the party played on popular sentiments against taxes, bureaucracy and preferential treatment of groups like immigrants and welfare clients. Pending on the electoral issues in focus, the party has had a mixed fortune with 13 percent of the vote in 1989 and 15 percent in 1997 as its best results. In the autumn of 2000 the party was for several months the largest party in Norway according to the polls. It entered, however, a period of fierce infighting over positions and policies, returning in the spring of 2001 to its 1997 election result in the polls. Because of Mr. Hagen's one-man performance on behalf of the party, its fate is very dependent on his ability to keep the party in the media as well as to keep its various segments together. In the early 1990s, the parliamentary group split over the relative importance of classical liberalism and populist causes in party policies. Nevertheless, Mr. Hagen and the Progress Party managed to maintain their level of voter support. In fact, opinion polls in the autumn of 2002 consistently put Mr. Hagen's party ahead of all the other parties in terms of popular support, also in Northern Norway. It remains to bee seen whether this is a passing mood or an emerging change of the electoral landscape. In the latter case, a revolution may be about to happen in Norwegian politics.

The old Communist Party (*Norges Kommunistiske Parti*), on the far left in Norwegian politics, was created when the Labour Party split in 1923. This was an old-style communist party with strong links to the Soviet regime. Its all-time high came just after the Second World War with 12 percent of the vote, but it soon dwindled due to the climate of Cold War and internal feuding. After 1961, the Communist party has not won representation in the Storting. At the 1993 election another far left representative from the tiny marxist-leninist inspired Red Election Alliance (*Rød Valgallianse*) was elected from the capital. His election was, however, mostly a personal tribute since the candidate had been active in uncovering a financial scandal within the municipal authorities.

Twice in the post-war period special county lists have managed to get their candidate elected to parliament. It happened the first time in 1989 when a People's Action Movement favouring the northernmost county, Finnmark, succeeded. The second time was in 1997 when a whaling skipper, resenting the restriction on whaling and seal-hunting, organized a "Coastline Party" in the Nordland county and managed to be elected to the *Storting*.

The national question in party politics

Norwegians have long been aware that they belong to a small nation. Up till 1905 they fought to leave the union with Sweden and to establish an independent state, knowing fair well that they never would gain parity with their Swedish brethren. The feeling was also strong that Norwegian history and culture, even the economy, gave the foundation and the need for an independent nation state. The recent independence – almost within living memory – is often taken as an explanation for why Norwegians were so reluctant to join another union in the 1990s. The debate over EU-membership also drew its strength from the old centre – periphery conflict and the "counter cultures" in Norwegian history (lay Christianity, New Norwegian language and teetotalism). In this debate, there were elements of a long-standing coalition in Norwegian political history, namely that between the rural districts and parts of the urban intelligentsia. Added to that was the anti-capitalist resistance against the "moneycratie" of Brussels – rooted in parts in the trade union movement and nostalgic socialism – and the defence of the traditional welfare state (supported in particular by female voters).

In some ways it may look odd that the national question should re-emerge so explosively during the EU debate. The process of nation-building was successfully completed long ago. Nation and state had merged into an institutionalized democracy – the Labour movement was integrated into the nation as well as the state during the 1930s and 1940s. Norway is even today basically an ethnically homogeneous country with comparatively few immigrants. About 6 percent of the

Norwegian population are immigrants in the sense that both parents were foreign citizens. Roughly half of these, however, came from Nordic, North European or North American countries and do not deviate much from standard cultural patterns in Norway. Traditional minorities – like the Lapps, which make up less than 0.01 percent of the population – are extremely small. Still it is important to note that – however small – these minorities challenge the strong institutional and cultural imperatives of treating everyone equally – in schools, at the workplace, in politics and in civil society generally. Their presence are forcing politicians and voters to confront the dilemmas of a multicultural society as well as to face the challenges presented to a traditionally homogeneous nation – ethnically, culturally and to a fair extent also socially.

The old project of nation-building so eagerly pursued through the 19th and most of the 20th century has, however, not only been challenged from the inside. The major challenge has come from the outside. The manifestations of this challenge has not come so much in the economic and cultural fields, in spite of fashionable arguments about "globalization", "Americanization" and the "communication revolution". The major challenge has been political in the shape of the European Union. The enormous success of the EU in terms of building a transnational institutional framework for economic and political co-operation between an increasing number of European states has forced politicians and voters alike to reconsider the very foundation of the Norwegian nation state. The EEA arrangement locks Norwegian public debate into a continuous discourse on the sustainability of Norwegian democracy, security, economy and culture. The "national question" today is not about secession, rebellion and multi-national state building – as in 19th century Europe. It is about building viable political, economic and cultural arrangements to sustain democracy, prosperity and a "Norwegian" way of life. Or in the shorter version: It is about membership of the EU.

The parties' international relations

Traditionally, political parties have borrowed and learnt from parties abroad. The rhetoric of "the third way", "neue Mittte" and "education, education, education" is about issues and style, just as the parties have followed closely the new campaign techniques developed by electorally successful parties in other countries. More recent to most parties is increased transnational co-operation and contact between ideological "sister parties". The contact pattern of Norwegian parties falls in three fairly distinct categories: The Nordic, the European and the Global (Heidar et al., 1997). Clearly, the Nordic contacts are both most frequent and most important. The contacts most useful to the parties are, furthermore, the bilateral relationships, even though these sometimes flourish inside the multilateral organization of "party families". The party leaders themselves see the personal contacts as the most useful part of the co-operation. Studies also show that there are the internal political needs of the parties that guide the agenda for these meetings. And the general pattern from "high politics" is reproduced: It is the central party leaders who are in charge, often closely co-ordinated with the activity of the parliamentary party group.

Overall activity on the international arena is small. However, in all parties it is on the increase and attributed increasing importance by the leadership. The Labour Party has without comparison the most frequent international contacts. The Nordic social democratic parties have a long-established tradition of co-operation across national borders. These parties have their own Nordic organization with regular meetings and congresses, mutual guest representation at their congresses, and cross-national committees working out policy recommendations. Also the Conservative Party has in later decades worked systematically to extend its international co-operation, and both Labour and the Conservatives hold membership in their European umbrella organization, the Party of European Socialists and European Peoples' Party respectively. This is the case even though these organizations in principle are reserved for parties from EU countries. They were let in during the Norwegian application for membership in the EU in 1994 – and not kicked out again.

Still, there is little evidence that the general increase in international contacts during the latter decades has affected the political parties to any significant extent. Clearly, this it quite rational party behaviour as all major forces having an impact on their political and organizational success are to be found within the national borders: The voters, the nomination process of party candidates, the political agenda, parliament and government. International contact is focused on the exchange of ideas, building leadership networks and boosting credentials to be used in national politics. But the fact that busy, overworked party leaders give high priority to these contacts is a reason to believe that at least lack of such activity sends negative images that is detrimental to the party and the leader in the struggle for national power. Some party leaders explicitly argue that an increased contact with the institutions and parties in the EU is necessary to compensate for the lack of Norwegian membership. However, the level of "europeanization", not to speak about "globalization", is still fairly limited among Norwegian parties.

Elites on trial

Political elites are always on trial in democracies. Their power may end abruptly at election times or through parliamentary actions. In this Norway is not a special case. We may still ask whether the party politicians are particularly exposed in Norway?

It may be argued that political forces were crucial in shaping Norwegian society and that this has possibly left a lasting legacy (Heidar 2001). The construction of "Norway" as a modern state and nation was to a large extent the project of a tiny 19th century elite of politicians, bureaucrats, artists and academics. This elite and the institutional defences entrenched in the "official's state" were not, however, able to stem the tide of the peasant's movement in the 1880s. Actually, the old elite was split and some of them joined the new wave of challengers. Later – in the 20th century – the rising Labour movement toppled the new "bourgeois" power elites. Contemporary Norwegian institutions do clearly not make any solid defences against new challenges. The complaint of the conservative elites of the 1880s was precisely that the plebiscitarian elements were not sufficiently contained and delayed in the political process. There was no federalist structure, no first chamber in parliament and no royal veto in legislative matters after 1884. Today the PR electoral system and the decentralized party nomination of candidates for parliament give central elites few instruments in "guiding" the electoral process. The formidable power of the media is unpredictable. It is, of course, possible to argue that the fixed parliamentary term of four years, without the possibility of calling new elections, makes up a defence for the rulers of the day, but that argument may equally well be put the other way round: that the fixed-term election period removes another instrument from the elite's tool-box.

The strength of politics is evident in the public budgets and in the corporate networks. In spite of the strong impact of market ideology since the 1980s and the Thatcher-Reagan crusaders that also have been active in Norway, more than 50 percent of the entire economy still goes through public budgets, and the state coffer is well-filled. Even if privatization and increased market exposure of many public enterprises has been the dominant political trend during the latter decades the state is no doubt still strongly entrenched in the economy. A major issue in Norwegian politics at the turn of the century is still – just like in the first two decades of the 20th century – how to secure national interests in a changing, increasingly internationalized economy. Corporatist structures are of major importance in a small, open economy like the Norwegian. The mix of public and private structures is still a central characteristic of the Norwegian society. Finally, the strong impact of politicians is evident in the public policies pursued in areas like welfare, health, the districts and gender equality.

The proposition that Norwegian politics is particularly important is, of course, difficult to prove and must remain a hypothesis. Politics is, on the face of it, not more important in Norway than in the neighbouring welfare societies Sweden and Denmark. Certainly, the consorted industrial strategies of Germany, the consensual politics of the Netherlands and Belgium or the French dirigisme are challenging cases confronting the argument of a special Norwegian "primacy of politics". Still, Norwegian elites may be more "on trial" than politicians are in many other comparable democracies. No doubt political institutions expose them strongly to voter judgments. That is not unique. Electoral participation is also consistently high. That is not unique either, although the combination of weak institutional defence and high electoral exposure is less common. Add the ingredient of having a small population and the potential for elite challenges increases. However, the most demanding factor for Norwegian elites during the 1990s has been the mismatch between elite and voter opinions on the European issue—the dominant elites in favour, the dominant electorate against. Furthermore, the political parties did not reflect the electorate well as a clear majority of the members of the Storting were in favour. This makes for crossing political allegiances and antagonisms that again make stable parliamentary government in line with party programmes and public opinion extremely difficult. This is not an elite "trial" that is likely to trigger a major breakdown in Norwegian politics. The consensual elements in politics and culture are too strong to make that likely. The major challenge facing Norwegian democracy in the years ahead – outside or inside of the EU – will be that of accountability, to sustain a democratic system where the electorate might vote for alternatives — and to where they can expect to get what they voted for.

References

Furre, Berge (1992). *Norsk historie 1905 – 1990.* Oslo: Det Norske Samlaget.
Heidar, Knut (2001). *Norway. Elites on Trial.* Boulder, Co: Westview Press.
Heidar, Knut and Einar Berntzen (1998). Vesteuropeisk politikk, Oslo: Universitetsforlaget.
Heidar, Knut, Hanne C. Pettersen and Lars Svåsand (1997). "Norske partiers internasjonale forbindelser', in Knut Heidar and Lars Svåsand, eds., *Partier uten grenser?* Oslo: Tano.
Rokkan, Stein (1970). 'Nation-Building, Cleavage Formation and the Structuring of Mass Politics', in Stein Rokkan, *Citizens Elections Parties.* Oslo: Universitetsforlaget.
Stavang, Per (1964). *Parlamentarisme og maktbalanse.* Oslo: Universitetsforlaget.
Valen, Henry and Stein Rokkan (1974). 'Conflict Structure and Mass Politics in a European Periphery', in Richard Rose, ed., *Electoral Behavior: A Comparative Handbook.* New York: The Free Press.

Notes

[1] In the Norwegian political vocabulary "bourgeois" has no derogatory associations. The conservatives in particular considered themselves and their coalition partners from the 1960s onward as proponents of "bourgeois policies".

[2] The story is somewhat simplified in covering only still existing parties; the "offspring" also generally had a more complex background than that of emerging from the Liberal Party alone.

[3] Of the Cold War 1950s and 1960s, not the British "Third Way" of the Blair government of the 1990s.

Chapter 7

The One and Indivisible Republic? The Constitutional Debate on Corsican Autonomy

Raino Malnes

Introduction

In France, as elsewhere, constitutional debates usually come in the wake of major political crises, but they are staple events even in the settled context of the Fifth Republic (Carcassonne 1999; Duhamel 1999: 31-43).[1] Do they stand apart from debates over more mundane matters? Are they more infused with ideas? Are they conducted in a more open-minded manner?

These questions evoke certain misgivings about modern democracies. They allude to the complaint that – in Jeremy Waldron's (1999) phrase – there is not enough *dignity* to democratic politics. Machinations, stratagems and tactical manoeuvres are the rule of the day; politicians are schemers and plotters who engage in horse-trading, log-rolling, interest-pandering, anything but principled political activity; their weapons are not arguments, but schemes and bluffs – or so the argument goes.[2] Is all of politics – even constitutional debates – like this?

In theory, neither constitutional debates nor politics in general have to be like this. At its best, Waldron (ibid.: 2) says, democratic politics – in particularly legislative activity – can be "something like the following: the representatives of the community come together to settle solemnly and explicitly on common schemes and measures that can stand in the name of them all, and they do so in a way that openly acknowledges and respects (rather than conceals) the inevitable differences of opinion and principle among them". Waldron avers that it is a rosy, perhaps naive picture, but to him it is an aspiration: something worth having. This view is presumably as widespread as disappointments with the alleged darkness of real politics. John Dryzek (1992: 115) makes the point by contrasting "adversary democracy" with "a different kind of political interaction" in which "collective choice proceeds discursively rather than strategically". The latter kind of politics has two characteristics. First, politicians espouse values; second, "values [are] subject to rational public discourse" (ibid.). For "[m]ost Western political systems", Dryzek argues, "a thorough overhaul might be in order", and the "most prominent alternatives ... emphasize discussion oriented towards consensus" (ibid.: 118).

It will be clear by now that two images are enmeshed in what one may call the dignified picture of politics. First, there is an image of politicians as *principled* actors – men and women who stand for something and can be trusted to speak their minds. They display conviction and sincerity. This image contrasts with what Stuart Hampshire (1989: 175) calls scepticism about practical reasons. "The sceptic says that such reasons are always rationalizations, that is, they are without effect, dynamically inert, mere decoration, designed to make the agent respectable in the eyes of others." The idea that politicians are principled actors also goes against the assumption that they are opportunists. The predominant motive of opportunists is a naked interest in winning elections. They cater to people with a view to capturing votes (or other kinds of support) and have no genuine commitments. Their interest in electoral success may make them wary of how well their actions and utterances go home with voters who, on their part, have commitments, but this is only to say that shrewd opportunists are good at faking principled attitudes. Posturing is stock of their trade. By contrast, politicians of principle can be taken on their words.

The second image that shows in the picture of dignified politics is commonly called the *deliberative* conception of democracy. While democracy is often defined in procedural terms, as a system of equal voting rights and majority rule, this conception gives pride of place to substantive aspects of decision-making. It implies that the value of democracy lies in a free, explicit and open-minded exchange of ideas. Without that, democracy has little to say for itself in normative terms, or so the argument goes.

A process of deliberation has two characteristics. First, decisions are taken only after people have offered "justifications for the exercise of collective power framed in terms of considerations that can, roughly speaking, be acknowledged by all as reasons" (Cohen 1998: 186). Issues are debated in good faith. Second, political opinions are affected by the exchange of them. Thus, "public reasoning itself can help to reduce the diversity of politically relevant preferences because such preferences are shaped and even formed in the process of public reasoning itself" (ibid.: 199; italics deleted). The contrast to deliberation is *confrontation*. Opinions are marshalled, sometimes with rhetorical skill, but there is no real discussion. Politicians do anything to outwit opponents and a partisan spirit reigns. Those who are shrewdest win the day.

Two questions may be asked about the picture of dignified politics. First, are the twin images of principled politicians and deliberative decision-making only an aspiration or even an approximation to reality – if not all of it, then at least discernible parts? Second, how strong is, all things considered, the normative force of this picture? Does its *prima facie* attractiveness stand up to scrutiny? The first question is raised in this article; the latter is a subject for another occasion.

The empirical focus is the debate about the constitutional status of Corsica, which is one of France's regions. This debate dominated French politics in long periods in 2000 and 2001. The government proposed the transfer of limited but significant legislative autonomy to local authorities on the island. In itself, such a proposal is an extraordinary event in a centralised state whose constitution embodies the ideal of the "one and indivisible republic". Thus, the purpose of this chapter goes beyond the theoretical exploration that was prefigured above. I also hope to shed some light on the tension between centralization and decentralization in contemporary France. The conflict between Paris and the provinces is of long date (Knapp and Wright 2001: ch. 12). What follows is a close look at the interplay between principles and political expediency in the current state of this conflict.

Corsica and the constitution

A lengthy, sometimes violent conflict has pitted successive French governments against a varied lot of Corsican "nationalists": organizations and clandestine groups that demand greater autonomy for Corsica. Some want full political independence, others limited exemption from principles that otherwise regulate national legislation and administration. Independence for Corsica has been on no government's agenda, but the government of Lionel Jospin, which came to power in 1997, soon broached the possibility of a special status for the island among France's regions. At the end of 1999, Jospin launched negotiations that were meant to cure the "Corsican malaise". Known as the "Matignon process" – named after the building that houses the offices of the prime minister – these negotiations brought together the government and the elected members of the Corsican Assembly, including nationalists. In July 2000, the government proposed a law granting Corsica a greater say than other regions in legal and regulatory matters. It also wanted the teaching of the local language to be made an integral part of primary education on the island.

Parts of the proposal for a special law on Corsica were subject to textual refinements right up until the text was formally presented to parliament. In its final wording, it said that the National Assembly may authorize the Corsican territorial assembly to "adapt" certain laws and regulations to the specificities of the island, and it was "suggested" (*proposé*) that the Corsican language be taught in primary schools. The first vote on the law took place on May 22, 2001, and a majority in the National Assembly adopted it. I shall concentrate on the events that preceded this vote. What came after – the subsequent hearing of the law in the Senate, the final vote in the National Assembly, and what happened after the national elections of 2002 – will be briefly discussed in the last section of the article.

The government that put forth the proposal for limited Corsican autonomy consisted of five parties. All belonged on the left in the conventional left-right spectrum of French politics. *Parti Socialiste (PS)* was the senior partner. In the debate over Corsica, it had been somewhat divided among itself; yet, nearly all its representatives ultimately cast a favourable vote. One junior partner, *Les Verts*, had always supported the initiative for limited autonomy, while another, *Parti Communiste Française (PCF)*, housed more opponents than supporters, and its representatives in parliament all abstained from voting. The proposal of the government met with vehement opposition from a third partner – *Mouvement des Citoyens (MDC)*. The smallest party in the government, *Parti Radicaux de Gauche*, had been split in the debate and was split in the vote.

The parliamentary opposition, which consisted of four parties on the right, was also a site of dissonance. The leader of *Democratie Libérale (DL)* – Alain Madelin

– early spoke out in favour of autonomy, but most *députés* of his party took the opposite view. Most Gaullists, in *Rassemblement pour la Republique (RPR)*, as well as centrists, in *l'Union pour la Democratie Française (UDF)*, opposed the government's proposal from the start. Yet, in the last days before votes were called in May, some leading Gaullists and centrists made conciliatory moves. Some of them went on to cast a favourable vote, while others abstained from voting.

The Gaullist president, Jacques Chirac, was a case of his own. He long signalled an accommodating attitude, but in February 2001, when the government took the proposal to the council of ministers (to prepare for its presentation to parliament), Chirac came out against it, only – seemingly – to soften his opposition at the time of the ultimate parliamentary debate.

Both left and right were, accordingly, in disarray. There were disagreements and shifting attitudes. Whence did these discords and shifts arise? In view of the previous distinction between different kinds of politics, the question breaks down into two. First, do divergent positions reflect principled divergences, or are they expressions of crosscutting tactical considerations? Second, do shifts of attitude stem from deliberation that make people change heart, or are they spurred by opportunism? In a short article, I can come nowhere near to an exhaustive answer. The anecdotal bent of the analysis will be evident, but the anecdotes are, hopefully, clues to a more comprehensive truth.

Three questions

The analysis will revolve around three questions. The first question turns on the *coherence* of a political position. Is it settled and consistent or an amalgam of mixed convictions? Is it steeped in ideology or an expression of a fragmented and variable frame of mind? (I borrow the last phrase from Blackburn 2000: 36.) On a standard definition, an ideology is a discreet and relatively coherent system of beliefs (Thompson 1993: 409). But a principled stand needs not amount to an ideological point of view. Convictions sometimes want consistency, and a fragmented frame of mind is not necessarily one that wants convictions. Incoherence is, arguably, a pronounced feature of mental reality. "Values may easily clash within the breast of a single individual" (Berlin 1990: 12).

The second question is best introduced by an imaginary example. Let's assume that I am a member of government in a democratic state, and political freedom is among my most cherished concerns, but democracy and freedom have come under threat from a group of fanatics who are, with some reason, suspected of plotting a *coup d'état*. This is my choice: "I may seek to promote political freedom by using my power in government to suppress [the] dangerous group of fanatics. Or I may honor it [freedom] by renouncing measures that themselves violate people's freedom" (Pettit 1997: 127). Drawing on the contrast between *promoting* and *honouring* a value, one may distinguish between two kinds of attitude. On the one hand, politicians may incline towards *pragmatism*, regarding their values as goals to be put into effect as far as circumstances permit. Results are what counts; actions and policies are means that do not matter in their own right. Thus, a pragmatist is a person of principle who is ready to opt for a policy that dishonours her principles provided it promises to further the same principles better than a honourable policy would do. She is willing to trade principles against expediency for principles' sake. In a democracy, expediency has a lot to do with capturing positions of political authority through electoral contests. Pragmatic politicians may be expected to strike electoral deals with a view to obtaining representation for their parties. They are willing to enter into awkward coalitions and forge alliances of convenience in order to gain political influence.

On the other hand, politicians may want to honour their principles and be bent on fashioning their whole activity after them. They will, in particular, promote these principles only in so far as it can be done without tampering with them. The principles are seen partly as aspirations, partly as constraints. They represent values that are to be realized as well as rules of proper conduct that limit instrumental calculations about ways and means of realising these values. For want of a better term, I shall call this attitude *purity*.

One might think that only a penchant for purity can have a place in the picture of dignified politics, but this is not so. Power is needed to translate principles into policies, and those who take their principles seriously, will not be unconcerned about ways and means of getting what they want. A principled politician should not be confused with an unworldly dreamer. The point is rather that some objectives go well with pragmatism while others are easily compromised – pejoratively speaking – by political compromises (Benjamin 1990: ch. 2). Think, for example, of the difference between a socialist's aim of equalising net income and a Catholic's endeavour to outlaw abortion. The former aspiration sits well with pragmatism; the latter does not.

The third question that I raise in this article relates to the *purpose* of political activity. Democratic politics is largely a matter of words: verbal acts, such as declarations, statements, interventions in debates and discussions. What are they aimed at? On the one hand, they may be contributions to an open-minded exchange of opinion, in which people argue with each other, trying to persuade opponents, but also listening to them with the intention of giving in if and when they meet with better arguments. This attitude corresponds to the deliberative image of democracy. On the other hand, political statements may be akin to means of fortification that nurture confrontation. Then, as Diego Gambetta (1998: 29) says, they admit "neither doubts nor nuances", but are "packaged in such a way as to silence the audience rather than to invite further argument". In the latter case, there is no deliberation, but confrontation is not the absence of principled politics. It is rather a clash between heartfelt principles.

Purity and pragmatism on the left

Sometimes, a political party stands united behind its leader to such an extent that its positions are virtually at one with what the leader says and does. *Mouvement des Citoyens (MDC)* – the Citizens' Movement – was a case in point. Its founder and leader, Jean-Pierre Chevènement, personified the party. Minister of the interior from 1997 until August 2000, he resigned in protest over the proposal for limited Corsican autonomy. Jacobinism was written all over his every opinion about the issue. His opposition to autonomy rested on the idea that France ought to remain a unitary and indivisible state. In an interview with *Le Monde* (July 19, 2000), he warned against "l'effet de contagion": the risk that inflated powers for Corsica will precipitate a general devolution of legislative power from the National Assembly to regional assemblies, resulting in a "patchwork" of local laws and a return to the conditions of *l'Ancien Régime*, i.e. pre-revolutionary France. He also argued that Corsican autonomy would violate the principle that all citizens should be equal before the law: "It is this attachment ... to France as a community of citizens, which are not to be distinguished according to their origins, that has been brought to the fore by the issue of Corsica" (Chevènement 2000: 21). During the parliamentary debate, he was even more outspoken, placing the government's proposal in the context of what he called "la victoire des ethnismes" (*Le Monde*, May 17, 2001).

A statement of principle may be a sham and a posture – a false pretence intended to conceal true motives. But Chevènement's stand was, to all appearances, honest. Take his resignation form the government. Such an audacious act resonated well with the public, and predictably so, in a country where political mavericks are often appreciated. Chevènement may not have been blind to this prospect, but it can hardly be imputed to him as the motive of his resignation. The ideological coherence of everything he said and did before and after suggests an attitude of purity rather than pragmatism, let alone opportunism. His statements were clear and rounded and they rhymed. While it seems that he hesitated for a while before concluding that he could not serve as minister in Jospin's government, his resistance to Corsican autonomy was non-negotiable: "I have many convictions. Lionel Jospin knows them. He knows exactly where I refuse to go" (*Le Monde*, July 19, 2000).

If we are to judge from Chevènement's interventions in the constitutional debate, he was always intent on confrontation rather than deliberation. He rejected autonomy for Corsica as a matter of unbending principle. Every piece of behavioural evidence tells about a staunch, if not a closed, mind, made up for good. This illustrates that the two images that come together in the picture of dignified politics – principled politicians and political deliberation – may well come apart in reality. Chevènement was a politician of principle, but there is no indication that he saw the debate on Corsica as an occasion for a frank and open-minded exchange of opinions.

We may contrast Chevènement's purity to the attitude of communist *députés*. Consider what happened when the government first wanted to present the parliament with the proposal for Corsican autonomy, in February 2001. Chirac frustrated the effort by refusing to have the proposal on the agenda of the council of ministers. This – if we are to believe *Le Figaro* (February 15, 2001) – is how the situation was seen "at Matignon" by an anonymous member of Jospin's staff:

> With the exception of Alain Madelin and his friends, the opposition will seize on this occasion to demonstrate that they stand united behind the President. ... This may

motivate our people to stick together ... For the *chevènementistes*, Corsica is an existential issue and they are not going to yield, but the communists who criticised us at the beginning of the process will certainly think twice before they lend their voices to the chorus of protests that come from the right.

According to the same newspaper, an unnamed socialist representative saw things likewise: "Chirac's initiative may prevent deep and real divergences on the left from unfolding". As far as MDC is concerned, this analysis was apt. While the creation of this party was spurred by the reorientation of French socialists in economic matters and foreign policy, it subsequently owed its grip on public attention – which at times was significant, if not much rewarded by votes – to its high profile in constitutional debates. If MDC were to compromise on an issue like Corsica, its *raison d'étre* would come in question. Thus, opposition to the government's proposal was an existential matter.

Things stood differently with the Communist Party. To be sure, there is no denying the Jacobin allegiance of PCF. Its leader in parliament expressed "strong reticence" on the eve of the debate on Corsica, implying that the proposal jeopardised "the foundation of the Republic" (*Le Figaro*, May 16, 2001). Still, there was reason to expect that the Communist Party would rather shelve its misgivings about Corsican autonomy than risk an association with a protest trumpeted by Chirac. This assumption alludes to the major predicament of the party. In the early 1990s, revisionism took hold of it. The communist leadership distanced itself from Marxism and soon made ready for electoral cooperation with the socialists – who, on their part, opened themselves increasingly to liberal ideas about social and economic policy. Cooperation with PS has obvious attractions to PCF. In 1997, it yielded tangible results in the form of more *députés* than the party would have been capable of capturing on its own. It also brought ministerial posts. But there are indications that revisionism takes its toll in terms of dwindling electoral support. Some communists have long raised a concern about ideological effacement. This was, in particular, invoked to explain the losses of PCF – as well as the gains of *l'extrême gauche* (two genuinely Marxist parties) – in the municipal elections of March 2001. The presidential and the parliamentary election of 2002 added to the losses (which is not to say, of course, that the PCF would necessarily have fared better of it had not embarked on revisionism).

There was, arguably, two ways in which PCF might have boosted its left-wing credentials during the period we are studying. On the one hand, it might have distanced itself from government policies that were liable to elicit vocal protests from the far left. On the other hand, it might have stayed clear of causes that meant much to parties on the right. The latter imperative came to the fore when Chirac showed signs of pronounced opposition to Corsican autonomy – or so, at any rate, the two anonymous analysts plausibly suggest. Several communist *députés* vented strong reservations, but none came out against the government's proposal in parliament. The entire group abstained from voting. In the light of the communists' predicament, this comportment has an air of respectability to it. The communists' choice, like that of the Citizens' Movement, had an existential bearing; only in their case, existentialist concerns nurtured pragmatism rather than principled behaviour. Moreover, the concerns of the communists were incidental to the Corsican issue as such. The Jacobinism of PC notwithstanding, the fate of the party had little to do with whatever it said on constitutional matters and everything to do with the credibility of its claim to be a radical antidote to all that came from the political right.

Many communist parliamentarians were opposed to Corsican autonomy and made no secret about it. They resolved not to vote according to their true preferences so as not to add their votes to those of the parliamentary opposition. It was no opportunist manoeuvre. The pragmatic nature of their motivation is apparent from the transparency of their conduct. Their open betrayal of principle did not betray their status as principled actors.

When it comes to the other aspect of dignified politics – deliberation – the communists have little to show for themselves. Their Jacobinism did not share the zeal of the Chevènement's, but nothing suggests that they ever prepared for anything but confrontation in the debate over Corsica. Their abstention from voting in the National Assembly was a calculated ruse, not an ideological concession.

Puzzles on the right

The moderate French right takes its ideological cues from two sets of values. One of them may be called bonapartism; the other is an undiluted from of liberalism. The former involves a commitment to unity and indivisibility under a central government, headed by a strong executive power that takes active part in economic life. The latter is a commitment to the virtues of political decentralization and the market. In both theory and practice, these values are hard to reconcile. Yet, the Gaullist party has found room for both. (In 1999, some prominent members of RPR, disgusted with liberal tendencies, broke out to form a new party, but it did not take long before most renegades were back.) *Democratie Libérale*, by contrast, has come close to displaying uniformity under the banner of undiluted liberalism. The centrists in *l'Union pour la Démocratie Française* are, by and large, wholehearted *décentralisateurs* and half-hearted champions of economic liberalisation.

When the debate over Corsica began, the liberal democrats almost immediately parted with each other. Their leader, Madelin, thought that Corsican autonomy might pave the way for a general devolution of political power. He said: "The course that has been taken with regard to Corsica seems to go in the right direction: It will oblige on all politicians ... to face the question of regionalisation" (*Libération*, Sept. 11, 2000). But this argument made no headway amongst his own, and eventually most representatives of DL voted against the government's proposal or abstained from voting. On the face of it, their behaviour makes little sense. In constitutional matters, the liberal democrats are staunchly opposed to the Jacobin cult of unity and indivisibility. Why didn't they all seize on the occasion to promote devolution of power?

One may argue that their predicament was akin to that of the communists. Principles came up against considerations of expediency and the result was pragmatism. The liberal democrats knew that standing firm would amount to breaching the unity of the right, as the Gaullists overwhelmingly rejected Corsican autonomy. But decentralization has such importance to French liberals that one would expect them to see it as something of an existential issue. Why, then, did only a minority of liberals favour of the government's proposal?

A similar puzzle is presented by the behaviour of many centrists, including most representatives of UDF in the National Assembly. Anti-Jacobinism is, more than anything else, what centrism is about in France. Francois Bayrou, the leader of the party, is a federalist who scents mischief even in talk about "decentralisation".

> In the Jacobin mind ... power comes from above and does not devolve to lower levels save by way of delegation from the top. When one says that 'decentralisation' or 'deconcentration' are required, one also says that power belongs above and one should beg the State to delegate some of it, and the State retains the right to take power back. The spirit of federalism is the opposite of this. According to the spirit of federalism, legitimacy lies at the ground level of society. Power is most legitimate when it is closest to people. (Bayrou 2000)

It is no surprise, then, that Bayrou lauded the government's policy, suggesting that it be extended from Corsica to other regions. But it surprises that he subsequently had a change of mind, chiding the government for "an ethnic approach" (*Le Monde*, Sept. 5, 2000). And there is more. While some centrists in parliament supported the government, those who opposed it far outnumbered the rest. What we have is another apparent discrepancy between principle and practice among *decéntralisateurs*. Why did most representatives of UDF fail to honour their commitment to decentralization?

Here are two hypotheses as to why they, as well as a majority of liberal democrats, opposed a policy that ought to have resonated well with their principles. First, both groups may have acted in good faith. Call this the *honourable* hypothesis. It is reported, for example, that countervailing considerations pertaining to the turbulent history of Corsica surfaced in internal discussions in DL. One representative argued: "Corsica is not the best governed community. If it is taken as a model of decentralization, one really starts off badly!" (*Libération*, Sept. 11, 2000). Some liberal *députés* worried, more particularly, about insufficient provisions for the protection of the Corsican coastline. Similar consternations were voiced among centrists: "Corsica is not the best site for experiments in decentralisation" (*Le Monde*. May 17, 2001). As far as the centrists are concerned, pragmatic considerations of a political nature may also have made themselves felt. UDF, alone amongst parties on the right, had sided with Jospin's government on an issue of import just before the law on Corsica came to the National Assembly.[3] In view of this, some centrists may have worried that another failure to fall into line would throw doubt on where they belonged in the political landscape. (After all, UDF's predecessor in the Fourth Republic – *Mouvement Républicain Populaire* – regularly allied with the socialists, and remnants of the centre-left alliance were briefly resurrected in late 1980s.) Thus, the qualms of the centrists may have had something in common with those of the communists (cf. section 4). Some of them even felt obliged to foreswear tactical objectives of any kind (*Libération*, May 9,

2001).

Yet, a second hypothesis suggests itself. It may be that, among centrists as well as liberal democrats, many were willing to forget about principles in the hope of dealing the government a conspicuous blow. The preparation of the new law had taken enough time and work to make its adoption a matter of political prestige. If it were to be defeated in the National Assembly, this would, in all likelihood, detract from the government's reputation for getting things done. It would be no small calamity a year from national elections. Here, according to the second hypothesis, lies the motive behind opposition from UDF and DL. Call this the *dishonourable* hypothesis.

The honourable hypothesis fits in with the dignified picture of politics; the dishonourable hypothesis does not. Both resolve the puzzles on the right, but two problems remain. This first is, obviously, that the hypotheses conflict and so cannot both explain what took place. The second problem is that both hypotheses smack of concoctions. They border on what Jon Elster (1985: 460) calls "frictionless speculation": creative interpretation of events that have enough complexity to reward a modicum of hermeneutical ingenuity.

Puzzles are disconcerting. Both the picture of dignified politics and the dark picture preserve what Brian L. Keeley (1999: 125) calls "human meaning" and "rational accounting". They trace actions to comprehensible motives and thereby dispel absurdity. But an impression of puzzling behaviour may be true to the facts, while attempts at explaining absurdity away by "making sense" of what was done distort reality. Keeley argues that "[s]ome people just do things", and "[t]oo strong a belief in the rationality of people in general ... will lead us to seek purposive explanations where none exists" (ibid.: 126). In the present case, politicians were torn between ideological principles and considerations of expediency, and it need not come as a surprise that such a practical conflict fosters behaviour that has no broad meaning.

Government and opposition: deliberation or machination

The Jacobinism of the Citizens' Movement, which was the subject of section 3, belongs to a venerable tradition of French socialism. It has adherents even in the echelons of the Socialist Party. During the debate on Corsican autonomy, Henri Emmanuelli, who headed the finance committee of the National Assembly, confessed to "a moderate Jacobinism". Although he voted in favour of the government's proposal, he was sceptical of it, and his scepticism echoed the protests of Chevènement: "I am very worried ... about the rise of nationalism among basques, corsicans and others ... [T]hese nationalisms have an ethnic connotation that troubles me a lot" (*Libération*, August 24, 2000). Emmanuelli predicted the ascension of "spirit of right-wing regionalism". Jack Lang, by contrast, spoke favourably about "une reconnaissance des particularismes et des originalités" (*Le Monde* July 23-24, 2000). Lang was among those who rose to power with Mitterand and wielded influence when local democracy was virtually created in France in the 1980s (Safran 1995: 260-4). Some in his generation have made political decentralisation their creed (Rocard 2000; Mauroy 2001). It is *de rigueur* among younger socialists. The Jacobin voice has, accordingly, been muted for decades.

One is somewhat surprised, then, to find that the government waited long before it made something out of the linkage between Corsican autonomy and a general devolution of political power. It was, apparently, a late and laggard realisation. In an interview in *Libération* on May 15, Daniel Vaillant – the minister of the interior – alleged that the justification of a special status for Corsica lie in the particularities of this insular territory. He argued: "the circumstances and the aspirations differ. Corsica isn't the laboratory of decentralisation". Eight days ahead, however, he struck a different cord: "certain dispositions that are included in the project and that resurrect the classical transfers of competence might be extended to other regions on the mainland" (*Le Figaro*, May 23, 2001). He drew a line between the proposal for Corsican autonomy and a broader project that the government was about to launch in the name of "la démocratie de proximité".

Vaillant invested the new cast of the proposal with further significance. It was, in his view, a basis for building consensus between government and opposition. Alluding to an incipient "dialogue" with the likes of Valéry Giscard d'Estaing (UDF) and Eduard Balladur (RPR), he said: "Why make decentralisation into a political bone of contention, as the right has come to terms with the left on this issue?" (*le Figaro*, May 23, 2001). At the time, there were reports that Balladur and Giscard d'Estaing, as well as the gaullist Nicolas Sarkozy and the centrist Raymond Barre, would vote in support of the government's proposal (which Balladur and Barre eventually did, while Sarkozy and Giscard abstained). In view if this, one may wonder whether the modalities of the debate were about to change. So far, it had taken the shape of a confrontation. Was it transmuting to a frank and honest discussion? Had the scene been set for deliberation?

Robert Goodin (2000: 81-3) distinguishes between the "internal-reflective" and the "external-collective" mode of deliberation. The former takes place when an individual reconsiders and revises his point of view. He may come to understand certain alternatives in new ways and thus become aware of merits or demerits that previously went unappreciated. This, it seems, was the case with Vaillant. The proposal for Corsican autonomy took on a new gestalt in his mind, and the same may have happened to others, including some who were previously bent on rejecting the proposal. It appears that this internal-reflective process ran parallel with an external-collective process – an informal discussion between the government and members of the opposition. Individual reflections were sustained by discussion and sustained it in turn. The final days of the debate on Corsican autonomy saw a bout of deliberative democracy, or so it seems.

But another hypothesis offers itself. It was, indeed, seized on right away by members of the opposition, who rejected Vaillant's bipartisan overtures. Francois Fillon, principal spokesman of RPR in the parliamentary séances, said: "The government has taken no initiative on decentralisation in four years. Suddenly it tries to wipe out its Jacobin image" (*Le Figaro*, May 19, 2001). Francois Sauvadet, spokesman of UDF, perceived a "political manoeuvre aimed at assuring those who are tempted to modify their votes" (ibid.). This is to say that the internal-reflective aspect of deliberation was nothing but a pretence and the external-collective aspect nothing but a series of stratagems. But none goes free of the kind of suspicion that comes with Sauvadet's hypothesis. It is apt to place every utterance and action under a cloud. The government was charged with machination, but those who questioned its motives are themselves open to the charge of subterfuge. Their allegations of duplicity may have been a cover for partisan unwillingness to judge the government's initiative on its own merits.

Both hypotheses are credible. Vaillant's sudden recasting of the issue looks a bit like a ruse, but may, on the face of it, have been perfectly honest. Those who cast doubt on his motives may, for all we know, either have acted in bad faith or been truly doubtful about the motives. Which hypothesis has most to say for it? As long as the government tried to win over opponents in its own ranks, it had good reason not to make anything out of the linkage between Corsican autonomy and the general objective of decentralisation. As the MDC and many Communist representatives were hostile to this objective, brandishing it would have been counterproductive on the part of the government. However, as the parliamentary vote drew closer and opposition among *chevénementistes* and communists seemed insurmountable, it was left with the option of courting centrists and gaullists. This may explain the sudden shift of approach: It was motivated by expediency and smacked of opportunism.

Such an hypothesis may also be invoked with respect to centrists and gaullists who purported to call the government's bluff. While their cynicism was not without justification, it also indicates that they placed political advantage above principles. Whatever motive Vaillant had for linking Corsican autonomy to a general plan for "la démocratie de proximité", this linkage gave the *decéntralisateurs* in RPR and UDF an opportunity for furthering decentralization. With a few exceptions, they made nothing out of it, but were more intent on frustrating the government's legislative effort with respect to Corsica.

The nature of the conflict

To conclude, principles mattered to the positions politicians took in the conflict over Corsican autonomy. Jacobins were pitted against more or less wholehearted *decéntralisateurs*. Moreover, the debate was not without deliberation. In the final days before the proposal for Corsican autonomy was put to the vote, a meeting of minds took place when the government held talks with parliamentarians of UDF and RPR. But the two aspects of dignified politics did not go together. When the government tried to initiate deliberations over the issue, its initiative smacked of opportunism. By contrast, the comportment of the staunchest Jacobins illustrates that principled politics need not make for deliberative politics. In all political quarters, there are illustrations of the role pragmatism plays in politics. The conflict over Corsican autonomy brings out the truth of the general proposition that there is normally no prospect of promoting a political principle without compromising it. Pragmatism showed, for example, in the communists' abstention from voting against a proposal that most of them opposed. Thus, principled politicians do not always honour their principles, and while a penchant for purity is the surest sign of a principled point of view, calculations of expediency should not be taken as a sure sign of unprincipled politics. Finally, the analysis also indicates that politicians who are caught on the horns of the dilemma that sometimes arise when principles and expediency collide, may act in ways that defy purposive explanation.

The contents of regional policy

After its adoption by the National Assembly in May 2002, the law on Corsica's status was sent to the Senate, where a large majority – made up mainly by Senators of the Right – rejected the core of it: the proposal for limited autonomy in legal matters. During the senatorial proceedings (November 2001), Jean-Pierre Raffarin – a liberal democrat – chastised the government for its general approach. It had, he said, brought Corsican nationalists into the process of negotiations and thereby placed the debate in an undesirable context: "What could have been a debate about regional issues, became a debate about the national issue" (*Le Figaro*, Nov. 9, 2001). In Raffarin's view, the constitutional quandary that came with the proposal for legislative autonomy served to "obstruct the development of decentralisation" (*Libération*, Nov. 7, 2001). The general drift of his statements seems to be that decentralization is a worthy cause, but the government betrayed it in the Corsican case by provoking unnecessary constitutional conflict.

The next episode took place in December, when the legislative initiative of the government went back to the National Assembly. Here it met with final approval (267 votes for, 234 against, and 30 abstentions). This was, by and large, a reiteration of what happened in the first hearing (in May), but some representatives of the Right who originally supported the proposal – like Eduard Balladour – abstained from voting in December. Then the opposition instructed the Constitutional Court – which oversees French legislation – to assess the constitutionality of the law. In January 2002, the *Conseil constitutionnel* censured the article that authorised the transfer of legislative power to local authorities. Thus, the core of the government's proposal came to nothing. The Court allowed only that Corsican authorities might be given extended powers in adapting national regulations to local circumstances. (This, to be sure, is more than any French region on the mainland is entitled to; it constitutes an unsurpassed exception from Jacobin norms, but it is "extraordinarily timid" in comparison to the practice in most European states (Duhamel 2002).)

The spring of 2002 was election time in France. The terms of both the president and the parliamentarians in the National Assembly expired. As a candidate for the presidency, Lionel Jospin campaigned in Corsica on the promise that if he were elected, he "would stick to his commitments" (*Le Monde*, April 7 – 8, 2002). He said that he wanted "a revision of the constitution that was not only valid for Corsica, but for all territorial collectivities" (*Le Figaro*, April 8, 2002). But Jospin was not elected. Chirac received a new mandate, and the parliamentary election brought his supporters to power. The Socialist Party and its allies lost control of the executive, and Raffarin – the former senator – was appointed prime minister in a government of Gaullists, centrists and liberal democrats. (In the course of the election and its aftermath, a new party came into being in an effort to unite RPR, UDF and DL, but this development need not concern us here.)

It seems (September 2002) that Raffarin intends to stand by the belief in decentralization that he professed during the Senatorial debate. He has foreshadowed "experiments" in transferring authority on specific matters to departments and regions, and proposes that the "right of experimentation" be inscribed in the constitution. But Raffarin avers that he will not go as far as the former government allegedly did: "I do not want that the unity of the republic once again comes in question" (*Le Monde*, July 12, 2002). Others on the Right have pleaded for decentralization that is "constitutionally anchored" (*Le Monde*, July 27, 2002). Patrick Devedjian, who is delegated responsibility for *Libertés locales* in Raffarin's government, speaks of a French model in which there is "a unitary state that recognizes the growing role of local collectivities" (*Libération*, Sept. 11, 2002).

What kind (and amount) of decentralization can be had within the limits of the "one and indivisible republic"? What kind of autonomy will constitutionally anchored decentralization confer on Corsica (and other regions)? Some are wary, if not sceptical, about the outcome. José Rossi, a liberal democrat who currently heads the Corsican Assembly, says that the "whole query ... consists in knowing the margins of the right of experimentation promised by Raffarin" (*Le Monde*, July 26, 2002). Others doubt that experimentation can be put into practice without harm to the values associated with political unity. "The principle of equality may suffer", predicts the socialist Jean-Pierre Balligand (*Libération*, Sept. 11, 2002), alluding to the different prospects of rich and poor regions in what he calls "a bazaar without name". It remains to be seen whether or not decentralisation without constitutional controversy is a piece of wishful thinking.

References

Bayrou, Francois (2000). 'Une chance pour féderer l'Europe', *Libération*, May 23 (www.liberation.com/quotidien/debats/mai/00/20000523f.html).
Benjamin, Martin (1990). *Splitting the Difference*, Lawrence, Kansas: University of Kansas Press.
Berlin, Isaiah (1990). *The Crooked Timber of Humanity*, London: Fontana Press.
Blackburn, Simon (2000). *Ruling Passions*, Oxford: Oxford University Press.
Carcassonne, Guy (1999). 'Amendments to the French constitution: one surprise after another', *Western European Politics*, 22, 4.
Chevènement, Jean-Pierre (2000). 'La Corse au miroir de la France', *Le Monde*, Nov. 24.
Cohen, Joshua (1998). 'Democracy and liberty', in Jon Elster (ed.), *Deliberative Democracy*, New York: Cambridge University Press.
Dryzek, John S. (1992). How far is it from Virginia and Rochester to Frankfurt? Public choice as a critical theory, British Journal of Political Science, 22.
Duhamel, Alain (2002). 'La peur des régions'. *Libération*, January 26, 2002 (www.liberation.com/quotidien/debats/020126-110046010REBO.html).
Duhamel, Olivier (1999). *Droit constitutionnel. 1. Le pouvoir politique en France*, Paris: Éditions du Seuil.

Elster, Jon (1985). *Making Sense of Marx*. Cambridge: Cambridge University Press.
Gambetta, Diego (1998). '"Claro!": an essay on discursive machismo', in Jon Elster (ed.), *Deliberative Democracy*, New York: Cambridge University Press.
Goodin, Robert E. (2000). 'Democractic deliberation within', *Philosophy & Public Affairs*, 29, 1.
Hampshire, Stuart (1989). *Innocence and Experience*. London: Allen Lane.
Knapp, Andrew and Wright, Vincent. (2001). *The Government and Politics of France*. London: Routledge.
Mauroy, Pierre (2001). 'Fédéralisme non, d´centralisation oui', *Le Monde des Débats*, 21, January.
Nelkin, Dorothy (1984). 'Science, technology, and political issues: analyzing the issues', in Dorothy Nelkin (ed.): *Controversy. Politics of Technical Decisions*. Beverly Hills: Sage.
Pettit, Philip (1997). 'The consequentialist perspective', in Marcia W. Baron, Philip Pettit and Michael Slote, *Three Methods of Ethics: A Debate*, Oxford: Blackwell.
Rocard, Michel (2000). 'Corse: jacobins, ne tuez pas la paix!' *Le Monde*, August 31.
Safran, William (1995). *The French Polity*, White Plains, N.Y.: Longman.
Thompson, John B. (1993). 'Ideology', in *The Oxford Companion to Politics of the World*, Oxford: Oxford University Press.
Waldron, Jeremy (1999). *The Dignity of Legislation*, New York: Cambridge University Press.

Notes

[1] Thanks to Harald Baldersheim, Lawrence Rose and Emmanuelle Vignaux for helpful comments on earlier versions of this article.

[2] This view of politics is omnipresent. Here is a small, assorted sample of illustrations: In the gravedigger scene in Shakespeare's Hamlet (act 5, scene 1), the prince says about one of the skulls that is dug up that it "might have been the pate of a politician ... one that would circumvent God". In a discussion of Edmund Burke's shifting and contradictory opinions, Alan Ryan (1992: 40) writes: "Burke was a professional politician in an age when preferment was the way to wealth. He was a man of humble origins who made his way in the world by making himself useful to the grandees who found him a seat in Parliament, gave him a pension, and kept him loyal by dangling before him a peerage and a civil list pension to establish his family in the landed gentry. What would be more plausible than that he said what his employers wished to hear and changed allegiances when profit lay in a new direction?" (Ryan 1992, p. 40). the assertion that "protest groups ... exploit technical expertise to challenge policy decisions", and that "[t]he way project proponents or citizen groups use the work of 'their' experts reflects their judgments about priorities or acceptable levels of risk. Whenever such judgments conflict, this is reflected in the selective use of technical knowledge. Expertise is reduced to one more weapon in a political arsenal". (Nelkin 1984: 16 and 17).

[3] This issue was the alteration of the electoral calendar for 2002. If events were allowed to run their course, the parliamentary election would come before the election of a new president, but the government proposed that the order be reversed. While a majority approved the proposal, both Gaullists and liberals were unanimously against it.

Chapter 8

French Regional Leadership and Economic Strategies in a Globalizing World

Michel-Alexis Montané

Introduction: regional leadership and development policies in France

Globalization[1] gives rise to competition between the public authorities of the various levels of government: local, regional and national. This competition mainly occurs in the economic field. Globalization also produces institutional dissemination or governance practices such as growth coalitions, city networks or the conversion to new public management (NPM) methods. Consequently, we have to question[2] the changes in political configurations and the responses to globalization, bearing in mind that governance situations are characterized by a complex distribution of roles among public, private and "third sector" actors (Stoker, 1998).

The policy responses to the new economic deal are already well analyzed by numerous scholars (Amin and Thrift, 1994). However, there is also the question of territorialized interests, linked with the problem of political power legitimization, especially at the regional level. The notion of leadership makes it possible to integrate these dimensions (territory, legitimacy) into the analysis (Daloz and Montané, 2000). In France, regional leadership has recently been constituted within the framework of a complex political and administrative system, which initially gives little importance to the regional level. Between the local level, where one finds the many municipalities (or *communes*), and the national level (that of the central state), the most significant tier used to be the *département* whose elected assembly is named the *conseil général*. A hundred *départements* make up the French territory today and, despite criticisms against them (insufficient size, outmoded ways of electing their assemblies), they have been reinforced with numerous civil servants and financial means. The decentralization legislation of 1982 was not based on notions of community. Worse still, it did not clearly attribute responsibilities nor tax resources. Even today, economic competencies are largely shared by all government tiers in France, now increased by a whole series of inter-municipal structures.

The regions, however, were established (Nay, 1997). Larger and fewer than the departments, the twenty-two French regions resulted from an initiative (1956) which responded to the State's concern over improving the scale of its economic policy (Ohnet, 1996). The size of regions is well adapted to development policies. The establishment of the twenty-two French regions took mainly economic realities into account. They correspond to "relevant" economic areas, drawn around regional *métropoles*. These *métropoles* were selected among the cities (Bordeaux, Toulouse, Marseilles, Lille, Rennes, etc.) with economic weight and dynamism (in particular technological dynamism) that already made them regional capitals. In this cutting of the regional pie, history or geography had little influence (except the case of Alsace). In budgetary terms, the regions are less well equipped to conduct development policies. They do not have more resources than a big city or *département*. Moreover, when the regions became directly elected bodies, following the act on decentralization, the legislator acknowledged an economic obligation towards them, but this does not prevent cities and *départements* from implementing their own development policies.

Since the first direct election of regional assemblies in 1986, the regions have gradually established a room of their own, not least thanks to quite aggressive communication policies. They have become a part of the French political system and increasingly play the European card (Balme, 1996), under the benevolent eye of Brussels and the europhile *régionalistes*, often wary of the *départements*, which they regard as too closely linked to the central State (Alliès, 1989).

In the economic field, however, the regions still have little substantial control over public policy. Apart from joint measures, one may say that the municipalities seek to assist private companies and support the creation of economic activity, and that the *départements* initiate local development projects and support marketing of local firms. At the end of the day, everyone intervenes in everything. The State, in particular, preserves its decisive role. For major projects, the regions must act within the framework of the *Contrats de Plan* known as "State-Region" long-term plans where regions negotiate with the central administrations. They also depend on the *schémas de services* and national frameworks organizing public intervention in many areas such as transport and infrastructures. Even the management of European structural funds, intended for the implementation of regions under State supervision, is not entirely entrusted to the regions. In the budgetary field, the tax reforms have separated the regional tax returns from regional economic activity. The regions do not take advantage of the budgetary results from the possible success of their economic initiatives. This is not very encouraging, as regional leaders have pointed out.

For their development policies, the regions must find partners for each project among the other public bodies and come to agreements with various ministries, thus reducing their freedom or autonomy. Despite this, they try to innovate institutionally, to support the local economy and develop new sectors. Indeed, with regard to the events arising from the globalization of the economy, the regional leaders are compelled to act, as is shown in the following example.

A meso government facing the challenge of globalization

The concrete example presented below of confrontation between the political leaders of a region and the heads of a transnational corporation (reorganizing their firm after a merger), provides a good illustration of the room of manoeuvre for regions (cf. Sharpe, 1994) in a globalization context.

On the crucial day of Wednesday the 16th of April 2000, at 16.15 p.m., a highly symbolic and consequential meeting took place in Paris, in the Elf headquarters at *la Défense*, the atmosphere being heavy with expectation. This meeting brought together, yet again, the super-boss of a transnational corporation (TNC), and the most important political leaders of one of the many areas where this company is located, namely Aquitaine.

The "super-boss" was the Frenchman Thierry Desmarest, CEO of Totalfina-Elf, a transnational oil corporation resulting from the recent merger of those two companies (more precisely Totalfina's take-over of Elf). The political leaders taking part were the President of the *Conseil régional d'Aquitaine* (regional council) Alain Rousset (a socialist), the President of the *Conseil général des Pyrénées-Atlantiques* (a *département*, smaller than the region) François Bayrou (UDF – moderate, rightwing), and the mayor of the town of Pau, André Labarrère (a socialist). These three elected officials were concerned with the possible departure of Elf from *Béarn* (the district around Pau), and from the *département* of the *Pyrénées-Atlantiques*, south of *Aquitaine*. They were particularly mindful of the industrial employment and fiscal resources produced by the local activity of this oil company with transnational shareholders (mainly but not exclusively Belgian and French) quoted on the world stock markets. This is a world-wide company.

The problem of relocating part of *Elf Aquitaine's* activities already existed before Totalfina's take-over. Previous relations between the regional political leaders and company heads had never been very fruitful. There was genuine anxiety before the meeting of the 16th of April 2000. This meeting, according to the elected leaders as well as the heads of Totalfina-Elf, was quite satisfactory for both. The elected leaders obtained some guarantees to maintain TNC activities in Béarn. They demonstrated their bipartisan unity and showed their willingness to form a united front in economic matters. They had invited Thierry Desmarest to come to Béarn, and they were at pains to point out the importance of his firm for the regional economy. They were very concerned about the social implications of any change in the company's local activities.

The TNC's concern was quite different. *Aquitaine* was not the only region where the firm was established. If we look more carefully, we see that the policy of Totalfina-Elf regarding local authorities, political leaders and their territories, is a global policy, for all the French regions as a whole and perhaps beyond. The heads of Totalfina-Elf never miss the opportunity of pointing out that they are present in *"many regions"*. Indeed, they *"understand"* the concerns of the Aquitaine or Béarn inhabitants. But this statement certainly did not suffice to restore the regional leaders' confidence.

We observed a fundamental contradiction between the position of elected officials defending the economy of a region, and the approach or attitude of a TNC, which is constantly pressurized by the complaints made by representatives of the various regions and areas where it is operating. The contradiction is between the elected officials' accountability to their own particular area and a TNC's accountability to its global prosperity, but for no region in particular. The negotiation is not a balanced discussion, the balance of forces being in favour of the TNC: significantly, the political leaders came to the CEO's Paris office, and not the contrary.

We could also take the case of the recent oil slick, after the sinking of the "Erika" tanker carrying oil – coincidentally – for Totalfina, that polluted the beaches along the French Atlantic coast. In this case as well, the local and regional political leaders were weak when up against a TNC, and had to ask for assistance from the French State. But as usual, the State was slow to react, particularly when handing out financial relief, and in any case it is virtually powerless faced with dominant economic interests. Totalfina, for its part, has only accepted to award money to meet local problems, but with very little effect.[3] The regional political leaders, in this case, too, carry little weight when dealing with a firm, which does not depend (or depends very little) on their territory (as a market or a resource), and have little need of their policies.[4]

The meso government is linked to territory, but economic matters are less and less territorialized

Notwithstanding the limits of decentralization, a representative democracy (such as the French political system) remains in all respects a territorialized structure (Parri, 1988 ; Ritaine, 1991). In other words, representative democracy is contained within spatial boundaries, and depends on its inherited institutions, on the political culture and its local supports. At the same time, the economy, with all its social implications, tends to become dependent on globalization, i.e. less and less anchored, with fewer territorial links. A part of it, the new communication economy, becomes completely "extra territorial".

Two main long-term changes have been noticeable in France since 1982, even before the effects of globalization became as crucial (and felt) as today:

- Decentralization, which has major consequences for the territorialization or the localization of public policy,[5] as well as for the accountability of the local and regional political leaders.
- Economic matters have become increasingly crucial in local politics. It is also a very sensitive issue linked to local employment and to the fiscal resources of the local and regional authorities. In France, we have to remember that the scarcity of employment (and a weaker mobility of the workers) is considered more acute than fiscal matters or the overall prosperity and well-being of the community. This is certainly the main difference in comparison with the North American context (cf. Peterson 1980 on "city growth"), or perhaps the North

European countries. We should add that, in France, the interventionist tradition of the State is duplicated locally.

If the territorialization of politics continues or is reinforced, the meso government also faces some structural changes that can be linked to globalization, concerning the field of public policy and the other dimensions of the public sphere. Globalization, over and above the competition between the public authorities and a greater public/private overlap, could also locally bring a "new" civic or political culture (Clark & Hoffmann-Martinot, 1998), the conversion to liberal methods for the modernization of the public sector through market mechanisms (Walsh, 1995) and more participation of the users/consumers/citizens. This is the idea of New Public Management (NPM) (Ferlie & al., 1996). According to these ideas, globalization does not only bring some constraints or new uncertainty, but also provides instruments to increase the capacity of public authorities to handle those negative aspects. It offers models of action/policy (projects, contracts, quasi-markets, etc.), models of success (German or Italian regions are pointed out as examples to follow), models of association among public and private sectors, and models of participation – or perhaps political protest (José Bové in France). In the field of economy and policy adaptation to globalization, the most famous regional models are to be found in Germany, e.g. Baden Württemberg, or in Italy, e.g. Emilia-Romagna (Cooke & Morgan, 1994). What kinds of effects are to be expected from these more positive or creative influences of globalization, both on political leadership and regional policies?

The implementation of the NPM is characterized by "faith in leadership" (which implies more responsibilities for leaders, results-related contracts, etc.), more use of indirect control than of direct authority (in the form of management through objectives, exposure to competition, etc.), and a concentration on the user or the citizen through freedom of choice, neighborhood committees, etc.[6]

As concerns the leadership of urban and regional regimes, traditionally dominated by private organized interests (Stone, 1989), we may ask, are we in the future going to find stronger representation of organizations working at the public/private interface in alliance with "the new social movements" in the broader sense?[7]

The shift to "indirect control" may leave leadership unchanged, but it may also affect its composition, its resources, its autonomy, and its social reputation. Is the generalization of comparable situations or management methods able to reduce the specificity that each leadership was given by its social and political context, through various combinations (Montané, 2001) of its constitutive dimensions (territory, political party, institution, etc.)?

Let us take the urban and regional case as an example. Today, it is not enough, for a city leader, to strike a neat balance between opposite forces (change and conservation) or the unity of the community, and build visible infrastructures. During the 1980s, the question of economy, in particular, brought some events to the political agenda, which were more and more concrete, measurable and comparable from city to city, region to region, election to election. The "personalization" of the executive power in the regional councils tends to place leaders in the same situation as urban mayors. All levels of meso governments have become more complex and considerably developed. Previously, political leaders only encountered opposition from within their own parties and local opponents. Now they also have to compete with other leaders, those of similar (Bordeaux versus Toulouse) or distinct but superposed territories (Region, *département*, city, etc.). The urban and regional leaders have the same weapons in this competition,[8] notably institutional communication very much in fashion during the 1980s (Montané, 1994), and access to regional media (TV, press), whilst the political opposition in the city is traditionally powerless due to its lack of resources (except in the case of regions, where the Law tries to change their situation) and the "vicar of Bray syndrome" (*"légitimisme"*) of the local and regional media – at least in France.

So, the regional political leaders face the consequences of globalization in an uncomfortable situation and, at the same time, we are concerned about the fact that the new methods of public intervention have not completely proved their relevance at the meso level in France.[9]

The adaptive responses of regional political leaders

In the wake of globalization, the context of public intervention is now characterized by the relocalization of public policies, the fragmentation of the public sector, a partial withdrawal of the national State (Hassenteufel, 1998), competition between cities and territories in the European area. Keeping its strategic role, the State is shifting onto the local leadership some of the policies seeking to ameliorate the social effects of globalization, or to make the territories more competitive (Benoit-Guilbot, 1991).[10] But the regions still ask for more autonomy and resources in order to build a proactive development policy.

When a private company decides to set itself up somewhere in a country, the elected officials of this area are inclined to cover all the expenses (infrastructures, fiscal tax credits, etc.), and ensure media coverage of this. Often, no serious evaluation is made as to the positive effects for the territory (local jobs, activity, and local tax incomes). These positive effects are deliberately exaggerated, even when they are actually lower than the new expenses involved in setting up the new company. The area's local authorities are the victims of a public policy fashion, which is a direct consequence of the influence of globalization, and the "diktat" of the economy (more precisely of the market and the private corporate model).[11] The public funds used for such occasions could have more positive effects if they were invested in local development (linked to the local culture, the economic networks of SMEs, the educational, tourist and agricultural resources of the territory) or in the improvement of solidarity between different areas (urban policy, or policy for weak rural zones). But the elected officials "love" TV cameras and need to present the idea that they are doing useful things, acting for the public good:[12] the arrival of a big company gives them such an opportunity. In the same way, regional leaders meeting the head of a TNC in his office (which is again proof of the official's powerlessness) is paradoxically presented as something positive in the regional press – as a good point for the territory.

When the political leaders are already involved with the media with regard to regional development, and when their involvement in economic matters is well-known by the local public opinion, they are unable to change this fact if, sadly, the economic situation becomes less favourable. Now, for a local or regional representative, a big setback or bankruptcy, the relocation or the closure of a factory, which occurs within the boundaries of his constituency, may turn out to be the major event of his/her whole political career.

Employment still remains the key problem, in particular for the semi and unskilled industrial workforce in factories or, also, in service industries – jobs that are directly threatened by globalization. The workers (and their families) are far less mobile than financial assets, and capital. They stay behind but continue voting in the area when employment has gone away.

Box 1: Norsk Hydro and the socialists

> Another example is the current problem of the Socadour fertilizer factory in Tarnos in the Landes. The Landes is a *département* of Aquitaine led by the socialist party. This factory is a branch of HYDRO AGRI, whose holding is the Norwegian corporate NORSK HYDRO. The TNC tend to favour its activities in another French region: Brittany. The socialist leaders of the Landes, together with Henri Emmanuelli, former minister and former national leader of the French socialist party, have warned the State (the ministry/department of Industry) as usual. But they also met the heads of HYDRO AGRI. The latter only confirmed the next closure of their factory. Consequently, the political leaders can only demand that economic activity be maintained in the area.

We should add that, when employment is threatened, nobody cares about attributing economic responsibility or not to the various authorities or government levels; nobody cares about the actual ability of the representatives to act in this field. Concerned inhabitants appeal to all their authorities, irrespectively, and expect some decisions, clear statements and a continuous involvement. Political leaders understand this phenomenon and, since 1982, have continually developed their resources and capabilities in the economic field: in all decentralized structures and not solely at the regional level. This complexity of public policy is not helpful and can reduce the efficiency of regional initiatives. Having a multi-level technocracy is not enough to halt the decline in regional industrial employment, to overcome the persistent depression of a city, or to invent some development where there is no development at all.

In this case, the powerlessness of the political leaders demonstrates a twofold problem: a problem of political legitimacy, and a problem of political accountability (already involved at the meso level), both inextricably linked (Coicaud, 1997). The legitimacy of those in leadership is affected when they are no longer "responsible" for changes within their territory, meaning that their action has increasingly less of an effect, and becomes virtually negligible.

In order to keep their local legitimacy, regional political leaders develop several responses to globalization. We note widespread policies aiming at counterbalancing the effects of firms' relocation or bankruptcy, and more generally the impact of globalization. But this raises the issue of financial resources and the long-term question of what fiscal income there will be for the future. Consequently, leaders are also interested in policies that preserve or introduce economic activity[13] (tax dumping, support for firms, external communication, etc.), but competing with all the other regions or authorities – almost a no-win game (Madies, 1999).

Regional leaders are more and more speaking about developing better rooted economic activities in an endogenous way through: 1) the relation between scientific research, local universities and regional companies; 2) "risked assets" (*capital-risque*) in the region; 3) an intelligent economic use of the city's or region's heritage.

Box 2: Priorities of the economic policy of the Regional Council of Aquitaine

"The struggle for employment leads the Regional Council to give the priority to the development of a dense network of small and medium-sized firms (SMEs), and of a strong industrial sector."

The Regional Council supports the firms, their potential of innovation and creativity, and backs them in their strategies for improvement of their competitiveness. This regional intervention takes various forms:
- financial support to the individual projects, in particular for the creation and the development of activities;
- involvement in programmes initiated by other regional actors of the economic development;
- implementation of "contracts of progress" or specific assistance for the "sectors of excellence" of the region: aeronautics, chemistry, wood-paper, electronics, etc.;
- financing structures of search and technology transfer;
- financing training programmes for workers or job seekers.

"Economic development requires more and more financial, technical and human means, that are difficult to pool without partners. Creativity and partnership: two keys to develop employment and the economy."

When a crisis occurs, which concerns a specific economic sector, the regional Council can set up emergency plans, in exceptional circumstances.

In the region of Aquitaine, the recent promotion of research on viticulture and training for occupations in the wine-growing sector in general is a good example of regional economic policies prompted by increasing international and global exposure: the Regional Council, in collaboration with an agency of the State in charge of agronomic research (INRA) and multiple other partners, tries to make up for lost time compared with other regions in this respect.[14] More widely, wine constitutes one of the strong pillars of the regional development policy of this region (cf. also chapter 10). Previous regional leaders had somewhat neglected this sector, that now seeks to combine traditions and a modern profile at the same time.

Conclusions

We should not overlook the State bureaucracies (Rouban, 1990), or the meso government ones, that take part in the adaptive or proactive policies, with variable degrees of administrative or political success (Clark, 1995). It is true that the adaptive policies related to globalization carry elements of convergence, for example in French urban planning (Levine, 1994) or management (Iribarne, 2000). On the whole, however, it seems that if the new methods grouped under the term "New Public Management" are increasingly being adopted in many countries, they are applied with more difficulty in France both at the local and regional levels. This is due to many reasons, like the recent constitution of a territorial civil service, less qualified and even more politicized or clientelist than other State bureaucracies. The central role maintained by the State and its traditional modes of regulation, or the priority given to institutional partnerships over public/private ones, also restrict the diffusion of NPM methods. For the same reasons, regional plans or programs are more encouraging than constraining, more indicative than mobilizing, and are added to those of the *départements* or the various ministries.

Today, the problem of the globalized economy is the major preoccupation in meso government. As elected officials try to react to globalization, there is no complete separation between economy and politics. But if the present time is a period of discourse on public/private partnership in public policy, it is also a cycle of relocation or non-territorial economy that many political leaders must undergo.

In this context, it is necessary to look at the new types of relationships between public authorities (particularly political leadership),[15] and economic interests more or less organized and represented at the territorial level. In the context of the declining influence of political leaders over the strategic decisions of TNCs, whose activities are critical for entire regions, the collaboration between public and private organizations is less idealistic than before.

This point considered, some questions still remain, giving research directions that seem promising. What are the precise perceptions of the globalization process? Do the urban and regional leaders sometimes align their strategies in consequence, in France as in Norway? We find some elements of trans-national convergence regarding political concerns, economic events and regional policy models, but the local situations and perceptions remain largely context-bound. For example, when the dynamics of regions in both countries are contrasted it seems that, in France, regions try to reinforce their institutional and policy role (or their political capacity, cf. Ritaine, 1997); in Norway, according to Harald Baldersheim, one is "more critical" as regards their role – Norwegian regions or counties seem to be on the decline (cf. chapter 9). However, the common challenges to regional leaders as they struggle to frame adaptive responses to globalization is well summarized by the following statement: *"Of key importance to both understanding and policy prescription is the recognition that contemporary regional economic success is inseparable from cultural, social, and institutional accomplishment"* (Cooke, Morgan, 1994). The recognition of these relationships, while coping with the growing separation of economy from territory, is a major challenge to leadership.

References

Allies, P. (1989). "Territoire régional et représentation des intérêts", *Politix*, 7/8.
Amin, A., Thrift, N., eds. (1994). *Globalization, Institutions, and regional development in Europe*, Oxford University Press.
Aprallange, C., Montane, M.-A. (2001). "La politique de la ville: du management public saisi par la démocratie. Velléité ou réalité?" in Allies, P. *Démocratie et management local*, Paris: Dalloz.
Baldersheim, H., Balme, R., Clark, T. N., et al. (1989). *New leaders, parties and groups: comparative tendancies in local leadership*, Les Cahiers du CERVL, Bordeaux.
Balme, R. ed. (1996). *Les politiques du néo-régionalisme, Action collective régionale et globalization*, Paris: Economica (politique comparée).
Benoit-Guilbot, O. (1991). "Les acteurs locaux du développement économique local: y a-t-il un 'effet localité'?", *Sociologie du travail*, 4.
Blondel, J. (1987). *Leadership: towards a general analysis*, London and Beverly Hills: Sage.
Briquet, J.-L. (1994). "Communiquer en actes. Prescriptions de rôle et exercice quotidien du métier politique", *Politix*, 28, pp. 16-26.
Burns, J. MacGregor (1978). *Leadership*, New York: Harper and Row.
Clark, T. N. (1995). "Les stratégies de l'innovation dans les collectivités territoriales: leçons internationales", *Politiques et management public*, 13/3, septembre.
Clark, T. N., Hoffmann-Martinot, V. eds. (1998). *The new political culture*, Westview Press.
Coicaud, J.-M. (1997). *Légitimité et politique. Contribution à l'étude du droit et de la responsabilité politiques*, Paris: PUF (Questions).
Cooke, Morgan (1994). in Amin, A. and Thrift N. eds. (1994). *Globalization, Institutions, and regional development in Europe*, Oxford University Press.
Daloz, J.-P., Montane, M.-A. (2000). "Polysémie et évolutions d'un concept: retour cavalier sur la littérature consacrée au leadership", Colloque international du CERVL, IEP de Bordeaux, *Leadership politique et pouvoir territorialisé*, 18-20 Oct.
Ferlie, E., Pettigrew, A., Ashburner, L., Fitzgerald, L. (1996). *The New Public Management in Action*, Oxford University Press.
Fitoussi, J.-P. (1997). in Francois-Poncet, J. (1997). *La mondialisation: fatalité ou chance?*, infra.
Francois-Poncet, J. ed. (1997). *La mondialisation: fatalité ou chance?*, Les Rapports du Sénat, Commission des Affaires économiques, no. 242.
Hassenteufel, P. (1998). "*Think Social, Act Local* – La territorialization comme réponse à la crise de l'Etat-Providence?", *Politiques et Management Public*, vol. 16, no. 3, September.
Iribarne, P. (2000). "Management et cultures politiques", *Revue française de gestion*, Les cultures nationales à l'heure de la mondialisation, no. 128, pp. 70-75.
Jones, B. D. ed. (1989), *Leadership and Politics: new perspectives in political science*, Lawrence: The University of Kansas Press.

Le Bart, C. (1989). *L'imputation au maire du développement économique local: l'exemple de trois villes moyennes de l'Ouest intérieur*, Ph.D. Thesis in Political Science, Université de Rennes I.
Levine, M. A. (1994). "The transformation of urban politics in France. The roots of growth politics and urban regimes", *Urban Affairs Quarterly*, vol. 29, no. 3, March, Sage Pub. Inc., pp. 383-410.
Madies, T. (1999). "Les collectivités locales se livrent-elles à une concurrence fiscale sur la taxe professionnelle?", *Revue française d'économie*, vol. XIV, 4, pp. 191-234.
Maquard, D. (1998). *Maîtriser la mondialisation*, Desclée de Brouwer.
Montane, M.-A. (1994). *Communications politiques locales*, Mémoire de DEA Gouvernement local, IEP de Bordeaux.
Montane, M.-A (2001). *Leadership politique et territoire, Des leaders en campagnes*, Collection "logiques politiques", Paris: L'Harmattan.
Nay, O. (1997). *La région, site institutionnel. Les logiques de représentation en Aquitaine*, Thesis in Political Science, IEP de Bordeaux.
Ohnet, J.-M. (1996). *Histoire de la décentralisation française*, LGF.
Parri, L. (1988). "Dimension territoriale de la politique et dynamiques d'échange", *Revue française d'administration publique*, no. 48, Oct-Dec.
Peterson, P. E. (1981). *City limits*, Chicago: University of Chicago Press.
Peterson, P. E. (1987). "Analysing developmental politics, a response to Sanders and Stone", *Urban affairs quarterly*, vol. 22, no. 4, June, pp. 540-547.
Ritaine, E. (1991). "Territoire: espace du jeu politique", *Quaderni* 13/14, printemps.
Ritaine, E. (1997). "La capacité politique des régions en Europe du sud: parcours réflexif", *Colloque CERI-CRAP*, Rennes, 1996. In Le Galès (Patrick)., Lequesne (Christian), *Les paradoxes des régions en Europe*, La Découverte.
Rouban, L. (1990). "La modernisation de l'Etat et la fin de la spécificité française", *Revue Française de Science Politique*, 40/4, pp. 521-545.
Sanders, H. T., Stone, C. N. (1987). "Competing paradigms, a rejoinder to Peterson", *Urban affairs quarterly*, vol. 22, no. 4, June, pp. 548-551.
Sanders, H. T., Stone, C. N. (1987). "Developmental politics reconsidered", *Urban affairs quarterly*, vol. 22, no. 4, June, pp. 524-539.
Sassen, S. (1999). "La métropole: site stratégique et nouvelle frontière", *Cultures & Conflits*, Les anonymes de la mondialisation, L'Harmattan, no. 33-34, pp. 123-140.
Schramm-Nielsen, J. (2000). "Dimensions culturelles des prises de décision", *Revue française de gestion*, Les cultures nationales à l'heure de la mondialisation, no. 128, pp. 76-87.
Sharpe, L. J., ed. (1993). *The rise of Meso Government in Europe*, London: Sage.
Stoker, G. (1995). "Urban governance in Britain", *Sociologie du travail*, 2, note de recherche, pp. 301-315.
Stoker, G. (1998). "Theory and urban politics", *International political science review*, vol. 19, no. 2, pp. 119-129, 1998.
Stone, C. N. (1989). *Regime politics: governing Atlanta 1946-1988*, Lawrence: University of Kansas Press.
Walsh, K. (1995). Public Services and Market Mechanisms, Competition, contracting and the new public management, Public Policy and Politics, Macmillan.

Notes

[1] According to Daniel Maquard (1998), *mondialisation* and globalization are almost synonymous terms.

[2] This chapter is based on a doctoral research on the constitution of political leadership at the territorial level (Montané, 2001), and on some ongoing research relating to regional development policies.

[3] Desperate, the associations of volunteers and victims went to the General Assembly (the corporate shareholders meeting) of Totalfina-Elf on the 25th of May 2000, and questioned the actual authority, namely the shareholders. These associations have joined a co-ordination (*"coordination"*) of the anti oil slick "collectifs" (groups). An activist had bought a share, and was consequently allowed to speak for 2 minutes. He asked the shareholders to assume their responsibilities, to be accountable (*"prendre leurs responsabilités"*). Denis Baupin, from the French Green party (*"les Verts"*) was there. The co-ordination has asked for an appointment (not a rendez-vous...) with the President of the Republic, Jacques Chirac.

[4] In Alaska, in contrast, local authorities have enforced some laws on TNC's activities, including very strict legislation for safe oil transport. These laws are well respected. As a major oil producer, this territory is therefore able to coerce oil TNCs.

[5] There is a double movement: State public policies abandon the "all sector" (*tout sectoriel*) organization, and tend to take up territorial or transverse patterns (i.e. the policy's territorialization); and local authorities develop their own policies, more or less autonomously (and not necessarily with a transverse pattern: local policy sectors also exist!).

[6] Baldersheim H., Seminar Paper, CERVL-IEP de Bordeaux, May 1999.

[7] Including the questions on water tariffs, urban transport, and various public services or public goods.

[8] Especially the struggle for the assignment/appropriation of public achievements (Le Bart, 1989).

[9] For instance in French urban policy (*"politique de la ville"*). Cf. Arpaillange, M. (2001).

[10] These are the two faces of a single effort of adaptation to globalization, through counterbalancing and competition.

[11] One could be tempted to speak in terms of the *référentiel de marché* (general market-oriented pattern) when considering all these elements related to the NPM.

[12] It is actually a prerequisite role (Briquet, 1994) that applies to politicians and particularly to the leaders. It is combined with the struggle for the assignment/appropriation of public achievements, characteristically the economic ones (Le Bart, 1989).

[13] For example, 565 million French francs listed in the 4th *Contrat de plan Etat-Region Aquitaine 2000-2006* (the contract between the State and the Region), concerning the "industrial excellence" and the competitive SMEs.

[14] With the foundation of the *Institut des sciences de la vigne et du vin*.

[15] But not only political leadership, also administrative leadership, or even party activists.

Chapter 9

Norwegian Regions as Development Agents – County Councils on the Defensive

Harald Baldersheim

Regional councils on the defensive

The position of regions in Norway is becoming increasingly ambiguous. The growing unease of regions is something of a political enigma. Norway has a long regionalist tradition. The post-war period has been one of increasing regionalization, with important welfare and development functions allocated to regions. The regional structure of popular governance – with the county councils as the institutional backbone – dates back to 1837. Since the 1990s, political opinions on the county councils have become increasingly polarized, however. A split between abolitionists and revivalists has emerged. Lately, the abolitionists have been gaining the upper hand. Why are the county councils on the defensive? Are weaknesses of regions and their leadership being exposed in a climate of increasing globalization? Have regions proven unable or unwilling to respond to new challenges? Or do we have to seek the answers in a more specific Norwegian political context?

The disenchantment with the regions is a rather surprising development. First, Norway has been somewhat of a leader among the Nordic countries in terms of regionalization, including the control over important instruments of regional development. Second, as pointed out above, the regions have long historical roots both in the institutional structure of Norway and in terms of cultural distinctiveness.[1] Third, since the 1980s, the national government as well as the county councils have very much embraced the change in regional policy thinking known as the emergence of "the endogenous model" of regional development, characterized by regional initiatives and "bottom-up" development efforts. Against a background of a globalizing economy the dirigiste, state-centred model of regional development has come to be seen as an insufficient guarantee of jobs and welfare in peripheral regions (Amin and Thrift 1994, Keating 1997). In the Nordic countries as well as in most West European countries, elective regional bodies have acquired a greater say in regional development policies (Sharpe 1993, Leonardi 1999). Analyses of these trends under the umbrella slogan of "Europe of the regions" are fast becoming an academic industry (Balme et al, 1994, Keating & Loughlin 1997, Kohler-Koch 1998).

The politico-administrative regional structure of Norway is in the main made up of 19 directly elected county councils. The regional agencies of the state are largely conterminous with the county councils. So far, the 19 counties have been essential service providers and development agents. They have been responsible for hospitals, secondary schools, regional communications and ancillary services. Regional planning and development initiatives are also important county functions. County councils have been directly elected since 1976 but have a history of more than 160 years. The role of regional state agencies has, with some exceptions, been that of bodies of supervision and appeal whereas elected county and local councils have been responsible for service provision, planning and development. As a result of this division of work between state and regional/local bodies, the latter have accounted for nearly two thirds of all public spending and have employed a similar proportion of all public employees. In consequence, a highly regionalized and localized system of governance has evolved since the 1970s. In this respect, however, Norway has been very much a member of the Nordic "family" of polities as similar patterns are found also in the other Nordic countries. Developments along the lines suggested by the slogan of "Europe of the regions" may in fact have been more of a reality in the Nordic area since the 1970s than on the Continent where the slogan originated. However, Norway may be in the processes of breaking with the Nordic model with respect to regional governance.

In the early 1990s, the abolition of the county councils was a cause espoused only by The Progress Party, a party on the extreme right of the political continuum. In 1995, this stance was adopted also by the Conservative Party. The argument of the Progressives and the Conservatives is simply that for a country as small as Norway, three levels of government represent too much bureaucracy, local and national governments should be enough. In 2000, similar opinions suddenly began to be heard in several other parties. Criticism focused in particular on hospital management (other county functions were largely overlooked). Even the Labour party seemed to be in doubt with regard to the county councils before its Congress in November 2000. However, in contrast to the anti-bureaucratic attitudes of Conservatives, leading Labour figures speculated that what Norway needed might be something quite different from the county councils, say four or five really large regions to lead the way into the 21st century.

The present county councils survived the Labour Congress as a result of a compromise: the county councils would be granted additional functions in regional development but would have to relinquish responsibility for hospitals. Hospitals were to be allocated to a new, independent hospital authority, somewhat along the lines of the British National Health Service. The Labour government, with unusual speed, introduced a bill already in February 2001 to achieve this reform before the parliamentary election that was to take place in September. The bill was passed against the opposition mainly of the region-friendly Centre Party and the Left Socialist Party. The promised new regional development functions for the counties have taken longer in appearing, however. The national elections of 2001 resulted in the formation of a centre-right government. At the time of writing, the government is proposing to relieve the county councils of even more functions. So the future of the county councils is in serious doubt.

In the other Nordic countries regional governance is being restructured and energized in the wake of European integration, especially so in the new member states of Finland and Sweden (Sandberg and Ståhlberg 2000). While Norway used to be the most decentralized of all the Nordics, with service provision and regional development functions integrated under the control of the county councils, Sweden is now regionalizing its governmental structures beyond the Norwegian model in the form of a series of experiments in bottom-up control over regional policy instruments. Finland's traditionally state-dominated and fragmented regional governance is being infused with bottom-up elements in the form of 20 regional councils with roles in policy development in conjunction with state bodies.

So why are Norwegian county councils on the defensive? Is the reason that they have not been able to respond to the pressures of globalization and international competition? Are they still in the policy approaches of the industrial and dirigiste era? Is the political leadership of regions stuck in outmoded attitudes and styles? Below, these issues are examined with material from case studies in selected regions and surveys that permits a comparison of Norwegian regions with those of neighbouring Nordic countries. Can the explanation of the Norwegian case be found in inertia and deviance from regions in other countries?

The role of the county councils in regional development: illustrations

As mentioned above, during the 1980s, thinking on regional development policy changed from a dirigste to an endogenous model of regional development (Isaksen 1997, Bukve 1998). Development was no longer seen as mainly a question of the state guiding private and public investments to regions most in need of jobs and welfare. It was increasingly seen as dependent upon mobilization of local and regional ideas and initiatives. This shift naturally led to a more important role for regional and local institutions, such as county and municipal councils. New theoretical perspectives further emphasized the embeddedness of regional development, e.g. theories of "social capital" (Putnam 1993), "human capital" (Reich 1991), or "learning economies" (Lundvall 1992).

Can these insights also be traced in the organization of regional development in Norway? In my opinion, the answer is "yes". Since the 1970s, *the Comprehensive County Plan* was the county council's traditional instrument for development purposes. The county plans were supposed to co-ordinate the investments of the county council's various branches, those of regional state agencies and also municipal development plans. Ambitions such as these of course required time-consuming efforts of co-ordination and negotiation. The County Plan was clearly a product of the dirigiste era. During the 1980s, the County Plan came increasingly under criticism for bureaucratic wastefulness and lack of achievement. In the early 1990s, focus shifted to more targeted and programme-oriented development initiatives. Such programmes might aim at helping small firms innovate or market products abroad, stimulate young people to return to the home region, develop cooperative ventures between regional universities and local entrepreneurs, establish cross-border projects with opposite numbers in other countries, etc. Most county councils had established their own departments for regional development. These typically encompassed a unit for economic initiatives, a unit for communications and in many cases a unit for cultural affairs.

The introduction of the logic of endogenous development did not indicate the abdication of the state in regional affairs, however. The state through the Ministry of Local Government and Regional Development financed and continues to finance substantial proportions of regional development programmes in individual regions. The financial support is used as an incentive to promote a particular instrument of regional development, *the Co-Ordinated Regional Development Plan* (COREG for short). This is an investment programme and action plan that brings together the major public actors in the region in a supposedly concerted programme that is intended to align state as well as regional resources. The influence of the organization of EU regional development projects is clearly visible, especially the "partnership" approach.

Two examples may illustrate the sort of policies that in practice make up the COREG. For the year 2000, the county of *Hedmark* developed seven sub-programmes under the COREG Plan:

- aid for restructuring of economic branches[2]
- support for experimental economic projects
- the establishment of networks of expertise among firms
- institutional development (primarily to enhance efficiency in local government)
- cultural projects
- place development (the "embellishment" of particular localities)
- internationalization of the regional economy.

The county of *Aust-Agder* initiated four sub-programmes in this respect:

- support for experimental economic projects
- place development
- internationalization of the regional economy
- a special programme for peripheral districts.

The two examples suggest both similarities in policy development as well as regional distinctiveness. These programme labels could also be found in the corresponding plans of other counties. The similarities may suggest the guiding hand of the state but may also indicate learning across borders. The latter issue will be discussed later.

Case studies (unpublished) of three counties demonstrated that the *procedures* they followed varied markedly with regard to mobilizing partnerships in order to identify priority areas and target groups. The three development "regimes" identified were labeled "business", "bureaucratic" and "deliberative" regimes respectively. The business regime was identified in the county of *Hedmark*.

Working procedures were characterized by a deep involvement of business elites and the establishment of independent arenas (*Viking Venture*) for business for the mutual exchange of ideas between business people but also for the open discussion of regional development issues. *BioInn* represented another arena for businesses, in this case for companies in biological and food production.

The bureaucratic regime was characteristic of procedures in the county of *Aust-Agder*. Here, input to the COREG Plan came mostly from the designated institutions of the public sector through the established channels of communications. Little effort was made to involve "outsiders". Project implementation was also seen as largely the responsibility of public agencies (labour market exchanges, municipalities, social services).

The deliberative regime of the county of *Sogn og Fjordane* was a set of procedures that aimed at involving and stimulating discussion in a wide network of discussion groups. These groups involved not only businesses but also civil society (voluntary associations and individuals). Sogn og Fjordane also gave more of a role to research institutions than other counties did.

A traditional corporatist element was not wholly absent from the procedures observed in the three counties. The regional branches of the Trade Union Congress and the Employers' Association respectively were regular participants in the processes leading up to the adoption of the plans. However, as indicated by the examples of Hedmark and Sogn og Fjordane corporatism could not be said to be the most pronounced feature of regional development planning, the networks of participation extended well beyond what would be expected in a strongly corporatist set-up.

The examples illustrate that the county councils certainly have made efforts to establish endogenous development policies. In doing this they have also established partnerships with regional elites, although partnerships with the private sector are not as widespread as the declared ambitions might have suggested. Partnerships with state agencies are perhaps the most conspicuous feature of the programmes being established at the county level.

Although new development initiatives have been taken by the county councils, and new ways of organizing development projects have been found, the vigour and audacity of these initiatives may not be enough to impress the voters or the elites that matter. To what extent is the regional political elite involved? Does it demonstrate leadership in the face of globalization? These issues are addressed below.

What policies for the future? Policy preferences of the regional political elite

Can the declining role of the county councils be explained by a lack of policy visions for the future? Have they lost energy and drive, concentrating on the day-to-day management of services such as schools and hospitals instead of the long-term challenges of the regions? Are the challenges of globalization and European integration absent from the agenda of the county councils? To answer these questions, a yardstick is needed with which to assess the county councils as development agents. Below, these questions are discussed in a comparative perspective drawing on data for the four Nordic countries of Norway, Denmark, Finland and Sweden. Elected county council members of all Nordic regions have been surveyed (usually members of the county council's policy committee).[3] The questions posed covered policy preferences for regional development, participation in policy networks and views on European integration. Were the Norwegians so different from the other Nordics? May such differences explain the beleaguered position of the Norwegian county councils?

The analysis is guided by *a model of policy learning*. As a point of departure, it is assumed that europeanization and globalization lead to increasing competition between regions nationally and across national borders. Competition exerts a pressure on regions to develop new policies to deal with the new situation. This pressure triggers a learning process in which regions look beyond their own boundaries for inspiration in the policy process and also for resources for implementing the policies. Thus, a series of more or less wide-ranging networks may emerge as channels for learning. Learning, in turn, results in new policy preferences being formed, and this again leads to new policies being adopted.

The establishment of cross-border networks represents the *leadership* dimension of the model. The more and deeper the members of regional councils engage in networks of various sorts, the more they are said to exhibit *cosmopolitan* leadership (as against *localist* orientations).[4] Cosmopolitan leadership is expected to favour preferences for "new" types of policies.

Basically, the analysis focuses on the following elements:
European integration/globalization ⇒ *regional competition* ⇒ *network formation/leadership* ⇒ *policy learning* ⇒ *new policy preferences*

The subsequent section of the chapter deals with the emergent policy preferences among regional councillors. Next, features of network formation are described and then policy learning processes. Finally, the interconnections between these three elements are analyzed.

Policy preferences

Perhaps the most fundamental question to be addressed is whether sub-national governments feel any increasing pressure of competition at all, and if they do, whether they see any point in trying to respond. Perhaps they think such issues should be left to the national government, or perhaps forces of the market should be left to run their course. The answer can be found in figure 9.1. Respondents were asked to take a stand on the statement that "European integration has led to an increasing competition among regions and cities". Comparisons on a national basis show that the proportions of regional policy-makers agreeing to the statement range from 70 percent in Finland to 35 percent in Norway. Norway is only a halfway member of the EU, so the pattern of answers might be taken to demonstrate that EU membership has led to an experience of growing competition: a more competitive climate is felt more strongly in member state regions than in those of non-member states. However, Danish regions are not much more prone to experience a climate of competition than the Norwegian ones despite Danish EU membership since 1972.

The Norwegian responses may also be interpreted against the actual extent of "the regional problem" in the Nordic countries. If the territorial distribution of levels of unemployment is taken as a measure of immediate regional crises, then Norway comes out as a country in a class of its own. In Norway in 1995, regional levels of unemployment varied from a low of 3.6 percent to a high of 7.3 percent. In contrast, the Finnish variation was from 5.5 to 22.7 percent. Swedish levels of unemployment ranged from 6.5 to 14 percent and Danish levels from 6 to 11 percent.[5] Clearly, both in terms of actual levels of unemployment and in terms of regional variations Norway was confronted with much less of a "crisis" than the other three countries, which may also account for less pronounced feelings of vulnerability among Norwegian regional councillors. In Norway, this situation of high levels of employment and small regional contrasts continued throughout the 1990s and into the 2000s.

Figure 9.1 "European integration has led to increasing competition among regions." Responses from regional policy committee members. Percentage agreed

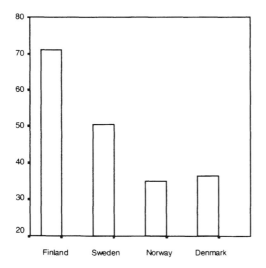

What sort of *policies* do regional elites see as relevant responses in order to promote the interests of their respective areas? Respondents were given a list of 18 different policy options and asked to state their preferences for these options. A five points scale was used to measure preferences (from "disagree strongly" to "agree strongly"). Based on factor analysis these alternatives could be grouped into four categories:

- internationalization/cross-border alliances/learning languages, etc.;
- "new" modernization (better electronic communications, upgrading R&D and educational facilities, alliances universities-business);
- functional decentralization (more functions to regions and/or cities);
- better service provision (of traditional services).

What are the preferences of regional councillors with regard to these policy types? How eager are they to adopt such policies? Is it internationalization, "new" modernization for the information age, functional redistribution or better service provision that have the highest priority as measures to improve competitiveness? This is brought out in figure 9.2.

Figure 9.2 Policy choices of regional politicians. Percentage in favour of indicated policy type

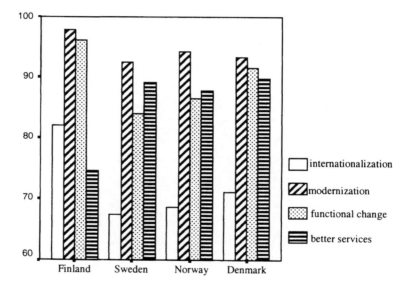

Figure 9.2 shows that strategies of modernization have a clear priority among regional policy-makers in all four countries, most of all in Finland, but also in the other three countries. The challenges of the emergent information economy are taken very seriously. In Finland and Denmark, policies of institutional reconstruction and functional redistribution take second place. Norway and Sweden put more emphasis on better service provision than Finns and Danes do. The various forms of internationalization receive less support, including such measures as cross-border alliances and improving the capacities of elected

Norwegian Regions as Development Agents 145

members and civil servants to engage in international contacts. However, this sort of activity is certainly not being discarded by the regions; more than two thirds of elected members in all countries favour such policies. Overall, the policy preferences of the Norwegians do not deviate much from those of their Nordic colleagues.

There is also a potential for further conflict in the policy choices of regions. The potential for conflict appears in particular when the strategies for functional redistribution are analyzed more in detail. In all Nordic countries, the distribution of functions between levels of government has been a widely discussed topic in recent years, and especially the allocation of responsibilities for development policies. Figure 9.3 presents the pattern of responses to the statement that *more responsibility for regional development should be transferred from regions (counties) to municipalities.* In this figure, results are also given for cities in Norway and Denmark (the municipal council of the capital city of each region was also surveyed in the same manner as the regional council). This is a proposal that is very much supported by the cities while the regions do not think this is a good idea at all.

Figure 9.3 "More responsibilities for development functions should be transferred from regions to municipalities." Responses of regional and urban politicians. Percentage agreed

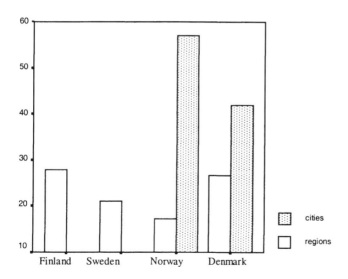

Figure 9.4 shows attitudes to the transfer of development functions from *state* bodies to regions. Not surprisingly, this suggestion is strongly supported by regions

in all countries. With regard to attitudes among city policy-makers concerning such reforms an interesting contrast emerges between Danish and Norwegian cities. Danish cities also support further regionalization of development functions whereas *Norwegian cities are much more reluctant in this regard.*

Figure 9.4 "More responsibilities for development functions should be transferred from state bodies to regions." Responses of urban and regional politicians. Percentage agreed

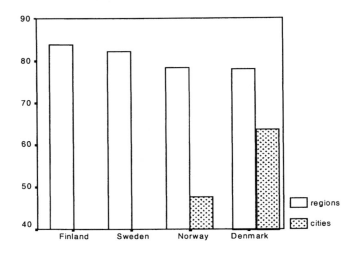

What may be reflected in this pattern is the weakening position of Norwegian counties over the last five years or so. As mentioned above, in the Norwegian debate on institutional reform the position of the counties is being seriously questioned. The cities have been especially vociferous in this respect. Many cities are now declaring to be ready to take over county functions. It should be added, however, that Norway also has champions for further regionalization. And the regions' own attitudes certainly suggest a willingness to take on an enhanced role in development issues.

Networks, internationalization and policy learning

Policy learning takes place through various channels, both of a formal and informal nature. Increasingly, policy is developed outside traditional governmental hierarchies; instead the policy process unfolds through networks of various kinds (Rhodes 1997). It seems reasonable to expect that the more extensive networks that cities and regions are involved in, the more policy learning will take place, which again may lead to more vigorous and sophisticated policy responses. Participation in international networks may be especially important for policy learning. Are the tribulations of Norwegian counties a reflection of an unwillingness or lack of capacity to take part in national and international networks?

The questions asked in the survey deal with the extent to which policy committee members were involved in co-operative ventures with other municipalities and regions (and state bodies) at home as well as with cities and regions abroad. They were also asked about visits to their twins abroad and participation in international conferences dealing with regional and municipal issues. The most common type of network participation is that of ventures with other municipalities or regions in the home country (inter-municipal and inter-regional ventures of various kinds, often of a developmental nature). Going on visits and study tours to twin cities and regions in other countries is also common. Participating in projects with regions and municipalities abroad or going to international conferences are more rare occurrences (interestingly, the pattern is the same for regions and cities). The emphasis is on cross-boundary involvement at home and short visits abroad. The more demanding international networking is performed by a select few.

In figure 9.5 a summary measure[6] of networking is presented. At the same time the data are broken down by country.

Figure 9.5 Participation in networks international and overall. Regional politicians. Mean scores, scale 0-3

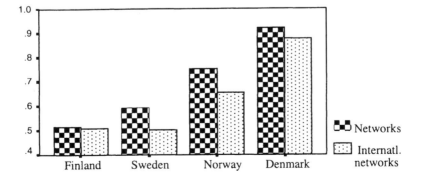

Figure 9.5 deals with *regions* in the four countries. The darkest bars represent overall networking whereas the more lightly shaded bars focus on the international

contacts. Regional policy leaders in Denmark and Norway seem more involved in cross-boundary networks of all kinds than the Swedish and Finnish counterparts do. This also goes for the international networks. The reason for the lower density of networking in Finland may partly be the specific nature of the Finnish regions with their concentration on the developmental functions, which may result in a more narrow array of functional networks than in the other countries. The more reserved attitude of the Swedes is harder to explain in this way, however, since Swedish regions have much the same functions and position as the Norwegian and Danish ones.

How much *learning* does in fact occur through the networks that have been described above? Do councillors go on visits and study tours without having much to tell when they return home? Is it just empty exercises in municipal tourism? Do they learn anything from their contacts across borders and boundaries? The question posed in the survey in order to address this issue was *whether the councillors, taking the whole of the Nordic area into account, could name one or more municipalities or regions they would consider as pioneers and paragons with regard to policy development on issues related to internationalization.* The rationale of the question was that if the councillors could name pioneering municipalities or regions, then this would be an indication of retention of information that had a high likelihood of influencing subsequent policy formation when they came back home.

The results as indicated by table 9.1 are not very impressive. Around 70 percent of the councillors (from regions and cities combined) cannot name a single pioneering authority that they think could be emulated. At the other end of the range 13 percent of councillors are able to name *both* regions and municipalities, from whom they think something could be learnt.

Table 9.1 Policy learning: How many politicians are able to nominate pioneering regions/cities. Percentage of total who can identify pioneer

		Nomination of min. 1 city (percentages of total)		Total
		no	yes	
Nomination of min. 1 region (percentages of total)	no	70.8	5.2	75.9 percent
	yes	11.5	12.6	24.1 percent
	N	765	165	930

In figure 9.6 a *policy learning index* has been computed. The index summarizes the extent to which councillors are able 1) to name a pioneering municipality at all,

2) to indicate a pioneering municipality in another Nordic country, 3) to name a pioneering region at all, 4) to name a pioneering region in another Nordic country. Thus, the index can take on values from 0 to 4. Figure 9.6 presents mean scores on the index by country. On the whole, councillors from regions in Finland and Sweden have the highest scores and therefore seem the more eager policy learners. The Norwegians seem less well informed than their Finnish and Swedish colleagues. The Danish regional councillors are decidedly the ones least interested in developments in other places. Or perhaps they feel they are themselves the vanguard and don't have so much to learn from others? The explanation could also be that the Danes look outside the Nordic area to find inspiration for new policies. The survey would not cover such a case. However, we know from previous studies that Nordic municipalities primarily learn from each other and only to a lesser extent from outside the Nordic area (Baldersheim and Ståhlberg 1999). Therefore, we think that also the Danish results of this survey are valid.

Figure 9.6 Policy learning index: Ability of regional councillors to nominate pioneering region/city. Scale: 0-4

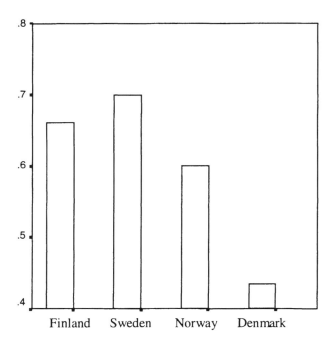

In terms of *leadership* types (cosmopolitans versus locals), the data suggest that Norwegian regional councillors are not less cosmopolitan in their orientations than their colleagues in other Nordic countries although the indicators yield a somewhat ambiguous picture. The Norwegians participate more in international networks than Finns and Swedes do but less than the Danes. The Norwegians *know* more than the Danes about what is happening in other places but not quite as much as Finns and Swedes. Overall, the Norwegians do not stand out as markedly different from their Nordic counterparts; they are not, however, the international champions among Nordic regions.

Do networks and policy learning matter?

The next question is: Do networks matter for policy learning? Are those councillors most involved in networks *also* those more aware of developments in other places and thus more able to point out pioneers? There is indeed a strong correlation between the indices of network formation and the index of policy learning. The correlation coefficients between *policy learning* on the one hand and *total network participation* and *international network participation* on the other hand are r=.323 and r=.307 respectively, both significant at the .01 level. So participation in networks certainly matters for policy learning. Those who are involved do have something to show for their efforts.

But does policy learning have any impact on *policy formation*? Does it matter for the further steps of the policy process? With the data available this issue can only be explored partially. We do not have information on policy *outputs* or *outcomes*, only on the *policy preferences* of councillors as presented in the preceding section. So we ask: Are policy preferences influenced by policy learning as defined above? Again we find positive correlations. The three "new" types of policy responses described above were internationalization strategies, "new" modernization, and redistribution of functions across levels of government. A preference for these strategies is positively related to policy learning. *The greater the awareness of pioneers in other places the stronger the preference for new policies.* However, the relationships are not as strong as those between networks and learning. The correlation coefficients between policy learning on the one hand and the policies of internationalism, modernism and governmental reorganization on the other hand are r=152, r=.072 and r=.079 respectively (the first relationship is significant at the .01 level and the two others at the .05 level). When regions and cities are analyzed separately, these relations are somewhat more pronounced for the regions compared to the cities, which indicates that the model works better for regions than for cities. When analyzed separately for countries and unit types, the strongest relationship between policy learning and policy preferences is found among Danish regions, with r=.314 (significant at .01 level). However, knowledge of a pioneering region also motivates the policy makers of *Norwegian* regions: the more they know about pioneers, the more they favour e.g. internationalization as a competitive strategy and the more eager overall development policy enthusiasts they become. In other words, leadership orientation matters for the policies that regional councillors wish to pursue. Cosmopolitanism drives internationalization and "new" modernization.

Conclusions

Norwegian regions are on the defensive. They are losing functions and support. In this respect Norway differs not only from the rest of the Nordic area but also from important trends in the rest of Europe. A "Europe of the Regions" may not be a quite realistic description of the present situation, but in most countries of the EU regions have become more important players over the last decade or so (Sharpe, 1993). Relations to the state have taken on more of a partnership character. Regions have also become partners of the European Commission through programmes such as the structural funds or Interreg. The establishment of the Committee of the Regions is a reflection of these developments. "Multi-level governance" (Marks et al, 1996) is a phrase coined to capture the role of the regions at the European level, emphasizing the role of regions in European integration from below.

The growing importance of regions is driven by a climate of increasing competition between regional economies (Amin and Thrift 1994; Clarke and Gaile 1998). In this competitive climate an endogenous model of development has gained prominence, placing regional actors in the natural locus of initiative and mobilization. In many respects, the Norwegian county councils as development agents act their part in this scenario. Norwegian counties have also been affected by European integration. Their cross-border and international contacts have been substantially extended and deepened in the 1990s. They have become partners of regions in neighbouring countries that may seek EU-funding for cross-border project from the Interreg programmes. They have applied successfully in their own right for projects in other programmes (e.g. Leonardo). In their modus operandi as development agents the county councils have imported many of the features of their EU partners: partnerships, additionality, etc. in their own development programmes. The policies favoured by Norwegian regional policy-makers largely mirror those of regional champions in other countries. It is hard to detect a particular Norwegian model of regional development or modus operandi. Learning – copying, dissemination of information, exchanges of experiences, study tours – helps spreading innovative methods of work among regions. Some are faster learners than others, but in the end the commonalities dominate. This is europeanization from below. Norwegian regions take part in this process.

So what is different in Norway? Why are not the county councils celebrated here? Perhaps the answer lies in the difference detected in figure 9.1. At least compared to Finnish and Swedish regions, the Norwegians feel much less exposed to competition from other regions. The Norwegian deviance may in fact make sense against the absence of immediate regional crises, as suggested by the low levels of unemployment in Norwegian regions. If there is no strongly felt competition and no immediate crisis, there may be less of a demand for the endogenous development model, and so there is less perceived need for regional actors with a mandate from below to mobilize the region. So whatever the county councils do, however effective policy-makers they are, if their efforts do not correspond to acutely felt needs, their efforts may not be appreciated. Exit the county councils?

References

Amin, Ash. and Nigel Thrift, eds. (1994). *Globalization, Institutions and Regional Development in Europe*. Oxford: Oxford University Press.

Baldersheim, Harald and Krister Ståhlberg, eds. (1999). *Nordic Region-Building in a European Perspective*. Aldershot: Ashgate.

Balme, Richard, Philippe Harraud, Vincent Hoffmann-Martinot og Évelyne Riaine. (1994). *Le territoire pour politiques: Variations européennes*. Paris: Éditions L'Harmattan.

Bjørklund, Tor (1996). "The Three Nordic Referenda Concerning Membership in the EU", *Co-operation and Conflict 1996*, vol. 31: 11-36.

Bjørklund, Tor (1999). *Periferi mot sentrum: landsomfattende folkeavstemninger i Norge*. Oslo: Institutt for statsvitenskap, Det samfunnsvitenskapelige fakultet, Universitetet i Oslo.

Clarke, Susan and Gary Gaile (1998). *The Work of Cities*. Minnesota University Press.

Goldsmith, Michael and Kurt Klaudi Klaussen, eds. (1997). *Europeanisation of Local Government*. London: Frank Cass.

Harvie, Christopher. (1994). *The Rise of Regional Europe*. London: Routledge.

Isaksen, Arne ed. (1997). *Innovasjoner, næringsutvikling og regionalpolitikk*. Kristiansand: Høyskoleforlaget.

Keating, Michael and John Loughlin, eds. (1997). *The Political Economy of Regionalism*. London: Frank Cass.

Kohler-Koch, Beate, ed. (1998). *Interaktive Politik in Europa. Regionen im Netzwerk der Integration*. Opladen: Leske+Budrich.

Lipset, Martin.S. and Stein Rokkan (1967). *Party Systems and Voter Alignments. Cross-National Perspectives*. New York: The Free Press.

Lundvall, B.A. (1992). *National Systems of Innovation: Towards a Theory of Innovation and Interactive Learning*. London: Pinter.

Marks, Gary, Francois Nielsen, Leonard Ray and Jane Salk (1994). "Competencies, Cracks, and Conflicts: Regional Mobilization in the European Union". Chapter 3 in Gary Marks, Fritz W. Scharpf, Philippe C. Schmitter and Wolfgang S. Streck, eds.: *Governance in the European Union*. London: Sage.

Putnam, Robert (1993). *Making Democracy Work. Civic Traditions in Modern Italy*. Princeton: Princeton University Press.

Ratti, R., A. Brmanati and R. Gordon, eds. (1997). *The Dynamics of Innovative Regions. The GREMI Approach*. Aldershot: Ashgate.

Reich, Robert (1991). *The Work of Nations*. N.Y.: Alfred Knopf.

Rhodes, R. A. W. (1997). *Understanding Governance. Policy Networks, Governance, Reflexibility and Accountability*. Buckingham: Open University Press.

Rokkan, Stein (1975/1987). "Dimensions of State Formation and Nation-Building: A Possible Paradigm for Research on Variations within Europe". I Charles Tilly, ed. *The Formation of National States in Europe*. Princeton: Princeton University Press.

Sandberg, Siv and Krister Ståhlberg (2000). *Nordisk regionalförvaltning i förendring*. Åbo Akademi.

Sharpe, L.J. (1993). "The European Meso: An Appraisal". In L.J. Sharpe, ed. *The rise of Meso Government in Europe*. London: Sage.

Notes

[1] Political scientists have frequently pointed out the important place that regional contrasts and identities have in Norwegian politics. Distinct regional voting patterns have survived to this day (Bjørklund 1999). Indeed, the celebrated centre-periphery model of nation-building was "invented" by Stein Rokkan based on his observations of regional political contrasts in Norway (Lipset and Rokkan 1967, Rokkan 1975). Regions of the South and West, for example, are noted for their support of the so-called "counter-cultures" (fundamentalist religion, teetotalism, language issues), whereas the North represents a more radical or socialist tradition.

[2] The county councils do not offer financial support or extend credit to individual companies located in districts eligible for this type of support. This is the function of a state agency with branches in all counties (SND). The county councils are expected to formulate strategic guidelines for the state agencies in this respect and are also represented on the board of the agencies. Whether these guidelines are actually heeded is debatable, however. Micro credit of this nature was the responsibility of the county councils until 1997, when the state took over. The loss of the micro credit function and the direct contact with local companies that this function entailed was much regretted by the county councils. It was a hard-fought battle and an early warning of coming skirmishes.

[3] The number of regions are: Denmark 14, Finland 20, Norway 19, Sweden 24.

[4] The distinction is based on Robert Merton's famous pair of "locals" and "cosmopolitans". The former build their leadership on localised networks and sources of information, the latter rely on national and international sources and contacts. Cfr. Merton 1947/1968.

[5] Variations in regional levels of unemployment in the Nordic countries. 1995. Percentage.

	Mean	Minimum	Maximum	Range
Finland	17.5	5.5	22.7	17.2
Sweden	9.2	6.5	14	7.5
Norway	6	3.6	7.3	3.7
Denmark	8.8	6	11.3	5.3

[6] Councillors may score from 0 to 3 points on each of the types of activities described in figure 9.6. These scores are summarised and divided by no. of activities. The total networking score is based on the sum for all six activities. The international networking score excludes inter-municipal/-regional networks at home.

Chapter 10

Interest Group Leadership and Territory: The Case of Bordeaux Wine Producers

Andy Smith

Used as an analytical concept and by linking it to that of territory, political leadership can usefully be applied to studying power and legitimacy not only within public authorities but also within interest groups. More precisely, such an approach encourages research to focus upon the link between three overlapping dimensions of leadership –intra and inter-organizational competition, problem shaping and decision-making, evocation and dramatization (Genieys, Smith et al., 2000). By concentrating upon processes, choices and, above all, identifiable actors, this approach to interest formation and representation is an attempt to dynamize a field of study which, at least in Europe, is often excessively descriptive (Greenwood, 1997).

Such theoretical and empirical ambition is particularly important at a time when interest groups in much of Europe are facing the threefold challenge of "globalization", European integration and decentralization. The first of these terms synthesizes a process of liberalizing, and sometimes reregulating, markets which amongst its many effects tends to modify the balance of power within and between interest groups. Through changing public decision-making procedures, European integration and decentralization also often alter the nature of longstanding relationships between three representatives of private interests and guardians of the public interest. However, it is crucially important to see that these trends and their effects are neither automatic nor inevitable. Instead, they are the result of accumulations of strategies, choices and non-choices which produce patterns which vary in the extent to which they determine intra and inter-organizational mediation. Although interest group politics has arguably always contained a multi-level dimension, the addition of European and worldwide regulatory challenges seems nevertheless to have accentuated this aspect and thus generated a "new" object for research (Smith, 2001).

In order to tackle the dynamics of contemporary interest representation as a research question, this chapter applies my conceptualization of political leadership to structure empirical evidence generated into the way the wine producers of the Bordelais region today define and defend their interests. Put succinctly, in this region's wine sector, "globalization", European integration and decentralization have led producers to position themselves on a continuum. At one extreme, there are ardent defenders of a highly detailed, place (*terroir*)-linked and European-wide regulatory regime. For the last decade or so, these actors have strongly been resisting change at local, national and European levels. At the other extreme of the continuum, one finds protagonists who have fought for a reduction in the legal regulation of wine production, but also for the strengthening of producer-set regulation designed to position the wines of Bordeaux in a changing worldwide market. Between these polarized positions, and largely unbeknownst to outside observers, a battle for sectoral leadership has been raging. This chapter sets out my interpretation of this battle and suggests that although the battles fought are obviously specific to the sector and territory under study, in many respects they mirror what is currently shaping interest group politics in other sectors and other regions. Put simply, the point of view expressed here is that "economics" or "market conditions" have not been the causes of interest group change. Instead, the causal story that we have sought to unravel is one of actors, ideas and leadership.

Competing leaderships

Wine producers cannot simply vote for a regulated or deregulated future. Instead, they elect representatives whose rise to office can be analyzed in terms both of personal social trajectories and of leadership as a collective activity. The power of these leaderships can in turn be examined by looking in some detail at two aspects which contribute to perceptions of their eligibility for office: team-formation and network building. In abstract terms, what will be analyzed here is the degree to which leaderships generate active or latent followers. In empirical terms, our overall research project will attempt to show how competing leaders have progressively won, or sought to win, office at one or several of the local *syndicat viticoles*, regional, national and European levels. In this text, the demonstration will be limited first to analysis of leadership struggles that have taken place at the "regional" level: the Bordelais. However, one can only really understand the shift in power that has taken place at this level by looking at leadership struggles in the "micro-region" which has largely been the "winner" in Bordeaux's wine politics over the last twenty-five years: the area where relatively low priced, "Bordeaux" and "Bordeaux supérieur" wines are produced.

Leaderships of the Bordelais

The first point an outsider to this subject or region needs to grasp is that "the Bordelais" is not a natural or even an administrative region. Rather it is a socio-political construction, a category, which groups together the wines produced in most of the Gironde *département*. Over the years, this category has been institutionalized in a number of ways, in particular through the establishment of two interest groups: a producers' group – the *Fédération des grandes vins de Bordeaux (FGVB)* – and a producer-wholesaler group – the *Comité interprofessionnel des vins de Bordeaux (CIVB)*. By looking briefly at the changes in leadership of these two bodies, one can get an initial idea of the conflicts and compromises that have structured this level of wine politics.

Based in Bordeaux itself, the FGVB brings together representatives of each of the 35 *syndicats viticoles* which represent in total 57 certificates of origin (A.O.C.: *Appellation d'origine contrôlée*). Founded in 1939, an initial way of examining changes in its leadership is to set out the presidents of this organization and the *syndicat viticole* where they began their careers (see Table 10.1).

Table 10.1 The presidents of the FGVB

Period	President	Syndicat Viticole
1939-	Maurice Salles	Saint-Croix-du-Mont
1944-64	Bertrand de Lur-Saluces	Sauternes
1964-75	Jean Capdemourlin	Saint Emilion
1975-77	Paul Glotin	Graves de Vayres
1977-78	Henri de Lambert	Pomerol
1978-82	Paul Glotin	Graves de Vayres
1982-86	Hubert Bouteiller	Médoc et Haut-Médoc
1986-89	Pierre Medeville	Bordeaux and Bordeaux Supérieur
1989	Hubert Bouteiller	Médoc et Haut-Médoc
1989-90	Pierre Medeville	Bordeaux and Bordeaux Supérieur
1990-97	Jean-Louis Trocard	Bordeaux and Bordeaux Supérieur
1997>	Xavier Carreau	Côtes de Blaye

Focusing upon the President of this organization runs the danger of analyses in terms of leaders rather than that of leadership. Nonetheless, this table clearly shows that over the past 25 years the presidency has essentially been held by men who have had their electoral base in areas of relatively lower quality and lower priced wine. This change reflects what a local historian, Philippe Roudié, has called a switch from representation of Bordeaux's wines by an elite of top-quality producers, to the FGVB becoming "the emanation of the syndicats viticoles".[1] This change came about in dramatic fashion in 1975 when a group of representatives from different syndicats, mobilized by a drop in prices and the perceived helplessness of the FGVB, ousted the sitting president, Jean Capdemourlin. Apart from a few exceptional years, the Federation has since been led by men who have clearly favoured the development of red wine production at the expense of white and, above all, have sought to put into place incentives and constraints to encourage improved quality of medium-priced wines not produced in the four best known areas in the Bordelais: the Médoc, Saint-Emilion, the Graves and the Sauterne.

We will return to these policy priorities in the next section. But first it is important to stress the collective and reticular dimensions of the leadership of

Glotin, Trocard and Carreau. A first point to underline is that although these individuals are very much associated with one *syndicat viticole*, they personally also have had strong connections with others. Apart from his connections with wine merchants, Glotin also owned land in the Médoc whilst Trocard owns vines which are within the Saint-Emilion and Pomerol *terroirs*.[2]

The second and probably more important point is that these presidents of the FGVB have simultaneously sought to hold office within other regional and national organisations. Setting aside for the moment the national dimension, a major battleground has been the second principal organization in the wine politics of the Bordelais: the CIVB. Although created as long ago as 1948, as with the Federation, the CIVB was revamped in the mid-1970s, largely by producer representatives.

Table 10.2 The presidents of the CIVB

Period	President	Producer or merchant ?
1975-77	Jean-Pierre Jauffret	Merchant
1977-78	Paul Glotin	Producer
1978-79	Jean-Pierre Jauffret	Merchant
1979-80	Henri de Lambert	Producer
1980-82	Jacques Theo	Merchant
1982-84	Paul Glotin	Producer
1984-86	Jean-Pierre Jauffret	Merchant
1986-88	Hubert Bouteiller	Producer
1988-90	Francis Fouquet	Merchant
1990-92	Hubert Bouteiller	Producer
1992-94	Philippe Casteja	Merchant
1994-96	Hubert Bouteiller	Producer
1996-98	Philippe Casteja	Merchant
1998-2000	Jean-Louis Trocard	Producer
2000>	Eric Dulong	Merchant

Although the Presidency switches from the merchants[3] to the producers each year (see Table 10.2), what is important to grasp is that producer representatives have been in the vanguard of changing the dominant action logic of this organization. Initially set up to establish economic interventions (e.g. threshold prices) in order to stabilize producer revenue and wine prices, the CIVB has become a body increasingly devoted to promoting the wines of Bordeaux.[4] This in part reflects perceptions of more competitive world market conditions. But more generally it also reflects the emergence of a central debate within the region over the definition of "quality" production, how it can be encouraged within the profession and with what form of public support.

Leadership of generic wine production: Bordeaux and Bordeaux supèrieur

The debates around the notion of "quality" are particularly important because they are essential to understanding the resources and constraints of the leadership of the Bordeaux and Bordeaux supérieur (BBS) *syndicat viticole* (Drouillard, 2000). Covering an area of some 60,000 hectares and thus 55 percent of "the Bordelais", the 3,800 producer-members and 3,000 members of co-operatives which belong to this *syndicat* each year produce more than 350 million bottles of medium-priced red wine (more than half of Bordeaux's total production). Over and above these consolidated statistics, it is important to grasp three points. First, over the last twenty years wine the quantity of wine produced in this region has increased considerably, and in particular through the replacement of white by red wine.[5] This level of production means that the *syndicat viticole* is particularly well positioned in terms of voting rights in the FGVB.[6] Second, the average price has increased dramatically (figures), a change that reflects not only trends in external market conditions, but the effect of norms established and policed by the syndicat and symbolized by the name given to its new headquarters opened in 1979: *La maison de qualité*.

We will return to the question of norms in the next section. What we want to stress here is the inextricable relationship between a policy of improving wine quality and competition for the leadership of the *syndicat*. Two leaderships in particular need to be understood. The first was that led by Louis Marinier from 1974 to his death in 1985. During this period, Marinier clearly set out to build himself a reputation as the defender of the small producer and the simple label of "the Bordeaux". Described by journalists as "le père des petits châteaux", in his first year as president he was in open conflict with the leadership of the FGVB and played a part in its downfall. At the same time he also took on opponents in the BBS region by arguing in favour of red as opposed to white wine. More generally, his leadership is an important part of our study because he was one of the first representatives to argue in favour of policies to improve the quality of generic Bordeaux wine.[7]

Son of a well-known county councillor (*conseiller général*), over a mandate that lasted more than 10 years, Jean-Louis Trocard developed this discourse on quality and made it his central policy. Elected president at the age of only 36, Trocard rapidly also became president of the FGVB, the CIVB and the national CNAOC. From this "multi-position", he was able to argue with effect for policies that we will return to in section 2. In addition, this result was in part achieved by using a discourse marked by the terminology of the enterprise, which will be picked up on in section 3.

These points on the Bordelais in general, and on the BBS in particular, clearly need more development. Nevertheless, we have seen that change within the BBS area and syndicat viticole have had a decisive impact upon the wine politics of the whole Bordelais region.

Problem shaping and policy making

A second dimension to this analysis of competing wine leaderships is how the groups concerned have sought to aggregate and defend their interests. Called upon to take positions on precise questions such as planting quotas, labeling and promotion, Bordelais wine leaderships are constantly confronted with the question of how to regulate their sector at a time of great market uncertainty. By process tracing a number of key decisions, our research as a whole will endeavour to show how different actors have sought not only to define what constitutes "the problem" for them and their fellow producers, but also how they have tried to get this definition shared by representatives of other regions at the national and European level. In this chapter, we will limit the demonstration firstly to how different leaderships have sought to regulate the production of wine in the Bordelais region and, secondly, to their visions of how this product should be marketed. In both cases, connections between leaderships and actors outside the region need to be understood.

The regulation of production

As alluded to earlier, until the 1980s wine producers in this region tended to consider that there was a direct link between the amount of wine on the market and its price. At times of low prices (e.g. 1973-75) this postulate from neo-classical economics led producer representatives to try to reduce the size of the market by setting up systems of guaranteed threshold prices and storage (*stock régulateur*). This approach was pushed for even harder by producers from other regions such as the Midi (Genieys & Smith, 2000) and other countries, in particular Spain and Italy. Indeed, it became the basis of the European Communities wine policy until the mid-1980s (De Maillard, 2001). However, most representatives of Bordeaux's wine producers have rarely been entirely comfortable with this level of public intervention. Rather than accept the culturalist explanations offered by these representatives themselves,[8] the role of ideas here is better seen through how the perception of public problems contributes to the way these problems become defined and institutionalized through negotiation, custom and contracts. From this perspective one can better understand how the algorithm of "controlling production levels to keep prices high" has been replaced by that of "improving wine quality to attract higher prices". Without going into the detail of a highly complex issue, the politics of this change can be looked at by examining two points: controls on quality and rights to plant.

Labeled by some as organized "self-censorship", controls on wine quality work through a system of criteria that wine has to meet in order for a producer to have the right to bear the AOC name on his or her bottles (the *agrément* procedure). Without going into great detail, these norms have become increasingly strict, pushed by leaders such as Marinier and Trocard.[9] But collective action of this type has also been accompanied by the establishment of state-funded oenological and agronomic laboratories in this region. Although some of the actions in this direction taken by the leadership of the BBS have been contested by representatives of the nationally dominant farming union (the FNSEA), they have consistently been able to rely for support upon the *département*-level Chamber of Agriculture and local delegates from the bank *Le Crédit Agricole*. To give some idea of the success of this route to improving wine quality, in 1970 only 70 percent of the wines produced in Bordeaux were sold under AOC labels. Today this figure is nearer 100 percent, a change which serves to highlight how important low quality "vins de table" used to be in this region and no longer are.

A second issue we have looked at in detail as a case study of wine leaderships in actions concerns the rights of producers to plant new vines. In Europe, new plantings are strictly controlled by civil servants of the French state acting within limits set by EU legislations. If our evidence shows that Bordealais actors are active in the setting of European quotas, here we are more interested in two other issues related to this subject. First, we have looked at how new rights obtained "in Brussels" by representatives of the French government are redistributed between French regions. Here the manner through which Bordealais leaderships operate at the national level, particularly by putting forward their contribution to French exports and GDP, is highly revealing of the strength of the networks they are able to activate at this level. Second, Bordealais representatives have also been highly active to influence the norms governing the implementation of infra-national, and infra-regional, quota distribution. Issues such as how rights unsold in one region can be sold to producers from another have provoked serious and sometimes violent conflicts. Indeed, within the Bordealais itself, the issue or reselling rights has on occasions threatened solidarity between large and small producers, particularly those who live and work in the area that comes under the authority of the Bordeaux and Bordeaux supérieur synidcat.

Both these aspects of market regulation have thus involved the leaderships under study in a form continuous activity that elsewhere I have labeled "multi-interest representation" (Smith, 2001). In short, these sorts of issues illustrate how in analytical terms the strength of interest group leaderships in the Bordealais cannot be separated from their relationship to sources of influence at national and European levels.

Promotion and marketing

In the politics of wine, two aspects of promotion and marketing make this activity a potentially conflicting issue: generating a budget and spending it.

As regards the generation of revenues for promotion and marketing, this has in large part been channeled through the CIVB, an organization where promotion now accounts for over 75 percent of its annual budget. In 1999, its then president, Jean-Louis Trocard, campaigned successfully to increase subscriptions to this organization by no less than 50 percent. Although the president himself plays down the difficulty of this exercise,[10] considerable efforts were made to get to a situation where 90 percent of producers voted to accept the subscription increase. Two points explain in part this result. The first is the importance of a discourse on the danger of underestimating competition from other producers.[11] In newspaper interviews and professional magazines, this "context" is symbolized as a struggle between the (noble and unsuspecting) Bordelais and (crafty and unscrupulous) producers from an amorphous but dangerous "New World". The second is that the increase in subscriptions was linked to a change in the rules giving more autonomy on promotion to each *syndicat viticole*.[12]

Table 10.3 The CIVB's promotion budget

Year	Promotion budget (francs)
1971	7,500,000
1978	12,000,000
1981	18,400,000
1983	39,000,000
1988	65,000,000
1991	80,000,000
1994	89,000,000
1998	108,000,000
2000	125,000,000

As the last point suggests, spending the CIVB's promotion budget is another issue where bargains need to be struck and where leaderships can be contested or, conversely, gain legitimacy. Here it is important to understand that funds for the promotion of wine are redistributed to each type of wine on a pro rata basis linked to the total value of sales. Again, this system favours the promotion of generic red wine, and the BBS syndicat in particular.[13] Indeed, more generally the choices made over promotion by the FGVB and the CIVB often cause resentment in other areas where finer quality wine is produced and high prices seem almost guaranteed. One representative of the Sauterne, for example, grumbled to us about the hidden social policy that supports some producers in the Bordelais, producers of wine that he denigrated as "du Bordeaux social". Other issues concern the choice of target export markets and, as we shall see below, the images used to communicate to the general public.

Discourse, symbols and legitimation

As we have already seen, wine policy is not just the result of competing technocratic designs for dealing with self-evident visions of contemporary "market crises" and the resulting "need" for public intervention. Instead, "expert" and less expert opinion is divided and the winners of the debates which structure the making of wine policy have in reality not only advanced more or less sophisticated action theories, but also appealed to values that strike a chord with producers and public actors. This question of the role of values in public problem shaping and policy making overlaps strongly with the final dimension of our approach to political leadership: how the actors involved have attempted to legitimate themselves and their actions through communication, or what Marc Abélès has conceptualized as "evocation" (1989). In this respect discourse and symbolic acts, and in particular the use of lexicons of tradition and modernity, needs to be given specific attention. At least in this field, leaderships appear unable to use just one of these lexicons. Instead, judicious cocktails of both are used to justify policies and priorities whilst legitimating leaders and their forms of leadership.

The lexicon of tradition

A product like wine is repeatedly linked to a history that is said to go back thousands of years. In the Bordeaux region time is more often counted in centuries but is still very much a part both of promotional activity and of discourse used to justify particular forms of interest aggregation and market regulation.

In terms of collective action in the field of promotion, one can cite the plethora of brochures that emphasize the temporal anchorage of wine production in this region and, implicitly or explicitly, compare this favorably with the "virtualness" of wine from "the New World".[14] As the creation of a wine festival in Bordeaux itself as late as 1998 serves to testify, history can also be invented or reshaped for "commercial reasons" that have as much to do with reinforcing leaderships as they do about conquering markets.

But an appeal to tradition is also often used by leaders to convince producers that they must take steps to improve or maintain the quality of their production. In Saint-Emilion, for example, leaders have often linked the question of quality to the uniqueness of an architectural heritage recently consecrated by UNESCO in June 2000 as a "world heritage site" (Roudié, 2000).[15] More generally, the reference to tradition that most often seems to strike a chord with producers is that of the *terroir*, an area that corresponds to the limits of an A.O.C. (Boisseux & Leresche, 2000). In such cases the elements that make up the unity of a terroir are played up (the soil, the proximity to a river, etc.), allowing leaders to play down, where necessary, other factors that strike and symbolize discord, in particular oppositions between members of the same *syndicat viticole*.

The lexicon of modernity

At the same time, no leadership can rely purely upon the lexicon of tradition because of the danger of being seen as insufficiently dynamic, nostalgic or even reactionary. Instead, a blend needs to be found between references to the past and words, symbols and arguments from a lexicon of modernity. Here, as in many other sectors and regions, the key terms revolve around the notion of "enterprise". Three examples help to show this discourse in action and allow us to return to the central hypothesis of this chapter concerning the importance of the leadership of the BBS to understanding the wine politics of the Bordelais.

The first concerns the way leaders in this region have sought to update the A.O.C. as a policy concept whilst maintaining its historical and sociological resonance. Here the public discourse of Jean-Louis Trocard is of particular significance. Reminiscing in a professional magazine about his mandates as president of the FGVB and the CIVB, this actor declared that he had consistently sought to orientate these organizations towards issues that relate as much to the individual wine producing enterprise as to the AOC.[16] What this actor deliberately left unstated is that today the AOC is as much a brand for marketing as it is for regulating the quality of production. In addition, it the concept of the AOC remains a powerful means with which to counter the desire by a number of wine merchants to create a generic Bordeaux *vin de cépage* that would be free of the constraints of the AOCs, and therefore beyond the control of the leadership of wine producers. In particular, of course, such a wine would potentially be a threat to BBS wines and its leadership.[17]

The second example of the use of the modernity lexicon concerns the creation of an international trade fair: VINEXPO. Created by the FGVB-CIVB leadership in 1981, this faire is held in Bordeaux every two years and attracts exhibitors, merchants and other buyers from around the world. What is important to highlight, however, is that when the idea to hold such an event in Bordeaux was first mooted it attracted considerable scepticism and even opposition. In particular, inviting producers from the "New World" was seen as "putting the wolf in the sheep-pen".[18] Nevertheless, the leadership of the day prevailed and their successors now reap the benefits of an institutionalized and successful event where they can theatralize their commitment to modernization and the entrepreneurial spirit.

The third and final example of the use of the lexicon of modernity concerns a decision to focus advertising for Bordeaux wines upon the young consumer.[19] Using young wine producers as models, this campaign deliberately set out to break with the image of Bordeaux wines as produced by ageing farmers and drunk by old cigar-smoking men in armchairs. Instead, the "consumer of tomorrow" is shown that the producers of Bordeaux are now very much men and women of today.

Conclusion

We clearly still have a great deal of empirical work still to do on our study of the politics of wine in the Bordelais region. Nevertheless, the story we have so far been able to piece together has led us to develop in some detail two points that I hope will be of more general interest to readers of this book.

First, this case study shows that "globalization" is not an all-encompassing and anonymous trend which causes automatic and across the board change in political priorities and practices. Instead it is more a term that synthesizes a number of developments in contemporary capitalism which can cause the challenges for collective and public action to be redefined. Looking at precise case studies is a means of discovering who is engaged in this redefining and the extent to which the changes observed actually reflect significant shifts in the distribution of power.

Second, this chapter has also attempted to show that, when used as an analytical concept, leadership is an effective and stimulating way of investigating these "who" and "how" questions. In testing the claim made here that interest group leadership struggles revolve around three identifiable poles – electoral competition and eligibility, collective and public action and evocation – this chapter has also set out to show how research can be designed in order to grasp the different but interdependent dimensions of sectoral power.

References

Abélès M. (1989). *Journées tranquilles en 89*, Paris: Odile Jacob.
Boisseux S., Leresche J-Ph. (2000), "les terroirs européens face à la globalisation: entre corporatismes et néo-régionalismes", Communication au congrès de l'IPSA, Montréal, août.
De Maillard, J. (2001). "La Commission, le vin et la réforme", *Politique européenne*, vol 2 (2).
Drouillard V. (2000). "Histoire du syndicat viticole des appelations Bordeaux: Bordeaux supérieur de 1965 à nos jours", in Fédération historique du Sud-Ouest, *Vignes, vins et vignerons de Saint–Emilion et d'ailleurs*, Bordeaux, Maision des Sciences de l'homme d'Aquitaine.
Genieys W., Smith A. (2000). "Idées et intégration européenne: la grande transformation du Midi rouge", *Politique européenne*, vol 1 (1).
Genieys W., Smith A., Baraize F., Faure A., Négrier E. (2000): "Pour une sociologie du rapport entre leadership et territoire", *Pôle Sud*, no. 13.
Greenwood J. (1997). *Representing interests in the European Union*, London: Macmillan.
Roudié Ph. (2000). "Terroir et histoire à Saint-Emilion ou les éléments du succès mondial d'un site, d'un produit, d'une société", in Fédération historique du Sud-Ouest, *Vignes, vins et vignerons de Saint–Emilion et d'ailleurs*, Bordeaux: Maison des Sciences de l'homme d'Aquitaine.
Smith A. (2001). "Interest Groups and Territorial Governance: The Multi-level Representation of Agriculture in Two French Regions", forthcoming in J. Bukowlski, M. S. Piatonni and M. Smyrl, eds.

Notes

[1] *L'Union girondine des vins de Bordeaux*, July-August, 1999.

[2] A factor which has led some actors in the region, and within his home Bordeaux and Bordeaux supérieur area, to question Trocard's representativity. Trocard's predecessor, Pierre Médeville, was also from the BBS but also had vines in a more lucrative area: the Graves.

[3] Today the Bordedaux *négoce* is made up of 400 companies employing around 5000 people. However, one should note that 30 companies account for 80 percent of the turnover made by these wine merchants. Source : Cocks, *Bordeaux and its wines*, (15th edition), Bordeaux, Editions Féret, 1998. The anonymous authors of this famous annual consider that "the Bordeaux négoce has the power of a large scale enterprise and the flexibility of a small one" (p. 1941).

[4] Figures – The CIVB's annual budget is 130 million francs.

[5] In 1975, the 33 percent of the wine produced in the Bordelais as a whole was white. Today this figure is only 10 percent.

[6] Voting rights are linked to the total value of the wine produced within each syndicat's area. This system has produced some resentment in other parts of the Bordelais. A representative of the Sauterne, for example, bemoaned this situation and, paradoxically for a syndicat with probably the best profitablity per vine, claimed to prefer a federation that was organized more along the lines of a trades union! (Interview, December, 2000).

[7] For example, see an interview in the regional newspaper *Sud-Ouest* from as long ago as the 20th of July, 1983. Through this medium, Marinier argued for an individualization of the CIVB's promotion strategy and changes in its subscriptions before underlining that the only solution to low prices was "quality and more quality".

[8] "L'Etat, moins on le voit, mieux on se porte. On s'auto-organise et on le fait très bien (…) Nous somme girondins et on préfère régler nos affaires entre nous" (interview with ex-president of the FGVB and of the CIVB, November, 2000).

[9] In 1999, as much as 15 percent of wine presented for agrément in the BBS area was refused this status on their first application. The corresponding figures for 1997 and 1998 were 11.6 and 8.7 percent. (*Sud-Ouest*, article "Le rappel à l'ordre du Président").

[10] "L'augmentation est passée plus facilement que je ne le pensais. Mais c'étais mon travail et de toute façon on n'avait pas le choix". Interview, November, 2000.

[11] Our interview with Trocard was frequently punctuated by this "context". for example, "n'oublions pas que l'Europe est le premier marché mondial, les autres visent l'Europe" (November, 2000).

[12] Whereas beforehand a syndicat that devoted one franc to a promotion activity received one franc from the CIVB, since the rise in subscriptions one franc from the syndicat has to be matched by two francs from the CIVB.

[13] A representative of the Sauterne syndicat is highly critical of this system : "Nous pensons que ce système est aberrante, surtout pour la promotion extérieure qui coûte la même chose pour tout le monde. On nous dit que les liquoreux ne pèsent que de 2 percent des chiffres d'affaires du Bordelais mais on a déjà 10 percent du budget promotionM. Moi je dis qu'on est un des 6 groupes organiques du Bordelais et qu'on devrait donc avoir 16 percent: un sixième !" (interview, December 2000).

[14] See for example the brochure "A la découverte du pays des Bordeaux et Bordeaux Supérieur" produced by the BBS syndicat viticole in 1999.

[15] A former President of the *Collège des vins de Saint-Emilion* told us in an interview "quand j'étais président, on était dans la salle de réunion... et moi je leur disais en montrant le clocher de l'église : 'regardez ce dont vous êtes porteurs... vous vous devez être les meilleurs, de défendre cette mémoire" (November, 2000).

[16] "Il faut les orienter vers des préoccupations qui sont d'abord celles de l'entreprise viticole et pas seulement de l'AOC. Plus justement, peut-être, je dirais que la gestion de l'AOC tend de plus en plus aujourd'hui, à ne s'envisager que dans la sécurité des entreprises." *L'Union girondine des vins de Bordeaux*, July-August, 1999, p. 6.

[17] Trocard's successeur as president of the BBS, Jean-Louis Roumage, has repeatedly spoken out publicly against the *vin de cépage* project by using the regional newspaper *Sud-Ouest*. This issue again resurfaced in June, 2001 during the VINEXPO trade fair when a number of wine merchants spoke up for the idea of a 'Girondin' brand.

[18] Interview with former FGVB and CIVB president, June, 2001.

[19] Bordeaux International, no. 3, June, 2001, p. 18.

Chapter 11

Proximity and Social Cohesion in French Local Democracy: Answers to the Increase in Abstention and Political Disaffection?

Laurence Bherer

A foreign observer of French municipal life may find it surprising how few studies there are on participation in local politics.[1] In comparison with other countries where there is a strong tradition of electoral studies of local democracy,[2] local electoral turnout has not been a central issue in the French political science literature.[3] Furthermore, France was not covered by some of the early comparative research programmes on participation. For example, Almond and Verba preferred Great Britain, Italy and Germany to France as European cases for their study on civic culture (1963). The comparison of seven countries published by Verba and his colleagues in 1978 included Austria, the Netherlands and Yugoslavia in Europe but not France. The absence of France from international surveys partially explains why there is little research of a quantitative nature devoted to political attitudes, participation and involvement at the local level.

However, political participation in general is an important topic of French political science. Many French scholars have worked on problems of collective action or electoral turnout from a national or a more general perspective (notably: Lancelot, 1968; Perrineau, 1994). Nevertheless, it remains a fact that there are few studies of participation at the local level. Is local democracy not an issue in France? Actually, the opposite is the case, as demonstrated by the following observations. First, since the important decentralization reform in 1983, the local system has progressively become an important object of investigation, with the development of original research. The interest concerning the process of adaptation of local representatives in a new context of accountability was first the objective of early research in the period following decentralization. In this kind of study, the status and behaviour of local representatives was the object of analysis (for example: Garraud, 1989). The transformation of the links between the State and local government has also received a good deal of attention in research on local politics. Policy analysts especially have taken an interest in the latter topic, pointing out that the new role of the State in the local context is characterized by a construction of negotiation space for the numerous actors involved in the local democratic process (Duran and Thoenig, 1996; Gaudin, 1999). It is also since decentralization that the subject of local democracy has become an issue in the political science literature (Dion, 1984; Mabileau et al., 1987). To sum up, with decentralization, French political scientists have rediscovered the local level and more precisely, the local democratic process.[4]

Second, it would be exaggerated to say that local participation does not interest France, as one of the most important issues in French politics during the Nineties was "participative democracy" and "local democracy".[5] This flood of speeches, laws and policies relating to "participative democracy" and "local democracy" is directly connected to a more general debate on the crisis of the representative institutions and the effect of globalization on democratic practices in national and local democracy. The interest in "participative democracy" touches upon three issues at the core of the French political debate. First, the increase in the abstention rate for all types of elections (European, presidential, legislative, regional, cantonal and municipal) is seen as an expression of serious disaffection of electors and dissolution of trust between citizens and politicians. In this context, "participative democracy" is seen as a measure to move representatives closer to citizens. As municipalities represent the governmental level reputed to be in closest contact with the people, the development of "participative democracy" is particularly intensive at the municipal level. Both national government and municipal councils have promoted participation in local democracy by adopting public policies, legislation and local level experiments. Furthermore, in a desire to re-establish and to create a good social climate, particularly in the poor neighbourhoods bordering some French cities, the development of "participative democracy" fits into schemes for improving social cohesion. In this latter approach, the local level also becomes the space where citizenship could be reconstituted on a new basis. Thus, the creation of local participative tools in the Nineties is justified by these two important frames of reference – proximity and social cohesion – in a desire to foster political trust among French citizens.[6]

Taking into account the widespread discussion focusing on local democracy and participation, it is thus unfair to think that local participation is not an issue in France. French political scientists are increasingly interested by this phenomenon that has also led to the development of local experiments.

In this chapter, we will outline concrete effects of the concern with proximity and social cohesion on the development of local participative institutions. In a context where intensive innovation in participatory institutions is taking place, we deliberately choose an institutional approach to local democracy. We will present a range of participative instruments, which are emerging in French municipal democracy and the issues concerning each one. To do this, we have adopted a comprehensive approach: instead of asking if participative tools represent "real" participation, we will investigate what French public authorities understand by "participative democracy" in the context of local democracy. In the first part, developments concerning electoral participation in local elections and referenda will be presented. The presentation gives an opportunity to review the main hypotheses concerning local electoral turnout in a context of increasing abstention.

We will see that the drop in electoral participation is directly connected to the development of participative institutions at local level. The local participative experiments carried out between elections will be the object of the second part, in respect of the frames of reference (proximity and social cohesion) that are highlighted in national public policies and legislation. In conclusion, we will briefly develop a line of reasoning with regard to the possibility of truly institutionalizing participation in the present-day French municipalities.

Local election turnout and referenda: elusive data

The number of municipalities in France is exceptional. With 36,763 municipalities, the French municipal level is very fragmented. Furthermore, the majority of these municipalities are very small: 33,915 have less than 3,500 inhabitants. Altogether, there are only 37 French cities, which have a population of 100,000 inhabitants or more. This count includes the three biggest ones: Paris (2,147,857), Marseille (807,071) and Lyon (453,187).[7] Even if the idea of amalgamation returns regularly to the political scene, there is not a strong and clear political will to initiate this reform. To reduce the number of municipalities would be seen as an attack on an important symbol of the French Republic. In addition, the legitimacy of national representatives is partially rooted in their mandates as local representatives: for deputies or ministers, to have some local a responsibility demonstrates a degree of contact with the people. This is why the accumulation of mandates is so important in the French political system. It is a way of preventing a strong centralism around Paris and the isolation of the national political institutions from local issues.[8]

The local electoral system reflects the heterogeneity of French municipalities. In those of less than 3,500 inhabitants, the municipal council is elected by a majority plurinomal electoral system with two rounds. The electors have to choose from fixed lists of candidates, but they can also: 1) change the order of candidates in the lists; or 2) replace a candidate by a person who is not on the list; or 3) compose a new list on the basis of the fixed lists.[9] To add to the complexity of the local electoral system, the rules for determining the winning candidates are not the same for the first and the second rounds.

Since decentralization in 1983, the municipalities of 3,500 inhabitants or more are subject to an electoral system, which combines proportional, and majority rules. The electors choose from fixed lists, with no right to change the order and the name of the candidates in the same way as in the small municipalities. The distribution of the number of seats in the local councils depends on whether the winning lists have won the majority in the first or the second round. The principle is based on the idea that the winning list should have a good majority, but that the opposition lists obtaining at least 5% of the votes should also have some seats.[10]

In this context, the local level turnout is hard to gauge. The number of French municipalities and the disparity of the local electoral systems make it difficult to give a general overview of local electoral participation in France. The compilation of results is arduous. This is why we found few general and comparative studies on electoral turnout in France. Furthermore, studies, which seek to cross a group of variables, are almost nonexistent. Usually, researchers prefer to focus on some categories of municipalities, referring to the larger ones and seldom the smaller. In addition, the analysis of election turnout is undeveloped because it is often part of a study, which aims to present all the ins-and-outs of local elections.[11] Fortunately for this brief review of local democracy in France, the analysis of municipal election campaigns and their results is systematic for each election.[12] To compensate for the lack of electoral data, we will, first, briefly present the data available and, then, a number of hypotheses to explain local electoral participation will be reviewed.

Table 11.1 shows the electoral turnout in the 10 municipal elections since the end of the Second World War. The reduction in the participation rate from the Eighties until now is particularly striking: since the municipal elections of 1989, it has dropped successively from the record established in 1959, each electoral turnout being lower than the previous one. In addition, electoral participation could actually be lower, because as Hoffmann-Martinot has pointed out, this statistic does not take into account citizens who are not registered on any electoral list (1999:119).[13] In fact, the municipal electoral turnouts follow the national downward trend, which has been observed in all types of French elections for over ten years, after a decade of strong electoral participation (1974-1986) (Subileau, 2001A: 1). This line of analysis tends to confirm the strong links between French national and local politics: the results of the local elections are partially explained by the issues of national politics. We shall return below to this type of argument.

Table 11.1 Electoral turnout in municipal elections 1947-2001 (percentages)[14]

Year	1947	1953	1959	1965	1971	1977	1983	1989	1995	2001
Turnout	77	80	75	78	75	79	78	73	69	67

Sources: Martin, 2001a: 176 and Martin, 2001b: 364.

As many electoral studies have shown, electoral participation is higher in the smaller municipalities than in the larger ones. This is also the case among French municipalities (Martin, 2001B; Le Bart, 2001). The literature on French rural municipalities has characterized the political scene by: 1) a low degree of competition in electoral campaigns (Nevers, 1992); 2) a system of transferring power among mayoral candidates chosen from local dignitaries and family members (Faure, 1992; Abélès, 1989). The low level of politicization of villages and towns was described by Kesselman in 1966 as an "ambiguous consensus" ever present in the rhetoric of the contemporary French rural actors (Kesselman, 1966). Indeed, in the rural municipalities, the party system is not very well developed. But, to compensate for this fact, the rural political scene offers a political context easier to understand for the voters. The right to change the fixed list of candidates is a tool which could give a voter greater influence on municipal life. The social control, stronger in small municipalities, also explains the high level of electoral participation. For the individual voter, anonymity is impossible: the choice not to carry out the "civic duty" of voting is socially more costly (Subileau, 2001B: 49).

A 2001 paper from Le Gall gives us a comparison of electoral turnouts according to the size of the municipalities. An analysis of table 11.2 demonstrates that the participation in elections in small municipalities is greater than in the larger ones. Whereas in the rural municipalities the participation rate is around 80%, the electoral turnout is approximately 60% in cities of over 30,000 inhabitants. The electoral turnout is thus in inverse proportion to the size of the municipalities: the smaller a municipality, the higher the participation of its inhabitants. However table 11.2 shows that abstention is not only an urban reality: as in the cities, electoral participation had also been dropping continuously since the Eighties in rural municipalities. The urban political apathy seems to have to spread to the rural political process (Le Gall, 2001: 7).

Table 11.2 Electoral turnout in municipal elections 1983-2001, according to the number of inhabitants[15]

	1983	1989	1995	2001
Under 3,500	85.6	82.0	79.1	76.5
From 3,500 to 9,000	80.4	74.5	71.3	65.4
From 9,000 to 30,000	74.7	67.6	64.2	61.3
Over 30,000	70.1	62.0	57.9	56.9
Mean	78.4	72.8	69.4	67.4

Source: Le Gall, 2001: 7.

How do French scholars explain municipal electoral participation? In a context where the electoral data is elusive, it would appear to be useful to look at the different hypotheses that have been offered to explain the results of local elections and more particularly, the participation rate. First, few studies seek to define the profile of the participant and abstentionist voters in the context of a local election. Usually, scholars suggest that the local abstentionists will be of the same profile for both local and other types of French elections. Subileau gives some information on the local abstentionist electorate. The non-voters belong predominantly to the following groups: people in social difficulties (unemployed, low salary and non-graduate), the young between 25 and 39 years old, single people, students, workers and new residents of a community. But as the drop in electoral turnout has been noticed in all types of elections, it is tempting to talk about "a nationalization of electoral behaviour" (Subileau, 2001B: 50). Municipal electoral participation cannot thus be isolated from the national context.

This debate on the influence of national politics is a recurrent theme in analyses of French municipal elections: are electors' choice and participation rates influenced by national or by local political events? Is it possible to analyse 36,763 different municipal elections, each with specific issues, by a national approach? In fact, two positions exist regarding this issue, sometimes opposed and sometimes complementary. One line of analysis, which was inspired by the model of the "midterm elections" in the USA, shows that the results of local elections are directly connected to national electoral issues (Parodi, 1982). It is in the nature of municipalities (lack of an autonomous party system) that municipal elections will largely be influenced by the national situation and, in this context, local elections could be seen as "second order" elections. Two scenarios related to the electoral cycle have been outlined. If municipal elections are held just before national elections (presidential or legislative elections), the choice of the voters would be determined by their degree of (dis)satisfaction with the record of the President or that of the government. In this scenario, participation in local elections would be high. On the other hand, if municipal elections are held *after* an important national election, the electoral climate is pacified. It is then an election "without obligation and sanction" for the representatives. In this kind of "intermediate election", electoral turnout is lower. Without a national issue and with a high level of satisfaction, neither the opposition nor the majority electorates are mobilized. The local context would be more important for the choice of the voters. This is why an intermediate election is less predictive of the results of the next national election than the first scenario, which may be a good indication of the voters' mood. Thus, the position of the municipal election in the national electoral cycle is vital for understanding the behaviour of electors (Jadot, 2001). Martin has successfully tested this model for the municipal elections since 1945 (2001A). According to him, the larger the municipality, the closer the municipal electoral issue is related to national politics.

The second approach prefers to localize the municipal elections, namely to interpret the electoral results according to the local political process specific to each municipality. Lehingue states that "the most fragmented municipal poll in Europe" cannot be the object of a simple analysis, which tends to gather together a jumble of different local contexts (Lehingue, 2001). For example, the meaning of an electoral success is not simple: a victory could hide a protest vote more than demonstrate allegiance to the successful team. Only a local analysis can reveal this fact. Furthermore, the average rate of participation does not reflect the strong geographical, political and social disparities that characterize French municipalities as a whole. This approach is an invitation to take French municipal variety into account and to render more complex the analysis of the municipal election results. In other words, the municipal poll has to be read by a bottom-up approach. This field of research prefers case studies, of which the book of Dolez and Laurent (2002) is a good example. However, this approach tends to focus on the game surrounding local political teams and gives few details about the local factors in the electoral turnout.

The study of Hoffmann-Martinot is atypical in this literature. He also rejects the national approach to interpreting local voting but, unlike the "political localists", he does not limit his analysis to political life in each municipality. Hoffmann-Martinot rather tries to widen the study of voting to a group of factors that serve to differentiate municipalities and that may describe the abstentionist and the participationist municipalities. Based on a range of explanations from literature on voting behaviour, he has tested 10 hypotheses relating to the political context, spatial factors, political culture and social situation (Hoffmann-Martinot, 1992). Furthermore, Hoffmann-Martinot takes into account the full electorate (18 years old and more) and not only registered voters, to calculate the electoral turnout. With correlation and multivariate regression analyses, he found that three variables can explain the French municipal election turnout: 1) the degree of social cohesion of the territory of a municipality (hypothesis based on the "urbanness continuum" model of Verba and Nie, 1972); 2) the intensity of political competition (the greater the number of political lists during an election, the lower the electoral turnout); 3) the kind of local political culture present in a region (clientelism or strong democratic roots and the presence of an influential group of owners). In a comparative study, these hypotheses have been also tested with success in Great Britain: the same variables determine variation in electoral turnout in both countries (Hoffmann-Martinot, Rallings and Thrasher, 1996).[16] The perfect French participationist and abstentionist cities could thus be described:

> The participationist city *par excellence* – a Northern or Southern medium-sized municipality, isolated from major intermingling of populations, and characterized by strong opposition between Left and Right – as opposed to a radically abstentionist city, defined by the opposite characteristics: ill-defined historical, territorial and demographic autonomy, with a unclear or floating political space (My translation: Hoffmann-Martinot, 1992: 34).

This kind of analysis remains exceptional in French literature on municipal democracy. It would, therefore, be interesting to conduct follow-up analyses with the same hypotheses to ascertain the evolution of the vote. As the data of Hoffmann-Martinot came from the 1983 municipal election of cities of over 20,000 inhabitants, the abstention was not as marked as today. A new analysis could help gain a better understanding of this fast-growing phenomenon.

The presentation of the local vote would not be complete without a discussion of *local referenda*. Are referenda possible at French local level? Is the referendum a practice integrated in the local democratic process? The answer is ambivalent. Even if the law has evolved since the Sixties, the practice of local referendum is moderate. First, the French Constitution indirectly restricts the use of a local referendum to a consultative role: direct democracy is forbidden since the local council cannot transfer its legitimate decision-making power to citizens (Raséra, 2002: 116-117). The first attempt to codify the local referendum is the law of 1971 on municipal amalgamation.[17] In this framework, the referendum was a tool that could be initiated by the Prefect, if some of the local councils involved in a project of amalgamation included several municipalities particularly hostile to the idea of municipal merger. In fact, this is a measure of last resort in a complex process of amalgamation. An observer of the time already pointed out the inefficiency of this referendum procedure. According to him, the merger referendum would be an infrequently used tool (Becet, 1971). With the lack of amalgamation projects, events proved him absolutely right (Aubry, 1989). Marion Paoletti, who has done very interesting work on local referenda and the French approach to local democracy, counted 157 local referenda between 1971 and 1991 (Paoletti, 1997:

85-86).[18] In a country which includes 36,763 municipalities, this number is very low. In addition, Paoletti has shown, using a survey, that the majority of these local referenda were developed in municipalities of under 3,500 inhabitants. The referendum is usually a political tool used by the mayor to reject a project initiated from outside municipal life (for example, from the State, train or electricity companies, property developers, etc.) or to settle a question which divides the local council or the population. In the first case, the referendum is used as a means of exerting symbolic pressure and in the second case, as a way to legitimize a decision and to pacify the social climate in the municipality. In 1992 and 1995, new laws extended the application of the local referendum and recognized legally a practice, which already existed in a few municipalities. Now the mayor and the local council can initiate a referendum and, in the exceptional case of a planning project, the local population can request a referendum. In the latter case, the rules are strictly defined and in this sense, popular initiatives are rare. After the promulgation of the 1992 law, the number of referenda has increased although the local referendum remains an exception: since 1993, about 200 referenda have been held, which is an interesting but still limited increase (Raséra, 2002: 117-119).

Nevertheless, the legal recognition of the referendum bears witness to French interest in local and participative democracy, particularly evident during the Nineties and which still continues today. The 1992 and 1995 acts have helped to develop and legitimize the issue of participative democracy. Both laws and the creation of several participative tools in local democracy are directly connected to the political explanation of the increase in abstention as a French national movement, which, as mentioned above, can be observed in all types of elections. Political discourse on abstention is concerned with finding the roots of voter disaffection. Many observers have noted that French institutions have lost their transparency. For citizens, it is becoming increasingly difficult to develop clear political opinions faced with a fragmenting party system: since the Eighties, the electoral lists have grown in number, indicating an erosion of the traditional dichotomy of the Right and the Left. The political parties on each side find it difficult to create a coalition for each type of elections. During the 2002 presidential election, a new record was reached: 16 candidates for the mandate. Furthermore, French electors were called to the polls on a record number of occasions during the Nineties. In addition to the usual seven types of elections, French electors have known two national referenda and with the dissolution of the National Assembly, one legislative election in addition. In this context, abstention would be the confirmation of the Swiss syndrome: too much voting produces a weariness among electors. Furthermore, the progress of the Europeanization of French politics and the uncertainty engendered by phenomena of globalization (for example, workers' redundancies in factories in the North) add to the institutional confusion. In this context, the political actors are looking for new solutions. The development of participative institutions in local democracy is one of the most important political responses to the problem of rebuilding proximity between citizens and representatives and social cohesion among citizens.

Proximity and social cohesion: a 'gentle command' to participate in local democracy

Participation and local democracy have become important issues in France. In the traditional Presidential New Year message for 2001, the President, Jacques Chirac, called for greater local involvement: "Everyone's participation in the life of his/her city is too limited. We need to open it up to everyone" (*Le Monde*, January 4, 2001). The Prime minister, Lionel Jospin, also broached the topic of participation, by announcing, almost at the same moment, new legislation on local democracy. The initiative became known as the Proximity Act. During the 2001 municipal elections, two issues were particularly highlighted: the problems of insecurity in French cities and the need for greater proximity between political institutions and citizens. The latter issue was developed by the main political parties, but also by a new kind of municipal candidature: the "citizen lists". Initiated in Toulouse (Southern city of 398,423 inhabitants) and presented in about twenty French cities, these lists are interesting because of what the proponents claim about local democracy in France.[19] The "citizen lists" reject the professionalization of political life, which is seen as a cause of a growing gap between "ordinary citizens" and representatives. Their members present themselves as a disillusioned people of the Left and, more generally, of the party system. They come from the world of voluntary associations, from the poor suburbs inhabited in large part by people of different ethnic origins, and from a variety of Left wing parties. The "citizen lists" demand greater participation and direct democracy as a way to bring citizens and representatives closer to each other. As Guionnet pointed out, they wish to restore a link and an exchange between the local community and its politicians (2002). In short, they want to ensure that the "top" hears the rank and file by giving a voice to people in participative forums.[20]

Without exaggerating the influence of the "citizen lists" on the 2001 municipal elections, the emergence of this kind of non-politicized groups in an election, with clear claims for participative democracy, is symptomatic of how the issue of local democracy is formulated in France. This phenomenon is all the more interesting because the people who initiated this movement come from the poor suburbs, where a policy against social exclusion – the Urban Policy Programme – has been implemented since the Eighties. The Urban Policy Programme[21] has a clear objective of "participation of inhabitants" but the initiators of the "citizen lists" were not accepted in the measures of the Urban Policy Programme, even though they were encouraged to participate at the beginning – and they also managed to organize interesting events (in particular, a pop festival). This experience of non-participation served as a foundation to organizing the "citizens lists": according to their proponents, projects have to come from the neighbourhood and should not be defined for its inhabitants from outside the neighbourhood (Visier and Zoïa, 2001).

The "citizen lists" of 2001, with their participative discourse, belong to a wider French movement, promoting participation and local democracy. This is clearly evident in national policies as well as in participative experiments carried out in several French cities. The flood of legislation and policies on participative procedures was interpreted by some French analysts as an emergence of a new norm for public policy (Blondiaux, 2002). The legitimacy of political decisions is now based on a "deliberative norm", discernible in various public policies (ethics and sciences, health, environment, planning, and so on).[22] These participatory arrangements – such as consultative committees, national hearings, forums, special surveys, etc. – have few common points concerning how they work, but they all demonstrate a desire to find new ways of more closely involving citizen and groups in policy elaboration. A "gentle command" to participate is thus obvious in French public life: the citizen is invited via many channels to be involved in public affairs. The local experiments and the policies concerning local democracy also contribute to the recognition and the strengthening of the participative norm in public policies. In the following paragraphs, we focus on how the participative norm is displayed in the local process, in respect of the frames of reference detailed in the introduction (social cohesion and proximity). Some types of representative local experiments are also presented in order to evaluate the impact of the "gentle command" to participate in local democracy.

Participation and social cohesion

The desire to rebuild social links by the promotion of participation is particularly evident in the Urban Policy Programme. This policy was born at the beginning of the Eighties in response to violence and social difficulties in the poorer French neighbourhoods (mainly in the suburbs). Its objectives were ambitious: to combat social exclusion and spatial segregation. With an area-based approach, the Urban Policy Programme made use of a range of social indices to identify the most disadvantaged neighbourhoods. It has four main principles: 1) comprehensive measures in the territory selected; 2) multilateral processes of co-ordination are established among the public sectors involved, with a sharing of information by the different actors and a federation of the different initiatives; 3) the Urban Policy Programme encourages "participation of the inhabitants"; 4) it is the object of a periodically-renewed contract between the actors. The first measures of the Urban Policy Programme gave priority to housing renovation and the building of neighbourhood facilities (sport, community equipment, leisure, and so on). In addition, the Urban Policy Programme was progressively integrated with the State, with a creation of a Ministry of Urban Development, inter-sectorial delegation to be in charge of the links between ministries on policy issues and a consultative organization. In the wake of criticisms about the measures being limited to housing and facilities, subsequent programmes were drawn up with a local development approach to well-integrated economical and social actions.

The Urban Policy Programme is unusual because, contrary to traditional policies, it aims not to define contents but to put in place a new process, or a negotiating space between the actors present in the disadvantaged neighbourhoods. The contracts are negotiated between the territorial actors (City Hall, Prefect, Département, region, associations, decentralized ministries, etc.) resulting in the fact that interpretation of the Urban Policy Programme objectives is specific to each territory, with some degree of autonomy. This last remark is particularly true for the application of the will to participate. It is the responsibility of each contract to define the way in which participation will be encouraged and developed. This is why the participative experiments are so different and difficult to list. The cases cited by the French literature show how subjective the term "participation" is and relative to the context in which it is promoted. In the Urban Policy Programme, participation and citizenship are brought together: participation is seen as a means for citizens to develop their citizenship. Poverty is understood as a situation characterized by lack of both financial and social resources. In fact, in the Urban Policy Programme, participation is less a way to influence public authorities than to experiment with empowerment. In this context, involvement in public life is interpreted as a demonstration of social integration (Helly, 1999: 36-37). With its objectives of "participation of the inhabitants", the Urban Policy Programme seeks to take into account the voice of the "have-nots" in order to restore their membership in society. Its participative aims are thus ambitious. It is not surprising that under the umbrella of participation, the managers of the Urban Policy Programme group together several different experiments: 1) parents are approached to be involved in helping homework workshops for children; 2) the creation of posts of mediators, with the task of bringing in everyday worries; 3) the establishment of exchanges between social housing administrators and their residents; 4) a range of consultative tools (neighbourhood councils, special "dialogue days", special purpose committees, information meetings); 5) decentralization of municipal offices; 6) formal recognition of the role of associations in charge of social issues; and so on. Box 1 gives an example of initiatives with the hallmark "Urban Policy Programme" in Bordeaux.

Nevertheless, the degree of success and efficiency of the Urban Policy Programme's objective of participation is difficult to evaluate. First, as we have said, the municipalities are free to interpret this objective as they wish. Sometimes, measures proposed are far from a traditional definition of participation, where the citizen is an active partner. Second, the conception of participation is so all-enveloping that the range of actions which addresses the objective of citizenship, is very wide. Third, the political culture of each city has to be taken into account. In a municipality where City Hall is traditionally open to participation, participative experiments are more audacious. In a more cautious city, the participative issue has a long way to go. However, experts in the Urban Policy Programme are very critical about the objective of participation. Blanc and Legrand emphasized from 1987 the pitfalls of the Urban Policy Programme concerning participation (1987). Given the case of Nancy (105,830 inhabitants), they judged that the consultative tools for housing renovation were disappointing for citizens: representatives and civil servants are undecided about entering into dialogue with inhabitants. In addition, for disadvantaged citizens, it is not easy to speak publicly as a group, especially in a context where the authorities have their strategies to discredit or to avoid citizens' requests: 1) culpability (the problem in the neighbourhood must come from its inhabitants); 2) expertise (implying that they, as technicians, possess superior knowledge); 3) a tendency to shift the answers to a problem to another entity. Warin concurs, stating that social housing managers (like other actors, according to us) are more interested by the additional grants brought by the Urban Policy Programme than by open dialogue and consultation with inhabitants: "Their attitude can be summed up in this way: we must involve the inhabitants from time to time for administrative purposes, but without the emancipatory aims of a permanent or wider participation" (Warin, 1995: 153, our translation). Participation remains a pious wish. The absence of certain social groups is also criticized: young people, unemployed people and people of other ethnic origins. In this context, the objective of re-building social cohesion can only be partially realized because the primary target groups are not reached (Bacqué and Sintomer, 2001). This situation is reflected in the flood of intermediaries appointed to take care of mediation.[23] Mediation is an interesting effect of the Urban Policy Programme but its widespread application tends to diminish the objective to empower citizens (Arpaillange, Darlon and Montané, 2001: 20). Finally, it may seem paradoxical to seek to develop citizenship in disadvantaged neighbourhoods, but not in other neighbourhoods, where there is no greater level of participation. Is the lack of social cohesion only a problem of the poorest of our society? Is the enhancement of citizenship just for people in social difficulties?

However, the Urban Policy Programme has also contributed to the development of new channels for the local democratic process. Observers generally agree that participation in the framework of the Urban Policy Programme represents progress, even if the results are not those expected. The participative experiments have opened up a new public space, which allows associations and activists to meet public authorities. Furthermore, with the role of social development agents, the participative tools strengthen a neighbourhood approach to local policies. With the designation of the poorest neighbourhoods, the spatial definition of other neighbourhoods has been progressively put in place in the municipalities where neighbourhoods were not yet of political significance.[24] This last point is important for understanding the development of participative tools related to "proximity".

Example 1

The Urban Policy Programme: examples of participation

As we have seen, the objective of participation is interpreted in different ways by the municipalities. It is impossible to give a complete overview of experiments that are classified as "participative" by French City Halls. In Bordeaux, four consultative experiments are closely related to the Urban Policy Programme. Bordeaux is an example of a city where a participative tradition was totally absent. In this context, the participative tools of the Urban Policy Programme remain limited. The objectives of participation still have to gain legitimacy amongst representatives and municipal employees.

The Dialogue Groups: first degree of mobilization in neighbourhoods

Groups of professionals have been created in some of the five neighbourhoods of Bordeaux covered by the Urban Policy Programme (out of a total of 13 neighbourhoods). These groups organize on a community basis people who normally work in different domains, with the aim of sharing information and co-ordinating their actions (social workers, police officers, youth workers, managers of social structures, and so on). Citizens are not involved in this network, but the members of the groups are responsible for ensuring an efficient two-way flow of information. For City Hall, it was necessary to begin with the professionals and not the citizens because of the lack of civic life in these neighbourhoods. Furthermore, the senior civil servants decided that establishing direct links with "ordinary citizens" is the responsibility of the elected representatives whereas municipal employees need to meet professionals. This is why the "Dialogue Groups" are interesting for the professionals, but it appears that it is not a place where municipal employees can be in touch with citizens. The Dialogue Groups remain organizations that are suitable for addressing emergency problems and not developing permanent measures.

The Think Tanks on Participation: a way to highlight the participative issue among representatives and citizens

Bordeaux was chosen by the consultative organization of the Urban Policy Programme's inter-sectorial delegation to conduct a pilot experiment with the objective of evaluating the implementation of the Programme in Bordeaux (Dunkerke and Strasbourg were also chosen). Led by an expert in participation engaged for this purpose, the group was composed of three representatives, some municipal employees, associations particularly recognized for their democratic life and "dynamic" citizens. City Hall had to seek out associations and citizens from each of the five Urban Policy Programme neighbourhoods. Associations and citizens selected were personally invited to be involved in the Think Tank by the representative in charge of the Urban Policy Programme in Bordeaux. The process was not generally open. Rapidly, the subject of discussion shifted towards general participation of citizens in public life instead of participation in the limited framework of the Urban Policy Programme. However, some members of the three "colleges" did not stay in the group. A core of 10 people came to each meeting. The schedule (meetings held during the day) was not convenient for ordinary citizens and associations. Furthermore, the objective of the group was confused: the group never had any clear tasks. In reality, the "Think Tank" was a way to make use of participatory instruments to enhance the legitimacy and visibility of City Hall. The need for recognition was a subject discussed by the members of the group. Recently, the mandate of the group has been renewed in order to establish clear links with each department of the City Hall.

The Citizens' Dialogue Group: how to involve people in difficult circumstances

French municipalities have limited powers in the social domain. They are responsible for emergency and front-line social measures, such as emergency housing for the homeless, housing, food bonds, and so on. With the adoption by the National Assembly of an Act Against Exclusion, which encouraged participation, in 1999 Bordeaux's authorities decided to form a group of citizens or associations that were users of social services managed by the municipality.[25] The group is a mix of people in difficulties and people involved in charity associations. The aim of the group is to start a dialogue between municipal employees and citizens, in order to improve services. But this user approach was rapidly rejected in favour of a "citizen" approach: dialogue and expression were promoted to a greater extent. Workshops were formed for housing, social laws, public transport. Two problems appeared: first, the municipal employees viewed this initiative as an indirect way for the managers to evaluate and criticize their work. They were extremely suspicious. Second, the citizens had a secret hope to resolve their problems by participating in the Citizens' Dialogue Group: to find accommodation, to get a job or to obtain French nationality papers. Some of them expressed their disappointment: even if they were totally involved in the Group, their efforts did not lead to solutions to their own problems. This experiment shows to what degree participation is limited for the "have-nots": is it possible to think of the quality of life when you are in crisis situation? Furthermore, the group aims to improve Bordeaux's social services whereas the involved citizens seek to get out of their difficult condition. Nevertheless, some of them agree that Citizens' Dialogue Group has allowed them to familiarize themselves with their rights through the workshops.

The project 'How to live together better': experimentation or last resort project?

In two neighbourhoods, Bordeaux has a pilot experiment to elaborate a "neighbourhood plan" with all the actors who work and live in these neighbourhoods. The aim is to establish priorities concerning welfare services, planning and facilities. Consultation was conducted by two elected representatives, with the help of the development agent of these neighbourhoods. Each group (citizens, professionals from institutions and social workers) was consulted separately during the course of one day. The consultative process was attractive for everyone but the participants did not know what the next step was. When will the "neighbourhood plan" be implemented? At present they do not understand the objectives of the municipality because they have no news. Is participation an end in itself or is it a tool for transformation?

Participation and proximity

The distinction we have made so far between participative tools for the enhancement of social cohesion and proximity respectively may be difficult to maintain in actual practice. In fact, the two arguments are mixed, especially in the Urban Policy Programme neighbourhoods. In the latter, we find some "proximity tools" also with clear objectives concerning social cohesion. But, contrary to the social cohesion framework, the proximity experiments are territorially extensive and restrictive on people involved in the participative relationship: on the one hand, proximity frameworks are found not only in neighbourhoods in difficulty: each area of the city is covered by these initiatives. On the other hand, the proximity rhetoric put the emphasis only on the links between representatives (sometimes the public authorities as a whole) and citizens. The creation of social links among citizens is not the first priority of proximity measures.

In the proximity discourse, participation is seen as a complementary tool of representative democracy (Bacqué and Sintomer, 1999: 126). Participation and representation are two sides of the same coin: local democracy. Participative procedures are a means for representatives to get closer to citizens, and in this sense, to better exercise her/his role as a politician. As Lefebvre pointed out, the discourse on "proximity" is seen as a means to manage the "crisis of representation". It reveals a new conception of political legitimacy: the conduct of politics in the immediacy of "ordinary citizens" is a way of keeping politics more humane (Lefebvre, 2001). In a context of political disaffection where representatives appear far from the reality of "ordinary citizens", to profess a desire for nearness is a symbolic response to this problem. Under the umbrella of proximity, a wide range of public initiatives can be identified. First, we may find non-political measures, such as the "proximity agents"[26] and the "proximity police officers", but also new labels for well-known neighbourhood facilities: proximity parks, proximity car parks, and so on. Proximity has become the new term that serves to emphasize the need for local roots among public authorities. Participative organizations with a political mandate have also been set up (principally, the neighbourhood councils). They are put in place along with a range of other tools, such as representatives in charge of each neighbourhood, neighbourhood surgeries, decentralized municipal offices, departments in charge of neighbourhood life, etc. This movement can be interpreted as an attempt to "territorialize" representation. As city council representatives are normally elected by list, their territorial roots are unclear. With a neighbourhood approach to municipal political life, the local representatives try to create direct links with the inhabitants. In this sense, the symbolic aspect of neighbourhood reform is significant.

On the participative side, the concrete expression of the proximity initiatives is above all the creation of neighbourhood councils. Under the term "neighbourhood councils" (as used by City Halls), a broad range of experiments can be identified. A search on the web reveals that a variety of cities (in terms of size, population profile and region) have adopted neighbourhood councils during the last few years. This kind of experiment is difficult to evaluate: there is often a gap between the project as announced and as actually implemented by representatives and citizens.

Not only because the representatives try to embellish the experiment but also because the participative tools are the object of negotiation and empowerment of the "two" sides. The projects and the rules are re-interpreted by participants in order to find their place in participative institutions. Only direct observation and interviews enable the real functioning of neighbourhood councils to be understood. In the next paragraphs, we will give an outline of the principal types of French neighbourhood councils.

First of all, neighbourhood councils are not totally new in France. Some French cities adopted participative policies for their neighbourhoods during the Seventies and the Eighties. Neighbourhood councils have existed particularly in Left wing cities, for example in Roubay (Neveu, 1999), in Nanterre and in Grenoble. But the justification at that time was related to the "citizen self-determination" trend of the Seventies, then a desire for of proximity as now. Some of them still exist today and belong to a group of progressive cities that seek to give a voice to their citizens. These neighbourhood councils have often been granted a fairly high degree of autonomy. They are entirely managed by elected citizens, without the chairmanship of a city council member, and City Hall gives them a small annual budget (about 15 000 euros) to enable them to initiate their own projects. This is the case of Saint-Denis, Bobigny, La Roche-sur-Yon, Montpellier, Voisins-le-Bretonneux, Venissieux, Issy-les-Moulineaux, Villeurbanne, etc. A second group of cities gives less power to their citizens: 1) representatives control the agenda and the meetings of the neighbourhood councils to a great extent; 2) or if the autonomy is respected, no budget is distributed. Box 2 outlines the participative experiment of Bordeaux.

Neighbourhood councils are to be set up in each city with the adoption of the Proximity Act, which made the creation of neighbourhoods' councils obligatory in every city of more than 80,000 inhabitants. This Act, which includes a range of measures, such as the representatives' status, the operation of the fire service, the reorganization of the census, to the review of national public enquiries, was presented as a new step towards decentralization that started with the 1983 reform. According to the Home Office minister, proximity arose from a new demand for nearness from citizens. He held that increasing electoral abstention could be explained by the lack of proximity. Thus the objective of the Act was to promote local democracy by improving representative democracy (by reviewing the status of representatives) and participative democracy. The imposition of the neighbourhood councils is seen as a way to spread positive participative experiments in municipalities where there is some democratic deficit. The Proximity Act stipulates only a minimum of procedures and rules to set up neighbourhood councils. The municipality has room to maneuver to interpret this national "gentle command" to participate. In the years to come, it will be interesting to observe the impact of the Proximity Act on the general implementation of the neighbourhood councils in French cities.

However, the increase in the number of neighbourhood councils does not guarantee the quality of participation and the degree of democratization and empowerment. With regard to their actual impacts on local public life, the few researchers who have observed neighbourhood councils are not optimistic, even with regard to the most advanced experiments. First, the real will of City Hall is called into question. More often than not local representatives try to twist the objective of participation toward communication strategies. They hesitate to give power to participative institutions. This is why the proximity rhetoric is mostly symbolic. The debate on the Proximity Act demonstrates the fears of city councillors: they point out that by the nature of their status (local politicians), they are still in a position of nearness. Second, the representativeness of the representatives and the participants is uncertain (Blondiaux and Levêque, 1999). On the one hand, the opposition local councillors rarely have a clear-cut role in the neighbourhood councils. Consultation policy is first and foremost a policy which favours the links between City Hall/ citizens and not citizens/representatives. NCs are first of all concerned by City Hall priorities (above all, the mayor's initiatives). On the other hand, neighbourhood council members are usually more then forty years old and come from the middle class. Young people, people of other ethnic origins and women are almost wholly absent (Bacqué and Sintomer, 1999: 130-133). Some municipalities have tried to address the question of representativeness by randomly selecting some active members of the neighbourhood councils. But the "conscripts" rapidly lost their motivation because their legitimacy compared to active citizens and highly organized associations was considered ambiguous (Blondiaux, 1999). Third, neighbourhood councils often seek to avoid conflict in favour of a soft consensus (Bacqué and Sintomer, 1999: 133-136). For example, representatives point out that this is not the right place to discuss such-and-such a subject, or a citizen who is over-critical is accused by representatives or by other citizens of bringing partisan debates into a "citizen institution". The ideological debate is forbidden, which has the effect of putting the emphasis on day-to-day problems. In this context, the neighbourhood councils contribute to the development of particular interests rather than the general interest (Blondiaux and Levêque, 1999). Participants talk easily about problems in their street but more rarely from a neighbourhood or a city point of view. However, the implementation of French neighbourhood councils constitutes progress as regards citizen-oriented information. In a city with numerous large urban development and planning projects like Bordeaux, the neighbourhood councils and the other concomitant tools, represent a way to assure the circulation of information relative to the next construction site in the city. The citizens have the opportunity of interviewing representatives and municipal employees about their decisions and projects, and in this sense the representatives have to assume a minimum of accountability between elections (Quesnel, 2000).

Example 2

Neighbourhood councils in Bordeaux[27]

Origin

The neighbourhood councils (NCs) of Bordeaux were created in 1995 by the mayor, Alain Juppé (French Prime minister at that time). Bordeaux NCs were born out of a special local context: 1) Juppé took over from the previous mayor, Jacques Chaban-Delmas, who was at the head of City Hall for 48 years. 2) Juppé had decided to in initiate a range of large urban projects (building a tramway and bridge, renovating the quaysides, renewing the inner city, etc.), after a decade of inactivity. To set up these projects and to respect the wind of participation[28] the mayor needed an effective communication tool.

Functioning and process

At the beginning, only the "life blood" of each of the 13 neighbourhoods served as members of the NCs. In fact, the NCs gathered former sympathizers of Chaban-Delmas, representatives of some institutions (schools, social organizations, etc.) and some active citizens. Rapidly, resident associations and citizens asked to be listened to by the mayor. For five years, the NCs have been open to everyone. At least a hundred people are always there. The mayor chairs the assembly, accompanied by the neighbourhood representatives, the Planning and Neighbourhood life deputy mayors and sometimes, the Département representatives (always from the majority side). At the start of a meeting, the mayor presents the future projects of the neighbourhoods or of the city and the progress of current projects, with the help of municipal employees. Then citizens ask questions and make comments on every subject, but under the control of the mayor who selects people to speak who put up their hand. Usually, the meeting lasts one and a half hours. Three neighbourhood meetings are organized every year. The mayor chairs a general meeting of every NC every year.

Effects

Even if the Bordeaux NCs are limited participative tools, their creation has improved democratic life in two ways. First, in order to put the NCs in place City Hall had to adapt its organization. A Neighbourhood Life Department and a deputy mayor in charge of it have been created to organize meetings and respond to citizens' complaints. The mayor also appointed a representative (of his team) responsible for each neighbourhood. The formation of NCs is also accompanied by the creation of various supplementary participative tools: small consultative meetings, commissions by subject (Associative Life, Education, Culture, Health, Ethnic groups) and planning workshops (the most interesting participative organization). However, the success of most of them remains limited and they serve first and foremost the communication strategy of the mayor. Nevertheless, the NCs have indirectly encouraged the creation of some resident associations. A kind of new opposition has arisen in a city where it has traditionally been weak. Bordeaux's citizens and associations consider NCs to constitute a bare minimum of participation and think that they now have a right to be consulted. City Hall could not backtrack.

Conclusion: too high ambitions for local participation?

The development of local participative institutions in France is marked by the preeminence of the State in the promotion of participation. The adoption of participative tools is indeed first and foremost a national movement. Through national policies such as the Urban Policy Programme or the Proximity Act, the French State is present in the local democratic process. The intervention of the State in local public life is driven by the desire to address the problems of abstention and political disaffection. The municipality is seen as an appropriate locus for rebuilding political legitimacy and ameliorating social apathy. However, there are also problems associated with participation as a route to better social cohesion and more proximity.

The national attention devoted to local participation may reflect an overidealization of the democratic values of local government. By virtue of its small scale, the local level is accorded democratic superiority. As Dahl and Tufte have demonstrated, "smallness" is often expected to facilitate closely knit relationships and co-operation. Proximity between representatives and citizens is a guarantee of efficient and democratic local politics (1973: 13-16). The examples of the Greek cities or a reference to some early modern philosophers usually serve to support this consensual image of local democracy. This idyllic nature of local democracy is a widespread myth (Paulette, 1999). One may ask, however, whether, in a complex political system, the local level is the right one to begin a renewal of democracy? A series of observations show that this cannot be assumed to be the case. First, in a context where the metropolitan district is becoming more powerful, to limit participation to municipalities also limits the reach of citizen influence. For example, in Bordeaux, representatives often point out that many projects depend on the joint decision of the group of municipalities that constitute the metropolitan area, and once taken, it is difficult to change the decision. The powerlessness of the municipalities is thus often raised as an issue in the participative meetings. This raises the question of the appropriate level for participatory processes (Basque et Intoner, 1999: 139-140). As municipalities are losing some of their autonomy in metropolitan government, it might be interesting to consider the democratization of the latter.

The permanence of the participative tools created in the last years is second issue. Are the conditions favourable for the development of these instruments into mature institutions? Blondiaux has already suggested that neighbourhood councils remain poor institutions (1999). Without clear procedures and a transformation of the municipal policy process, the outlook may not be good for the empowerment of citizens or representatives in the context of the participatory processes. Complete institutionalization comes through a change in rules but also through new practices. Is the national promotion of local participation an appropriate way to influence local practices? In addition, participative tools, even in a context of clear representative democracy, call into question the principles of representation and expertise (accountability and responsibility) central to representative democracy. If participatory tools become widespread, we will have to consider new principles more compatible with representation, expertise and participation at the same time. As representation is an established principle of the municipalities in France (Mabileau, 1994), the permanence of the participative organization is uncertain. The temptation for representatives to hijack the participative movement is already evident and we are witnessing a development towards communication rather than participation.

Finally, to return to our starting point, electoral abstention and political disaffection, we should ask if local participation can resolve such complex issues that are really of a national character. With its limited resources it is doubtful that local government can identify a new road towards citizenship. The issue of citizenship extends far beyond the local arena. Perhaps it is this overly large ambition of social cohesion and proximity that will threaten the institutionalization and the permanence of French local participative tools. Even if the democratization of local politics is somewhat enhanced through better communication between representatives and citizens, other steps will also have to be taken, including improvements in the conception of local participation, to really make a difference with regard to local and national democracy.

References

Abélès, Marc (1989). *Jours tranquilles en 89. Ethnologie politique d'un département français*. Paris: Éditions Odile Jacob.
Abélès, Marc (2000). *Un ethnologue à l'Assemblée*. Paris: Éditions Odile Jacob.
Almond, Gabriel A. and Sidney Verba (1963). *The Civic Culture. Political Attitudes and Democracy in Five Nations*. Princeton: Princeton University Press.
Andolfatto, Dominique (1992). "Quand les abstentionnistes s'expriment". *Revue politique et parlementaire*. Juillet/août. No 960: 40-46.
Arpaillange, Christophe, Catherine Darlon and Michel-Alexis Montané (2001). "Small is beautiful". Le quartier est-il aujourd'hui le lieu d'une refondation de la culture et de la pratique démocratiques?". 5e conference Ville-Management *Cultures et pratiques de la démocratie locale*. Bayonne. 6-7 september.
Aubry, François-Xavier (1989). "L'avenir du référendum local". In Conac, Gérard and Didier Maus ed. *Le référendum, quel avenir?* Paris: Éditions STH.
Bacqué, Marie-Hélène and Yves Sintomer (1999). "L'espace public dans les quartiers populaires d'habitat social". In Neveu, Catherine, ed., *Espace public et engagement politique*. Paris: L'Harmattan.

Bacqué, Marie-Hélène and Yves Sintomer (2001). "Affiliation et désaffiliations en banlieue". *Revue française de sociologie*. 42 (2): 217-249.

Becet, J.M (1971). "Le référendum intercommunal et l'article 8 de la loi du 16 juillet 1971 sur les fusions et regroupement de communes". *La Revue Administrative*. 143, September/October.

Blanc, Maurice and Monique Legrand, (1987). "La participation des habitants dans la réhabilitation des quartiers d'habitat social". In Colas, Dominique ed., *L'État de droit*. Paris: Presses universitaires de France.

Blatrix, Cécile (1999). "Le maire, le commissaire enquêteur et leur "public". La pratique politique de l'enquête publique". In CRAPS/CURAPP ed., *La démocratie locale. Représentation, participation et espace public*. Paris: Presses universitaires de France.

Blondiaux, Loïc (1999). "Représenter, délibérer ou gouverner? Les assises politique fragiles de la démocratie participative de quartier". In CURAPP/CRAPPS ed., *La démocratie locale. Représentation, participation et espace public*. Paris: Presses universitaires de France.

Blondiaux, Loïc (2002). "La délibération, norme de l'action publique contemporaine?". *Projet*. January.

Blondiaux, Loïc and Sandrine Levêque (1999). "La politique locale à l'épreuve de la démocratie. Les formes paradoxales de la démocratie participative dans le XXe arrondissement de Paris". In Neveu, Catherine ed., *Espace public et engagement politique*. Paris: L'Harmattan.

Boy, Daniel, Dominique Donnet-Kamel and Philippe Roqueplo (2002). "Un exemple de démocratie participative. La "conférence de citoyens" sur les organismes génétiquement modifies". *Revue française de science politique*. 50 (4-5).

Callon, Michel, Pierre Lascoumes and Yannick Barthe (2001). *Agir dans un monde incertain. Essai sur la démocratie technique*. Paris: Seuil.

Chabanet, Didier (1999). "La politique de la ville au défi de la participation des habitants à Vaulx-en-Velin". In Balme, Richard, Faure, Alain and Albert Mabileau ed., *Les nouvelles politiques locales*. Paris: Presses de Sciences Po, 345-364.

Dahl, Robert A. and Edward R. Tufte (1973). *Size and Democracy*. Stanford: Standford University Press.

Dion, Stéphane (1984). "Les politiques municipales de concertation: néo-corporatisme et démocratie". *Sociologie du travail*. No 2.

Dolez, Bernard and Annie Laurent ed. (2002). *Le vote des villes. Les élections municipales des 11 et 18 mars 2001*. Paris: Presses de Sciences Po.

Duran, Patrice and Jean-Claude Thoenig (1996). "L'État et la gestion publique territoriale". *Revue française de science politique*. 46 (4): 580-623.

Faure, Alain (1992). *Le village et la politique. Essai sur les maires ruraux en action*. Paris: L'Harmattan.

Fourniau, Jean-Michel (1997). "Figures de la concertation 'à la française'". In Gariepy, Michel and Michel Marié ed., *Ces réseaux qui nous gouvernent?* Paris: L'Harmattan.

Garraud, Philippe (1989). *Profession, homme politique: la carrière politique des maires urbains*. Paris: L'Harmattan.

Gaudin, Jean-Pierre (1999). *Gouverner par contrat. L'action publique en question*. Paris: Presses de Sciences Po.

Guionnet, Christine (2002). "Les listes d'extrême gauche et le discours de 'la politique autrement'. Cas des listes Motivées et Tous Ensemble À Gauche aux élections municipales de mars 2001 à Rennes". Arising from a conference organised by CRAPS and CURAPP. Lille, January, 10 and 11.

Helly, Denise (1999). "Une injonction: appartenir, participer. Le retour de la cohésion sociale et du bon citoyen". *Lien social et Politiques – RIAC*. 41 (spring): 35-46.

Hoffmann-Martinot, Vincent (1992). "La participation aux élections municipales dans les villes françaises". *Revue française de science politique.* 42: 3-35.
Hoffmann-Martinot, Vincent (1999). "Les grandes villes françaises: une démocratie en souffrance". In Gabriel, Oscar W. and Vincent Hoffmann-Martinot ed., *Démocraties urbaines. L'état de la démocratie dans les grandes villes de 12 pays industrialisés.* Paris: L'Harmattan.
Hoffmann-Martinot, Vincent, Colin Rallings and Michael Thrasher (1996). "Comparing local electoral turnout in Great Britain and France: More similarities than differences?". *European Journal of Political Research.* 30: 241-257.
Jadot, Anne (2001). "Élections intermediaries". In Perrineau, Pascal and Dominique Reynié ed., *Dictionnaire du vote.* Paris: Presses universitaires de France.
Kesselmann, Mark (1966). "French local politics: A statistical examination of grass roots consensus". *The American political science review.*
Lancelot, Alain (1968). *L'abstentionnisme électoral en France.* Paris: Colin.
Le Bart, Christian (2001). "Élections municipals". In Perrineau, Pascal and Dominique Reynié ed., *Dictionnaire du vote.* Paris: Presses universitaires de France.
Lefebvre, Rémi (2001). "Rhétorique de la proximité et 'crise de la représentation'". *Cahiers lillois d'Économie et de Sociologie.* Paris: L'Harmattan.
Le Gall, Gérard (2001). "L'étrange consultation électorale de 2001 ou l'invention d'une défaite". *Revue politique et parlementaire.* 103 (1011): 2-32.
Lehingue, Patrick (2001). "Faire parler d'une seule voix? Les scrutins municipaux des 11-18 mars 2001". *Regards sur l'actualité.* April (270): 3-18.
Mabileau, Albert (1994). *Le système local en France.* Paris: Montchrestien.
Mabileau, Albert, Moyser, George, Parry, Geraint et Patrick Quantin ed. (1987). *Les citoyens et la politique locale. Comment participent les Britanniques et les Français.* Paris: Pedone.
Martin, Pierre (2001a). *Les élections municipales en France depuis 1945.* Paris: La Documentation française.
Martin, Pierre (2001b). "Les municipales et cantonales des 11 et 18 mars 2001". *Commentaire.* 24 (94): 361-371.
Muller-Quoy, Isabelle (2001). *Le droit des assemblées locales.* Paris: Librairie générale de droit et de jurisprudence.
Nevers, Jean-Yves (1992). "Entre consensus et conflits. La configuration aux élections municipales dans les communes rurales". *Revue française de sociologie.* XXXIII: 391-416.
Neveu, Catherine (1999). "Quel(s) espace(s) public(s) pour les 'habitants'? Réflexions autour de l'expérience de comités de quartier à Roubaix". In CURAPP/CRAPP. *La démocratie locale. Représentation, participation et espace public.* Paris: PUF.
Paoletti, Marion (1997). *La démocratie locale et le référendum.* Paris: L'Harmattan.
Paoletti, Marion (1999). "La démocratie locale française. Spécificité et alignement". In CURAPP/CRAPP. *La démocratie locale. Représentation, participation et espace public.* Paris: PUF.
Parodi, Jean-Luc (1982). "Dans la logique des élections intermediaries". *Revue Politique et Parlementaire.* 903: 42-70.
Perrineau, Pascal ed. (1994). *L'engagement politique. Déclin ou mutation?* Paris: Presses de la Fondation nationale des sciences politiques.
Quesnel, Louise (2000). *La consultation des citoyens comme outil de la démocratie locale.* Toronto: Presses du CIRUR.
Raséra, Michel (2002). *La démocratie locale.* Paris: Librairie générale de droit et de jurisprudence.

Subileau, Françoise and Marie-France Toinet (1993). *Les chemins de l'abstention. Une comparaison franco-américaine*. Paris: Éditions de la Découverte.
Subileau, Françoise (2001a). "Abstention". In Perrineau, Pascal and Dominique Reynié ed., *Dictionnaire du vote*. Paris: Presses universitaires de France.
Subileau, Françoise (2001b). "L'abstention aux élections municipales de 2001: rupture ou confirmation?". *Revue politique et parlementaire*. 103 (1011): 33-54.
Verba, Sidney, Norman H. Nie and Jae-on Kim (1978). *Participation and Political Equality. A Seven-Nation Comparison*. Cambridge: Cambridge University Press.
Visier, Laurent and Geneviève Zoïa (2001). "Motivé-e-s. Les quartiers, la culture et le politique". *Mouvements*. 18 (November-December): 62-67.
Warin, Philippe (1995). "Les HLM: impossible participation des habitants". *Sociologie du travail*. 2: 151-176.

Notes

[1] As a Canadian, I have been studying French local democracy for three years with the aim of making a comparison with Quebec local democracy, with particular interest in Bordeaux and Quebec city. I would like to thank Kate Holiday who helped me to correct the English translation of this text and Vincent Hoffmann-Martinot for his helpful advice.

[2] In this text, "local level" is understood as the *municipal* level.

[3] Of course there are some interesting exceptions which we will see later in the chapter.

[4] Before 1983, we can find very interesting analyses of local politics, which remain a research classic in the local field. But it is true that after 1983, we can observe an increase in the number of studies which are interested in the local level.

[5] We use inverted commas to put the emphasis on the fact that the terms "participative democracy" and "local democracy" are used by French political actors. These expressions are totally integrated in political speeches in France.

[6] Syntomer and Bacqué maintain that a third frame of reference is also evident in the French discussion concerning participative democracy: participation would be a means to improve public management and to take better decisions (1999). This is, in fact, the case but by comparison for example with Canada where this is a central argument for implementing participative policies, this kind of argument is a maringal one in France.

[7] Figures from the Home Office (*ministère de l'Intérieur*). 2001. *Les collectivités locales en chiffres*. www.dgcl.interieur.gouv.fr .

[8] See two books from an anthropologist, Marc Abélès, who has closely observed the work of national and local representatives: 1989 and 2000. He explains how the accumulation of mandates is perceived by the representatives.

[9] In French, this practice is named *panachage*.

[10] For more details, see for example Muller-Quoy, 2001: 15-17.

[11] A data bank from Grenoble university gives data on electoral results. They are not accessible by internet but its Website gives some information on the data available. See the *Centre d'information des données socio-politiques* (CIDSP): www.cidsp.com .

[12] The synchronization of municipal elections every six years encourages this kind of analysis.

[13] The rate of non-registered electors has been estimated at about 9% (Andolfatto, 1992: 40). Furthermore, some observers have analysed that the phenomenon of increasing abstention has been recorded, together with a rise in the non-registered voters, particularly for the 2001 municipal elections (Dolez and Laurent, 2002: 20).

[14] Results for the first ballot in all the French municipalities, on the basis of the percentage of registered voters.
[15] Results for the first ballot in all the French municipalities, on the basis of the percentage of registered voters.
[16] The differences between the two countries are based on the electoral participation of working-class cities (higher in France) and an average electoral participation (also higher in France).
[17] Before this date, some municipalities had used the local referenda concerning internal management of local affairs but without legal recognition.
[18] A relatively low number of these referenda concerned amalgation.
[19] This kind of list was not completely new. The literature reports one case for the 1995 municipal election near Lyon. See Chabanet, 1999.
[20] The "citizen lists" did not propose concrete participative tools. As non-professionals, they preferred to define their desire for greater participation rather than formulate substantial tools and policies. This is why they had no platform.
[21] Its name in French is confused: *la politique de la ville*, namely the Urban Policy Programme. However, only some neighbourhoods (with great social difficulties) are concerned by it. In the rest of the text, we will use the name Urban Policy Programme to designate this policy.
[22] On French experiments in these sectors, see for example: Blatrix, 1999; Boy, Donnet-Kamel and Roqueplo, 2000; Callon, Lascoumes and Barthe, 2001; Fourniau, 1997; Vallemont, 2001.
[23] To refer to this kind of position and the other positions devoted to the Urban Policy Programme, the term "urban development positions" have been introduced (in French: *les métiers de la ville*).
[24] Bear in mind that in France, the election of local councillors is not based on territorial representation, with the consequence that neighbourhoods were not given so much attention. We will see that with the development of "proximity" tools, the neighbourhood is being taken over by the representatives.
[25] The Citizens' Dialogue Group was partially financed by European programmes (Urban and Objective 2), as was the Think Tank on participation.
[26] They have vague responsibilities: mediation and information. They are generally visible by walking around in the city. Depending on municipalities, the "proximity agents" were a short-lived experiment.
[27] At present, we are studying the case of the Bordeaux policy consultation.
[28] For example, the Environmental minister of Juppé's government had adopted a Charter of participation.

Chapter 12

Local Political Participation in Norway: Does Globalization Make a Difference?

Lawrence E. Rose

Observers of local government and politics in Norway awaited the outcome of elections to municipal and county councils held in September 1999 with more than the usual sense of anticipation. Not only was there the usual uncertainty regarding what the results would portend for the fortunes of political parties competing for the voters' favor. There was in addition a sense of curiosity, indeed even trepidation, as well. Grounds for this apprehension lay in the election outcome four years earlier. In 1995 little more than 62 percent of eligible voters had cast a ballot in municipal elections, and even less cast ballots in county council elections (59 percent).[1] While this level of voting may be quite respectable by international standards, it gave rise to sharp concern in the Norwegian context. It was, after all, the lowest level of electoral turnout recorded in the entire postwar period. To find a lower turnout in municipal elections for the nation as a whole one had to go back to 1922.[2] Every bit as noteworthy as the low turnout, however, was the fact that this outcome extended and strengthened a trend that had prevailed since 1963, at which time turnout had reached a historical high for local elections in Norway – fully 81 percent (see figure 12.1).[3] In a little over 30 years, in other words, the percentage of those who chose to pass up the opportunity to vote in local elections had roughly doubled, increasing from 19 to 38 percent. Non-voters, or what Norwegians call "couch voters" referring to the fact that these voters choose to stay at home on their couches rather than going to the polls, had become the single largest block of voters.

The electoral outcome in 1999 did little to allay the apprehensions of observers. On the contrary, voter turnout continued to decline, falling to 60 percent for municipal elections and just above 56 percent for county council elections. Efforts to lower the electoral threshold and make voting easier by permitting postal balloting prior to election day, and to stimulate electoral participation by means of experiments with the direct election of mayors conducted in 20 of Norway's 435 municipalities, appeared to be largely for naught – or to have had marginal effects at best.[4] The trend of declining electoral involvement in local elections continued unabated.

Figure 12.1 Voter Turnout in Local Elections in Norway, 1901-1999

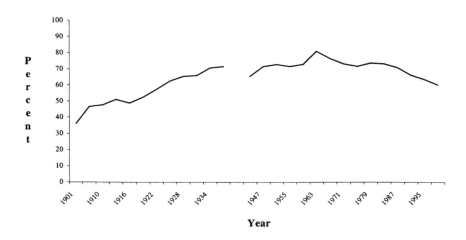

This trend is something of an enigma: how can it be explained? Certainly not by suggesting that the status of local government within the Norwegian political system has been diminished and that there is therefore less at stake to motivate voters. On the contrary, as measured by both public expenditure and public employment, local government has exhibited substantial growth throughout the period in question. From the early 1960's until the late 1990's, for example, local government expenditure as a proportion of all public expenditure expanded from roughly 50 to 60 percent. Similarly local government employment grew from 50 to roughly 75 percent of all public employment.[5] These figures reflect a long-standing national policy under which local governments at both the municipal and county levels have been used as a primary tool in developing and shaping the Norwegian welfare state (cf. Nagel 1991, Rose 1996). Thus, although exceptions are to be found, the range of responsibilities assigned to local government has in general increased throughout the postwar period. At present municipalities exercise responsibility for primary schools and adult education, primary out-patient health care, care for the elderly, a variety of social welfare services, technical tasks such as water supply, sewage and garbage disposal, fire protection, the building and maintenance of local roads, and land use planning plus a number of cultural and leisure time activities such as libraries, parks and athletic facilities. The principal responsibilities of county governments, by comparison, have been secondary education, building and maintenance of trunk roads and, where necessary, other transportation facilities such as harbors and ferries, and, until recently, the operation of hospitals for in-patient care.[6] It must be emphasized, furthermore, that these responsibilities apply regardless of the size of the municipality or county in question. This is most noteworthy in the case of municipalities, inasmuch as over

55 percent of all municipalities (of which there are 434 at present) have less than 5,000 inhabitants, and only 10 have more than 50,000 inhabitants.

As these comments indicate, it is not an exaggeration to state that local government occupies an important position in the Norwegian political-administrative system. The public, moreover, appears to understand and appreciate this fact, as responses to questions posed in several national public opinion surveys clearly reflect (cf. Baldersheim et al, 1990:6-10, Rose & Skare 1996a:84, 1996b:138). Given this state of affairs, it is necessary to ask how long-term decline in electoral turnout is to be interpreted? How can the decline be understood and, perhaps by implication, what significance may it have for the viability of local self-government?

There are several ways of approaching these questions. In the present chapter attention is concentrated on investigating what impact, if any, globalization may have on citizen involvement in local politics. Is it the case, for example, that globalization serves to reduce a sense of identity with the local community, and thereby undermines the basis for local political involvement? Alternatively, does globalization perhaps have the opposite effect; does it strengthen the individual citizen's awareness of – indeed even appreciation for – his or her local ties and thereby serve to strengthen the basis for local involvement? Or is globalization without noteworthy significance for citizens' local political involvement, either in one direction or the other?

If the decline in participation in local elections in Norway is any indication, one might well be led to believe that the first alternative is the most appropriate interpretation – namely that globalization weakens local political involvement. But is this justified? Voting, after all, is only one of many forms of local political involvement, and evidence from many countries suggests that while electoral participation may be on the decline, citizen involvement in other forms of political participation – especially that which in many instances has been termed "unconventional political activity" – has been on the increase (cf. Borg, 1995; Dalton 1996:45 & 76; Gunderlach 1995; IDEA 1997; Lijphart 2000: Topf 1995; Verba et al. 1995:71-72). The same is also true in the case of Norway. As the results in figure 12.2 demonstrate, citizen involvement in a variety of non-electoral political activities at the local level has clearly grown in recent years. Although the findings in figure 12.2 reflect only a three-year time span, and the differences are not great, the percentage of citizens reporting the activities considered nonetheless shows a *consistent increase*, not a decrease. The same tendency is also reported by Bjørklund and Saglie (2000:83-86) based on analyses using data from other sources.[7]

Figure 12.2 Citizens reporting different forms of local political participation in Norway, 1993 and 1996 (percent)

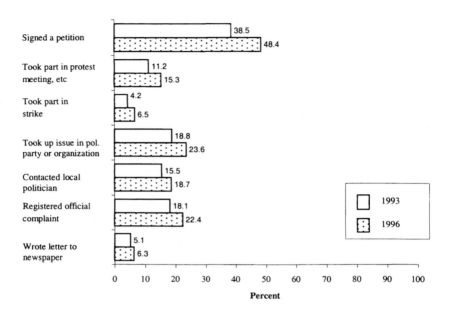

Given empirical findings regarding aggregate trends in citizen involvement across a broader spectrum of activities in Norway and elsewhere, in short, it is not readily apparent whether globalization has or will have any systematic impact on local political participation. To reach a more definitive conclusion on this issue, however, requires a more detailed approach, an approach that involves a number of difficult conceptual and methodological challenges. For one thing the concept of globalization is multifaceted and requires elaboration and specification to be understood and investigated correctly. For another, the issue in question is of a complex causal character; the argument is that changes in one factor (globalization) may underlie changes in another factor (local political participation). To investigate the potential impact of globalization in a rigorous manner, therefore, implies the availability and use of reliable diachronic data. And to assess the extent to which causal relationships are of a universal as opposed to more situational contingent nature, comparable analyses should be carried out in a variety of cultural settings.

These challenges are not fully met in this chapter. Not the least problematic is the lack of reliable time series data that would permit the investigation of dynamic causal effects over time. The inquiry reported here, moreover, is limited solely to Norway and hence represents only a small part of a larger global picture. For these reasons the present chapter must be seen as an exploratory probing of some of the issues and relationships that are involved. The strategy pursued in exploring these matters, furthermore, is indirect and partial rather than direct and comprehensive. No attempt is made to specify and empirically measure the various facets of globalization. Rather, as a surrogate indicator of what globalization might imply, the chapter uses responses to two questions posed in national surveys carried out in 1993 and 1996. These questions relate first to a sense of identification with different geographic areas and second to a sense of community with other persons living in these areas respectively. Finally, in considering what impact globalization may have on patterns of citizen involvement, the chapter focuses on individual political participation at the local level only. Hence, the strategy employed leaves a good deal to be explored in other contexts and by other means.

In what follows, first globalization and how this may relate to individual identity political behavior is briefly discussed, after which evidence is presented regarding the cognitive affiliations Norwegians express with respect to various socio-political units. The empirical links between these affiliations and local political behavior are then explored and the chapter concludes with a summary discussion of the findings.

Globalization, identity and political behavior

Globalization may be defined as a process of increasing international interweaving of social, economic and political life and the transactions that constitute these.[8] Evidence of such a trend may be found in a variety of spheres, ranging from commerce and communication to education and cultural activities. The extension of intergovernmental relations across boundaries – at the local and regional as well as national levels – may also be seen as evidence of this trend. Yet whether such developments have a behavioral impact, and if so how and at what level is a conceptual as well as empirical question. At the individual level the conceptual argument hinges on two links in a causal chain: the first link suggests that globalization serves to change the frame of reference which contribute to molding individual identities, whereas the second link suggests that once formed, these identities serve to shape or influence individual (political) behavior.

Figure 12.3a The interrelationships between globalization, identity and political behavior – a simple model

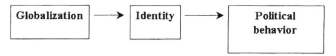

This fundamental line of reasoning is depicted in figure 12.3a. Globalization, however, is only one of any number of factors that may contribute to the shaping of identities. In reality, therefore, a slightly more complex model, such as that shown in figure 12.3b, better depicts the situation pertaining for most individuals.[9]

Figure 12.3b The interrelationships between globalization, identity and political behavior – a more complex model

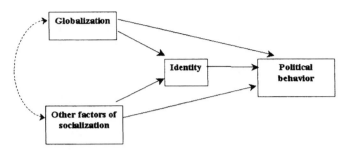

Both models are essentially of a social-psychological character; that is, individual identities are seen to be developed as a function of an individual's social ties and networks.[10] This feature is noted in Figures 12.3a and 12.3b by the arrows which represent the causal influences that are presumed to exist. However the strength and nature of these causal influences (whether they exert a positive or negative impact, for example, or what the direction of the causal influence may be) remain matters for further theoretical conjecture and subsequent empirical verification.[11] A variety of considerations make this a complex and hazardous endeavor. Foremost among these considerations is the fact that globalization, as it is commonly conceived, is a macro-level phenomenon that is seen as encompassing and effecting all individuals in a relatively uniform manner. Yet in reality individuals are likely to be embedded in a set of social circumstances that make them more or less subject to the potential impact of globalizing impulses. Retired individuals living on minimum pensions, for instance, are much less likely to be exposed first hand to a global environment than are employed and well-to-do individuals or, for that matter even young people who are more readily able to avail themselves of opportunities for international travel. Likewise individual work situations differ greatly in terms of the exposure they provide to the forces of globalization (e.g. use of the internet, professional conferences, commercial trade, etc.). These differences presumably have an impact on just how globalizing tendencies influence individual identities.

To date few research endeavors have attempted to specify and operationalize just how the relevant causal dynamics operate.[12] This is, of course, a formidable task, since the problem is not only one of identifying the specific "forces" of globalization, but also isolating and measuring the effects of these forces at the individual level without falling into the trap of assorted inferential fallacies. The present chapter is certainly subject to the same constraints and provides no breakthrough in this regard. It is rather a bootstrapping effort based on empirical materials gathered for other purposes.

The approach adopted

The approach employed here is essentially of an inductive character. Using responses to two questions asked in a panel study carried out in Norway among a cross section of the population in 1993 and 1996 respectively, differences in the degree to which individuals express (1) a *sense of identification with selected geographic areas* and (2) a *sense of solidarity with other persons living in these areas* are highlighted. Of particular interest is the strength of the cognitive-affective orientations individuals express with respect to their local residential communities and municipalities on the one hand and to broader international areas – the Nordic area and Europe respectively – on the other.[13] Clearly there is no reason to suggest that a strong orientation to one area necessarily precludes a strong orientation to the other – i.e. that there is an inherent "antagonism" among different identifications. Psychological identification, in other words, is not a zero-sum phenomenon. Citizens may have strong positive orientations to both levels. Individuals may also have weak and perhaps even negative orientations to both levels or, alternatively, they may have strong, positive orientations to one and weaker, more indifferent or negative orientations to the other.

Depending on the specific mix of orientations different individuals express (what might be termed cognitive-affective profiles), therefore, the population can be divided into a variety of groups. Once this is done, two interesting questions emerge: (1) are the characteristics of individuals displaying different cognitive-affective profiles consistent with theoretical ideas about the impact of globalization; and (2) to what extent do differences in orientations relate to patterns of political involvement at the local (or, for that matter, the national or international) level? These questions constitute the focus for the remainder of this chapter. Before taking these questions up in greater detail, however, it is critical to emphasize what is being done here is *not* to argue that differences in orientations are necessarily the result of the forces of globalization per se. Rather the focus is upon how, if at all, differences in individual political behavior relate to differences in specific cognitive-affective orientations. In undertaking the inquiry, the presumption is that differences in orientations, even if they are not specifically the result of globalization, may nonetheless be used to suggest what impact processes of globalization may *potentially* have were it indeed possible to demonstrate that globalization contributes to shifts in individual cognitive-affective orientations. If no relationships are found, then one possible conclusion is that globalization in its own right may not be of any further significance for (local) political behavior. If, on the other hand, different relationships are found, then one possibility is to extrapolate from this to predict future shifts in (local) political involvement as a result of further processes of globalization.

Cognitive affiliations among Norwegians

Just what affiliations do Norwegians express with respect to different geographic areas, and how do these affiliations relate to actual political behavior? A first glimpse into these issues is provided by the findings presented in figure 12.4. This figure shows the percentage of respondents who by their answers to the relevant survey questions suggest that they have a *strong* sense of identification with a set of selected geographical areas and similarly a *strong* sense of solidarity with other persons living in the same set of areas.[14]

Figure 12.4 Percentage expressing "strong" identification with selected geographic areas (1993) and "strong" solidarity with other people living in these areas (1996)

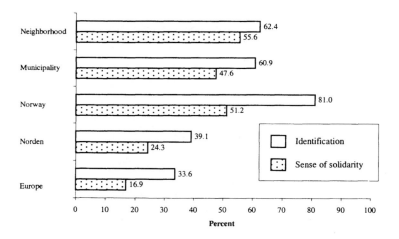

Several noteworthy features are to be observed in this figure. First, it is evident that the percentage expressing strong *identification with* different geographic areas is consistently greater than the percentage expressing *solidarity with* other people living in these areas. This difference is not at all surprising. To feel and express a sense of solidarity with other individuals in an area involves a much more substantial psychological commitment than does a sense of identification or attachment with an area. We should therefore expect that the proportion expressing a sense of solidarity would be lower.

In a similar vein it can also be argued that it is more difficult to experience and express a sense of solidarity with individuals living at a greater distance from oneself. This is because solidarity builds in part on familiarity and sympathy (or even stronger, empathy) with the other individuals involved.[15] With the exception of those for Norway as a whole, the findings presented in figure 12.4 are again consistent with this line of reasoning. Thus, whereas the difference in the two percentages relating to the neighborhood is about seven percent, the difference for the municipality is 13 percent, and for Norden and Europe it is roughly 15 and 17 percent respectively. The demands of or barriers to solidarity, it would appear, increase as one moves farther from "home". That findings for Norway as a whole are an exception (the difference is nearly 30 percent) merely underlines the fact that national identity in many cases may represent a special case. It may be quite easy (at least it is for Norwegians) to profess a strong sense of national identification, whereas experiencing a sense of solidarity with all those living in the country is quite another matter – and certainly something not equally readily realized.[16]

The other feature of note regarding figure 12.4 is that the areas for which both a sense of identification and a sense of solidarity with others tend to be uniformly highest are the neighborhood and municipality respectively. Just over sixty percent of all Norwegians express a strong affective orientation toward these areas and approximately half also express a strong cognitive affiliation with others living there. Comparable proportions regarding strong attachments to the Nordic area and Europe as well as people living in these areas are less than 40 and 25 percent of the population respectively. For many Norwegians, in other words, the local area where they live appears to constitute a very strong point of reference.

This is consistent with findings from the 1990-91 World Values Study in which individuals in over 30 countries were asked to indicate the geographic area with which they identified most. Respondents were given several options from which they could choose, including a category labeled "the town or locality where you live". Nearly seven out of 10 Norwegians (69 percent) selected this response as the area with which they identified most (cf. Figure 12.5). Among 16 countries in Western Europe and North America, this was the highest percentage to be found in any country, exceeding Sweden, the country with the next highest score in this regard, by 13 percentage points. In France, by comparison, only just over four of ten Frenchmen (41 percent) made a similar choice, indicating that the town or locality where they lived was the area with which they identified most. Just what accounts for these cross-national differences is an interesting question in its own right.[17] Whether it reflects differences in political institutions and ideas of local democracy, such as those Quantin (1989) highlights in his contribution to a comparison of local politics and participation in Britain and France, or rather some other set of circumstances and factors will not be pursued further here. It suffices to underline the fact that there seems to be a marked tendency for Norwegians to identify strongly with their local communities, and this tendency is documented by several different studies.

Figure 12.5 Percentage of the population in 16 countries expressing greatest identification with "the town or locality where they live"

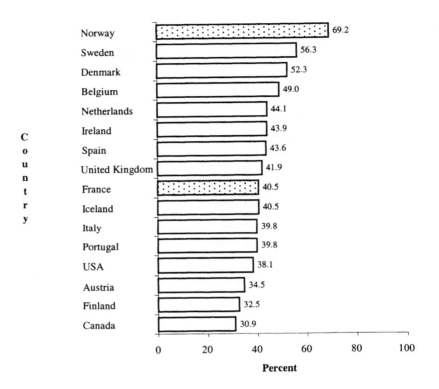

Source: World Values Study 1990-91, question 76a.

Local political participation in Norway – how much and by whom?

What difference, if any, do such cognitive orientations have for citizen involvement in local politics? It is reasonable to expect that a local identification and sense of solidarity should, if anything, be positively associated with local political involvement. The critical question at this point, therefore, is what impact, if any, an international orientation may have on this relationship? Does an international orientation serve to undercut and weaken whatever relationship may exist between a local cognitive affiliation and local political involvement, does it serve to strengthen the relationship, or is it of no empirical consequence? Arguably all three alternatives are possible. For example, individuals generally have limited resources available for political involvement – time being a primary example in this respect. An internationalist orientation, if acted upon, could therefore well reduce the resources available for local involvement. On the other hand a positive synergy effect might exist, whereby an international orientation would reinforce tendencies for political involvement associated with a local orientation. In this case activities with an internationalist bent may heighten interest and generate further motivation for local involvement (and vice versa). Finally, it could be that these or other considerations counterbalance or negate one another, in which case no effect would be observed.

In considering these alternatives, attention here is focused on *non-electoral* political participation. In theory *electoral* activity could also be considered, but for two reasons this will not be done. First, it seems likely that the impact of different cognitive affiliations would be most prominently registered in connection with non-electoral political involvement. Although turnout for local elections in Norway has declined markedly over the past three decades, voting continues to be perceived to be a "citizen duty" by a preponderant majority of citizens (cf. Bjørklund & Saglie 2000:79-80; Rose 2002). Hence, voting behavior is less likely to be subject to the influence of geographic cognitive affiliations than is non-electoral behavior. Second, aside from voting, the data set used for this chapter does not include measures of campaign activity or other forms of electoral behavior. The analyses reported here, therefore, are limited to various forms of local non-electoral participation.

Seven different forms of local non-electoral activity are considered.[18] These activities, and the percentage of the population that reports having engaged in these activities during the two years prior to the survey, are displayed in figure 12.6. The activities are ranked according to the proportion reporting each of them. As is evident, only participating in a volunteer project for the benefit of the neighborhood, local community or municipality and giving money to a campaign in connection with a local issue are activities that more than half of the population report having undertaken during a two year period (61 and 57 percent respectively). The remaining activities are reported by only a third of the population or less. And when it comes to what some may consider the core of local political activity – participating in a campaign regarding a local issue, taking up an issue in an organization, association or political party, or attempting to influence a decision of the municipal council in some other way – less than 20 percent of all Norwegians report having undertaken these.

This pattern of involvement is by no means extraordinary. Rather, it is quite typical for most empirical findings regarding citizen involvement in local politics (see, for example, Mabileau et al, 1989). Depending on the form of activity and the time frame involved in reporting these activities, rates of local political participation commonly vary from under five percent to not more than three-quarters of the population. For the present inquiry, however, the specific percentages reporting each activity is not of primary interest. The focus is instead on whether or not there is any evidence that the percentages vary according to the types of cognitive orientations to which people given expression.

Figure 12.6 Percentage reporting having undertaken selected forms of local political activity *

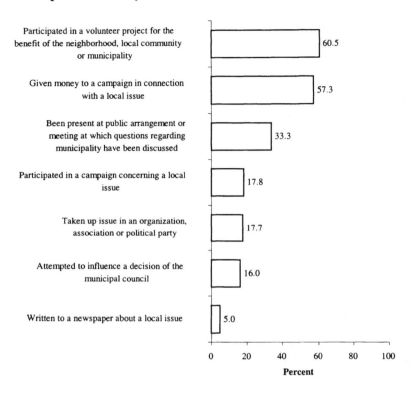

Source: Rose & Skare (1996b: 283-284)
* Minimum N = 1456

In order to explore this it is useful to develop a typology of cognitive orientations that highlights and distinguishes a little more clearly the different combinations of local and international cognitive affiliations expressed by people. The indices of local and international orientation already discussed provide the basis for just such a typology. By dichotomizing these two indices and then running a cross-tabulation of the resulting variables, we can identify four types or groups of individuals (cf. figure 12.7). For want of a better term, one of these groups may be labeled "the unattached". These are individuals who express a relatively low level of attachment to and little solidarity with other individuals living in their neighborhood and municipality and likewise a low level of attachment and solidarity with respect to the Nordic and European areas. As operationalized in this fashion, roughly 17 percent of the Norwegian population fall into this category.

Figure 12.7 A typology of citizens based on their cognitive orientations to local and international areas *

		Affiliation with neighborhood and municipality	
		Low	High
Affiliation with Norden and Europe	Low	"The unattached"	"Localists"
	High	"Internationalists"	"Cosmopolitans"

* A "high" or "low" with respect to affiliation with the respective areas is based on a dichotomization of scales constructed from two items relating to a sense of identity with the areas involved and a sense of solidarity with other persons living in these areas. For additional details, see the methodological appendix.

A second group of individuals are those who express a relatively *strong* sense of identification and sense of solidarity with others living in their neighborhood and municipality, but who express a relatively *weak* sense of identification and solidarity with others living in the Nordic area or Europe more generally. These individuals, whom may be considered "localists", constitute nearly half (47 percent) of the Norwegian population. By contrast, a third group express a relatively *weak* sense of identification and sense of solidarity with others living in their own neighborhood and municipality, but at the same time express a relatively *strong* sense of identification and solidarity with other individuals living in the Nordic area and Europe. This group is quite small (8 percent – less than one in ten Norwegians) and may be termed "internationalists". Finally, there is a fourth group consisting of those who express a relative strong sense of identification and sense of solidarity with others living in both areas. Roughly three out of ten (29 percent) of all Norwegians are found in this group, which may be termed "cosmopolitans".[19]

The question, then, is whether any differences are to be found between these groups with respect to the rates of local political involvement to be observed, and if so whether the differences are of statistical significance. This question may be approached in several ways. The approach that provides the most self-evident response is illustrated in figure 12.8. In this figure the percentage of individuals within each group that reports having participated in a volunteer project for the benefit of their neighborhood, local community or municipality is presented along with the coefficient *eta*, a statistical measure of the degree to which the percentages differ from one another.[20] As this measure indicates, the percentage of individuals reporting this activity within each group does differ (eta = 0.15) and the differences are statistically significant. Thus we see that whereas this form of local political involvement is reported by both localists and cosmopolitans in roughly equal proportions (64 and 65 percent respectively), it is less frequently reported by internationalists (55 percent). And among the unattached it is even less common (45 percent).

Figure 12.8 Percentage reporting having participated in a volunteer project for the benefit of their neighborhood, local community or municipality according to differences in cognitive affiliation (N=1470)

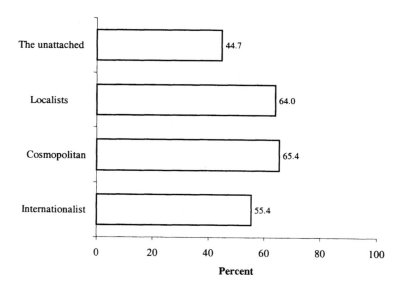

This pattern of findings is noteworthy in several respects. For one thing, it serves to support the contention that cognitive affiliations may be of some importance with respect to political behavior – if nothing else than as a conditioning factor. This is most evident in comparing the percentages of the unattached and the localists that report having participated in a local volunteer project. The difference is nearly 20 percentage points (45 versus 64 percent). Of course the direction of the causal effect, if that is indeed what is involved here, cannot be specified and documented from the materials reported here. It could just as easily be that participating in such volunteer projects, for whatever reason this is undertaken, contributes to strengthening the individual's sense of local identification and solidarity with others as the opposite. Were this to be the case, however, one would expect that the differences in participation among those with different cognitive profiles should be less pronounced. The reason for this is that barring a cumulative effect (something that of course cannot be done without closer investigation), it can be argued that anyone who has participated in such activities would be subject to the same socializing forces – forces that presumably encourage a sense of local affiliation – and should therefore have quite similar profiles of cognitive affiliation. Yet this is clearly not evident from the results presented in figure 12.8.

Another interesting aspect about the pattern of findings in figure 12.8 is that the percentage reporting having participated in a local volunteer project is nearly identical for localists and cosmopolitans, both of which have a relatively strong cognitive affiliation with the neighborhood and municipality. This serves to imply that a stronger international orientation per se does not inhibit local political involvement, at least so long as it is combined with a relatively strong local orientation. If the findings can be stretched a bit, in other words, it is possible to suggest that such cognitive orientations need not compete with one another and thereby have an impact on individual propensities to engage in local political activity. But neither is there any apparent synergy effect. Having a strong sense of cognitive affiliation in both directions does not appear to enhance the likelihood of undertaking specific forms of local political participation.

Finally, in what is perhaps the most significant finding in light of concerns about the possible implications of globalization for citizen orientations and political involvement, we must note that the percentage that report taking part in a local volunteer project is significantly lower among the internationalists than it is for localists and cosmopolitans. In the absence of a stronger local orientation, in other words, the likelihood of certain forms of local political involvement appears to be less. This applies, of course, to both the unattached and the internationalists. But depending on the dynamics underlying this tendency, which it is unfortunately not possible to determine with the present data, it can be suggested that the potential consequences are arguably of far greater import in the case of the internationalists than it is for the unattached. The reasoning here is that internationalists are more representative of those who have been "marked" by the forces of globalization.[21] Given this assumption, then to the extent that globalization (as part of a larger modernization syndrome) does serve to weaken local orientations, the implications seem quite clear: the foundation for local political involvement is undercut and prospects for local political participation decline.

Before jumping to such a pessimistic conclusion, however, it is worthwhile considering similar findings for the other forms of local political activity reported in figure 12.6. Rather than presenting six additional figures, each comparable to figure 12.8, the same findings may be combined and presented in tabular form (cf. Table 12.1). Each row contains the percentage of individuals within each of the four groups that report taking part in the activity in question, as well as the measure *eta* and its statistical significance. The first row of the table reproduces the findings from figure 12.8, whereas the remaining rows provide the same information for the six other forms of activity. For purposes of comparison, the percentage for the population as a whole is also presented in each case, as is the number of cases upon which the percentages are calculated.

Table 12.1 Rates of selected forms for local political participation among persons with different cognitive affiliation profiles. Percent and eta

Form of activity	The unattached	Localists	Cosmopolitans	Internationalists	Total population	N	Eta
Participated in a volunteer project for the benefit of your neighborhood, local community or municipality.	45	64	65	55	61	1470	.15*
Given money to a campaign in connection with a local issue.	44	61	62	49	57	1456	.14*
Been present at a public arrangement or meeting at which questions regarding municipality have been discussed.	20	39	37	18	33	1488	.17*
Participated in a campaign concerning a local issue.	11	18	23	13	18	1474	.10*
Taken up a local issue in an organization or political party.	10	19	21	12	18	1487	.11*
Attempted to influence a decision of the municipal council.	10	17	21	8	16	1490	.12*
Written to a newspaper about a local issue.	1	5	6	7	5	1497	.09*

* Significant at .01 level

The findings presented in Table 12.1 are highly consistent with those already discussed with respect to taking part in local volunteer projects. For most of the activities there appears to be a clear division: localists and cosmopolitans tend to be the most active locally, while the unattached and internationalists are less active. In fact, with only two minor exceptions, cosmopolitans are the most active, followed closely by the localists. But in one case (being present at a public arrangements or meeting at which questions regarding the municipality are discussed) localists report this activity slightly more than do cosmopolitans (39 versus 37 percent). And in another instance (writing to a newspaper about a local issue) the internationalists edge out both cosmopolitans and localists in reporting this activity (seven as opposed to 6 and 5 percent respectively). Internationalists, in other words, lag behind both localists and cosmopolitans in almost all forms of local political participation, and trail even the unattached in two forms of local involvement. The only form of local political activity where the internationalists appear to be slightly more involved that others is with respect to writing to newspapers about local issues.

Discussion and conclusion

Attempting to provide a summary assessment of the status and prospects for local democracy and citizen involvement in Norway in light of the findings presented here is a bit akin to judging whether a glass of water is half empty or half full. There is no clear answer, and how one responds depends upon what one may wish to emphasize. Trends in electoral behavior over the past three decades provide the basis for a more negative view, at least if one attributes declining turnout to a sense of increased disaffection and withdrawal of citizens from the local political arena. But evidence relating to other forms of local political participation provide the basis for a more positive view. Citizen involvement in a variety of non-electoral activities shows signs of being on the increase in much the same fashion as has been observed in a number of other countries. In this respect it would seem that the focal point of political involvement for many citizens is increasingly the non-electoral rather than the electoral arena.

What underlies this shift is a matter of discussion and conjecture in its own right. Among the factors suggested by some have been the changes in individual resources – especially the level of education which provides a foundation for involvement in a broader spectrum of political life. Associated with this has been an increase in levels of individual political efficacy and a greater potential for what Dalton (1984) has termed "cognitive mobilization" among broader segments of the population. Combined with changes in general value orientations (cf. Inglehart 1977, 1990, 1997) and new patterns of mass communication, which provide individuals not only with more information, but also better means to initiate political action, many citizens have in recent years been in a position to choose from among a broader repertoire of political activities. With an apparent strengthening of individual instrumental attitudes, some have even wondered if the changes in citizens' behavior may reflect a more fundamental change in the meaning of participatory activity (cf. Eriksen & Weigård 2000; Fuchs & Klingemann 1995; Habermas 1994; Rose 1999).

These are all possibilities that require further attention. The question posed in the sub-title to this chapter is one facet of this issue. Even if Norway has displayed tendencies of resisting some of the more overt consequences of globalization and international integration (for example by its rejection of membership in the European Union and a lag in the adoption of many New Public Management measures) and thereby reinforced the impression of a country existing on the periphery, it is indisputable that processes of globalization are being experienced throughout the country. The question is what do these processes portend for the future. Findings presented here do not provide a definitive answer to this question; they are merely suggestive. And the implication suggested is mixed. So long as globalization serves to strengthen an international orientation without undercutting local identities, there would seem to be little grounds for concern. Rather those who here have been termed cosmopolitans may well continue to offer a leading example of local citizen involvement through a variety of non-electoral channels. If, however, globalization contributes to a weakening of local orientations, then the prospects for broader citizen participation in local politics do not bode so favorably. This latter possibility is a matter of substantial normative and empirical importance for the future development of local democracy in Norway.

Methodological appendix

Description of the data and the operationalization of variables

Data used in this chapter were gathered in connection with the research project "Consumers, (tax)payers, citizens – The individual's relations to local government". This was a project funded by the Norwegian Research Council as part of a larger program of research on local government and politics. The intent of the project was to investigate the manner in which residents related to local government in the face of changing conditions of social and political life. Two national citizen surveys were conducted for this purpose – one in 1993, the other in 1996. Findings reported in this chapter are based on the panel of individuals that were interviewed in both surveys. The surveys conducted were in both cases based on a stratified sample that was designed to include respondents residing in all of the country's municipalities, in particular residents of the smallest municipalities which are otherwise represented by relatively few individuals in normal cross-section sample surveys. In both surveys data collection was carried out by a combination of telephone interviews and a follow up postal questionnaire sent to all those successfully interviewed by telephone. In 1993 a total of 3,820 persons were interviewed by telephone, and of these 3,005 completed and returned the questionnaire by the time data collection was completed. In 1996 a total of 3,833 persons were interviewed by telephone, and of these 2,994 completed and returned the questionnaire. Altogether the panel consists of 1708 persons who were interviewed and completed the postal questionnaire in both surveys. Based on an initial sample of 5,400 persons selected as a pool for telephone interviews, the figures for both surveys represent a response rate (or successful telephone interview completion rate) of 71 percent, and among those who were interviewed by telephone 79 and 78 percent completed and returned the postal questionnaire in 1993 and 1996 respectively. Analysis of selected socio-demographic characteristics of individuals who were interviewed and subsequently completed and returned the postal questionnaire show only a few significant deviations from population values for individuals residing in the various strata.[22] A review of the responses also suggests that the materials are of a generally high quality.

Sense of attachment or identification with selected geographic areas

Based on responses to the following question, which was asked in the 1993 survey: "In today's society people feel different degrees of attachment to or identification with various geographic areas. Can you indicate to what degree you feel an attachment to each of the geographic areas listed below? Place a checkmark for each geographic area."

The following list of seven geographic areas was then presented:

   a. The neighborhood or local area where you live
   b. The municipality where you live
   c. The county in which you live
   d. The region in which you live
   e. Norway as a whole
   f. The Nordic area
   g. Europe

Response categories were "None/little", "Some" and "A great deal".

Sense of solidarity with others living in selected geographic areas

Based on responses to the following question, which was asked in the 1996 survey: "In today's society people feel different degrees of solidarity with people living in various geographic areas. To what degree do you feel a sense of solidarity with persons living in the following geographic areas? Place a checkmark for each area."

The list of geographic areas presented was identical with that used in 1993. Response categories were "None", "Little", "Some", "Quite a bit" and "Very much".

For purposes of the analyses carried out in this chapter responses to this and the preceding attachment item from 1993 were recoded as follows:

None/ little = 0
Some = 1
A lot = 2

Indices of local and international affiliation

Responses to questions concerning a sense of attachment to and a sense of solidarity with others living in specific geographic areas were added to create indices for each area with values ranging from 0 to 4. The indices relating to neighborhood and municipality were then combined to create an additive index with values ranging from 0 to 8. The indices relating to Norden and Europe were likewise combined, again with values ranging from 0 to 8. Don't know responses were treated as missing data.

For purposes of establishing a typology of cognitive orientations for each individual, the indices of local and international affiliation were dichotomized with values from 0 to 4 being considered "low" and values 5 to 8 being considered "high". In essence this means that those individuals who received a "high" value had at least a value of 3 (i.e. had a response of "a lot") on one of the underlying indices.

Forms of local political behavior

Based on responses to the following item, which was asked in the 1996 written questionnaire: "Have you done any of the following things during the last two years?"

The following list of seven activities was then presented:

a. Participated in a volunteer project for the benefit of your neighborhood, local community or municipality.
b. Been present at a public arrangement or meeting at which questions regarding your municipality have been discussed.
c. Been present at a meeting for parents of school children or other meetings of a similar character.
d. Taken up a local issue in an organization, association or political party.
e. Attempted to influence a decision of the municipal council.
f. Given money to a campaign in connection with a local issue.
g. Participated in a campaign concerning a local issue.
h. Written to a newspaper about a local issue.

Responses were coded as follows ("Don't know" and "Don't remember" were treated as missing):
No = 0
Yes = 1

References

Baldersheim, Harald, Tore Hansen, Per Arnt Pettersen and Lawrence Rose (1990). *Publikums syn på kommunepolitikk og kommunale tjenester.* Bergen: LOS-senteret. LOS-rapport 90/2.
Bjørklund, Tor and Jo Saglie (2000). *Lokalvalget i 1999: Rekordlav og rekordhøy deltakelse.* Oslo: Institutt for samfunnsforskning. Rapport 12:2000.
Borg, Sami (1995). "Electoral Participation", in van Deth, Jan W. and Elinor Scarborough, eds., *The Impact of Values.* Beliefs in Government vol. 4. Oxford: Oxford University Press.
Dale, Trine (1993). *Prosjekt "Folks forhold til kommunen". Dokumentasjonsrapport.* Oslo: Statistisk sentralbyrå, Seksjon for intervjuundersøkelser.
Dalton, Russell J (1984). "Cognitive Mobilization and Partisan Dealignment in Advanced Industrial Democracies", *Journal of Politics* 46:264-284.
Dalton, Russell J. (1996). *Citizen Politics: Public Opinion and Political Parties in Advanced Western Democracies,* 2nd ed. Chatham, NJ: Chatham House.
Deutsch, Karl (1961). "Social Mobilization and Political Development", *American Political Science Review* 55:493-514.
Eriksen, Erik and Jarle Weigård (2000). "The End of Citizenship? New Roles Challenging the Political Order", in McKinnon, C. and I. Hampshire-Monk, eds., *The Demands of Citizenship.* London: Continuum.
Friedman, Jeffrey, ed. (1996). *The Rational Choice Controversy: Economic Models of Politics Reconsidered.* New Haven: Yale University Press.
Fuchs, Dieter and Hans-Dieter Klingemann (1995). "Citizens and the State: A Changing Relationship?" in Klingemann, Hans-Dieter and Dieter Fuchs, eds., *Citizens and the State.* Beliefs in Government vol. 1. Oxford: Oxford University Press.
Gunderlach, Peter (1995). "Grass-Roots Activity", in van Deth, Jan W. and Elinor Scarborough, eds., *The Impact of Values.* Beliefs in Government vol. 4. Oxford: Oxford University Press.
Habermas, Jörgen (1994). "Citizenship and National Identity", in van Steenbergen, B., ed., *The Condition of Citizenship.* London: Sage Publications.
Held, David, Anthony McGrew, David Goldblatt and Jonathan Perraton (1999). *Global Transformations: Politics, Economics and Culture.* Cambridge: Polity Press.
IDEA, (1997). *Voter Turnout from 1945 to 1997: A Global Report.* Stockholm: International IDEA.
Inglehart, Ronald (1977). *The Silent Revolution: Changing Values and Political Styles among Western Publics.* Princeton: Princeton University Press.
Inglehart, Ronald (1990). *Cultural Shift in Advanced Industrial Society.* Princeton: Princeton University Press.
Inglehart, Ronald (1997). *Modernization and Postmodernization: Cultural, Economic and Political Change in 43 Societies.* Princeton: Princeton University Press.
Keohane, Robert O. and Joseph S., Nye Jr. (2000). "Introduction", in Joseph S. Nye Jr. and John D. Donahue, eds., *Governance in a Globalizing World.* Washington, D.C.: Brookings Institution Press.
Larsen, Helge O. (2002). "Democratic Renewal or Constitutional Confusion?" in Caulfield, Janet and Helge O Larsen, eds., *Local Government at the Millennium.* Leverkusen: Leske + Budrich Verlag.
Lerner, Daniel (1958). *The Passing of Traditional Society.* New York: Free Press.
Lijphart, Arend (2000). "Turnout", in Rose, Richard, ed., International Encyclopedia of Elections. Macmillan, London.

Mabileau, Albert, George Moyser, Geraint Parry and Patrick Quantin (1989). *Local Politics and Participation in Britain and France*. Cambridge: Cambridge University Press.
Nagel, Anne-Hilde, ed. (1991). *Velferdskommunen: Kommunenes rolle i utviklingen av velferdsstaten*. Bergen: Alma Mater.
Norris, Pippa (2000). "Global Governance and Cosmopolitan Citizens", in Nye, Joseph S., Jr. and John D. Donahue, eds., *Governance in a Globalizing World*. Washington, D.C.: Brookings Institution Press.
Preston. P.W. (1997). *Political/Cultural Identity: Citizens and Nations in a Global Era*. London: Sage Publications.
Quantin, Patrick (1989). "In Search of Community Spirit", in Albert Mabileau, George Moyser, Geraint Parry and Patrick Quantin (1989). *Local Politics and Participation in Britain and France*. Cambridge: Cambridge University Press.
Rose, Lawrence and Audun Skare (1996a). *Dokumentasjonsrapport: Undersøkelse om folks forhold til kommunen, 1993*. Oslo: Institutt for statsvitenskap, Universitetet i Oslo.
Rose, Lawrence and Audun Skare (1996b). *Dokumentasjonsrapport: Undersøkelse om folks forhold til kommunen, 1996*. Oslo: Institutt for statsvitenskap, Universitetet i Oslo.
Rose, Lawrence E. (1996). "Norway", in Albaek, Erik, Lawrence Rose, Lars Strömberg and Krister Ståhlberg. *Nordic Local Government*. Helsinki: The Association of Finnish Local Authorities.
Rose, Lawrence E. (1999). "Citizen (Re)orientations in the Welfare State: From Public to Private Citizens?" in Bussemaker, J., ed., *Citizenship and Transition in European Welfare States*. London: Routledge.
Rose, Lawrence E. (2002). "Normer og roller – borgerpliktens endelikt?" in Aardal, Bernt ed., *Valgdeltakelse og lokaldemokrati*. Oslo: Kommuneforlaget.
Rose, Lawrence E. and Krister Ståhlberg (2000). "Municipal Identification and Democratic Citizenship: A Finnish-Norwegian Comparison", in Karvonen, Lauir and Ståhlberg, Krister, eds., *Festschrift for Dag Anckar on his 60th Birthday*. Åbo: Åbo Akademi University Press.
Rudlang, Hilde (1996). *Undersøkelse om folks forhold til kommunen - 1996*. Dokumentasjonsrapport. Oslo: Statistisk sentralbyrå, Avdeling for personstatistikk/ Seksjon for intervjuundersøkelser. Notater 1996 96/22.
Statistics Norway (1995). *Historical Statistics 1994*. Oslo/Kongsvinger: Statistisk sentralbyrå. NOS, series C-188.
Statistics Norway (2002). *Statistisk Årbok 2002*. Oslo/Kongsvinger: Statistisk sentralbyrå. NOS, series C-713.
Topf, Richard (1995). "Beyond Electoral Participation", in Klingemann, Hans-Dieter and Dieter Fuchs, eds., *Citizens and the State*. Beliefs in Government vol. 1. Oxford: Oxford University Press.
Verba, Sidney, Kay L. Schlozman and Henry E. Brady (1995). *Voice and Equality: Civic Voluntarism in American Politics*. Cambridge, MA: Harvard University Press.

Notes

[1] Elections for both bodies are held at the same time, so the marginal cost of casting a ballot in both elections is relatively low once a voter has decided to vote.

[2] Direct elections for the county councils were first introduced in 1975. Before that time representatives to county councils were indirectly elected by municipal councils.

[3] Turnout in the 1963 local elections was in many respects abnormal, since elections took place in the aftermath of a national cabinet crisis that focused and rallied the political interest of many citizens. The general point concerning a long-term decline in local election turnout nonetheless remains the same.

[4] For a discussion of these experiments, see Larsen (2002).

[5] These percentages are based on materials found in Table 23.1 and Table 23.3 in Statistics Norway (1995:586 and 588) and supplemented by data for more recent years from the statistical yearbook for 2002 (Statistics Norway 2002:278 and 283).

[6] Effective as of 1 January 2002 primary responsibility for the operation of hospitals has been taken over by central government.

[7] Findings reported by Bjørklund and Saglie (2000) are based on surveys carried out in connection with the 1995 and 1999 local elections in Norway and the 1985, 1989 and 1993 national parliamentary elections. The wording of questions asked in the national as opposed to local election surveys is not identical, but it is close enough to permit a careful comparison. And the trends, if not the absolute levels of political participation, are identical with those reported here.

[8] There is no universally accepted definition of globalization; definitions abound. But the definition offered here captures what seems to be the essence of many definitions found in the literature. See, for example, Held et al. (1999:14-15) and Keohane & Nye (2000:2).

[9] For a discussion of political-cultural identity that reflects the models displayed in Figures 3a and 3b, see Preston (1997), especially chapter 4.

[10] Other theoretical perspectives exist that seek to explain why people would identify with specific geographically delimited units, but in these alternative perspectives there is little, if any, reason to expect that processes of globalization per se should make a difference. In the social-psychological perspective, by comparison, there is good reason to believe that globalization may play a significant role. For a brief review of alternative theoretical perspectives regarding development of individual identities with geographic areas, see Rose and Ståhlberg (2000:261-263).

[11] It is important to stress that models depicted in Figures 3a and 3b both represent simplified synchronic snapshots that are merely intended to highlight the causal linkages of primary interest for the present chapter. This is not to deny, however, that there may be a variety of processes whereby the causal arrows may point in the opposite direction as well, especially when considered in a more diachronic light. This is particularly evident in thinking about political behavior at a higher political level where decisions taken by policy makers may in their own right have an impact on identities and aspects of globalization. This latter possibility is clearly underlined by Keohane and Nye (2000) in their introductory chapter to the book *Governance in a Globalizing World*. This is also a central tenet in what Held and associates label the skeptical thesis regarding globalization. As they note: "governments are not the passive victims of internationalization but, on the contrary, its primary architects" (Held et al, 1999:6). In a similar manner there is every reason to believe that also at the individual level the causal influences may in fact run in both directions, especially between identity and behavior.

[12] The work of Ronald Inglehart (1977, 1990, 1997) is a noteworthy exception to this statement, and Inglehart's work is hotly contested by many scholars. Among earlier work of some relevance, however, that of Deutsch (1961) and Lerner (1958) should also be mentioned.

[13] Question wording and procedures used in index construction based on these items are presented in the methodological appendix to this chapter.

[14] As noted in the methodological appendix, the questions on which figure 12.4 is based included both the county and the region in which the respondents lived. For purposes of simplification, however, these two additional geographical areas have been omitted.

[15] Basically this is an argument that familiarity builds understanding and respect (not, as some might suggest, contempt) for other individuals, and these considerations are important building blocks in establishing a sense of solidarity.

[16] That the two cognitive orientations considered here are not one and the same is also evident from the correlations that exist between responses to the two questions from the same individuals. For the four principal areas of interest here the magnitude of these correlations is roughly .30, while for Norway as a whole the correlation is only .22.

[17] For an exploration of the difference between Norway and Finland, see Rose and Ståhlberg (2000).

[18] Given the context in which the data were collected, the activities reported in figure 12.2 are also presumably local in character, although the *arena* or *object* of the activities was not as explicitly highlighted in the question as it was for the activities reported in figure 12.6.

[19] Note that this is a different and arguably more appropriate use of the term cosmopolitans than that found in Norris (2000).

[20] Eta is only a measure of differences, varying from a value of 0.0 (no difference) to a value of 1.0 (total difference) and says nothing about the direction of the differences.

[21] Findings from separate analyses not presented here do not provide a strong basis for making this assumption. It nonetheless seems more reasonable to make this assumption than the opposite – i.e. that the unattached are those who represent the product of globalization.

[22] There is no significant deviation with respect to gender for example. There is a slight tendency towards a systematic under-representation of the oldest segment of the sample (those from 67 to 80 years of age), but in only two strata is the deviation statistically significant in the 1993 survey. For a more detailed discussion of the surveys, sample composition and results achieved, see Dale (1993), Rose & Skare (1996a, 1996b) and Rudlang (1996).

Chapter 13

"Management" and Urban Political Leaders in France

Stéphane Cadiou

The aim of this article is to highlight the way local political leaders make use of the terminology and practice of *management* for political ends. New power constellations[1] and arrangements are emerging in French cities. A quest for legitimacy[2] is part and parcel of the processes of urban governance although it may not always be easy for politicians to assess exactly what the public expectations are, except in a rather roundabout way.[3] Increasingly, management discourse is serving the quest for legitimacy.[4]

"Public management" as a reference

A reflection of a "new spirit of capitalism",[5] management invades many politico-administrative fields. Above all stemming from the private sector and conveying a symbolic system of representations, it has subsequently gained specific attention in public organizations. Generally speaking, management discourse reveals a switch of political attention to *administrative* dimensions of governmental activity, which is indicated by the interest taken in the provision of services and in the financial aspects of their operation. Management, re-qualified as "new public management",[6] is characterized by its concern with the transformation of the internal functioning of city administrations but also by its focus on relationships with users and external partners. To achieve such objectives, managers rely on a combination of principles of action such as project logic, innovation, contractualization, competition, evaluation, participation... . The objective of the managerial approach is to reconcile financial skill (stabilizing fiscal pressure) with the maintenance of public services. The promotion, coherence and apparent necessity of these principles are conveyed in the form of an opposition to "classic" administration condemned for its "bureaucratic", "heavy" and "irresponsible"[7] ways. The promotion of "management" entails criticism of traditional administration, highlighting its presumed incapacity to meet "new demands". Therefore, management emerges as a response to sectorial divisions and administrative hierarchies, and more generally as a means of renewing modes of government. It becomes a real "accusation tool" allowing (in the name of financial orthodoxy) the denunciation of (for example) engineers as excessive spenders of investment budgets. It is equally a "disqualification" tool against the conservative administrative order and its personnel serving in highly fragmented organizations. Whether it is a technique or discourse for change, management is a power instrument, conveying a socio-political vision with a hegemonic objective (financial orthodoxy, making individuals responsible).

The symbolic and practical efficiency of management is measured by the fervour it arouses, beyond partisan affiliation, with diverse local, political and administrative political leaders, who quite often relate their credibility to their ability to promote new dogmas:

"It is evident that your reflections will take you to the frontier of the current restructuring, a reorganization in the functioning [of the administration of the Bordeaux Metropolitan Authority]. There are reallocations of resources to be envisaged"[8] (A. Juppé).

"Our administrative organization is still very divided, very vertical, whereas problems, and in particular a certain number of big issues concerning society, need a more global approach around projects"[9] (a communist mayor).[10]

As a power discourse, public management drives a certain number of local *reforms*. The service projects (the "communal project" in Bordeaux, "Nantes public services XXI" in Nantes) are implemented in order to transform existing administrations. Often materializing through a change in the organization chart, they go together with the formulation of "community projects" or "urban projects", intended to implement the mayors' political intentions. In a similar way, management allows for the legitimization of lower financial expenditure by prompting more constraining financial practices and controls (Centre for budgetary responsibilities, management control, evaluations, feasibility studies...). So it is definitely the "hegemonization" of an organizational schema we are witnessing in so far as management tends to re-orient the former practices. Seeing the elected officials turned "managers", or even a "mayor-manager", clearly testifies to a redefinition of political action and its main actors. The spread of management is facilitated by the fact that the latter does not constitute a theoretically hermetic structure, impervious to interpretations. Management principles are sufficiently vague to be adapted and implemented in very diverse situations but strong enough to maintain a coherent vision of institutions and public organizations.

Tensions around legitimacy

Here, we will look into the way urban leaders respond to management. This means understanding the politico-ideological situation that management reflects and aims to change. The use of management tools in urban governments is difficult to dissociate from questions about the identity and the legitimacy of political leaders who are subject to contradictory processes that demonstrate the limits of their leadership positions.

The management orientation has been all the stronger as the main French political parties (and in particular the Socialist party) accepted neo-liberal administrative approaches during the 1980s. It nevertheless seems that the penetration of management into France has not been as strong as in other countries, mainly because consultancy firms have been less active in this field in France.[11]

Below, two types of tensions are discussed that highlight the emergent nature of leadership, and more particularly the ideological function of management.

Responsibilities and complexity

One of the major effects of French decentralization since 1982 has not only been the redistribution of public responsibilities but also the relocation of social problems caused by the economic crisis of the 1970s and 1980s. The "crisis" has become increasingly urban. It was during this phase (qualified by some authors as a hegemonic crisis of State machinery[12]), that the elected officials in big towns had to elaborate and formulate responses to new economic constraints. Besides, urban political leaders were made more accountable also because (with the Socialists having won over positions at the national level) leftist local representatives could no longer denounce the State and ascribe the perverse effects of implemented policies to the state elite. Redistributing tasks is therefore related to a limitation of loopholes for urban leaders at a time when cities are considered as key actors of the (international) re-organization of the world. Indeed, the political responses of new urban leaders happen within a context of turmoil in the cities, and more particularly the major ones. The State has gradually lost its hegemonic place in urban services. Without giving in to the charms of a diehard localism, it is important to stress the structuring force of emergent lines of collaboration and communication between the major urban centers of Europe.

Whereas European towns were historically defined in relation to the State,[13] they are increasingly embedded in international urban networks, which drive the leaders to elaborate their programmes and to describe themselves in relation to exogenous constraints. The function of social integration, consequently, becomes more problematic and comes into conflict with definitions of "good governance" as advocated by international organizations such as e.g. the World Bank.

Parallel to decentralization, the cities have become a setting for a certain number of state or local public operations. The palette of urban policies has changed, from housing and infrastructure (which until now have made up the main grounds for public intervention) to social affairs, the economy or even ecology. What used to be termed urban politics is, in this respect, particularly revealing considering the juxtaposition of many operations and procedures (Social development of districts, urban contracts, large urban projects, local integration plans based on the economy...). In the same way, more or less experimental procedures for various sectors (Project for Urban transport, Local housing project, Environmental Charter, *contrat d'agglomération*), are added on top of each other without methods to adjust or to combine them being specified.

In the cites, numerous arrangements for public intervention are therefore heaped on top of each other, creating future problems of linkages and organizational integration. The international positioning strategies of cites, adopted by the leaders and largely supported by the managers of large private groups (network operators, public works...) have trouble adjusting to social programmes carried out in the so-called sensitive districts. How does one reconcile, for example, the restructuring (led both by the mayor of Bordeaux and the Chamber for Industry and Commerce) of the agency for urban economic development (formerly the Office for Research and Development) with interventions in the city's most disadvantaged areas? It is the same in Nantes, where the introduction of social development procedures for districts and the establishment of an economic development agency directed by aids close to the mayor, seem to pull the town in two opposite directions.

Recourse to a managerial approach is an ideological response to the contradictions and limits inherent in the leader's position, confronted with difficult adjustments between various public programmes at the local level. It is a way to partially ameliorate the dispersion of public operations and certainly also problems of interests, conflicts and competencies. Although it claims to reshape the functioning of administrations and more generally modes of government, management only provides a weak tool for mobilization. Elected officials simply aim at doing *better.* Management is thus a form of demonstration of the their powerlessness with regard to the problem of enhancing social integration in urban spaces.

In the wake of decentralization an increasing degree of specialization has taken place in urban administration. Even if the competencies of the cities did not really increase, decentralization led to a partition of certain administrative spheres. For example, in many cities, urban development is divided between operational urbanism, road networks, green spaces, etc. The implementation of service projects, inspired by *New Public Management* (to which the majority of the main political and administrative leaders rallied in the city councils of Nantes and Bordeaux) partly shows a concern with functional fragmentation. Management is presented as a means of providing an "efficient and innovating" organization:

"Beyond an ever increasing technicality, the management of projects and problems requires a new expertise, the ability to manage complexities. The stance of our fellow citizens, their expectations and their involvement in the very life of our town not only hold us to a wider accountability but also oblige us to build a high-performing organization for the public services for which we are responsible"[14] (*Community Project*, The Bordeaux Metropolitan Authority).

"In 1997, the town of Nantes initiated a wide "quality" approach within its services, "Nantes Public Utility Services XXI", with a view to improve the services rendered to the *Nantais* and to adapt the services to social changes [...] Eventually, it meant generalizing and making durable a "municipal culture of change"[15] (*Activity Report*, Ville de Nantes, 1999).

Actually, across the service projects, it is not really a question of setting priorities but rather of showing how they complement each other, in such a manner that service coordination becomes (for those in charge of politico-administrative affairs) proof of a "working" administration. Instead of dealing with the question of overload, the managerial teams resort to inevitably unstable organizational arrangements and compromises: new departments are created, subsequently giving rise to a proliferation of inter-departmental meetings. So, in Nantes, since 1989, the focus on "urban development" led to a specialization of policies (between urban town-planning, dealing with public areas and town policy) and departments creating a split within the former compact organization. A new department, "Development and Neighbourhood Affairs", was created as from 1995 and was placed under the Chief Executive Officer's authority.

Moreover, the local leaders always seem to be waiting for tools able to give minimal coherence to disparate expertise and services. This is the reason why they willingly resort to new management techniques, like computer processing or expert systems. These techniques are used to bring out the complementarity between the departments.

Public recognition and criticism

The "service projects" give rise to numerous coordination meetings between departments, but also between elected officials and civil servants or external partners. In Nantes or Bordeaux, "decentralization" and "proximity" projects have led to the setting up of ward committees throughout the city (cf. also chapter 11). The implementation of procedures derived from these urban policy generate both their own committees in which elected officials, technicians and inhabitants meet each other, as well as evaluation procedures.

In short, whilst *relational systems* vary, political leaders constantly find themselves more and more subject to external and possibly contesting arguments and remarks. D. Gaxie underlines that (for the elected officials) one of the consequences of these systems is to reduce the "field of the possible"[16] by increasing opportunities for assessment of policies, which contributes to weakening the position of elected leaders. The projects aiming at transforming government methods have thus engendered a certain continuity (beyond the electoral periods) of the views on political activity. The latter is consequently subject to a more and more incessant flux of comments, criticisms, reports or rumors. Without precisely studying the influence of relational systems, we can at least suggest that they compel the elected officials to increasingly justify themselves.

"We can no longer initiate projects without involving the population... it is something very complicated and not obvious....still, this has always existed but the population's capacity to accept things is becoming more and more of a concern."[17]

The tools used in the name of a "new" urban management encourage controversies, never completely mastered by the elected officials and therefore potentially destabilizing. But, on the other hand, they provide them with many occasions to show their adjustment to expectations – whether actually achieved or constructed.

Effects on urban leadership

A new technocracy?

The use of a managerial rhetoric is a sign of the redistribution of power relations within administrations. This tends to reveal the incapacity of traditional methods of local government to meet financial constraints. The risk-sharing objective is inconsistent with the logic of public programmes (cf. the case of "régies directes") and skills, which have constituted the functional field of urban engineers. In a similar way, objectives of rationalization, networking and evaluation seem incompatible with practical and traditional (administrative/technical) hierarchies. Nevertheless, the recombining effects of administrative functioning are difficult to perceive, and (very rarely) expressed radically. The most perceptible effect is the growth of new administrative elites, able to embody financial constraints through their profiles and assets. One may mention two evolutions affecting the internal equilibria and the organizational capacity of urban leadership.

On the one hand, it is undeniable that, at the head of the municipal services, an elite of specialists in organizational matters has emerged. Some authors have therefore examined the reinforcement of the Chief Administrative Officer's role – the latter having "put on the clothes of the manager": "in many towns the establishment of a general management of services is one of the signs of the pre-eminence acquired by the CEO".[18] The CEO's strengthened position also goes hand in hand with the development of new profiles, corresponding to administrative know-how. Hence, the rise to power of senior management employees (senior civil servants) recruited from urban enterprises. Knowledge of the city is not a priority in their recruitment, unlike their capacity to manage and apply knowledge and techniques largely independent of the local context, in order to run projects according to the criteria of "managerial governance". In Bordeaux, since Juppé took the reins of the town-hall in 1995, a complete change of department heads took place in the course of two or three years. Their mainly external recruitment particularly aimed at breaking with promotions by seniority having led to a lack of managers in the Bordeaux town hall. To this effect, the present general manager of departments is a former E.N.A. (National School of Administration) student and sub-prefect. It should also be stressed that the rise of management has engendered a *differentiation* process within local administrations, with an increase in agents expected to take on tasks prompted by the new managerial style: management controllers, assessors, experts in internal communication... agents more often placed close to the CEO who regards them as new tools to strengthen his power. At present, next to the CEO for the Bordeaux Metropolitan Authority, there is for example an "evaluation committee, a prospective and advisory committee" (with diverse departments: "evaluation and planning" "organization and methods", auditing, "management supervision and advice", quality control, negotiation counseling) regrouping experts with administrative knowledge and experience with management (to this effect, one of the committee's members is a former management employee of a private company).

The growing reference to management goes with an abundance (alongside political leaders) of experts working *with* and *for* administrative "rationalization". For the management experts policy methods and administrative criteria are at the top of the agenda: such a perception, consequently, tends to change government activity into an affair of "technical" procedures, entrusted to a body of modern day *missionaries*: the "managers". It happens all the more easily as it is conceived as a pragmatic response to a group of problematic dysfunctions, described by the management experts as the symptoms of a "governability" crisis. Without embarking upon a discussion of this nature, it must be stressed that it makes up an indispensable support for the promotion of new actors of local administration.

Alongside the "managers" a new set of professional figures has emerged, responsible for converting the managerial principles of action into operational practices within and next to the departments. These are the so-called "project leaders", whose origin is linked to the so-called "urban policy" projects. Conveying a rhetoric emphasizing project logic, comprehensiveness and networking the new prerequisites for administrative action, the project leaders are often seen as actors and carriers of innovation. Between municipal institutions and local societies, between theorized discourses on management and implemented actions, they appear as the *go-betweens* likely to renew methods of intervention. Because of the hopes that they represent to local leaders and scientists, project leader posts have been extended to more traditional areas of action (transport, urban development, economy...). In Nantes, the system of project leaders (at first set up in the wards "at risk" in accordance with urban policy) was extended to the whole of the town area as of 1995. The duty of project leaders (and others in charge of similar missions) is above all to express the managerial watchword through actions, to mobilize and propel (public or private) "partnership" networks around systems of public action.

From this perspective, the consolidation of urban regimes is strictly dependent on new administrative elites, conveying and defending managerial standards. Mastering new skills as regards management and organization becomes a crucial concern in exercising government activity. Consequently, urban regimes tend to encompass more complex organizational settings, the integration of which still remains problematic. Actors become increasingly interdependent. As a result, leadership comes out reinforced but also proves to be less transparent. Each actor contributes to the consolidation of the regime but with effects limited by the presence of many participants.[19] In this respect, leadership is a collective product, imperfectly controlled by the elected leader on account of the existence of multiple interactions. For the leaders, the risk is to see the tools of power dispersing.

Finally, we wish to emphasize that the constitution and consolidation of regimes is weakened by the personalized nature of the activities of the new managers and professionals. Called to implement systems of public action or to rationalize administrative organization, the new administrative elites are doomed to permanently tinker with managerial principles in order to adapt them to local contexts.[20] To this effect, the remarks of an internal note from the administrative hierarchy, during the implementation of the departmental project of the Bordeaux Metropolitan Authority, are particularly revealing:

"The community project as a reference document must be implemented by the new organization. To maintain its relevance, it must be adapted for implementation suited to the evolution of the Authority's needs and resources. Furthermore, its implementation can only be gradual, especially so as to take into account the time needed for an end to resistance that is inevitable in a context of major change."[21]

The redefinition of political skills

In the larger French cities, the political and administrative leaders' acceptance of "new management principles" is undeniable. The reorientation of managerial practices is also partly the product of a *competition effect* expanding (beyond the borders under state control) the limits of the local political arena. In this respect, leaders increasingly see themselves as ed actors committing their town in a widened, mainly European urban space with relatively vague contours: "If there is an ambition that we must set for ourselves today, it is to assert ourselves as the great urban pole of the Atlantic front. By relying on our history, talents, know-how and simply adapting ourselves to rapid world evolutions. That is the goal of a metropolis."[22]

"Owing to its wines, Bordeaux enjoys real international fame. But the city has to be extended to enable it to compete with other major cities."[23]

The adoption of managerial strategies is partly explained by the need to be positioned in relation to transnational networks for the circulation of assets and resources (information, skills...). But it also results from the "imposition effect" (wrapped up in a semi-learned appearance[24]), of a discourse on the necessary "urban European governance". This discourse is based on watchwords turned into hegemonic standards[25], e.g. references to "partnership", "projects", "cooperation", but also "flexibility", "efficiency", "transparency" etc. The terms favoured are connected to each other and operate in a circular way to make up a kind of *autonomous* rhetoric, whose originator and conveyor can never really be identified. Rendering discourse autonomous enables the origin and dominant interests on which it is based to be partially erased, reinforcing its authority and apparent neutrality.

This is how a more prescriptive than descriptive rhetoric, with managerial inspiration, which leaders tend to cling to, is asserted. As a result, we are witnessing a symbolic redefinition of methods of political representation shared by diverse (political, economic, intellectual) national and international[26] elites. For elected officials concerned with asserting their leadership and seeing it acknowledged, the interest is to appropriate and master this managerial rhetoric. In other terms, to be heard in the public sphere, and therefore recognized as a legitimate partner, the dominant language (in this case the managerial language) needs to be mastered. We are therefore dealing with a redefinition of *political skill* in the sense that the latter is now closely associated with the capacity of the leaders and their parties to record their actions in registers and forms inspired by managerial standards. This is why political leaders today associate their names, or even their fate with the assertion of new managerial demands structuring the representation of what political action should be like. The present mayor of Bordeaux's stance is, on these grounds, highly committed to promoting the "*redynamisation*" of the town through administrative reform. Eisinger's characterization of the regimes of American cities also captures developments in French cities, "leaders must first and foremost demonstrate skills in managing scarce resources [...] the new mayors speak the language of modern public management and run their administrations accordingly".[27]

The question of political distinctions

Finally, one may wonder whether one of the effects of constant references to managerial issues will be to erase or at least to attenuate political distinctions between urban leaders. Political leaders seem on the way to becoming "super co-ordinators", managing the town's resources, contracting with foreign partners, PR agents for their cities...The leaders' discourse tends to avoid references to social conflicts, and instead makes "coordination" an objective in itself. Management methods thus tend to define new perspectives with regard to political struggles and public recognition. In other terms, political credibility is sought and obtained by focusing on *methods* and *means* of action. Political cleavages are now centered on attitudes to "new" managerial methods as a discriminant criterion. The "new" public management is often presented in opposition to "former" governmental practices[28] thus (re-) establishing a political distinction. On the whole, placed in a position as public rulers, within a context where financial margins are reduced, urban political leaders are renegotiating their political identity according to new positions, in this case according to ways of managing public institutions.

The constitution of political regimes in French cities today increasingly relies on professionals that master a set of techniques and arguments intended to change the way local administration has traditionally functioned. Spreading managerial watchwords has been made easier as urban political leaders have had to face both an extension of public tasks and responsibilities and a decrease in financial means. The success of the managerial rhetoric is thus explained by the possibility it has given leaders to define a new foundation for their political credibility. The emergent image of the *mayor-manager* is suggestive with regard to the transformation under way. The other side of the coin is a "globalization" of political practices, which results in a blurring of political distinctions and a concomitant loss of transparency and urban autonomy.

References

Bailey, F. G. (1971). *Les règles du jeu politique*, Paris: PUF.
Boltanski, L. and E. Chiapello (1999). *Le nouvel esprit du capitalisme*, Paris: Gallimard.
Bourdieu, P. and L. Wacquant (1998). "Sur les ruses de la raison impérialiste", *Actes de la recherche en sciences sociales*, 121-122.
Eisinger, P. (1998). "City Politics in an Era of Federal Devolution", Urban Affairs Review, 33: 3.

Elias, N. (1991). *Qu'est-ce que la sociologie?*, Paris: Ed. de l'aube.
Gaxie, D. (1996). "Gouvernabilité et transformations structurelles des démocraties", in *Curapp ed. La gouvernabilité*, Paris: PUF.
Hood, C. (1991). "A Public management for all seasons?", *Public administration*, Vol. 69.
Lagroye, J. (1985). "La légitimation", in *Traité de science politique*, Tome 1, Paris: PUF.
Lagroye, J. (1993). "Estimation assez grossière sur la base d'indices ténus", *Sociologie politique*, Paris: PFNSP.
Le Galès, P. and A. Harding (1996). "Villes et Etats", in V. Wright and S. Cassese, eds. *La recomposition de L'Etat en Europe*, Paris: La Découverte.
Lowndes, V. (1997)."Change in Public Service Management: New Institutions and New Managerial Regimes", in *Frontières*, 9.
Poulantzas, N. ed. (1976). *La crise de l'Etat*, Paris: PUF.
Préteceille, E. (1991). "Paradoxes politiques des restructurations urbaines", *Espaces et Sociétés*, 59.
Prior, D. (1993). "In search of the New Public Management", *Local Government Studies*, 19: 3.
Roubieu, O. (1994). "Le modèle du 'manager'. L'imposition d'une figure légitime parmi les hauts fonctionnnaires des collectivités locales", *Politix*, 28.
Saint Martin, D. (1998). "The New Managerialism and the Policy Influence of Consultants in Government: A Historical-Institutionalist Analysis of Britain, Canada and France", *Governance*, 11: 3.

Notes

[1] Whence frequent recourse to the term "équipes politiques" (political teams) used by F. G. Bailey, cf. *Les règles du jeu politique*, Paris, PUF, 1971.

[2] "acquérir une légitimité durable", J. Lagroye,, "La légitimation", in *Traité de science politique*, Tome 1, Paris, PUF, 1985, p. 396.

[3] "estimation assez grossière sur la base d'indices ténus", J. Lagroye, *Sociologie politique*, Paris, PFNSP, 1993, p. 396.

[4] We will mainly depend on reflections developed during research carried out for a doctorate relating to expertise in the management of towns. We will particularly consider the cases of two major towns, Nantes and Bordeaux, run by two mayors of different political camps. One is a gaullist mayor (Bordeaux), the other is a socialist mayor (Nantes).

[5] "nouvel esprit du capitalisme", L. Boltanski, E. Chiapello, *Le nouvel esprit du capitalisme*, Paris, Gallimard, 1999.

[6] "nouveau management public", C. Hood, "A Public management for all seasons?", *Public administration*, Vol. 69, 1991. D. Prior, "In search of the New Public Management", *Local Government Studies*, Vol. 19, 3, 1993.

[7] L. Boltanski, E. Chiapello, *Le nouvel esprit du capitalisme*, op. cit.

[8] "Il est évident que vos réflexions vont conduire à des modifications de frontières, à une réorganisation dans le fonctionnement [de l'administration de la Communauté Urbaine de Bordeaux] Il y a des réallocations de moyens à envisager."

[9] "nous avons une organisation de l'administration qui est encore très cloisonnée, très verticale, alors que des problèmes, et notamment un certain nombre de grandes questions de société nécessitent une approche plus globale autour de projets."

[10] "La pratique et la réalité du management public dans les collectivités territoriales", *Les Cahiers du CNFPT*, 43, 1995. This journal is particularly revealing with regard to managerial ecumenism.

[11] This is an argument developed by D. Saint Martin, in "The New Managerialism and the Policy Influence of Consultants in Government: An Historical-Institutionalist Analysis of Britain, Canada and France", *Governance*, Vol. 11, 3, 1998.

[12] See also for a more general presentation of theses on State defiance, N. Poulantzas, dir., *La crise de l'Etat*, Paris, PUF, 1976. Cf. also E. Préteceille, "Paradoxes politiques des restructurations urbaines", *Espaces et Sociétés*, 59, 1991.

[13] P. Le Galès, A. Harding, "Villes et Etats", in V. Wright, S. Cassese, ed., *La recomposition de L'Etat en Europe*, Paris, La Découverte, 1996.

[14] "au-delà d'une technicité toujours croissante, le traitement des dossiers et des problèmes fait appel à un savoir-faire nouveau, la gestion de la complexité. Les comportements de nos concitoyens, leurs attentes et leur implication dans la vie même de notre agglomération nous obligent non seulement à une plus grande responsabilisation mais aussi à doter les services publics que nous gérons d'une organisation performante."

[15] "En 1997, la ville de Nantes a engagé une vaste démarche qualité au sein de ses services, 'Nantes Services Publics XXI', avec pour objectif d'améliorer les services rendus aux Nantais et de les adapter aux évolutions de la société [...] A terme, il s'agit de généraliser et pérenniser une 'culture municipale de changement.'"

[16] D. Gaxie, "Gouvernabilité et transformations structurelles des démocraties", in CURAPP, dir., *La gouvernabilité*, Paris, PUF, 1996.

[17] "on ne peut plus maintenant faire des projets sans associer la population.. c'est quelque chose de très compliqué et de pas évident.. enfin cela a toujours existé mais il faut toujours se préoccuper effectivement de capacité de la population à accepter les choses." Interview with an administrative director.

[18] "la mise en place dans de nombreuses villes de directions générales des services est un des signes de la prééminence acquise par le secrétaire général", O. Roubieu, "Le modèle du 'manager'. L'imposition d'une figure légitime parmi les hauts fonctionnnaires des collectivités locales", *Politix*, 28, 1994, p. 46.

[19] N. Elias, *Qu'est-ce que la sociologie?*, Paris, Ed. de l'aube, 1991.

[20] V. Lowndes, "Change in Public Service Management: New Institutions and New Managerial Regimes", *Frontières*, 9, 1997.

[21] "Le projet communautaire, document de référence, doit être mis en œuvre par la nouvelle organisation. Pour garder sa pertinence, il doit être adapté pour une mise en œuvre en adéquation avec l'évolution des besoins de l'Etablissement communautaire et de ses moyens. Par ailleurs, sa mise en œuvre ne peut être que progressive notamment pour tenir compte du temps nécessaire à la levée des résistances inhérentes à un contexte de changement majeur."

[22] "S'il est une ambition que nous devons nous assigner aujourd'hui, c'est de nous affirmer comme le grand pôle urbain de la façade atlantique. En nous appuyant sur notre histoire, nos talents, nos savoir-faire, et en nous adaptant sans complexes à la rapidité des évolutions du monde. C'est tout l'enjeu métropolitain", J. M. Ayrault, *Nantes Passion*, octobre 1998.

[23] "Bordeaux bénéficie, grâce à ses vins, d'une véritable notoriété internationale. Mais elle doit être élargie pour lui permettre de rivaliser avec les autres capitales", *Bordeaux Métropole*, 97, décembre 1999.

[24] We want to point out the mobilisation of researchers as "experts" and the euphemisation of conflicts that is engendered by this combination of practical and academic actors.

[25] P. Bourdieu, L. Wacquant, "Sur les ruses de la raison impérialiste", *Actes de la recherche en sciences sociales*, 121-122, 1998.
[26] Such a rhetoric is, for example, widely taken up and promoted by the World Bank and the United Nations as was shown at the world conference for the towns of Istanbul, Habitat II. Its diffusion, constitute an area of collaboration with relatively vague outlines.
[27] P. Eisinger, "City Politics in an Era of Federal Devolution", *Urban Affairs Review*, Vol. 33, 3, 1998.
[28] V. Lowndes, "Change in Public Service Management", art. cit.

Chapter 14

Is Local Democracy Under Pressure from New Public Management? Evidence from Norway

Morten Øgård

Much of the reform and development which has occurred within public administration in the western world during the last twenty to thirty years has taken place under the heading of "New Public Management" (NPM).[1] In this connection Christensen and Lægreid (1998) refer to a new administrative-political movement, while Hood – which for many purposes is regarded as a standard reference to the NPM concept – characterizes this development as "the most striking international trend in public administration" (Hood 1991:3).

The above-mentioned authors point out the emergence of an administrative-political doctrine with importance attached to the efficiency of marketing and management. According to Christensen and Lægreid (1998, 2001), NPM concepts are presented as universal and apolitical principles. The key words are "competition, privatization, freedom of choice, efficiency and output motivation, contract management, incentives". But this is far from saying that NPM-inspired reforms have been entirely unopposed. In connection with the development of a new administration policy a number of interesting debates have taken place. For example, intensive debates have been pursued in political parties, interest organizations, and not least in the many municipalities and regions where this type of measure has been launched. In addition, the lines have been drawn up within the academic community. The extent of the argument is considerable and a number of lines of debate can be traced:

- Is it possible to refer to universal leadership principles, which may be applied to different social segments (public, private and voluntary), and service areas (school, health and social services, culture, technical services etc.).
- Management by objectives: Is it possible to manage through the formulation of unambiguous goals?
- The use of the market as a control mechanism in order to achieve productivity efficiency in the public sector.

- The conceptual content of NPM and its implications seen in relation to traditional democratic values.

In this chapter I particularly want to focus on the latter debate[2] and to carry out an empirical test of impacts of NPM-oriented reforms in local government settings. Does a reorientation towards a market-based administrative policy (NPM) result in a displacement of traditional democratic values such as public participation and transparency in decision-making? Before proceeding with a closer consideration of this problem, I shall present some data on the actual implementation of various types of organizational-administrative reforms in Nordic cities and regions.

NPM in a Nordic context

In order to measure the degree of administrative innovation at the municipal and regional levels in the Nordic countries, I have developed eight indexes that measure the degree to which the municipalities and regions endeavour:

1. to introduce human resources-orientated personnel management;
2. to delegate authority internally to leaders at lower levels;
3. to redirect management towards goal/results/quality control;
4. to establish a market and competitive orientation;
5. to foster user-orientation;
6. to develop transparency;
7. to create opportunities for citizen participation;
8. to change political organization.

The data come from a survey of regions and cities in four Nordic countries (Denmark, Finland, Norway, Sweden – note that there are no regional data for Finland, as Finland does not have equivalents to the county councils of the other three countries). The cities chosen are the largest provincial city of the respective provinces/counties of the four countries. Results are presented in table 14.1.

Table 14.1 Administrative innovation: mean score of the indexes by country (all cases considered).* Scale 0 – 100

	Finland** Mean (Range)	Sweden Mean (Range)	Norway Mean (Range)	Denmark Mean (Range)	Total x
Increased focus on leadership/personnel management					
Personnel management	50 (22 – 100)	72 (0 – 100)	66 (22 – 100)	75 (44 - 100)	66
Delegated leadership responsibilities	53 (0 – 100)	68 (33 - 100)	72 (17 – 100)	85 (33 - 100)	70
Indirect management					
Management by objectives	77 (29 – 100)	62 (14 - 100)	50 (0 – 100)	52 (14 - 100)	60
Market/competition on orientations	90 (50 – 100)	76 (25 - 100)	61 (0 - 100)	61 (0 - 100)	72
The user in the centre					
User orientation	60 (27 – 91)	58 (18 – 100)	41 (0 - 82)	76 (55 - 100)	59
Changes in political organization/democratic processes					
Openness	51 (20 – 100)	57 (20 – 100)	28 (0 - 80)	45 (0 - 80)	45
Participation	65 (14 – 100)	37 (0 – 71)	24 (0 - 80)	41 (14- 80)	43

* Accumulated points in this and subsequent tables are calculated by aggregating the points allotted to the individual respondents as regards each question included in the various indexes. This score is then divided by the number of questions, and multiplied by 100. The higher the score, the greater the number of measures implemented by the municipality/region.

** Only the regional capitals are included in Finland.

In table 14.1 the eight indexes have been grouped into four broad categories that reflect the overall concerns of NPM: *human-resources-oriented* leadership, *indirect* management and control, *user-orientation*, and a reorientation of political steering. These main categories may again be related to broader theoretical perspectives (as suggested by Ståhlberg 1998a, 1998b), such as "managerialism", "liberalism", "communitarianism". Managerialism is reflected by the indexes concerning personnel management, delegation of responsibilities and management by objective. Liberalism is expressed through market-/competition-orientation and user-orientation. Communitarianism is reflected by the establishment of participatory channels.

If we consider the aggregated data in Table 14.1 in relation to these perspectives, an interesting pattern of development emerges within and between the respective countries. A managerial orientation is strongly represented in all of the countries. This particularly applies to Denmark and Sweden, but to a lesser extent in Norway. Finland, however, deviates somewhat from this pattern. If we look more closely, we find that this may be explained by a lower attachment to delegated leadership in Finland than in the other countries. On the other hand, within the framework of a managerial approach Finland appears to be more concerned with the introduction of new management models such as management-by-objectives, results indicators and quality management together with "benchmarking" to a greater degree than in the other three countries. In this connection it should be noted that Sweden occupies an intermediate position between Finland on the one side, and Norway-/Denmark on he other. My conclusion is that there is a strong managerialist development strategy in all four countries but that the importance attached to different elements varies between them.

Proceeding with an evaluation of the contribution of "liberalism" as a development strategy, it emerges that there are clear differences here. More precisely, we observe a tripartite division where Finland is the country where this strategy plays the strongest role. This is particularly associated with a market and competitive approach. Thereafter follow Denmark and Sweden, but notably ahead of Norway. With regard to Denmark and Sweden on this point, I would emphasize that these two countries attach importance to two distinctly different elements within the liberalist category. While Sweden appears to follow Finland in emphasizing marketing and competition, user-orientation characterizes the liberalist element in Danish development policy. Norway appears to occupy the last place regarding a liberalist element in development policy. While attaining a similar score to Denmark with regard to a market and competitive orientation, it is clearly the weakest in user orientation. In other words, we can conclude that a liberalist-inspired development strategy is strongest in Finland and definitively the weakest in Norway. In addition, it may be noted that Denmark distinguishes itself from Sweden in so far as the dominant liberalist component is user-orientation, while for the two other countries the focus is on a market and competitive orientation.

Considering "communitarianism", we note that this strategy in total is weaker in all the four countries than the other two. Having said this it is interesting to note that there is nevertheless a tendency towards a tripartite division. Finland is distinguished by being the most active while Denmark and Sweden (where Denmark lies a fraction ahead) occupy an intermediate position between Finland

and Norway. What I conclude on this basis is that the communitarian approach is least developed in these four countries; Finland, however, is the most active of the four in this field.

In summary, one could say that none of these countries reflect a unidimensional pattern in respect of the three development strategies outlined. In the Finnish case development policy can be discerned with roots in a managerial philosophy but with particular weight attached also to the market-oriented element in liberalism. I would also add that Finland goes further in pursuing elements of a communitarian-inspired development policy than the other three countries. The dominant Norwegian approach appears to be a managerialist "top down" philosophy. Sweden and Denmark are again in an intermediate position between Finland and Norway. Here it may be noted that while Sweden tends towards a managerial development strategy by establishing a market and competition-oriented profile, Denmark represents a further development of the managerial philosophy by particularly orienting itself towards increased user influence.

A weakness of the comparisons outlined above is that Finland is only represented by cities, not by the regional tier that is also included in the other countries. The more active reform orientation that characterizes the Finnish case may be due to this data bias. However, when only cities are compared (leaving out the regions of the other three cases) it emerges that the Finns are still more active in all types of reform than the municipalities of the other countries (the data for the latter comparison are not reproduced here). In other words, the Finns are the most active reformers in the Nordic area, across the board.

A line in the debate on New Public Management

Having looked more closely at the development of NPM in the Nordic countries, I shall briefly outline the debate, which has evolved around this theme. Some researchers such as Ferlie et al. (1996:9) have gone so far as to describe the inroad of NPM as a decisive turning point regarding management in the public sector. Lundquist (1998:137) speaks of this trend as an emergence of "economism" in the public sector. Lundquist's fear is that the preponderance of "economism" will consequently displace traditional values of the public sector, as expressed by Weber (1971). Klausen (1996a) largely follows Lundquist when he maintains that the NPM concepts reflect the classic conception of "economic man".[3]

However, this interpretation of the NPM concept has not stood unchallenged. In recent years a number of contributions have been made in the field of administration research which have questioned whether this view of the NPM concept does, in fact, capture actual reform trends in the public sector. I have already mentioned Ståhlberg's more nuanced outline of reform trends in the Nordic area – managerialism, liberalism and communitarianism (Ståhlberg (1998a, 1998b). Another researcher who has developed this theme is Jann (1997). Jann's point of departure is a consideration of the effect of NPM, or *Neues Steuerungsmodell* (NSM) in German public administration. Similarly to Ståhlberg, Jann argues that regarding NPM/NSM as just an attempt to achieve cost-effectiveness is too narrow. It is just as much a stage in the strengthening of democratic management of public administration.

In line with the critics of NPM/NSM, Jann holds the opinion that this concept does not comprise any homogenous theory of public administration. In Jann's view, however, the concept highlights circumstances which are of decisive importance for the future development of public administration, namely "how organizations can become more transparent, can be steered to achieve results, how organizations can learn and how they can change".

According to Jann, the challenge for political science is to conceptualize a dialectic between a strongly negotiation-focused concept associated with NPM/NSM and the traditional rules-and-hierarchy-understanding of administration as we know it from Weber. If these two approaches continue to oppose each other with normative arguments, Jann fears that one will not be able to reach a conceptual clarification, which could provide the basis for a new form of theoretical consideration concerning the administration of public organizations. Jann points out that,

> There is, until now, no evidence that NSM does not fit into such a new theory of governance. Indeed, there is quite a lot of evidence suggesting that it may fit much better than the classical Weberian image of the sovereign state, ruled exclusively by public law, bureaucracy and overhead democracy.

Against the background of somewhat disparate interpretations of NPM reforms, the interesting empirical question is whether local governments purse market-oriented lines of reform to the detriment of classical citizen-oriented local democracy. Or is NPM actually associated with a renewal of local democracy? If the latter is the case, there may be more to NPM than what has often been presented as a neo-liberalist market-oriented experiment.

What happens with traditional democratic values when NPM is introduced?

The purpose of this section is to demonstrate empirically what happens with traditional democratic values when a market-based administrative policy is introduced into local government in the Nordic countries. In order to operationalize democratic values,[4] I have chosen to focus on the dimensions of *transparency* and *citizen participation*. I have allowed NPM to find expression trough *user- and market-orientation*.[5] In order to test empirically the degree to which the two latter dimensions displace the first, I have developed four indexes based on the survey data presented above:

1. The Market-orientation index. This index comprises cover examples where functions have been transferred to private firms/voluntary organizations, whether share companies have been established, whether purchase and sale of services occurs within the municipal sector (internal pricing), and finally,

whether competition exists between the public and private sectors in contract tendering.
2. The User-orientation index. This index is constructed based on questions covering service declarations (citizens' charters), complaints procedures, freedom of user choice in the various services, user surveys, ease of access to service information.
3. The Openness index. This index is based on questions concerning the distribution of a municipal newsletter, general information meetings throughout the municipality or region, home pages on the Internet, the extent to which political documents are available on the Internet.
4. Participation index. This index is based on questions relating, for example, to public meetings, citizens surveys, establishment of citizens panels, creation of own web pages on the Internet for the individual politicians, placement of data terminals throughout the region for public use, question time at municipal meetings, active participation in planning and budgeting processes.

Results: Is democracy being displaced by New Public Management?

The research problem stated above is addressed through correlation analysis. The level of correlation between the various indexes are taken as expressions of the degree to which typical NPM reforms go together with or stand in opposition to democracy-oriented measures.

Table 14.2 Correlation matrix for the indexes' openness, measures directed towards citizen participation, used freedom of choice and market/competition orientation

		Openness	Participation	User-orientation	Market-orientation
Openness	Pearson Correlation	1.000	.380**	.315**	.271**
	Sig. (2-tailed)	.	.000	.000	.002
	N	130	130	130	130
Participation	Pearson Correlation	.380**	1.000	.278**	.267**
	Sig. (2-tailed)	.000		.001	.002
	N	130	130	130	130

** Correlation significant at the 0.01 level (2-tailed)

We observe that the index *openness* (measures directed towards providing information on events in the municipality/region, together with providing an insight into documents and political processes), not only shows a correlation with *participation*, but clearly correlates with *user-orientation* (measures directed towards user freedom of choice in respect of services available), and *market orientation* (competition and privatization). *Participation* (possibility for active citizen participation in the political processes) for its part, clearly correlates with *user-orientation* and *market orientation*.

In general, we may say that those municipalities and regions, which are innovative in so far as they are engaged in user orientation and market- and competition-orientation, are also innovative regarding citizen-oriented initiatives. These results concur completely with those of Gregersen (1999) who, in a major study of innovation in municipal social administration in Denmark, concluded that when a municipality was innovative in one area, the possibility was high that it was also innovative in other areas.

Other findings of a more qualitative character, which also support these findings, are case studies of the 'pioneer' Nordic municipalities (see, for example, Baldersheim et al, 1995, Henning 1996, Baldersheim and Øgård 1997, Hansson and Lind 1998, Baldersheim and Ståhlberg 1999, Ståhlberg 1998a, Solberg and Zäll 1999, Wahlquist 1999, Bäck 2000).[6] What these case studies show in brief is that pioneer municipalities that were innovative in the administrative political arena do not show a tendency to focus solely on a single model or solution. The local solutions usually reflected specific local conditions or problems It may appear as though the municipalities are quite selective in the measures chosen. They pick elements from various models available to them and assemble these as "local products" (model designations) that frequently bear the name of the municipality or the region. Thus, we find, among others, the Stockholm model, the Dalarna model, the Lunner model, the Larvik model, the Nordland model, the Farum model, and the Bohus model, to name a few. To illustrate this point, some of these "models" are sketched briefly below.

Frame 1: Key elements in the Oslo Model:

- Municipal parliamentarianism combined with urban district councils (udc) including experiment with directly elected politicians for udc's.
- Open competition concerning service production within the areas of refuse collection, cleansing, old persons' institutions, and parts of the public transport system.
- Freedom of choice: upper secondary schools.
- Increased user influence in services: establishment of management boards with representatives of parents/pupils in primary and upper secondary schools.
- Easy access to information for local citizens: realization of a design programme based on a broad information strategy for citizens.

The City of Oslo was one of the pioneers in the introduction of municipal parliamentarianism. In contrast to other municipalities in the Nordic countries, the emphasis was not placed on a pure purchaser–provider model. The distinction between the client and contractor became manifest through a steadily increasing focus on competitive conditions with the subsequent contract management of diverse service products. In addition to the increased focus on the citizen and the market, increased user-orientation was also a feature whereby increased freedom of choice was gradually introduced in certain areas, combined with the implementation of increased participation in school boards. In order to facilitate access to the various municipal activities, as indicated in the frame, the city council has introduced a design programme based on information and openness for the citizens. The city council is combining the development of the political administrative system based on citizen participation and involvement (such as direct elect of politicians to the urban districts within Oslo) with elements of NPM in the form of market- and user-orientation.

Frame 2: Key elements in the Tavastehus Model:

- Introduction of a Citizen's Charter (service guarantees).
- Development of a response system for users and citizens: Complaints Board.
- Enabling active participation for users and citizens through local evaluations where citizens evaluate the neighbourhood service and quality, open meetings in all committees and council meetings with question time; participation in planning processes, e.g. in the form of workshop for children and the elderly, citizens panel.
- On-going quality considerations based on user definitions of quality.
- Tendering with own units and private bidders for services.
- "Benchmarking" through extensive use of international and national comparison of service production, etc., and user/citizen-orientation.

An even more unadulterated and advanced project linked to the development of channels for citizen participation and response may be found in the Finnish municipality of Tavastehus which has been a pioneer municipality in the Nordic countries regarding the development of feedback systems for users and citizens (Naschold 1995, Baldersheim and Ståhlberg 1999). Central to this system are service guarantees and a locally based quality philosophy based upon what the user defines as quality. But neither has this municipality hesitated in its use of the market in order to ensure optimal use of resources. Another central feature of the Tavastehus model is "benchmarking" whereby a constant watch is held on progress compared with that made in other municipalities where comparison is natural in respect of cost and quality levels in service production. In summary, one might say that the Tavastehus model in Hirschman's terminology (1970) is constructed around the possibility and organization of letting the user's voice be heard in matters relating to political and administrative control.

Frame 3: Key elements in the Nacka Model:

- Freedom of choice for personal services such as schools, care of elderly and kindergartens.
- Increased citizen influence (enable them to "vote with the feet"). Establishment of "voucher" system where money follows the user.
- Create competition between own units internally and private bidders for local services such as: collective transport, cleaning, building maintenance and parks, school lunches, refuse collection, etc.
- Openness for citizens with insight into political processes and active participation in planning process.
- Extensive use of user surveys, which include on-going evaluation and quality control at the service unit level.

Whereas the Tavastehus model is constructed around the possibility for the citizens' "voice" to be heard, we may say that the Swedish municipality of Nacka is an exponent for "exit", i.e. that through a voucher system the municipality enables the citizen to "vote with their feet". In other words, the money follows the consumer's choice. In addition, the municipality has gone far in introducing competition within the collective services. On top of this market- and user-orientation it emerges in addition that the municipality has gone to considerable lengths in developing channels for active citizen participation in, for example, planning procedures.

Frame 4: Key elements in the Farum Model:

- Qualifying users to have real influence in the formation and development of services in the municipality: establishment of so-called "user panels".
- Freedom of choice in such areas as schools and kindergartens.
- Competitive tendering within areas such as technical operations and environmental services, including road-building and maintenance, parks, refuse treatment, management and development of treatment facilities for water and sewage, etc.
- Establishment of a municipal shop, citizens' shop and pensioners' shop with facilities for handling diverse matters so that the user will not have to go from one office to another.

The fourth frame illustrates the main elements in the development policy adopted by the Danish municipality of Farum. The entire political project, which provides the basis for this model, is based on a desire to reduce the municipal taxation level. (The aim was to achieve the lowest rate in Denmark, Brixtofte 1995). The manner by which this was to be achieved was to play on what Hirschmann characterizes as the *"loyalty* dimension". In order to motivate the service providing units, measures were taken to provide the system with legitimacy (citizens/users) through active participation of users in management at the service unit level. This was done by establishing so-called user-panels. In this manner an attempt was made to ensure both loyalty in respect of the framework set by the politicians simultaneous to ensuring users' influence in the design and content of service production. This is combined with a tendering and importance attached to freedom of choice.

How may these results be interpreted?

My findings and other studies outline innovative behaviour in local government as complex and multidimensional. Seen in relation to the lines of debate which formed the basis for this chapter, the results suggest that we should reconsider some of our impressions of the NPM concept. First, these findings suggest that the pioneer municipalities and regions (innovators) which followed the principles of NPM are far from being unilaterally focused on market- and consumerist ideals, as one might be led to believe from much of the administrative research publications of recent years. This implies that the advance of NPM in the form of market and user orientation in local government is linked to measures aimed at strengthening democracy and development – rather than aiming at displacing the latter. Whether we choose to characterize this as an extended NPM concept or not may be a matter of personal taste.

It is possible that the composite development policy identified here is an attempt to establish a *local legitimacy* in a society where, to an increasing extent, citizens regard the municipality as a service supplier just as much as a local democratic arena (Rose 2000). In this manner the new elements in administrative policy may be a signal that confidence in the municipality/local democracy may depend just as much on the individual citizen's or user's impression of the quality, availability, efficiency, supply and freedom of choice of municipal services and products as their satisfaction with the outcome of local elections held every fourth year. In other words, local governments may be seeking to establish a new – or perhaps more correctly, extended – form of accountability with regard to the local electorate.

References

Baldersheim, Harald and Øgård, Morten (1997). *Evaluering i kommunal organisasjonsutvikling*. Oslo: Kommuneforlaget.
Baldersheim, Harald and Ståhlberg, Krister (1999). Making Local Democracy Work. An evaluation of the Hämeenlinna model. Åbo Akademi.
Baldersheim, Harald, Hovik, Sissel, Tufte, Geir C., and Øgård, Morten (1995). *Kommunal reorganisering*. Oslo: Kommuneforlaget.
Boston, Jonathan, Martin, John, Pallot, June, Walsh, Pat (1996). *Public Management the New Zealand model*. New York: Oxford University Press.
Boyne, George A. ed. (1999). *Managing Local Services. From CCT to Best Value*. London: Frank Cass.
Budäus, Dietrich, Peter Conrad and Schreyögg, Georg (1998). *New Public Management*. Berlin: Walter de Gruyter.

Bäck, Henry (2000). *Kommunpolitiker i den stora nyordningens tid.* Malmø: Liber

Christensen, Tom and Lægreid, Per (1998). *Den moderne forvaltning.* Oslo: Tano Ascehoug.

Christensen, Tom and Lægreid, Per eds. (2001). *New Public Management. The transformation of ideas and practice.* Aldershot: Ashgate.

Clarke, John and Newman, Janet (1997). *The Managerial State.* London: Sage.

Clarke, Susan E. and Gaile, Gary L. (1998). *The Work of Cities.* Minneapolis: The University of Minnesota Press.

Cutler, Tony and Waine, Barbara (1994). *Managing the Welfare State.* London. Berg.

Du Gay, Paul (2000). *In praise of bureaucracy.* London: Sage.

Dunleavy, Patrick (1991). *Democracy Bureaucracy and Public Choice.* London: Harvester Wheatsheaf.

Ejersbo, Niels (1996). *Den kommunale forvaltning under omstilling.* Utgivelse i serien: Afhandlinger fra det samfundsvidenskabelige fakultet på Odense Universitet.

Eriksen, Erik O. (1993). *Den offentlige dimensjon.* Oslo: Tano.

Ferlie, Ewan, Ashburner, Lynn, Fitzgerald, Louise, and Pettigrew, Andrew (1996). *The New Public Management in Action.* Oxford: Oxford University Press.

Hansson, Lennart and Lind, Jan-Inge (1998). *Marknadsorientering i kommuner och landsting - erfarenheter och lärdomar från piojärernas kamp.* Stockholm: Nerenius and Santerus Förlag.

Henning, Roger (1996). *Att följa trenden.* Stockholm: Nerenius and Santerus Förlag.

Hirschman, Albert O. (1970). *Exit, Voice, and Loyalty: Responses to Decline in Firms, Organizations, and States.* Cambridge, MA: Harvard University Press.

Hood, Christopher (1991). "A Public Management for All Seasons?" *Public Administration* 69:3-19.

Hood, Christopher (1998). *The Art of the State. Culture, Rhetoric, and Public Management.* New York: Clarendon Press Oxford.

Jann, Werner (1997). "Public Management Reform in Germany; A Revolution without a Theory?" I Kickert, Walter J.M. ed., *Public Management and Administrative Reform in Western Europe.* Cheltenham: Edward Elgar Publishing Limited.

Klausen, Kurt K. (1996a). "New Public Management – falsk varebetegnelse med utfordrende indhold" *Ledelse i dag* 6:75-86.

Klausen, Kurt K. (1996b). *Offentlig Organisation, strategi og Ledelse.* Odense: Odense Universitetsforlag.

Klausen, Kurt K. and Ståhlberg, Krister, eds. (1998). *New Public Management i Norden.* Odense: Odense University Press.

Kleven, Terje (1997). "Kommunen som lokalpolitisk arena - inn i solnedgangen?" I Baldersheim, Harald, Bernt, Jan Fridthjof, Kleven, Terje og Rattsø, Jørn eds., *Kommunalt selvstyre i velferdsstaten.* Oslo: Tano Ascehoug.

Lane, Jan-Erik (2000). *New Public Management.* London: Routledge.

Lewin, Leif (1991). *Self-interest and Public Interest in Western Politics.* Oxford: Oxford University Press.

Lowdnes, Vivien, Stoker, Gerry, Pratchett, Lawrence, Wilson, David, Leach, Steve, Wingfield, Melvin (1998). *Enhancing Public Participation in Local Government.* London: Department of the Environment, Transport and the Regions.

Lundquist, Lennart. (1998). *Demokratins väktare.* Lund: Studentlitteratur.

Mclean, Ian (1986). "Review Article: Some Recent Work on Public Choice". *British Journal of Political Science* 16:377-394.

Minogue, Martin, Polidano, Charles, Hulme, David, ed. (1998). *Beyond the New Public Management. Changing Ideas and Practices in Governance.* Cheltenham: Edward Elgar Publishing.

Mitchell, William C. and Simmons, Randy T. (1994). *Beyond Politics: Markets, Welfare, and Failure of Bureaucracy.* Boulder: Westview Press.
Naschold, Frieder (1995). *The Modernization of the Public Sector in Europe.* Helsinki: Ministry of Labour.
Øgård, Morten (2000). "New Public Management – markedet som redningsplanke?", in Baldersheim, Harald and Lawrence Rose eds., *Det kommunale laboratorium.* Bergen: Fagbokforlaget.
Olsen, Johan P. (1990). *Fornyingsprogrammer og demokratiutvikling.* Bergen: LOS-senteret. Notat 90/19.
Perrow, Charles (1986). *Complex Organizations. A Critical essay.* New York: Random House.
Pollitt, Christopher (1990). *Managerialism and the Public Services.* Oxford: Basil Blackwell.
Pollitt, Christopher and Bouckaert, Geert (2000). *Public Management Reform. A Comparative Analysis.* Oxford: Oxford University Press.
Putnam, Robert D, (1993). *Making Democracy Work: Civic Traditions in Modern Italy.* Princeton: Princeton University Press.
Putnam, Robert D. (2000). *Bowling Alone. The Collapse and revival of American Community.* New York: Simon and Schuster.
Rao, Nirmala (1996). *Towards Welfare pluralism.* Aldershot: Dartmouth.
Rose, Lawrence E. (2000). "Demokrati – forventninger og virkelighet". I Baldersheim, Harald and Lawrence E. Rose, eds. *Det kommunale laboratorium. Teoretiske perspektiver på lokal politikk og organisering.* Bergen: Fagbokforlaget.
Self, Peter (1993). *Government by the Market? The Politics of Public Choice.* London: Macmillan.
Solberg, Bengt and Zäll, Fabian (1999). *Farum – en yndig kommun. Liberalt systemskifte i praktiken.* Lund: Timbro.
Stewart, John D. and Stoker, Gerry (1995). "Fifteen Years of Local Government Restructuring 1979-94: An Evaluation", in Stewart, John and Stoker, Gerry, eds., *Local Government in the 1990s.* London: Macmillan.
Stoker, Gerry, ed. (1999). *The New Management of British Local Governance.* London: Macmillan Press Ltd.
Stoker, Gerry ed. (2000). *The New Politics of British Local Governance.* London: Macmillan Press Ltd.
Ståhlberg, Krister (1998a). "Serviceförbindelser i kommunernas utvecklingspolitik", *Kommunal ekonomi and politik* 2:7-19.
Ståhlberg, Krister (1998b). "Utvecklingspolitiken i finländska kommuner. Vad, var och vem?" I Klausen, Kurt K. and Ståhlberg, Krister, eds. (1998). *New Public Management i Norden.* Odense: Odense University Press.
Wahlquist, Linda (1999). *Låt medborgaren bestämma! Kundvalsystem i Nacka kommun.* Lund: Timbro.
Wamsley, Gary L. Bacher, Robert N., Goodsell, Charles T., Kronenberg, Peter S., Rohr, John A., Stivers, Camilla M., White, Oliver F. and. Wolf, James F (1990). *Refounding Public Administration.* Newbury Park California: Sage.
Wamsley, Gary L. and Wolf, James F. eds. (1996). *Refounding Democratic Public Administration.* London: Sage Publications.
Weber, Max (1971). *Makt og byråkrati.* Oslo: Gyldendal Norske Forlag.
Yergin, Daniel and Stanislaw, Joseph (1998). *The Commanding Heights. The Battle Between Government and the Marketplace that is Remaking the Modern World.* New York: Simon and Schuster.

Notes

[1] See for example, Hood (1991, 1998), Budäus et al. (1998), Minogue et al. (1998), Klausen and Ståhlberg (1998), Lane (2000), Pollitt and Bouckaert (2000).

[2] For a more detailed review of the other lines of debate see, for example, Øgård (2000).

[3] Not only do Lundquist (1998) and Klausen (1996a, 1996b) argue that NPM represents a liberalist market element characterised by individualism, the market, competition, incentives, privatisation, and so forth in the development of the public sector, but this is also taken up by other Nordic researchers such as Eriksen (1993), Olsen (1990), Christensen and Laegreid (1998), Ejersbo (1996), Kleven (1997). The same arguments are also supported by British and U.S. researchers such as Hood (1991), Pollitt (1990), Stewart and Stoker (1995), Cutler and Waine (1994), Clarke and Newman (1997), Wamsley et al. (1990), Wamsley and Wolf (1996) and Paul du Gay (2000).

[4] The literature on the concept of democracy is extremely extensive and points in many directions, but according to Rose (2000:62) it is nevertheless possible to recognize three main profiles and individual variants of these: "1) thoughts concerning direct democracy, 2) thoughts concerning indirect or representative democracy, and 3) thoughts concerning communicative or deliberative democracy". The municipalities and regions in the Nordic countries have traditionally been founded on a democratic standpoint closely related to indirect or representative democracy, although in recent years we have seen several examples where the municipality has taken a step in the direction of measures with both a participatory democracy, deliberative and direct nature.

[5] There is broad agreement that those measures which have been launched to modernize the public sector and included in the concept of NPM, have largely been inspired by theories such as Public Choice, Principal Agent Theory, Contract Theory, and what Yergin and Stanislaw (1998) and Lane (2000) refer to as "Chicago School Economics". The keywords are: market orientation, competition, individual choice, results, etc. Hood (1998:98) defines this form of public administration as "Doing public management the individualistic way".

[6] What I would emphasize in connection with these studies is that initially these were not being considered being used to examine the problem as originally intended. However, it is interesting to note which the empirical matter presented in several of these case studies clearly illustrate the point about the multidimensional aspect in the innovative actions in these pioneer municipalities.

Chapter 15

Conclusions:
France – Return of the Girondins?
Norway – Rise of the Jacobins?

Harald Baldersheim and Jean-Pascal Daloz

Reforms engendered by pressures from globalization drive a new political agenda discernible in countries across Europe: European integration, cost-conscious institutional reforms, quest for political legitimacy, etc. At stake is the post-war welfare compromise. France, being at the centre of the storm, naturally experiences these pressures more strongly than Norway. The pressures set in motion centrifugal forces that open up the Jacobin state to new cleavages and rapidly shifting parties and constellations. Regionalization is part of the processes of change. Are the Girondins finally returning? The impacts on Norway, being at the margin of Europe, geographically and politically, are more of a centripetal nature. The combination of a rich state and European marginality makes the central government the focus of demands and hopes. Parties and cleavages have changed little. Regions are faded out; local government is colonized by state agencies. Have the Jacobins moved to Norway?

Globalization in France and Norway

The 1990s "discovery" of globalization was more of a shock in France than in Norway. Consequently, it led to stronger reactions, of which the formation of ATTAC is the most conspicuous one. The shock was greater because France's international prestige and world position was seen as being undermined, whereas Norway's traditional marginality and dependence were just more decisively confirmed. The cultural aspects of globalization – the invasion of the English language and the spread of Hollywood products – might be particularly hard to accept for France, a country so proud of its cultural achievements. Two further factors conditioned the Norwegian debate: the traumatic relation to European integration and Norway's affluence – public and private – that is so directly related to open world markets in oil, gas and fish products. Some political leaders were weary of talking about globalization for fear of opening up the wounds of the EU campaign that still fester in several parties. Furthermore, the well-filled state coffers mean that globalization can be used less convincingly in Norway as justification for public reforms and cutbacks than in many other countries with more strained state budgets. And the contradiction between world market dependency and an anti-globalization stance might be more difficult to overlook in Norway than in many other countries.

However, the globalization debate has many parallel features in the two countries. There is, first of all, a debate on how real or new globalization is. Second, it has to some extent followed a left-right cleavage. Those on the right tend to see it as bringing new opportunities nationally and internationally. Free trade brings growth to remote corners of the world and help lift backward countries out of the poverty they have been trapped in by archaic policies of self-sufficiency, the argument runs. In contrast, on the left, there is a tendency to see it as imperialism in new disguise. There is, however, also a far right or conservative reaction that deplores globalization as it weakens cherished national characteristics, such as language, identity or regional distinctions. The intellectual left shares some of the cultural concerns of the right, scorning globalization as macdonaldization and cultural leveling. Especially in France, anti-Americanism seems to have found renewed expression as anti-globalization.

In terms of leadership, globalization is almost uniformly seen as presenting a challenge to political leadership and the possibility of political control over national destinies. To the participants the debate also presents an opportunity to signal a stand on the grand issues of the day. The leader may point out directions towards a bright future that globalization entails, if only certain difficulties could be overcome, e.g. the low productivity of labour or the uncompetitive ness of companies. Other leaders may suggest a way to combat globalization or some of its expressions, e.g. the inroads of English or the appeal of foreign films. Generally, globalization is taken to signal a need for reforms of various kinds, often in the direction of New Public Management. Those who are suspicious towards the market orientation of NPM in their turn reject this type of reform as part of a globalization drive, seeking to emphasize the deeply sinister character of the venture in question. Finally, globalization may serve as a useful explanation for political failures, e.g. failure to save workplaces or obtain funding for certain projects. Who can win against the overwhelming forces of globalization or combat fate?

Parties and cleavages in France and Norway: the rise of the sovereignty issue

The polities of France and Norway share certain fundamental commonalities shaped by the formative struggles of nation-building so elegantly analyzed by Stein Rokkan's model of cleavage structures. Conflicts between State and Church, centre and periphery, labour and capital, town and countryside, gave rise to successive waves of party formations that still linger in today's party systems. New issues and parties have risen, old parties have waned, but basic structures have proved remarkably durable. The left-right divide still represents an overriding line of orientation in both countries although the meaning of this divide may vary somewhat. Other lines of division have been added to the political equations in both countries, e.g. post-material and "green" issues but these have not fundamentally altered the system. Interestingly, ecological concerns have been fairly easily absorbed by the system in both countries, although in different ways. In Norway, green politics has been integrated into the platforms of all parties although such issues form a more prominent part of the profile of some parties than of others. In France, a separate green party has been established that has found its position on left side of the political spectrum and even been included in the formerly governing coalition of the *gauche plurielle*.

One conspicuous contrast between the two countries is the more prominent role of the centre-periphery cleavage in Norwegian politics. This is not to say that France is a country without regional tensions or of a strongly homogeneous culture. France is certainly also today characterized by regional contrasts and prides. What is different in Norway is the elevation of the centre-periphery cleavage into a pillar of the political system, that has given birth to a series of institutions of the periphery that is part of the national institutional landscape (language rights, restrictive alcohol legislation, colonization of the state church by dissident opinion, strong local government, etc). In consequence, Norway has lacked the hegemonic, unified national elite and culture of France. In France, whoever is in power, it is the same elite that rules. It has to be admitted, of course, that in later years concessions have been granted to regional minorities over regional languages and that decentralization of power to regions and cities has taken place. Still, the bipolar character of the French party system has probably contributed to relegate the periphery more to the back seat in France than in Norway. Tellingly, the major cities and regions of France compete in enticing well-known national political figures to serve as their mayors. A Norwegian big-city mayor rarely considers a career in the national assembly as worthwhile. For a French city, a personal connection into the national elite is vital.

> The South West suffered manifestly from an under-representation in the cabinet of Jospin. One may hope that the team of Raffarin, the champion of the Atlantic Arc, will channel more investments towards the West, especially since the Prime Minister has secured the services of his friend Dominique Bussereau, who is from Charente Maritime, at the Ministry of Transport. Not to mention Alain Juppé, although it remains to be seen if his influence with Jean-Pierre Raffarain is as great as presumed. (*Sud Ouest*, 1 July 2002[1])

The quotation illustrates the centralized nature of the French state and also the mechanisms through which local and regional influence is brought to bear on national decision-making. However, Jacobinism is under pressure from demands for more regional autonomy. Malnes' analysis of the constitutional debate on proposals to extend more autonomy to Corsica demonstrates that while the Jacobin spirit is still strong among the political elite both of the Right and the Left, there are also profiled champions of decentralization. The dominant conception of republicanism – *France une et indivisible* – has given little room for a centre-periphery cleavage to develop as it has in Norway. Jacobin republicanism has been hegemonic. The Corsican debate may indicate that this is slowly changing. The new government that took office after the 2002 parliamentary elections seems pointed in a decidedly decentralist direction. In the programme presented to the National Assembly on the 3rd of July 2002, the Prime Minister, Jean-Pierre Raffarin, outlined four "pillars" of his programme. One of these was the extension of further powers to regions and communes. A constitutional reform was hinted at, which would give regions powers of "experimentation", opening up opportunities for regional adaptation of national legislation, somewhat on the Corsican model. Also his other "pillars" implied more active regions. It remains to be seen whether this part of the programme signals administrative experiments along the line of the Scandinavian "fee commune experiments" of the 1980s or amounts to more fundamental changes *à la* Spanish regional autonomy. Tellingly, the new Prime Minister is a former head of the region of Poitou-Charentes situated at the mouth of *La Gironde*. Are we witnessing the return of the *Girondins*?

The Norwegian Christian People's Party represents an oddity in need of explanation in the wider context of European politics. It has enjoyed electoral success and government power in the 1990s including the prime minister of the day. This party is clearly different from Christian democratic parties found on the continent, with the strongly puritan and fundamentalist streaks of the former. While religious values are also espoused by the continental varieties and by the smaller Christian parties of France, they usually combine such values with a more liberal platform than that of the Christian People's party. While the continental Christian democrats have been major forces in European integration the Norwegian party has been consistently anti-membership. In understanding the Norwegian phenomenon it is necessary to see it as another product of the centre-periphery cleavage of Norway, which is suggested both by the location of its regional strongholds (south-west) and its moral-religious platform.

For both France and Norway, the major challenge to the existing cleavage and party structure has come in recent years from issues related to nationhood, sovereignty and citizenship. In Norway, discussions on accession to the EU have had a prominent place in political debate and strife throughout the 1990s. The 1994 referendum split the Norwegians into two almost equal camps. Despite the Norwegian "no" of 1994 the issue has refused to go away like it did in 1972. In France, too, the issue of national sovereignty demonstrated its capacity for splitting the nation, as the yes-side came within a hairsbreadth of loosing the referendum on the Maastricht Treaty. The difference in outcome indicated that the French elite might be more in control of its citizenry than its Norwegian counterpart was, but the respective struggles also suggested that a new, difficult cleavage might be forming. This cleavage is creating havoc in the party structure.

Issues emanating from European integration are part of a wider set of questions about sovereignty and citizenship in the age of globalization. How far is the national elite entitled to go in its concession of sovereignty in the pursuit of common European goals? How fast is it advisable to go in the face of popular scepticism? In France, as in Norway, the political elite is more pro-European than the citizenry. However, this gap has also turned out to be a political opportunity for some parties and leaders that had led lives in the shadows of the establishment.

Increasing movement of people is another side of European integration and of globalization in general. Fast and far-flung financial transactions are a conspicuous ingredient of globalization. And so are the jobs lost or created as a result of those transactions. However, the other side of the coin is voluntary and involuntary movement of people that accompany the transactions of information and financial exchange. Some of those movements are welcome and encouraged. "Free flow of people" is among the four freedoms of the Maastricht Treaty. Paradoxically, as borders are opened (theoretically) for citizens inside the EU, borders are becoming more impenetrable for many on the outside wishing to come in to share in the (apparent) abundance inside. Clearly, maintaining such a double regime will give rise to institutional strain in the years to come, as the pressure on the EU borders will not abate. At the same time, many of those that have been let in, legitimately or illegitimately, are proving increasingly difficult to integrate for cultural reasons and for lack of social skills that are necessary on a modern job market. Permanent ghettos have grown up in or around major European cities, havens for cultures and lifestyles that many ordinary citizens find difficult to accept. These situations challenge notion of citizenship, that is, notions of the rights and duties of citizens in relation to the state. The challenge of citizenship is one of issues that are becoming the platform of new parties or new mainstays of existing ones around Europe. So far, they have often been classified as belonging to the extreme right. However, such a classification is proving increasingly difficult to uphold as these parties expand their appeals from those of xenophobic sound-bites to claims for social justice, taking increasing shares of the traditional working class vote. The *le pens* and *hedstrøms* are not going to fade away.

Party leadership is different in France and Norway. In Norway, parties choose their leaders. In France, leaders choose their parties. French leaders are party owners, Norwegian leaders are party servants (Carl Ivar Hagen may be the exception in Norway). In the whole post-war period, the range of parties has remained remarkably stable in Norway. Only two party-splits have occurred, and one of those has been healed again. Only one new party (not originating from a party split) has been formed, the Progressive Party. France has seen a succession of party splits and party formations. Characteristically, however, the same set of well-known figures has been at the head of the new formations. Party formations seem driven more by quarrels at the apex of parties than by disgruntled rank-and-file protest. Again, the elitist character of French leadership is evident, while in Norway party leaders have to present a man-in-the-street-image to maintain a political career. In France, careers are furthered through loyalty to the leader, in Norway through loyalty to party organs. In this respect, French parties more than Norwegian ones are based on leadership, whereas Norwegian parties are institutionalized platforms for causes.

Roots and regions

France and Norway are countries of regional contrasts in terms of geography, culture, dialects and economies. Regions have longer histories than the state. These regional distinctions are sources of pride and identity. They have formed the basis of durable centre-periphery cleavages in national politics, although more so in

Norway than in France. Interestingly, regions experienced a resurgence in the 1990s, giving rise to a discourse on the emergence of a Europe of the regions, characterized by strong European and regional institutions but with a receding role for the nation-state. This was a view much promoted by regional ideologues but appeared more doubtful in the light of analytical scrutiny. Undoubtedly, however, a wave of decentralization did take place in many European countries from the late 1970s on, with stronger regions emerging especially in Spain, Italy and Belgium, and later in the UK. With the assistance of European institutions regions have sought to take on an enhanced role in economic development policies. Theories of endogenous growth have informed the new policies, suggesting that regions can grow through the mobilization of internal potential and the formation of multi-level partnerships.

Norway upgraded the role of regional bodies with the reform of the county councils of 1976, introducing direct elections and giving the new bodies wider functions in health services and economic planning. Reforms with similar features were introduced in France from the early 1980s on, establishing 22 (mainland) regions as supplements to the existing 100 *départements*. Suddenly, a new class of hundreds of elected representatives was created in the two countries. The belief in the power of democratic politics was evident.

In France as well as in Norway, regions have sought to develop strategies in response to a more competitive world of globalization. A survey of Norwegian regional councillors demonstrated a keen awareness of international competition between regions. Strategies of their choice may include support to individual firms as well as more general policies aiming at marketing the regions as a whole. Regions are becoming particularly keen on policies reflecting the emerging information economy, such as supporting regional universities or partnerships between universities and local industry.

Both French and Norwegian regions are, however, still highly dependent upon the state for the implementation of their policies. The state controls many of the resources that are needed to realize development projects. Policy development as well as implementation are characterized by complex central-local partnerships in which politicians play a role as brokers between levels of government. This role is more highly developed in France. The *cumul des mandats* is an important integrative mechanism. Formally, the French rely on the *contrat de plan* to harmonize cross-level projects, whereas the Norwegians think in terms of broader, joint development plans (RUP). Here is an interesting contrast, with French regions pursuing pragmatic *ad-hoc'ry* while Norway's way is the grand plan (albeit in a down-scaled version). Again we notice a more room for political leadership in France than in Norway.

France and Norway also differ with regard to the outlook for regions in the respective countries. Norwegian regions – the county councils – are increasingly on the defensive. The right wing has wowed to abolish the county councils as superfluous bureaucracies in a small country, and the social democrats are wavering in their support. For now, hospitals have been transferred from the functional palette of the counties to that of the state, and their role in regional development is reduced. No parallel development is discernible in France. The regions may be state dependent but there is no discussion on their abolition. Indeed, as pointed out above, in France, regions may be headed for a glorious future under the new Raffarin government. Why is Norway different in this respect, not only from France but also from general European trends? It is near at hand to think that the persistent centre-periphery cleavage in Norwegian politics should serve to protect the county councils as expressions of regional variation. Apparently, it does not. Norway's non-membership of the EU may provide an alternative explanation of the faltering status of the counties: Norwegian counties do not benefit from the extra pull from Brussels that regions in member countries get. However, as Norwegian regions also participate in EU projects and are partners in the Interreg programme, this explanation also seems insufficient. Perhaps the comparison with France provides the answer: the political leadership of Norwegian regions is more weakly developed than that of France, and there is no politically integrative mechanism similar to that of the *cumul des mandats*. Although members of parliament often have experience as local or regional councillors they give up their local or regional careers when going to the Storting. Also end of contract with the regions?

However, the fate of regional political institutions is only a part of the story of regional development. Andy Smith's study of the Bordeaux wine producers demonstrates what scope of action there is for independent regional networks even in an industry heavily exposed to global competition. Although the Bordeaux producers have had to respond to the emergence of wine industries across the world, there was much scope for choice with regard to strategies of adaptation. In the Bordeaux region the battle raged between advocates of production controls (on volume) and quality controls (to enhance quality to obtain better prices). This was also in part a battle between the "famous" and the "ordinary" districts of the region. The latter won the day. The outcome was by no means a foregone conclusion. The strategy that subsequently guided development and marketing of the wine cannot be accounted for as a mechanic, market-driven response; it owes as much to personal leadership and dynamism of individuals and shrewd exploitations of positions and networks.

Local participation: Building social capital and discursive democracy

Both in France and Norway the level of citizen participation in local politics is considered an important indicator of citizen interests in local government. To many observers the falling level of voter turnout in local elections is therefore a worrying phenomenon. In France as well as in Norway turnout oscillated between 70 and 80 percent until the late 1980s, when it started to drop steadily. In the latest French local election (2001) only 67.4 percent of the voters used their democratic right. The level of participation (59 percent) was even lower in the 1999 local election in Norway. The lower level of voter participation in Norway is an enigma since the broader range of functions shouldered by Norwegian municipalities should lead to more citizen interest and participation in Norway.

There is a clear relationship between the size of municipalities and levels of turnout – in both countries, turnout is larger in smaller municipalities. So perhaps the higher level of turnout in France may be explained by the large number of very small authorities (Norway also has mostly small authorities, but the proportion of very small authorities is very much larger in France). It may be that small scale makes for greater transparency of governance and local politics therefore more comprehensible. Electoral methods may also play a part in explaining the contrast in turnout: the more bipolar political processes of France may make for more citizen interest. However, the general trend in both countries cannot be explained by contextual contrasts but has to be accounted for by common third factors.

Problems in recruiting candidates and absenteeism from council meetings are additional problems for Norwegian local parties. The turnover rate among Norwegian councillors is very high: two thirds of the elected candidates do not return for a second term, mostly because they withdraw voluntarily having served one term. The membership of political parties has also dropped substantially over the last two decades.

The French debate on proximity clearly indicates a concern with participation and a readiness to stimulate it as a channel for enhancing social cohesion. Security issues in the wake of social problems came to the forefront of the last local election. Both major blocks signaled a willingness to launch policies of integration in which citizen participation was to be major ingredients. One such policy was already in operation since the 1980s (*La politique de la ville*, or the Urban Policy Initiative). Examples of this policy can be found in the major cities of France. Bordeaux has a number of initiatives in this vein, such as The Dialogue Groups that initiate mobilization in neighbourhoods, the Think Tanks on Participation seek to establish bonds between citizens and elected representatives, the Citizens' Dialogue Groups that involve people in social difficulties, etc. The common denominator of these policies are a search for means to build social capital in areas that seem to be suffering symptoms of anomie.

Norway does not have inner city or suburban areas with similar levels of social conflict and has therefore not considered measures of the type associated with the French Urban Policy Initiative. Instead, Norway has focused more on institutional experimentation to stimulate interest in local politics. Among these, direct election of mayors is one of the more conspicuous experiments. Carried out in 20 municipalities during the 1999 election, levels of turnout did not rise dramatically but surveys said that people found that the direct mayoral elections had made local politics more interesting. Paradoxically, the experiments took place mostly in rather small municipalities where one would not think popular alienation would be a towering problem. However, Norwegian municipalities vary considerably with regard to locally initiated efforts to stimulate citizen interest. Some have introduced local ombudsmen as channels for better citizen communication, others have established neighbourhood councils, some try out user panels as a means for better client rapport, etc. There is also a rush to establish channels over the Internet, including chat pages as steps to discursive democracy.

Leadership and political styles: monarchic republic, republican monarchy

We have seen above that, in both countries, globalization, directly and indirectly, is driving a series of policy responses. Heated exchanges on the reality and merits of globalization are taking place. Issues of sovereignty and national cohesion have come to the forefront of the political agenda. Parties strive to adapt to the new agenda, their fortunes apparently changing more rapidly than before. The French election of 2002 of was a particularly vivid demonstration in this respect, although, in the end, the pendulum swung vehemently back. Regions and localities also find that their prospects are being affected by globalization and seek to develop their own responses to a new environment. To some extent, and especially in France, hopes are being placed in policies of decentralization and proximity. Is a Girondin revival under way? In Norway, national cohesion is pursued thorough a redistribution of oil revenues, driving a centralization of politics and institutions to the extent that the country seems in the grip of a Jacobin mood of uniformity and standardization.

Nevertheless, at the conclusion of this comparative study, we can only but be struck by the persistence of the political styles of the elites of the respective countries – styles remain distinctly French and Norwegian and seemingly unaffected by the new global context. In both cases, we observe highly institutionalized universes within which leadership is hardly preponderant. France retains its character of a "monarchic republic", Norway that of a "republican monarchy".

Despite apparent changes, Norwegians are not really abandoning the "Einar Gerhardsen" style (Einar Gerhardsen was the strong man of the Labour Party subsequent to the Second World War, who was to dominate the political scene right until the mid-1960s). His style was one of never appearing "above the masses" but being part of it. It also meant rejecting a certain theatricality of power and getting ones ideas and results to prevail without ever personally highlighting oneself. In other words, it is important to be modest while at the same time displaying efficiency. Of course, people sometimes remark on the growing importance of audiovisual media and a propensity for a growing personalization of politics, but stardom is not something that politicians should openly strive for. The format permeates even the style of the monarchy, epitomized by King Olav's famous journey on the tram into the Oslo woods for his weekly skiing trip during the 1973 oil crisis.

In the French case, it may be asked whether the political elite have ever left the Gaullist style, tinged with grandeur and strongly dependent on institutions. For two centuries, the country's history has constantly wavered between the royal model of Versailles (the French talk about their "Elysée Kings" or François Mitterrand's "court") and the correcting model of the 1789 revolution (Daloz 2002). During and shortly after his 1995 campaign, President Jacques Chirac wanted to present an image of simplicity by refusing for example motorcycle police escorts and opening the door of his car by himself. But he returned to a rather pompous style during the cohabitation period with a socialist prime minister, because he then needed to assert the superiority of his presidential office

(Fleurdorge, 2001). The recent failure of Lionel Jospin (who went as far as admitting to having been naïve during his campaign for the presidential elections) no doubt underlines the limits of an overly modest style, which contrasted sharply with French mores, even if many other factors must, of course, also be taken into account under the circumstances.

With everyone to his own style, the Norwegian and French political actors always prove to be ambitious on behalf of their countries. In the Norwegian case, this goes hand in hand with a great modesty and perhaps less mistrust in the globalization phenomenon. In the French case, it is more a question of asserting the desire to redirect this movement, perceived more or less as a threat, towards the interests and vision of a country which has never really stopped thinking of itself as a great nation and a model for others.

References

Daloz, Jean-Pascal (2002). "Ostentation in Comparative Perspective: culture and elite legitimation", *Comparative Social Research*, vol. 21.
Fleurdorge, Denis (2001). *Les rituels du Président de la République*, Paris: P.U.F.

Note

[1] "Le *Sud-Ouest* souffrait manifestement d'une sous-représentation dans le cabinet Jospin. On peut espérer que l'équipe Raffarin, le chantre d'Arc atlantique, va diriger d'avantage vers l'Ouest ses décisions d'investissements, d'autan plus que le premier ministre s'est assuré les services de son ami Dominique Bussereau, charentais-maritime, au secrétariat d'Etat aux transports. Sans parler d'Alain Juppé, dont on verra si l'influence qu'il a auprès de Jean-Pierre Raffarin est aussi importante qu'on le pretend." *Sud Ouest*, 1 July 2002.

Epilogue

Towards a Local-Global Leadership? A Research Agenda

Claude Sorbets

Heeding what local leaders actually say on the conditions of political leadership is a good point of departure for reflections on the meaning of political leadership in a global age. In the final report from the Unity Congress organized by the FMCU[1] and IULA[2] in May 2001,[3] four "questions" were raised:

- The question of *globalization* from an economic perspective: this trend was regarded as driving an "ineluctable inter-penetration of regions, cities and communities" as well as the "irresistible rise of the private sector".
- The question of *privatization*, focusing on public authorities' outputs (notably the services offered to citizens in a context where the market is predominant).
- The question of *local autonomy* which raises the ambiguous issue of political management (in a positive way when considering grassroots proximity and increased autonomy vis-à-vis the state; but in a negative way when considering the risks of isolation or the higher burden of expenditure for local governments).
- Finally, the question of *participation*: "the citizens' rights to be informed and consulted are fundamental to democracy ... but the definition of this in concrete terms remains disputable".[4]

Considering the present "global-City" heterogeneity, such a debate bringing together local government decision-makers from all over the world may appear idealistic or even surrealistic. However, the very fact that this debate took place at all demonstrates an evolution in perceptions of opportunities for political action since the fall of the Berlin Wall.

This debate has developed within a global forum under the auspices of the United Nations Organization. Since the key Congress organized in Istanbul "Towards a global charter for local autonomy" (30-31 May 1996) by the UN Centre for Human Establishments, Habitat, and the Coordination of World Associations for Cities and Local Authorities,[5] it has been continually followed up. The dynamics of the debate originate in a process whereby international organizations of local authorities (formerly highly divided due to post-Second World War political and social antagonisms) now seek to unite. The debate might lead to a search for new values, norms and regulations able to give a certain coherence to new political actors in an emergent world order simultaneously globalized and fragmented, polycentric and diversely organized. In any case, it would provide local actors with new possibilities and margins for manoeuvre when confronted with the era of information society and networks.

From the theoretical pioneer works of Jürgen Habermas or John Rawls to the ones for instance of Lester Thurow,[6] social scientists have contributed to this debate particularly on historical changes and conditions for the advent of "deliberative democracy". When reading specialized academic journals, especially English-language ones such as *Political Studies*, one finds that investigation of changes affecting the condition for local-global public action has been a persistent theme.[7]

The aim of this chapter is to propose a synthesized list of themes currently emerging in the field, and of the reflections conveyed by local government actors, elected representatives, administrative staff, private sector partners as well as association members. Most of these actors probably believe that perceptions of local politics have changed and must actually change. However, these evolutions also lead to certain confusion for everybody and above all for political actors.

The present success of the term "territorial" indicates the beginning of a new era for socio-political regulations. The latter are often considered as more and more complex due to the increase of levels and forms of systems and modes of action engendered by concertation – produced by organizational rationalization or democratic requirements. Consequently, power seems to be less distant. But from another perspective, political responsibility appears more dispersed or hazardously attributed to rather indistinct bodies difficult to identify.

In this new context, one important correlative is that the "métier politique" (political profession) evolves, can only but evolve and has to evolve in order to adapt to socio-political realities. But this necessary functional adaptation, individual and collective, which prompts the learning of a new way of "acting politically in context" is regarded as problematic. What we mean is that the prospect of a democracy "within everybody's reach" seems to be actually fading away. Should we not take into account that specific predispositions – notably intellectual and cultural – are required for one to adjust oneself to "a world political culture" (i.e. the one enabling action within "global" collectivities) (Sasken 1996), to propose new ways of "doing politics together", to know how to intervene in external "arenas" and "forums" and to think in terms of networks?

We shall distinguish several major components structuring this political scenario. The first one is "political intelligence" and the way it is made up. Another one is the thinking and acting of political decision-makers with responsibilities for specific territories, especially with regard to their presence in world arenas and networks. Our intention is to discuss how this new scenario gives a new tone to political leadership today with clear parallels from one country to another, whatever their traditional political culture and nature of their national/local relationships.

"Political intelligence" in the present world

The notion of political intelligence[8] refers to a specific *technè* on which a certain type of professional knowledge has been constituted over time. In representative democracies power relations are often denied. The usual attitude is to present political activities in a positive light by referring to amateurism, altruism, individual choice and free will, transparency, the ins and outs of actors and deeds. Neo-Machiavellian theoreticians, by observing the contradiction between an apparent political universe consisting in a confrontation of ideas and a real one consisting in the defense of material or statutory individual and social interests, can only but recall the timeless and universal nature of the power games in society – whether the latter depends on natural or socio-cultural inequalities between men and their possible groupings.

It is well known that the development of mechanisms regulating the competition for political power has tended to redefine political leadership and action. These depend on practical knowledge within the framework of a political profession, which is more and more technical and less within the reach of the "amateur" and "ordinary citizen". It is sometimes said that this managerial know-how, requested for the "skilled preparation of dossiers", identifying modes of action within our large bureaucracies, is based both on generalist and specialized competence. This technical skill is crucial for the politician in charge of acting through the framework of institutional positions, whether he deals with his peers, with the services directly or indirectly under him, or with external partners (other public or private authorities).

Political intelligence may undergo evolutions over time linked to the *zeitgeist*, the temporal context and its periodical vicissitudes, or from phase to phase. Referring to classical embodiments of political leaders – such as the "notable", the entrepreneur, the organizer – it would be easy to consider various ways of dealing with differentiated political activities. The professionalization of political activities seems all the more reinforced as the skilled knowledge available to the political actors – for instance, how to elaborate public policies or to adequately measure the opinions of the polity one claims to represents – presupposes a full-time activity and long, specialized training.

The notion of political intelligence leads to a certain way of perceiving and presenting things shared by the actors in question. The now dominant view according to which political action is no longer organized on a pyramidal but a network basis, or the division so commonly taken for granted by politicians between "actors" and ordinary people both illustrate the present political rhetoric. This common code helps to show who is actually an "actor" and who is not in the "comédie du pouvoir".

From pragmatic reflection, the "political intelligence" syntagma aims at expressing a particular meaning with its own logics (an original foundation of the power relation and thereafter a legitimate one) and its reason for being (expressing collective interests as a strategic, final goal).

Two dimensions relating to both the reason and dynamics of political activity should be distinguished in order to help us to specify its present forms in this era of globalization.

"Mobile power"

This term first suggests that power may refer to "the" or "a" legitimate object of competition as well as to actual power-holding. In this perspective, we are dealing with the motives for doing politics or for becoming involved in political militant activities. In this respect, strategic analyses of power would seek to identify the power resources pragmatically wielded by "political entrepreneurs". The "investor politician" (Lacam 1988) is seen as a rational manager handling "stocks" of power resources. Beyond this first meaning referring to a new attitude whereupon the desire for power traditionally repressed or denied is henceforth admitted, the term "mobile power" also allows one to see that power *loci* have moved, for instance due to decentralization and globalization. From this point of view, political power appears as a rare commodity that politicians should be able to locate and use for more or less defined purposes.

In the present context the common references to "public power" or "governance" take into account these changes that have occurred between the institutional public sphere and civil society with its multitude of associations. The uncertainties as regards representations of what exists within the *Polis* lead to unsure beliefs, for example some beliefs about erratic and more or less indistinct powers or about a territorialized power, which must find its roots and consolidations in public opinion (Laufer and Paradeise, 1982).

Considering the present technological revolution in the field of communication, of which Internet is the most obvious illustration, one could say that a myth has appeared, according to which "the center is everywhere and the periphery nowhere" (myth being understood here in the Sorelian sense, i.e. as a "driving image"). Consequently any place may potentially become the center of the world, and every local political actor may dream of this new communication utopia.

As a background to our reflections regarding the term "intelligence", it is useful to refer to theories inspired by Habermas' concept of "communicative action" and in particular to the concomitant joint search for "good understanding". The quest for agreements on values, horizons of meanings give a consensual orientation to the constitution of a predominantly deliberative new political world. More or less consciously, political leaders walk in their predecessors' footsteps, which predispose them towards "a-political" or clientelist relations in the name of their integrative roles.

Max Weber (1980) insisted on "communalization" as one of the major missions of the politician. The other mission, that of "sociation" of interests, i.e. arrangements and compromise between rival interests, is also discernible in the today's concern with making rational public policies subject to consultation and periodical assessments.

Before and beyond this pragmatic view of everyday political activity, political scientists could identify structural representations of nature – for instance, those of power as "reality" or "relation" – or culture – following B. Gracian (1980) one may speak of a "cité des egos", that is the political universe of the courtier who must know his way around. Political scientists may also identify what is believed in present-day societies as well as representations of what politics should involve and be judged for. In this respect, political intelligence must take into account what is possible, acceptable and feasible.

Local mobilizations

Going from "mobile" to "mobilization", the present political intelligence appears in its causal and finalized reality. One of the goals is to integrate and adapt societies. Another one is to instrumentalize identities and mobilize local resources in order to influence world trends, whether locally or globally, by seeking to have an impact on decision-making. In this perspective, it is important to possess (or to be thought of as possessing) "useful information" which may be transmitted to some other actors – certainly under the condition of exchanging information of the same nature at their disposal.

In the 1960s and 1970s what appeared, at least in France, as a derogation or even as a bypass of the State's principles (in this case of the Jacobin state's insistence on the territorial integrity of "The One and Indivisible Republic") is now understood as territorial differentiation according to which actors are entitled to be recognized as specific representatives of "his" or "her" territory. The consequent manipulation of representations is certainly structural. Researchers were therefore justified in proposing the hypothesis of a change in the dominant referential between these two levels of the State (Ion and Micoud 1989). At the local level, instrumentalizing mobilization and identity mobilization are related (like a couple of forces in physics): like an arm becoming intelligent because of an action conceived elsewhere or through the articulation of the conditions of an arrangement negotiated to be made acceptable.

It is within this kind of universe of political action that the leader must use the "cunning" intelligence once given by Metis to Ulysses, son of Laerte and/or Sisyphus, "the wittiest of men".

Reflexivity and activity of local authorities: Towards "thinking-acting globally-locally"[9]

The sociology of political actors must take into account their "reflexivity" as far as the process of action is constructed, the latter being shaped by evolving leadership configurations. In this regard, interpretations in terms of role games prove to be unsatisfactory as they tend to over-emphasize structural factors or in other words systemic effects.

Indeed, it is relevant to analytically consider voluntary actions. Even those compatible with the prevailing context may lead to various alternative solutions, exactly like in everyday life experiences. Bearing in mind the principle of a double adaptation – or a reciprocal adjustment – between the actor and the environment as well as its (relative) corollary of a double eligibility for politicians in relation to their area (i.e. expressing their environment and being recognized as doing so through actions and discourses) is in our view the best strategy to study political actors within their contextual framework.

Everybody should now acknowledge that differentiation among political actors is a variable *a priori* independent of concrete roles. Let us think for instance of innovative local leaders found in mid-sized towns at the end of the 1970s and their attempt to develop a new style playing on the managerial register (promoting rational public policies) and participatory involvement (promoting incremental politics "in public").

"Partnership action"

The notion of governance, even when the uncertainties of its meanings are kept in mind, helps us to reformulate a new ethos of politics in a modern way. Actually, what is at stake in the "government by contract" (Gaudin 1999) are new dimensions related to forms of actions and to the actor in political action. In this case, beyond new conceptual and mobilization modes linked to partnerships and decentralization, what is stressed is the complexity of territorial realities and the local ways of considering things hardly reducible to wider schemes.

The local and the global – in the light of neologism "glocal" – are perceived as the constitutive limits of one field both analytical (what leads us towards the actual reality) and synthetic (the reciprocal information of analyzed instituted things or of critical indicators of instituting parts, to refer to institutional analysis).

"Thinking-acting globally-locally"

This perspective aims at stimulating public actors' reflections in the sense of a more firm perception of their profession and condition. The proposition is to think-act globally, locally. This expression borrowed from Dubos' ecological thought should not just be a communicative slogan avoiding precisions on transfers and articulations from one level to the other whether one is in a contemplative or in an active mode and vice-versa.

Two complementary assertions illustrate this:

1) Thinking-Acting Globally, Locally (TAGC) because thinking is already acting.[10]
2) Because the global is in the local as a transferred present social dimension.[11] The TAGC principle is also a guide for every public actor for any of his specific actions.

In addition to the TAGC principle, singularities should be analyzed in contrast to excessive generalizations.[12] The idea is not to consider the local within the categories of the global or vice-versa – which would mean resorting to an unreasonable metaphor to characterize the actual reality. In other words, the local would be seen as signifying the global from which it would proceed metonymically. The former could be considered as a revealing criticism or as a specific analyzer of the latter, according to whether one prefers a neo-organizational or a neo-institutionalist perspective.

To elaborate a possible answer to the question: "What can be made here today?", that is, at a time of globalization, every actor is led to consider local problems, no longer thinking in terms of a national state - local dimension but a global-local one. From this perspective, everyone should be able to "say what can be read and said in one place".

Being present in world arenas:[13] Local action and "economic policy"

When thinking about national evolution regarding economic interest regulation, it is important to take into account the historical singularities of the countries concerned. As for France, when dealing with the relation between institutions and interests, it is crucial to consider what the positions of the various actors involved in the socio-political game have been for the last two centuries.

This collective background is essential to explain for instance the importance of modernizing state bureaucrats after the Second World War and also to explain why they have been actively contested – because of their omnipotence or their decay as "mirror of the nation" (Legendre 1999) – or the mythical importance associated with company "nationalization" and then "privatization" in French political debate during the last quarter-century. Due to European integration, one may certainly say that the French administrative organization and cultural references have greatly changed, thus making the old theme of the "French exception" a little suspect when considering present-day realities. What remains of the Jacobin State for a country durably engaged in political and administrative decentralization and confronted with the phenomenon of economic globalization?

However, just by considering the risk of a possible crisis regarding national unity and the inter-subjective struggle for recognition (Honneth 2000) organized by the state apparatus, it is certainly useful to emphasize aporia, even as far as the legitimation of public power, territorially recomposed, is concerned.

In interactionist or constructivist terms, the outcome of such a schematic approach to the national experience framework might amount to defining what French reflexivity can be (with its indexicality) and what the "inflexivity" of such a "common horizon of meaning" (Taylor 1994) can be, keeping in mind its effects on the national basic personality through present cleavages (the most persistent being the "right" - "left" axis).

Towards de-singularization?

It may be tempting to adopt a de-singularizing view, for instance when questioning the reality of "cultural exceptions" or the belief in a "de-differentiation" of various countries. Such a perspective may lead one to consider national singularities as mere epiphenomena. It is no doubt intellectually correct, whether by moving away from actors' reasons towards an epistemic one or moving away from repetitive stereotypes.

However, looking at things from the other side, i.e. taking into account specific local evolutions is also relevant. Actually, it is important to take into consideration national forms of political action and collective representations when studying the impact of a political culture over the members of a society. This appears useful when interpreting social political phenomena and is particularly crucial when anticipating other actors' actions or reactions. For instance, let us think about over-coding and decoding of what may be said in public or in private by a top civil servant such as a prefect. Local actors learn to interpret this in their interaction with him/her when they need to get their viewpoint accepted. Such knowledge is also part of the political intelligence at a certain time in a certain place.

The regulation of interests

In a study of the regulation of economic interests at the local level in France (Sorbets forthcoming)[14] – their identification, expression and legitimation – we propose to take evolutions regarding legitimate relations between the political power and interests as an indicator of changes in representations and an indicator of how the social interests are dealt with in the national polity.

In this regard, we may sum up these analytical propositions through two complementary hypotheses concerning institutional evolutions and cultural references:

– Hypothesis 1: local political intervention in the economic sector helps to analyze the level of political institutionalization of the French society polarized by the qualification and the localization of legitimate interests (general interests, local interests). What we mean here is that for a very long time, French local authorities have identified "local interests" or "proper interests", often perceived negatively especially when they seemed to be disguising clientelistic relations.

– Hypothesis 2: The ways of organizing economic intervention on behalf of a territory may provide pointers to socio-political games and the articulation of interests within new contexts (networking, globalization). What we mean here is that in contrast to previous decades (notably when development structures such as the *expansion committees* were set up in parallel with local administration or even from it) new forms of local actor involvement in the economic sector are now considered as the norm at the center of political activities.

Network involvement: Constituting globalized institutions

From a local perspective, the present political world is often perceived in terms of "challenges" coming mainly from the outside and the major concern would be to react to them. More than ever, everyone would see himself as belonging to One world – let us think about the success of the expression "global village" (McLuhan 1967) – simultaneously fragmented and globalized by more and more hegemonic networks. The latter are a critical indicator of societies which have reached a stage where the *noumena* of territoriality and temporality become more complex leading to a crisis of institutional and organizational structures. They are not only a critical indicator but also help us to analyze the institutional processes of reformed societies in relation to the "proximity" and the "mediate nature" of self-interested interactions.

What matters is to be able to respond to these challenges by finding the best voluntary adaptation, possibly by pretending to master what is beyond our control. We will just list a few dimensions structuring these representations currently debated.

The "network" dimension

In today's world, reference to networks has become a kind of "practical paradigm", that is a category related to this era, constantly used by all or part of a society. How could we presently speak of our own world, the political sphere or modernized political administrative systems as well as of communication without mentioning the term "network"?

From inter-municipal cooperation to territorialized governance (cf. the "pays", the "observatoires" in France), going through organized associations, the present world is full of networking, expressing a desire for both solidarity and flexibility, links and suppleness. International cooperation networks should be considered as an extension of this: for instance, twinning relations lead to claims to represent a new level of meso-governance (cf. the World Charter for Local Autonomy, extending the one previously adopted at the European level).

The limits of the state and communicative transfers

By reading Manuel Castells' recent works (1999), one understands the extent of the transformations that has happened in scholarly thinking as regards the conditions of efficient actions among societies recomposed on a globalized network basis. According to Castells, "one can no longer pilot economic development from the top" and "in this context, the European unification, first experience of a move from the Nation-State to the Network-State, must be considered as a historically important undertaking".[15]

Expressions such as governance, contract, partnership, public power... all characterize present ways of taking on public action. An authoritarian style would have been replaced by negotiation, force by the law, a distant decision-maker by a closer authority. These themes on changing regulation modes of present-day societies have been developed and popularized for the past twenty years, up-dating a "double hermeneutic" (Giddens) logic, underlining the return effects between the observer and the actor, taking into account not only identified principles but also the codes that become manifest[16] through enunciation.

Local power traditionally seemed to be like a zero-sum game with State power.[17] Some authors went as far as contesting its very reality (Sfez 1977) (Castells 1999)[18] or were just considering it as a localized conjuncture of forces.

Others would point out the emergence of "local political markets" with their differences and similarities from one place to the other according to "local cultural models" and their recurring particularities. In contrast to the subordinate and peripheral position ("sequentialized" and substantialized) of the local site of action, contemporary political intelligence (understood as a specialized knowledge related to a political professional practice) substitutes the action stance for possible centering with serialization and concatenation.

The sociological models which have been predominant in France for the last quarter-century: the one developed by the *Centre de Sociologie des Organisations* (CSO)[19] with a centre-periphery approach; institutional analysis (Loureau 1969) referring to the three notions "Instituting, Instituted, Institution"; or Marxist critical sociology as well as those referring to "post-modernity" all have come up against categorical problems that have forced them to acknowledge categories such as "levels", "actors", "networks", "equipment", etc. and are at the same time unsatisfactory due to their paradigmatic and syntagmatic uncertainties.

In this respect, the instability of meaning regarding terms like "local" or "territorial" demonstrates insufficiencies as far as the scientific construction of objects of research is concerned, too often driven by normative preoccupations of various types of interpretation: from the functionalist to the systemic going through structural-functionalist and structuralist phases.

Conclusion

To think about political leadership at a global age brings one to consider the town as the central point, democracy as the major reference, local autonomy as the key of sustaining development and territorial political action as the edge of a world which, thanks to information and communication technologies, is constantly within a potential or present state of virtuality and reality. Correspondingly, we would be tempted to say that what appears as more and more basic in our contemporary societies is demonstrations of a therapeutic paradigm which leads everyone, whatever his/her intellectual background, to think in terms of "problem-diagnostic-treatment".

Following this axiological orientation, analytical investigation of political intelligence prompts one to carry out research and to formulate propositions regarding questions about: the evolving *functionality* of local power and its *effects*; the *dynamics* and *forms* of the Institution and the Organization placed "between" social field conditions; *the localized changes* and the *type of change* implemented; the phasing and the distancing of constituted elements and entities.

References:

Auxiette, J. (2000). "Villes et mondialisation: pensée et agir localement et globalement", *Communes de France,* (September).

Castilles, M. (1999). *L'ère de l'information,* Paris: Fayard. 3 vol.: "La société en réseau", "Le pouvoir de l'identité", "Fin de millénaire".

Cooke, M. (1996). "Five Arguments for Deliberative Democracy", *Political Studies* (pp. 947-969).
Crozier, M. et al. (1974). *Où va l'administration française?*, Paris: Les Editions d'organisation.
Deleuze, G. (1969). *Logique du sens*, Paris: Les Editions du Minuit.
Dryzek, J. S. (2000). *Deliberative Democracy and Beyond*, New York: Oxford University Press.
Gaudin, J.-P.(1999). *Gouverner par contrat*, Paris: Presses de Sciences Po.
Gracian, B. (1980). L'Homme de cour, Paris: Editions Champ libre.
Gremion, P. (1976). *Le pouvoir périphérique: bureaucrates et notables dans le système politique français*, Paris: Editions du Seuil.
Honneth, A. (2000). *La Lutte pour la reconnaissance*, Paris: Les Editions du Cerf.
Ion, J. and A. Micoud (1980), "La commune entre l'Etat et le quartier", *Espace et Société*, no. 34-35.
Lacam, J.-P. (1988). "Le politicien investisseur", *Revue Française de Science Politique*, 38:1.
Laufer, R. and Paradeise, C. (1982). *Le Prince bureaucrate*, Paris: Flammarion.
Legendre, P (1999). *Mirroir d'une Nation: L'Ecole Nationale d'Administration*, Paris: Fayard.
Lourau, R. (1969). *L'instituant contre l'institué*, Paris: Anthropos.
Marsh, D. and Smith, M. (2000). "Understanding Policy Networks: towards a dialectical approach", *Political Studies*, vol. 48 (pp. 4-21).
McLuhan, M. (1967). *La galaxie Guthenberg*, Paris: Editions Mame.
Milar, Z. (ed.). (1992). *Globalization and territorial identities*, Aldershot: Avebury Press.
Rhodes, R. (1996). "The New Governance: governing without government, *Political Studies* (pp. 652 667).
Sasken, S. (1996). *La ville globale*, Paris: Descartes.
Sfez, L. (ed.). (1977). *L'objet local*, Paris: Christian Bourgeois.
Taylor, Ch. (1994). *Malaise de la Modernité*, Paris: Les Editions du Cerf.
Weber, M. (1980). *Economie et Société*, Paris: Plon.
Williams, C. H. (1993). *The Political Geography of The New World Order*, London & New York: Belhaven Press.

Notes

[1] Fédération Mondiale des Cités Unies.
[2] International Urban Local Authorities.
[3] Unity Congress FMCU - IULA, "Les priorités de la communauté locale", Rio - 3/6 May 2001.
[4] "les droits des citoyens à l'information et à la consultation sont au fondement de la démocratie... mais personne ne sait lui donner un contenu incontestable", M. M'Bassi (FMCU), ibid.
[5] Centres des Nations Unies pour les Etablissements Humains; Coordination des Associations Mondiales des Villes et Autorités Locales (CAMVAL).
[6] "Globalization: the product of a knowledge-based economy", The Annals: Dimensions of Globalization, July 2000.
[7] See for instance, Cooke (1996), Rhodes (1996), Marsh & Smith (2000), Williams (1993), Dryzek (2000), Milar 1992.

[8] "all the rules regarding a job, profession or a human activity" (ensemble des règles intéressant un métier, une profession ou une activité humaine), *Lexis*, p. 108.
[9] Auxiette (2000).
[10] Many political speeches are of a performative and illocutory nature: through their mere enunciation, as institutional or power discourse or because they correspond to an orthodox interpretation or because they give meaning to phenomena, they have real effects. Cf. Merleau-Ponty or Berger and Luckmann's constructivism.
[11] Consider the migrations of men and activities: they transfer at the very local level the forms and contexts of global experience, i.e. those of native identity cultures either undeveloped or disintegrating to the brink of being recomposed; those of instrumental positions according to the context which appear disconnected - cf. people or social groups in dual societies.
[12] Cf. William Occam, making a distinction between the singular, the series and the signs.
[13] F. de Bernard, "De la mondialisation aux mondialisations: domination ou partage du monde", Conference given at the University of Hamburg, Institut de France, 5, 2001.
[14] To be published in *Les crises des démocracies européennes*.
[15] "On ne peut plus piloter le développement économique par le haut", "Dans ce contexte, l'unification européenne, première expérience de passage de l'Etat-nation à l'Etat en réseau, doit être regardée comme une entreprise de portée historique."
[16] Deleuze, (1969), distinguishes the "attribut de la Proposition" (designation, manifestation, signification) and "L'attribut de l'énoncé de la Proposition" (the meaning).
[17] Cf. the Guichard report.
[18] Castells (1999) (vol. 2, chapter 5), shows a different reality: that of "L'Etat impuissant" (the powerless State) leading to a democratic crisis as a direct consequence of the rise in networks and of a disarrangement of the national shape of the State.
[19] (Crozier 1974), (Grémion 1976).

Index

Attac 58, 65

Christian Democratic, 67, 78-82, 104
Civil servants, 125, 145, 162, 179, 181, 223, 225
Cleavages, 3, 8, 24, 27-28, 62, 67, 83, 93-95, 245, 247, 250, 262
Collective interests, 258
Communication, 13, 42, 49, 62, 106, 126, 128, 130, 132, 164, 185-188, 197, 210, 221, 225, 253, 259, 264-265
Communities, 2, 22, 25, 27, 44, 46, 199, 202, 255
Competition, 3, 5, 12, 27, 37, 44, 49, 56-57, 64, 101-102, 125, 129-130, 139, 142, 144, 155, 160, 163, 187, 219, 227, 231, 234-235, 237-238, 240, 250-251, 257-258
Conservative, 13, 60, 65, 74, 76, 80, 82, 87, 95, 101, 103, 107, 138
Construction, 2, 47, 70, 78, 81, 107, 157, 169, 185, 265
Contract, 42, 178, 231, 237, 239, 251, 260, 264
Convergence, 1, 3, 26-27, 29, 56, 58, 100, 193, 217
Councils, 13, 137-142, 154, 170-171, 175, 179, 183-184, 186, 188, 222, 232, 238, 250-251, 253

Decentralization, 11, 111, 116-117, 121-122, 125, 126, 128, 144, 155-156, 169, 171, 179, 184, 221-223, 247-250, 253, 255-256, 262
Decision makers,
Decision-making, 5, 7, 10, 63, 100, 104, 110, 155, 175, 232, 248, 259
Democracy, 13, 24, 28, 30, 38, 55, 62, 100, 103, 105-106, 109-110, 112-113, 119, 128, 170, 175-178, 184, 187-188, 236-237, 241, 252-253,

255-256
Developments, 4, 12, 58, 70, 83, 149, 151-151, 170, 197, 228

Economic interest, 11, 13, 128, 133, 261, 263
EEA, 61, 64, 106
EEC, 60
Election, 11, 13, 30, 40, 68-71, 73-78, 83, 101-107, 115, 121, 126, 130, 138, 171-177, 193, 252-253
Elections, 11, 13, 22, 46, 68-78, 84, 86, 97, 102, 104, 110-111, 118, 139, 170, 172-173, 176, 185, 193, 195, 203, 241, 248, 250-254
Elites, 6, 17-18, 23-24, 27, 59-60, 93, 95, 107-107, 141, 144, 225-227, 253
Employment, 44, 48, 100, 127-128, 131-132, 143, 194
Endogenous processes, 58
Environmental, 58, 73, 104, 240
European Union (EU), 2, 4, 6, 9, 38-39, 49, 59-65, 71, 82, 94, 101-103, 105-107, 140, 143, 151, 162, 211, 246, 249, 251
Exogenous change, 56

Girondins, 245, 251
Global-local, 261
Governance, 1, 2, 3, 7, 8, 9, 10, 11, 12, 14, 39, 56-58, 63, 65, 70, 125, 137-139, 151, 219, 236, 252, 258, 260, 264

Identity, 3, 12, 26, 42-43, 49, 75-77, 79, 83, 195, 197-198, 201, 205, 221, 246, 250, 260
Ideology, 40, 45, 48, 72, 95, 102, 112
Immigration, 5, 14, 61, 63-64, 69, 76
Individual choice, 1, 257
Information society, 57, 256

Institutional change, 79
Institutionalization, 12, 21, 23, 25-26, 28-29, 72, 83, 188, 263
Instruments, 1, 75, 129, 137, 139, 170, 181, 187
Integration, 4, 5, 7, 10-12, 59, 61-62, 71, 75, 81-82, 139, 142, 144, 155-156, 179, 211, 221-222, 226, 245-249, 252, 262

Jacobins, 39, 120, 245

Labour, 13, 59-61, 65, 70, 94-95, 100-107, 138, 253
Leadership, 1-3, 6, 17-29, 64-65, 68, 71, 73, 77-78, 103, 106-107, 115, 125, 129, 130, 132, 137, 141-142, 150-151, 154, 155-158, 160-161, 164-165, 221, 225, 227- 231, 233-234, 255, 260
Left-right, 5, 9-10, 101, 103, 111, 246-247
Left-wing, 71, 101, 115
Legitimacy, 3, 7, 13, 19-21, 25-26, 28-29, 117, 125, 132, 155, 163, 219, 221, 240-241, 245
Legitimate interests, 263
Legitimization, 125, 220
Liberal, 2, 29, 3-40, 47, 56-57, 71, 75, 78, 80, 82, 94-95, 101-102, 115-118, 121-122, 129, 221, 248
Liberal democracy, 56
Liberalism, 2, 7, 38, 74, 78, 104, 116, 234-235
Local actors, 256
Local authorities, 13, 81, 110, 121, 127, 130, 256, 260, 263
Local autonomy, 255, 265
Local democracy, 13, 118, 169-170, 172, 175-177, 183-184, 187, 201, 210-211
Local government, 13, 140, 169, 187-188, 193-195, 212, 225, 232, 236, 241, 245, 247, 252
Local reform, 220
Localization, 58, 128, 263
Loyalties, 3

Management, 12, 14, 71, 126, 129, 133 138, 142, 219-223, 225-227, 231-240
Marginality, 5, 26, 245
Minorities, 4, 106, 247
Modernization, 12, 24, 26, 63, 129, 144-145, 151, 165, 207
Movements, 2, 49, 58, 60, 65, 79, 82, 94, 129, 249
Municipal elections, 77, 115, 172-174, 177, 193
Municipalities, 12-13, 77, 125-126, 141, 145-147, 149-150, 170-175, 179-180, 182, 184-185, 187-188, 193-194, 199, 212, 231-232, 235, 238-239, 241, 252-253

National state, 55, 57, 61, 63, 106, 261
Nation-building, 6-8, 11, 93, 105-106, 154, 247
Nation-state, 2, 13, 250
NATO, 5-7, 9, 59, 61
Neoliberal, 56, 58
Networks, 2-3, 10, 18, 27, 55, 56, 107, 125, 130, 140-142, 147-151, 154, 162, 198, 221-222, 226-227, 251, 256-257, 263-265
New Public Management (NPM), 14, 129, 133, 231-241, 246

Organization, 49, 56, 65, 68, 71, 76, 78, 82, 102, 106-107, 139-140, 157-159, 162, 178, 181, 186, 188, 203, 214, 220-223, 226-227, 232, 239, 262

Participation, 3, 13-14, 22, 61, 64, 72, 129, 141-142, 148, 151, 169-174, 177-188, 193, 195-197, 201-203, 207-211, 219, 232, 236-240, 252, 255
Partnership, 132-133, 140, 226, 264
Policy-making, 2, 57
Political actors, 176, 254, 256-257, 260
Political cleavages, 5, 7, 24, 93
Political competition, 3, 27, 175
Political fragmentation, 3, 6, 63
Political intelligence, 257-259, 262-265
Political leaders, 17, 20, 22-23, 27, 35-36, 38-39, 46, 49, 127-133, 139, 155-156, 164, 219-223, 226-227, 246, 251, 255-259, 265
Political leadership, 1, 3, 6, 18, 20, 22-23, 129, 133, 139, 155-156, 164, 246, 251, 255, 257, 265
Political management, 255
Political rhetoric, 258
Power relations, 17, 20-21, 55, 225, 257

Private sector, 38, 77, 129, 141, 219, 237, 255-256
Privatization, 231, 238, 255, 262
Professionalization, 24, 177, 257
Public actors, 140, 164, 261
Public authorities, 125, 129, 133, 155, 170, 179, 180, 183, 255
Public management, 125, 219-220, 224
Public opinion, 131, 195, 258
Public sector, 57, 60, 129-130, 141, 178, 232, 235, 244

Rationalization, 225-226, 256
Regional authorities, 129
Regional councils, 130, 139, 142
Regional development, 131, 133, 137-142, 145, 251
Regionalism, 3, 4, 8, 11-12, 118
Regions, 3-4, 11-14, 28, 38, 81, 110-111, 117, 119, 122, 126-130, 132-133, 137-140, 142-151 154, 156, 161-162, 165, 231-232, 234-236, 240-241, 247-251, 255
Regulation, 5, 40, 46, 133, 156, 161-162, 164, 156, 161, 162, 165, 261-264
Relations, 1, 5-7, 19, 21-22, 27-29, 61, 106, 127, 151, 197, 212, 259, 263-264
Reorganization, 151, 184, 220
Representations, 219, 258-263
Representative democracy, 10, 128, 183-184, 188, 244
Representatives, 17, 24, 29, 60, 81, 98, 109, 111, 116-117, 120-121, 128, 131, 155-162, 169-171, 174, 176, 176-188, 221, 238, 250, 251, 256, 259
Resources, 2, 40, 59, 61, 63-64, 100, 125-132, 140, 142, 160, 179, 188, 203, 210, 220, 227, 232-233, 239, 251, 258-259
Right-wing, 6, 39, 48, 70-71, 76, 102, 104, 118

Socialist, 62, 65, 71-72, 95, 100, 104, 113, 115, 122, 127, 131, 154, 254
Solidarity, 78, 130, 162, 199-202, 205, 207, 213, 264
Sovereignty, 7, 10, 59, 64, 71-72, 80, 246, 248, 253
Standardization, 3, 11, 18, 48, 253
State-building, 7-8, 11

Tradition, 4-7, 10, 13, 18, 20, 23, 65, 81, 107, 118, 129, 137, 154, 164-165, 169, 180
Transactions, 2, 21, 56-58, 63, 65, 197, 249
Transnational, 56-57, 61-62, 106, 127, 227

Uniformity, 3, 27, 116, 253
Urban policies, 221

Welfare state, 2, 5, 7, 12, 61, 63, 100-101, 105, 194
Wine, 155, 156
WTO, 2, 9, 64